T0192598

Pro HTML5 with CSS, JavaScript, and Multimedia

Complete Website Development and Best Practices

Mark J. Collins

Apress®

Pro HTML5 with CSS, JavaScript, and Multimedia: Complete Website Development and Best Practices

Mark J. Collins

ISBN-13 (pbk): 978-1-4842-2462-5
DOI 10.1007/978-1-4842-2463-2

ISBN-13 (electronic): 978-1-4842-2463-2

Library of Congress Control Number: 2017935969

Managing Director: Welmoed Spahr
Editorial Director: Todd Green
Acquisitions Editor: Todd Green
Development Editor: Laura Berendson
Technical Reviewer: Gaurav Mishra
Coordinating Editor: Jill Balzano
Copy Editor: Karen Jameson
Compositor: SPi Global
Indexer: SPi Global
Artist: SPi Global
Cover image designed by Freepik

Distributed to the book trade worldwide by Springer Science+Business Media New York, 233 Spring Street, 6th Floor, New York, NY 10013. Phone 1-800-SPRINGER, fax (201) 348-4505, e-mail orders-ny@springer-sbm.com, or visit www.springeronline.com. Apress Media, LLC is a California LLC and the sole member (owner) is Springer Science + Business Media Finance Inc (SSBM Finance Inc). SSBM Finance Inc is a **Delaware** corporation.

For information on translations, please e-mail rights@apress.com, or visit http://www.apress.com/rights-permissions.

Apress titles may be purchased in bulk for academic, corporate, or promotional use. eBook versions and licenses are also available for most titles. For more information, reference our Print and eBook Bulk Sales web page at http://www.apress.com/bulk-sales.

Any source code or other supplementary material referenced by the author in this book is available to readers on GitHub via the book's product page, located at www.apress.com/9781484224625. For more detailed information, please visit http://www.apress.com/source-code.

Printed on acid-free paper

To my beautiful and precious wife, Donna. Thank you for sharing your life with me.

Contents at a Glance

Contents

About the Author

Mark J. Collins has been developing software solutions for 35 years. Some of the key technology areas of his career include COM, .NET, SQL Server, and SharePoint. He has built numerous enterprise-class applications in a variety of industries. He currently serves as an application and data architect for multiple organizations. You can see more info on his website, www.TheCreativePeople.com. For questions and comments, contact Mark at markc@thecreativepeople.com.

About the Technical Reviewer

Gaurav Mishra is an expert in User interface Development and UX Design with more than 10 years of experience. He provides workshops and training in UI development, UX Design, and Drupal. Gaurav has played a key role in the success of many organizations and likes to build products and services from scratch. Gaurav lives in New Delhi, India, and likes to spend his leisure time with his baby Yuvika and wife Neeti. He likes all genres of music, from Indian classical to club music. Gaurav can be reached at mr.gauravmishr@gmail.com and also tweets at @gauravmishr.

Acknowledgments

First and foremost, I acknowledge my Lord and Savior, Jesus Christ. The divine and eternal perspective on life, which can only be found in You, is an anchor, steadfast and sure. I humbly conclude that Your hand has guided me, often carrying me, through every endeavor, great and small. I submit that nothing of any value or significance is possible without You.

I want to say a very big thank you to my beautiful wife, Donna. I can honestly say that I would not be who I am if it were not for what you have sown into my life. I am truly blessed to be able to share my life with you. Thank you for your loving support and for making life fun!

Next, I'd like to thank all the people at Apress who made this book possible and for all their hard work that turned it into the finished product you see now; this is truly a team effort. Jill, thanks for keeping everything rolling smoothly and for being patient with all the work; Gaurav, thank you for your input and critique, helping to improve the quality and accuracy of this book; and to all the other contributors at Apress, thanks for overseeing the many details. Everyone at Apress has made writing this book a pleasure.

Introduction

My goal in writing this book is to provide everything you need to know to be proficient in creating professional quality web applications that take advantage of all the great features in HTML5. I also wanted this to be equally helpful for both novices and seasoned professionals. I'll let you be the ultimate judge of how well I fulfilled those goals.

There is a tremendous amount of information presented in this book, and I knew that organizing it would be my top priority. The overall HTML5 umbrella encompasses HTML, CSS, and JavaScript; these can be thought of as the three legs of a tripod upon which your web application will depend. The first section of this book provides an introductory chapter on each one of these technologies. I recommend starting with these chapters, especially if you're relatively new to web development. Sections 2, 3, and 4 cover each of these three areas in more detail. The last section provides demonstrations of some advanced topics such as canvas, SVG, drag and drop, and indexed DB.

Thanks to some really helpful websites provided by Mozilla, W3 Schools, and many other organizations and individuals, there is an overwhelming amount of material readily available. This book is designed to augment these resources by focusing primarily on concepts. If you understand the basic principles, you can more readily, and effectively, apply the details of a particular feature. In keeping with my first goal, however, there are a lot of details provided as well. I have included reference materials in Appendix C to keep the narrative more readable.

There is an impressive set of frameworks available such as jQuery, Angular, Bootstrap, and Knockout. If you are doing any serious web development, you will want to use one or more of these. These frameworks don't provide any capability that you couldn't create yourself using the techniques I will be demonstrating. They will, however, make your job a whole lot easier if you choose them, and use them, wisely. In this book, however, I will focus only on the native capabilities of the web technologies and will not use any of these frameworks.

You can download the source code for each chapter from `www.apress.com`. Except for the last section, the amount of code is kept relatively short so you can enter it yourself as you follow along. However, the final code for each chapter is provided in the download for your convenience. In some cases, I may demonstrate two or three ways of accomplishing the same thing. The downloaded code will sometimes have portions of code commented out in these cases.

The technology that I'll be explaining is not platform or vendor dependent. The sample web pages that I'll be demonstrating should work on most major browsers. The files that you'll be editing – HTML, CSS, and JavaScript – are just simple text files that can be written with any text editor. Using a tool designed for web development will make your job easier by providing intellisense and context-sensitive formatting. I used Microsoft's WebMatrix to create the samples for this book. WebMatrix is free and easy to install and use. However, Microsoft is dropping support for WebMatrix in November 2017, offering a free, open source version of Visual Studio instead. That might be a bit of a pill to swallow unless you happen to already be in the Microsoft camp. There are plenty of alternatives. Your favorite browser probably provides basic editing capabilities as well.

Finally, as with most technologies, the landscape is constantly changing. I have carefully chosen to describe the capabilities that are supported by the majority of platforms and avoided those that have limited availability. By the time you are reading this book, things may have changed and you may find some information outdated. You may have to do your own research for a specific feature. I trust, however, with the foundations demonstrated in this book, you will be well able to leverage the HTML5 technologies, even as they evolve over time.

I wish you every success as you master all the wonderful facets of developing web applications. Never stop learning!

■ ■ ■

PART I

HTML5 Technologies

The term HTML5 encompasses a broad spectrum of technologies that together provide a compelling platform for building great web applications. These can be organized into three areas:

- 1) HTML – the web content, including markup instructions.
- 2) CSS – the styling rules that define how the content is presented.
- 3) JavaScript – provides client-side scripting and advanced capabilities.

Part 1 contains a chapter for each of these areas that introduces the fundamental concepts that you will need to understand in order to apply the material in the rest of the book. This section is a must-read for anyone relatively new to web development.

Each chapter also provides a broad coverage of the technology so, even if you are fairly experienced, you will likely find some tidbits that you weren't aware of or may have forgotten. I suggest every reader at least skim through these chapters. You may need to come back to review these chapters as you work through some of the more advanced chapters.

CHAPTER 1

■ ■ ■

Hypertext Markup Language

In this chapter I'll explore the first leg of the HTML5 triad, which is the actual content that will be rendered in a web page. In the next two chapters I'll explain how this content can be styled using CSS and introduce the JavaScript language. But we'll start with the content.

■ **Note**   I almost referred to this as *raw* content, but that would be an inaccurate description. A properly formed HTML document has a great deal of structure and organization.

Recall your earlier school days when your teacher returned your homework with red marks on it. Misspelled words, bad grammar, or other such mistakes would be circled or highlighted. You might call that a *marked-up* document, and generally the more marks, the worse the grade would be.

Similarly, a markup language is used to call out parts of the document and provide instructions or background information. The difference, however, is the audience. You may be good at reading HTML, and you certainly will be after reading this book, but you are not the intended recipient. The markup is provided to the browser as instructions for how this should be rendered. As such, this markup itself must be syntactically precise.

■ **Tip**   HTML5 is a relatively mature standard, or more accurately, a set of standards that is managed by the World Wide Web Consortium (W3C). For example, the overall HTML syntax is defined in `https://www.w3.org/TR/html5/syntax.html`. Much of the material in this book can be gleaned from these specifications, and I encourage that you look at some of them and be aware that they exist. These standards can be modified, or more likely extended, over time and these specifications are the definitive authority.

HTML Document

HTML is generally produced and consumed as a document. We may talk about snippets of HTML but in most cases, a web site will respond to a request with a complete HTML document, which is then parsed by the client and rendered on a device.

As a brief introduction into HTML syntax, let's look at a very simple HTML document. Listing 1-1 includes an HTML document version of Hello World.

© Mark J. Collins 2017
M. J. Collins, *Pro HTML5 with CSS, JavaScript, and Multimedia*, DOI 10.1007/978-1-4842-2463-2_1

Listing 1-1. Simple HTML5 Document

```
<!DOCTYPE html>

<html lang="en">
    <head>
        <meta charset="utf-8" />
        <title>HTML5 Sample Document</title>
    </head>
    <body>
        Hello World!
    </body>
</html>
```

Elements

Let's break this down a bit and look at the structure used for this document. These basic concepts are used for all of the remaining content that you'll write. The document is comprised of several HTML elements that are nested in a hierarchical fashion.

Like other markup languages, *tags* are used to annotate content with useful information. An HTML *element* generally follows this structure:

```
<tag attribute="value" ... > content </tag>
```

For example, the document title, "My First HTML5 Document" is identified by the opening and closing tags, `<title>` and `</title>`. In most cases each element has an open and close tag that are identical except the close tag is preceded by a "/" character. Sometimes the terms element and tag are used interchangeably; to be precise, however, an element is comprised of an opening and closing tag and the content that is found between these tags.

Elements will often contain other elements. Notice in the sample document that the `html` element contains a `head` and a `body` element. The `head` element also contains a `meta` and a `title` element. For better readability, this nested hierarchy is illustrated by indenting child elements.

DOCTYPE

The DOCTYPE element is an oddity and doesn't fit any of the standard element formats. There is a bit of history behind it as well. In the early days of web development (think IE4 and Netscape), web pages were developed against how the current browsers were implemented. As the HTML specifications evolved and matured, new browsers developed against the updated specifications would not work with the older web pages. The DOCTYPE element was introduced so each page could specify the version of the specification that it was written against. The browser would need to interpret this and provide the necessary backward compatibility.

I won't go into all the gory details, but as you can probably imagine, this was a big mess, for both browser vendors and web developers alike. Fortunately, with HTML5 the DOCTYPE can be essentially ignored. Just set it to html:

```
<!DOCTYPE html>
```

Attributes

An opening tag can include one or more *attributes* and there are two examples of this in the sample document. Later in this chapter I will explain the different attributes that can be used. Attributes are used to provide details about an element. The html element, for example, contains lang="en", which informs the browser that the content is written in English. The browser may use this to offer to translate the content if English is not the current language.

There is a set of attributes called *global attributes* that can be used on any HTML element. A complete list of these is provided with other reference material in Appendix C. The most common ones that you'll use are id and class. The id attribute defines a unique key for an element; it must be unique within the entire HTML document. This is often used when accessing an element in JavaScript. The class attribute is sometimes called the CSS class, because it is often used for applying styles to an element. Unlike id, the class attribute is a non-unique key; a single value is applied to elements that need to have identical formatting.

In addition to the global attributes, each element type may support other attributes. Notice that the meta element includes a charset attribute:

```
<meta charset="utf-8" />
```

The charset attribute specifies the type of character-set encoding that this page uses. You should always define the character set; however, this is particularly important if your page needs to display nonstandard characters.

There are some Boolean attributes that do not need a value; their existence indicates a true value and their absence means false. For example, a check box has a checked attribute if checked and this attribute is removed if not checked. You may see something like checked="checked", especially in dynamic HTML that is generated by server-side code. However, the browser will ignore the value and you only need to include the attribute; no value is needed.

Miscellaneous Structure Rules

Notice that the meta element does not have a closing tag. There are a few elements that do not have to use a closing tag, which are referred to as *self-closing* tags. It may be somewhat obvious, but these elements cannot have any content since the content is placed between the opening and closing tags. The "/" character at the end of the tag is technically optional, but the general consensus is that it should be included and some HTML validators will flag this as a warning if it's not there.

Keep in mind that whitespace characters such as tabs, carriage returns, and extra spaces are ignored by the browser. You can left-align all of the text and the rendered HTML will be identical. You could even put the entire document on a single line if you really wanted to. But the general convention and best practice is to format the HTML like it is shown here.

I want to make one additional comment before moving on: all of this structure is optional. In fact, if you entered the following as your entire HTML document, it would render the exact same content in the browser.

```
Hello World!
```

■ **Caution** Browsers are generally very good at using default configurations when details are omitted from the document. However, I assume that you're reading this book because you want to create professional-quality web applications. These additional elements provide important information, and you should be in the habit of producing well-formed documents to make your pages as useful as possible.

HTML tags are case insensitive. The general convention is to use all lowercase tags and I'll be doing that throughout this book. But you could use <HEAD> or <Head> and it would be just as valid.

Html Element

So, as you've already seen, the html element is the root node: the starting point of your document. There's not much to say about it. The html element can contain one head element and one body element. In addition to the global attributes, it also supports the manifest attribute.

```
<html manifest="www.mywebsite.com/cache.appcache">
```

The manifest attribute is used to define the application cache. The value of this attribute is the URL or address of the cache manifest, which is a text file that lists the resources that should be cached. This can be an absolute or relative URL. When these resources are cached on the client, your page will load correctly even when disconnected from the Internet. Caching these resources can also make your page load faster and reduce the load on the web server.

■ **Tip** The standard extension for the manifest file is .appcache. It is important that this file be provided by the web server with the correct MIME type, which is text/cache-manifest. This is configured differently depending on the type of web server you are using. For more information, look at the information provided in this article: http://www.html5rocks.com/en/tutorials/appcache/beginner/.

Head Element

There's not any real content in the head element; that's what the body element is for. In Chapters 4–8 I will explain all of the various elements that are used to define the body content. But for the remainder of this chapter, we'll explore the head element.

Now let's look at the elements that can be included inside the head element. You've already seen the title and meta elements, which I'll cover in a little more detail. There are a few other useful elements that belong here as well.

Title Element

The title element specifies the title of this page. This shows up in a couple of places:

- In the browser title bar or tab (see Figure 1-1)
- Search engines will usually include this in the search results
- When adding a page to your favorites or bookmark, the title is used as the name (see Figure 1-2)

Figure 1-1. *Displaying the title in the browser tab*

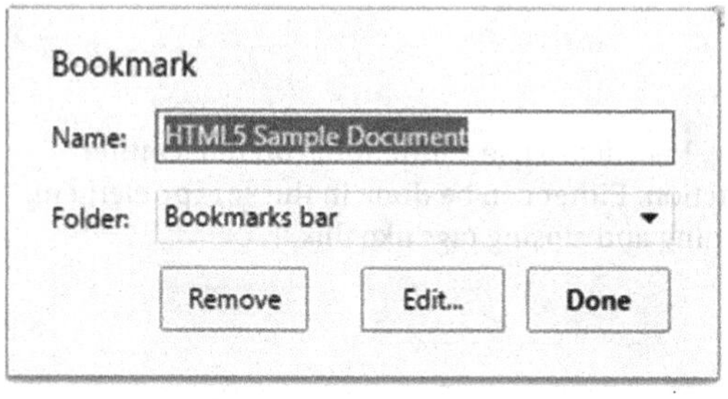

Bookmark

Name: HTML5 Sample Document

Folder: Bookmarks bar ▾

Remove   Edit...   **Done**

Figure 1-2. *Using the title in the bookmark*

Although somewhat obvious, you can only have one title element in your document. If you choose to ignore this rule, the browser will usually display the first title element and ignore the rest.

Meta Element

The meta element is an abbreviation for metadata, which is data that describes other data. In this case, the meta element describes the contents of the HTML document. The head element can include any number of meta elements, each providing a single data point using the name/value pair construct. For example:

```
<meta name="author" content="Mark J Collins" />
<meta name="description" content="Sample HTML document" />
<meta http-equiv="refresh" content="45" />
```

The value portion of the name/value pair is specified in the content attribute; however, the name portion is either defined in the name attribute or the http-equiv attribute, depending on the type of data being set. The name attribute is used for metadata that describes the content of the HTML document. The most common values for the name attribute are application-name, author, description, and keywords. These are all fairly self-explanatory. For keywords, the content attribute will contain a comma-separated list of keywords.

The http-equiv attribute is used to simulate an http response header. The more common values are these:

- content-type - the content attribute will specify a content type, typically text/html and a character set. For example, content = "text/html; charset=UTF-8".

- default-style - use this to specify the default style sheet.

- refresh - you can force the page to automatically refresh after a certain interval, which is specified, in seconds, in the content attribute.

As demonstrated in the sample document, the character set can also be specified using the shortened notation: `<meta charset="utf-8" />`.

■ **Note**   There are a lot of other `meta` names that you can use. If you're interested, check out the article at `http://www.html-5.com/metatags`. This site organizes these into logical groups such as search engine optimization (SEO), mobile devices, etc., and provides details on each one.

Script Element

The `script` element is used to load JavaScript in your page. In order to use a function, you must either define it or load an external script file that contains the function. Either can be done in the `script` element. To define JavaScript directly, include it in between the opening and closing tags like this:

```
<script type="text/javascript">
    function doSomething() {
        alert("Hello World!");
    }
</script>
```

The `type` attribute is optional and will default to `text/javascript` if not specified. This was required in HTML4 and you'll see it included quite often.

It is generally considered best practice to put JavaScript into a separate external file. One big advantage of doing that is to share the same script across multiple pages. To reference an external file, use the `src` attribute and do not include any content between the opening and closing tags. If you need to load multiple files, include each one in a separate `script` element. For example:

```
<script src="../scripts/sample.js" type="text/javascript"></script>
<script src="../scripts/demo.js" type="text/javascript"></script>
```

Normally, as the browser is parsing an HTML document, when a `script` element is encountered, the script is loaded and executed before continuing to parse the rest of the document. For external files, you can use the `async` or `defer` attributes to change this behavior. Both of these are Boolean attributes. If the `async` attribute is specified, the file is loaded and executed in parallel, while the parsing process continues. Alternatively, if the `defer` attribute is used, the script will be executed only after the page has been fully parsed.

```
<script src="../scripts/demo.js" defer ></script>
```

■ **Caution**   You should use the `defer` attribute if the script has code that executes immediately, which references any of the HTML elements. If it executes before the document is parsed, the script might fail because the elements are not yet available.

Link Element

The link element is used to reference additional external resources, which can be grouped into two categories. First, links are used to load resources that are used to render the source document – the most common of these being cascading style sheets. The second category is links to other related documents. The reader may choose to navigate to these documents but they are not needed to render the current page.

The link element uses a self-closing tag, and the linked resource is specified entirely through attributes. This is done through the href attribute that defines the address of the resource and the rel attribute. The rel attribute, an abbreviation for relationship, indicates the relationship between the source document and the linked resource.

Here are some typical link elements:

```
<link rel="stylesheet" type="text/css" href="Sample.css" />
<link rel="icon" type="image/x-icon" href="HTMLBadge.ico" />
<link rel="alternate" type="text/plain" href="TextPage.txt" />
```

This loads a CSS file named Sample.css and an icon file named HTMLBadge.ico. Notice the type attribute indicates the format of the file. For style sheets, this is optional since text/css is the assumed type. For others, such as the icon file, this is needed since a .png or .bmp file could be used as well. The last link references a text-only version of the page.

I will explain style sheets in the next chapter. The icon file is displayed in the browser tab as shown in Figure 1-3. It will also be used in other places such as bookmarks or favorites and also the history list.

Figure 1-3. *Displaying the specified icon in the browser*

■ **Note**   The link element can be used to reference many different types of resources for a lot of different reasons. Unfortunately, the term relationship does not always convey the best meaning of this attribute. For some of the most common values such as stylesheet and icon, this may be better interpreted as the type of resource rather than a relationship. For some, such as first, next, and alternate, relationship is indeed the proper term to use. However, for the sake of consistency, the rel attribute is used for all linked resources.

Tables 1-1 and 1-2 list the current rel values that are generally supported in the link element. There are other values that have been deprecated but may still be supported for some time. In addition, there are some that have been proposed but have not been adopted yet, as of this writing. The values listed here are the ones you should be using for new documents. The official specification for these can be found at https://www.w3.org/TR/html5/links.html#linkTypes.

Table 1-1. *Resource-type relationships*

Rel	Description
icon	Loads an icon used by the page as previously explained. With this relationship, a `sizes` attribute is supported to allow the desired size to be used, since an icon file often contains multiple sizes. The `type` attribute is expected to be an image file type such as "image/x-icon" or "image/png".
prefetch	Informs the browser that the external resource may be needed later and should be loaded when possible.
preload	Tells the browser that the related resource will be needed by the current document and should be loaded as soon as possible.
stylesheet	Loads a cascading style sheet; the `type` is optional and assumed to be `text/css`.

Table 1-2. *Reference-type relationships*

Rel	Description
alternate	References an alternate form of the source document. This can be used in different ways, which is explained in more detail later.
author	References a resource that provides information about the author of the source document. This is often a `mailto` reference such as `href=mailto://markc@thecreativepeople.com"`, which will send an email to the author. It could also be a link to a web page that includes details about the author.
help	References a page that provides help information about the current web page.
next	Used to reference the next document in a series.
license	Specifies a link to a page that provides licensing details.
pingback	Provides a link to a pingback service. This is used to notify a page when a link has been made to it from another page. This is primarily used on blogs and social media sites. See `https://www.w3.org/wiki/Pingback` for more details of this technology.
prev	A link to the previous document in a series.
search	The referenced document can be used for searching within the current document or web site.

■ **Note** The `rel` attribute can also be used in anchor (a) elements and `area` elements. This will be covered in Chapter 7. There are other `rel` values that can be used in these elements that are not supported in `link` elements. The values listed here are only the ones supported in a `link` element.

The `alternate` relationship link has many ways it can be used, but they all follow the basic concept of linking to another resource that provides an alternate form of the source document. There are basically two types of alternate documents:

- Type - the `link` references the current document in a different format. Use the `type` attribute to specify the type of the alternate document such as `type="application/pdf"`. A common use of this is to provide the document as a subscription feed such as ATOM. In this case, the `type` attribute is specified as `type="application/atom+xml"`.

- Language - the link references a translation of the current document into a different language. To do this, use the hreflang attribute to specify the language of the referenced document. For example, hreflang="es".

Both of these variations can be combined in a single link element. For example, if the French version of the current document is provided as a PDF document, use type="application/pdf" hreflang="fr".

The next and prev links are used to link documents that are part of a series: if you have an article, for example, that is published in three parts. The first and second document should provide a link to the next part using the next relationship. Likewise, the second and third documents should provide a reference to the previous document using the prev relationship. The previous relationship is still supported in many cases and works the same as prev. Some older values such as first, last, and up are now obsolete.

■ **Tip**   As I stated earlier, there is no actual content in the head element, although arguably the title element could be considered content. The purpose of the head element is to provide metadata about the document. This is also true of the link elements; adding them to the head element will not generate hyperlinks on your page that a user can navigate with. If you want an actual hyperlink, you'll need add an anchor element in the body. Providing the link element is similar to providing a title page in a book; no one generally reads it but it's a good practice to provide these details. It's even more important in an online document as search engines rely on these details.

The preload and prefetch relationships are similar. Both are hints to the browser that a resource should be loaded so it is available when needed. The difference is primarily in the urgency. The preload relationship indicates that the resource should be loaded early in the overall page rendering process. It will be needed by the current document so the instruction to the browser is to load it as soon as you can. In contrast, prefetch is used when the resource may be needed later, possibly in a subsequent page. The resource should be loaded but this should not slow down the current page load.

Style Element

The specific style attributes of an element such as color or size can be specified explicitly on the element, which is referred to as inline styles. The more common, and preferred, method however, is to define a set of rules that are used to determine the specific style attributes that are applied to the entire document. The next chapter will describe how these rules are implemented.

These rules are either included in an external style sheet (and referenced through the link element), or they are defined in a style element. In this regard, the style element is somewhat analogous to the script element, except it includes CSS content instead of JavaScript.

■ **Tip**   There is one big difference between the style element and the script element. The script element is used for including JavaScript either in the content of the script element, or by referencing an external file with the src attribute. When including styles, you use the style element to define styles; however, the link element is used to load an external file. Another difference is that a link element can only be used inside a head element; a style element can be used in either a head or body element, although this is not widely supported yet.

A very simple `style` element might look like this:

```
<style>
    html {
        color: red;
    }
</style>
```

This will set the `color` attribute to red for every element that is inside an `html` element, which as I've explained, is the root element for the entire document. This means that all of the content in the document will be red.

The `style` element supports the `media` attribute, which allows you to include a *media query*. A media query is a Boolean expression that can conditionally apply a set of styles. The styles are applied only if the expression evaluates to true. Media queries were originally intended to allow the same document to be formatted differently when rendered in print form. For example, the following style is applied only when printing a document:

```
<style media="print">
    html {
        color: black;
    }
</style>
```

However, media queries have been enhanced significantly giving you the ability to adjust the styles based on many different factors. One of the more common uses of this is in creating a responsive design where the format and layout of the page automatically adjusts depending on the screen resolution. Media queries will be covered in more detail in Chapter 9.

■ **Note**   Usually `style` elements are placed in the `head` element. The only exception to this is when the `scoped` attribute is used. The `scoped` attribute indicates that the `style` should apply to only the parent element and all its descendants. As of this writing, the `scoped` attribute is only supported by Firefox browsers.

Base Element

The `base` element is used to define the base URL that should be used for all other references in the document. This allows you to use relative URLs everywhere else. This saves a bit of typing but also makes it easy if you need to change the base address. The `base` element supports two specific attributes: `href`, which defines the base URL; and `target`, which specifies the default behavior when a link is selected. A `base` element might look like this:

```
<base href="www.thecreativepeople.com/html5" target="_self" />
```

■ **Caution**   The `base` element should be the first child of the `head` element, or at least come before any `link` elements so the base address will be applied to subsequent `link` elements.

As you can see, the base element uses a self-closing tag. Setting the target attribute to _self indicates that the link should be opened in the same window and tab as the current page. This can be overridden by assigning a different target in a specific link. The supported values for the target attribute are these:

- _blank - opens in a new window or tab

- _self - opens in the current window or tab (this is the default value if no target is specified)

- _parent - opens in the parent frame

- _top - opens in the topmost frame

■ **Caution**   The frameset and frame elements are not supported in HTML5 so the _parent and _top values are not applicable unless you are using an iframe. For details about browsing contexts, see the specification at https://www.w3.org/TR/html5/browsers.html#windows.

Summary

In this chapter I explained the basic syntax for creating the HTML document, often referred to as the markup. I also covered the details that can be included in the head element. Section 2 of this book will describe the elements that are available for the actual content of the document.

The next chapter will introduce Cascading Style Sheets (CSS) and how you can style the markup. Keeping the styling separate from the content will help you build a more maintainable web page.

As we work through this book in section 2, each chapter will build upon the web page created in the previous chapter. In this chapter, the focus was on the head element. Listing 1-2 shows a resulting sample web page based on the material presented in this chapter.

Listing 1-2. Sample HTML document

```
<!DOCTYPE html>

<html lang="en" manifest="sample.appcache">
    <head>
        <meta charset="utf-8" />
        <meta name="author" content="Mark J Collins" />
        <meta name="description" content="Sample HTML document" />
        <title>HTML5 Sample</title>
        <link rel="icon" type="image/x-icon" href="HTMLBadge.ico" />
        <link rel="alternate" type="application/pdf" href="MainPage.pdf" />
        <link rel="author" href="mailto:markc@thecreativepeople.com" />
        <link rel="author" type="text/html" href="http://www.thecreativepeople.com" />
        <style>
            html {
                color: red;
            }
        </style>
        <style media="print">
```

```
            html {
                color: black;
                }
        </style>
    </head>
    <body>
        <h1>
            Hello World!
        </h1>
    </body>
</html>
```

As expected, the resulting web page, shown in Figure 1-4, has minimal content, although the title and icon are displayed in the browser tab.

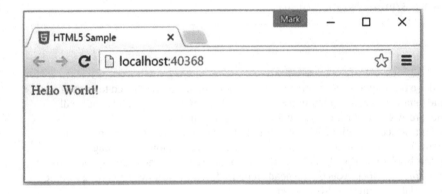

Figure 1-4. *The final web page for Chapter 1*

The complete solution, including the icon file, is available in the source code download. In the next chapter, we'll replace the style elements with external style sheets.

CHAPTER 2

■ ■ ■

Cascading Style Sheets

In this chapter I'll introduce the second leg of HTML development: the cascading style sheet. When creating an HTML document, it's always a good idea to separate the actual content from the styling rules. There are several reasons for this.

- Separation of concerns - This is often a good logical separation of responsibilities (and skill sets); a writer is good with words while a graphic designer knows how to apply fonts, colors, and layout to make an article visually appealing. That's not to say that a single person can't do both, but you'll usually find a person is better at one than the other.

- Consistency - Applying a standard set of styles across varying content will usually result in a more consistent look and feel.

- Reusability - An article can be re-purposed across multiple sites by simply applying different styles to the identical content.

- Maintainability - Content tends to be a lot more stable, while styles tend to come and go. You can give a web page an updated look without having to update the actual content.

Styling Guidelines

So how do you achieve this rich styling that is defined independently from the content? There are two parts to this solution. The process starts with well-organized content that is also properly annotated to provide contextual information. Then you must define a set of rules that specify how the appropriate style attributes should be applied to the desired set of elements.

Organizing Content

While there should not be any explicit formatting in the content, it is appropriate and desirable to identify text that should have special treatment. For example, a word or phrase that should be emphasized should be placed in an emphasis element. Likewise, when you want to make a strong emphasis about something, put it in a strong element like this:

```
<p>This <em>needs</em> to be emphasized, don't <strong>forget</strong> it!</p>
```

You may already know that the default style of an emphasis element is to italicize the font and a strong element is usually bolded. However, and this is the key point here, you're not using an emphasis element because you want the text in italics; instead, you're indicating that the text needs emphasis. The person creating the style sheet will determine how that emphasis should be made. They may choose to use a different font or color, instead of using italics.

© Mark J. Collins 2017

M. J. Collins, *Pro HTML5 with CSS, JavaScript, and Multimedia*, DOI 10.1007/978-1-4842-2463-2_2

■ **Tip**   Keep in mind that your style sheet may not be the only thing reading your content. A screen reader such as a Braille output device or text-to-speech software may interpret your emphasis and `strong` elements. Hopefully this will drive home the point that the contextual information provided in your content may be used in ways not yet imagined.

Another important point here is that the elements like emphasis and `strong` should be used consistently. I will cover all of the semantic elements that are available to you in Chapters 4–9. You should know what each of them is for and when to use them. Ultimately, deciding between emphasis and a strong emphasis is going to boil down to a judgement call. You will need to develop some guidelines so everyone knows when each is appropriate.

Applying Styles

Once you have a well-formed and amply annotated content, you can apply the desired styling. A style sheet consists of a set of *rules*. A rule is sometimes referred to as a *rule set* or *rule block*. A rule is comprised of a *selector* that defines a set of elements that the rule should be applied to, and one or more *declarations*. Each declaration sets the value of a single attribute. The general form of a rule is:

```
selector { declaration; declaration; ...}
```

A declaration includes a property and value separated by a colon, for example `color:red`, sets the `color` attribute of the element to red. The parts of a rule are shown in Figure 2-1; the selector is p, which selects all of the paragraph elements, and the declarations set the `font-size` and `color` attributes.

p { font-size:10px; color:red; }

Figure 2-1. *The parts of a CSS rule*

As with HTML, white spaces are ignored in CSS so this is often written as:

```
p {
    font-size:10px;
    color:red;
}
```

There is some debate as to the "best" way to format these rules; there are no right or wrong answers. However, I will follow this style as it seems to be the most prevalent.

Unlike HTML, CSS is not inherently hierarchical, so rules are not indented to show relationship with other rules.

■ **Tip** Here's a presentation made by Natalie Downe some years ago with a lot of suggestions for writing good CSS (http://clearleft.s3.amazonaws.com/2008/cssSystems_notes_small.pdf). Some of it is a little out of date but most of it is still very applicable today. I'd recommend skimming through it; it's a fairly easy read. But most of all, I hope some of her passion for CSS rubs off. Writing good software is as much art as it is science. I can teach you the science… the art is not as easily learned.

CSS3 Specifications

Like HTML, CSS capabilities are defined by an evolving set of specifications. The current published recommendation is CSS 2.1, and the next version being drafted is referred to as CSS3. However, CSS3 has been broken down into more than 50 "modules" with a separate specification for each. As of this writing, some of these modules have become official W3C Recommendations (REC); however, many are in Proposed Recommendation (PR) or Candidate Recommendation (CR) status. The W3C encourages the use of any of these specifications. There are still quite a lot that are in Working Draft (WD) status, which are not yet ready for general adoption.

■ **Tip** Since the status of each CSS module is ever-changing, for complete information about the current status of each, see the article at www.w3.org/Style/CSS/current-work.

So, the actual CSS3 "specification" is very much a moving target at the moment, and browser support for these specifications will also vary. However, there are already a number of cool features that are generally available, and I will demonstrate these in Chapters 9-15.

CSS Concepts

In the remainder of this chapter I will introduce the basic concept of how style sheets work. In Chapters 9-15, I will cover each of these in more detail.

Selectors

Selectors are very powerful, especially with the many improvements in CSS3, but can take some effort to master them. I will briefly explain them here and then in great detail in Chapter 9. One of the most common selectors is the *element selector*. In its simplest form, you specify the type of element that the declaration should apply to. For example:

```
em {
    font-style: italic;
}
strong {
    font-weight: bold;
}
```

Using this rule, all content in an emphasis element will use an italic font type. Likewise, a bold font will be used for all strong elements. As I mentioned earlier, these are the default styles for these elements. The browser has its own internal style sheet that defines these default styles. So even if you don't supply any style rules, the content is rendered in a reasonable fashion using the default rules.

Selectors generally cascade so the body selector will select all body elements as well as all elements that are inside a body element. Selectors can also be combined in various ways. The comma separator, for example, is used as a logical OR operator. So h1, h2, h3 will select all elements that are inside either an h1 element or an h2 element or an h3 element. Similarly, the space separator is a logical AND operator. So h1 p will select all elements that are both inside an h1 element and a p element.

Declarations

Selectors determine what elements a rule is applied to, but the declarations specify the style attributes that are applied to the selected elements. In many cases, each declaration sets the value of a single attribute. The name and value are separated by a color and the declaration is terminated with a semicolon; for example: color:red;. There is a seemingly endless number of style attributes that you can set, and I will demonstrate these in Chapters 10–15.

CSS supports shortcuts that allow you to specify multiple attributes in a single declaration. The margin attribute is a good example of this. The margin attribute specifies the amount of space between an element and its neighbors. The space above, below, to the left, and to the right can be specified independently. To set these all to 5 pixels you can use the following declarations:

```
margin-top: 5px;
margin-right: 5px;
margin-bottom: 5px;
margin-left: 5px;
```

CSS also allows you to set all four values in a single shortcut declaration:

```
margin: 5px 5px 5px 5px;
```

The four values in the declaration specify the top, right, bottom, and left margin values.

■ **Tip** The order of the values is important here since the values are not named but rather assumed based on order. To help remember the correct order, think of a clock. The day starts at midnight (top) and then continues in clockwise fashion to 3 (right) then to 6 (bottom) and finally to 9 (left).

The shortcut can be further shortened, however. If the right value is not provided it will be set as the same value of the left margin. Similarly, the bottom margin will use the same value as the top. So this can be also set like this:

```
margin: 5px 5px;
```

Here, only the top and right values are specified; the bottom is set to the same value as the top and the left is set to the same value as the right. Finally, since all values are the same, you can also use the simplest shortcut:

```
margin: 5px;
```

Units

In my previous examples, I have set the font size, color, and margin using some arbitrary units. Let's look at the most common units that are available.

Distance Units

The distance unit, sometimes called length or size, is used in many declarations and supports several types of units. The basic absolute units are inches (in), centimeters (cm), millimeters (mm), and 1/4 millimeters (q). Not much needs to be said about these; everyone knows what inches and centimeters are. However, their typographical cousins, picas (pc), points (pt), and pixels (px), seems to be much more prevalent. In 1 inch there are 6 picas, 72 points, or 96 pixels.

■ **Caution**   The unit pixel (px) does not equate to a device pixel, unless the resolution of your device just happens to be 96 dpi (dots per inch). To avoid the confusion, the term is called "visual angle unit" in the WC3 documentation. However, this unit is still commonly known as pixels. Its definition is 1/96 of an inch; be aware that the actual number of device pixels may be different.

One fundamental drawback to using these absolute units is that they seldom have any relevance to real-world dimensions. The actual size on one screen can be very different from another, depending on the device resolution. The absolute units are more useful when printing as the physical size is more accurately rendered. The relative units are recommended for normal screen presentation. There are two types of relative dimensions: font-relative and viewport-relative.

The font-relative units are relative to a font size, usually of the current font. These units are font size (em), character height (ex), zero width (ch), and root font size (rem). The term "em" comes from the field of typography, where the font size was once defined as the width of a capital "M". The font size is now defined as the height of the font, including the space above and below it. The em unit is equivalent to the font size. If the font size is 12px, for example, then 1em = 12px.

■ **Tip**   The em space character (   ) creates a space that is 1em wide. Likewise, the em dash character (—) creates a dash (hyphen) the size of 1em. Interestingly, the en space character (   ), creates a space = 1/2em.

The ex unit is defined as the height of the lowercase "x" character. In similar fashion, the ch unit is defined as the width of the zero "0" character. There are some special rules that are used when a particular font does not include an "x" or "0" character. If there is no practical way of otherwise defining ex or ch units, the value of 1/2em is used.

The em, ex, and ch units are all defined based on the current font. In a typical HTML document, different font sizes are used, and the font-relative units will adjust accordingly, depending on the font currently being used. The value of em in a h1 element, for example, will typically be larger than a paragraph (p) element. In contrast, the rem unit is based on the font size of the root element, which as I stated in the previous chapter is usually the html element. So the rem unit will always be the same everywhere in the document. So, if you want something to be sized based on the current font, use em (or ex or ch), but if the size should be constant, use rem.

The viewport-relative units are viewport width (vw), viewport height (vh), viewport minimum (vmin), and viewport maximum (vmax). These units represent 1% of the applicable viewport dimension. For example, if the viewport of the device (or browser window) is 600 pixels wide by 400 pixels high, 1vw = 6px and 1vh = 4px. The vmin unit is based on the smallest viewport dimension, in this case it is 400 pixels, so 1vmin = 4px. It doesn't matter how the viewport is oriented. Similarly, vmax is based on the largest dimension so 1vmax = 6px.

■ **Tip**   While not actually a "unit," a distance dimension can also be specified as a percentage, such as width: 20%;. When defined this way, the width is expressed as a percentage of the containing element. In contrast, vw and vh are a percentage of initial containing block, which is the total window size.

Color Units

The color attribute is defined by the value of the individual red, green, and blue components. The standard form is to specify each component as a hexadecimal value from 0 to xFF. The color is defined by a 6-digit number where the first two digits define the red component, the next two digits define the green component, and the last two digits define the blue component. When specified in this way, the hexadecimal number is preceded by the hash symbol ("#"). For example, black is defined as #000000 and white is #FFFFFF.

There are several alternative ways to specify a color attribute. The first is to use only a single digit for each component. For example, white would be defined as #FFF. When expressed in this format, the 2-digit form is derived by replicating the single digit. So #567 is converted to #556677.

For those who prefer to enter these as decimal values, the rgb() function can be used. The rgb() function takes 3 parameters, which are the red, green, and blue components expressed as decimal values between 0 and 255. (255 is the decimal equivalent of xFF.) Using this format, white is specified as rgb(255,255,255). To make this even easier, you can specify a percentage of the maximum value. Using this approach, white is defined as rgb(100%,100%,100%).

■ **Tip**   There is also an rgba() function that includes a fourth parameter called alpha, where you can specify the opacity. The alpha value can be between 0 and 1. A value of 1 means completely opaque and a value of 0 is completely transparent.

There are sixteen keywords that define specific color values such as red, blue, and black. You can use one of these instead of specifying the RGB values. These keywords are listed in the reference material in Appendix C, along with the RGB equivalent of each. In addition to these, CSS3 defines quite a few extended color keywords that are supported by many browsers. You can find the complete list at https://www.w3.org/TR/css3-color/#svg-color.

The use of RGB to define colors started when the first color cathode-ray tubes (CRTs) were introduced. CRTs had three colors that it was able to display: red, green, and blue. The intensity of each of these three colors could be varied for each dot or pixel on the screen. Consequently, the notion of using RGB terminology was based on the existing hardware capabilities. While we may need to end up with RGB values to render a particular color, using hue, saturation, and lightness (HSL) is a more intuitive way of expressing a color.

The hue is expressed as an angle. Picture a color wheel with red at 0°, green at 120°, and blue at 240°. The colors in between are relative compositions of the adjoining colors. Saturation indicates how intense the color and is expressed as a percentage with 100% being full saturation and 0% being gray. Lightness is also expressed as a percentage where 100% is white and 0% is black. A typical value would be 50%. As you increase the lightness, the color gets washed out and starts looking white. As the lightness fades, the color looks darker and eventually black.

To define a color in terms of hue, saturation, and lightness, use the `hsl()` function. A solid red color would be expressed as `hsl(0,100%,50%)`. The first parameter is assumed to be specified in degrees so no units are necessary. You can also use the `hsla()` function that includes the alpha parameter for specifying the opacity.

■ **Note**   The W3C specification on units can be found at `https://www.w3.org/TR/css3-values`. For more details on color units, see `https://www.w3.org/TR/css3-color`.

Keywords

There are a few keywords that you can use as "units" in most style declarations. These are `auto`, `inherit`, `initial`, `revert`, and `unset`.

- `inherit` - the `inherit` keyword indicates that the property should use the value of its parent element. Most properties are inherited by default so setting the value to `inherit` doesn't actually change anything; it would inherit the parent's value anyway. Adding it may improve the documentation of the author's intent. You may want to create a rule that uses `inherit` to override the value of another rule.

- `initial` - the `initial` keyword is used to set a property back to the initial default setting. In many cases, this is the browser's default value. For example, the default color is usually black so `color: initial;` will set the color to black. As of this writing, this is not supported by any version of Internet Explorer.

- `auto` - The `auto` value is a bit tricky and its behavior will change depending on where it is used. For example, setting the `padding: auto;` will automatically adjust the left and right padding to center the content. Setting `height: auto;` will cause the height to grow to fit the content inside.

- `revert` - The `revert` keyword specifies that the browser should ignore any author styles and use the browser default values. It is not supported by many browsers, as of this writing.

- `unset` - the `unset` keyword is a combination of `inherit` and `initial`. Basically, it works like `inherit` for all inheritable properties and like `initial` for the remaining properties. Like `revert`, the `unset` keyword is not supported by some browsers.

Precedence

Selectors return sets of elements and these sets can overlap. The result is that multiple rules can be applied to the same element. If one rule sets the font size, another sets the color, and a third sets the background, then there is no conflict. However, if one sets the color to red and another sets the color to green, what will happen? Here's where the precedence rules are applied.

Style Sheet Sources

First of all, there are three sources of style sheets:

- Author: These are the style sheets created by the web developer and what you normally think of when referring to a style sheet.

- User: A user can also create a style to control how web pages are displayed for them specifically.

- User Agent: A user agent (web browser) will have a default style sheet. For example, if you create a document with no style rules, the browser will display the content using a default font family and size. These are actually defined in a style sheet that is specific to the browser.

When rendering a page, the browser has to process styles from all of these sources to determine the appropriate style for each element. When there are conflicting rules, the author style sheet takes precedence over the user style sheet, which takes precedence over the user agent styles (browser defaults).

■ **Tip**   You might find it useful to look at the default browser style sheets. They are generally available although you might have to do some searching to find them. For example, you can use this link to see the style sheet used by Chrome: `http://trac.webkit.org/browser/trunk/Source/WebCore/css/html.css`

Specificity Rule

In addition, consider that even within a set of author style sheets there may be conflicting declarations. For example, a style sheet may include the following:

```
p {
    color: black;
}

header p {
    color: red;
}
```

A p element within a header element is selected by both rules, so which one is used? In this case, the specificity rule applies, which states that the more specific selector is used, which is the header p selector. With all the selectors that are available, determining which one is more specific is not as straightforward as you might think. ID selectors are considered more specific than class or attribute selectors, which are more specific than element selectors.

When applying the specificity rule logic, the browser will analyze each selector and give it a score based on the type of selector is used. This score is represented as a set of four values:

1. The number of inline styles (elements that include the style attribute)

2. The number of ID selectors

3. The number class, attributes, or pseudo-class selectors

4. The number of element selectors

The analysis compares the first value and only goes on to the next value when there is a tie. So if one selector includes an ID selector and the other doesn't, no further analysis is needed. The one with the ID selector wins. Finally, if all 4 values are the same, the tie is broken by taking the rule that appears last.

■ **Tip**   Understanding these precedence rules is important because conflicts will occur and you'll need to know how to deal with them. However, you should plan your style sheets to avoid conflicts.

Important Keyword

The one sort of "ace-in-the-hole" is the !important keyword. If this is used in a style rule, this trumps all other rules. You can add the !important keyword like this:

```
p {
    color: red !important;
}
```

Keep in mind that the !important keyword is applied in the declaration, not the rule. It only applies to a single declaration and must be repeated on each declaration that you want it applied to.

If two conflicting rules both have the !important keyword, then the precedence is determined based on the rules I already mentioned. However, when it comes to the source of the style sheet, they are applied in reverse order. The important rules in the user style sheet override important rules in the author style sheet. This has an important application (no pun intended). This allows the user to override the author styles for certain properties. For example, someone who is visually impaired may need to increase the font size. The !important tag will ensure that this style does not get overridden.

■ **Caution**   You might be tempted to use the important keyword to make a quick fix and override a cascaded style rule. With all the precedence rules that I just described, you shouldn't need to do this. I recommend using this as a last resort. Overuse of the !important keyword can make your style sheets difficult to maintain.

Box Model

Each element in the document takes up a certain amount of space, which depends on the content of that element. In addition, factors such as padding and margin affect this. Padding is the space between the content and the element's border. The margin is the space between the border and adjacent elements. This is illustrated in Figure 2-2.

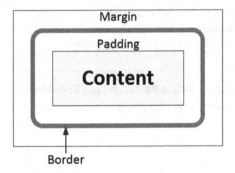

Figure 2-2. *The box model*

I explained the margin attribute earlier. In the same way, you can specify the padding with the padding declaration. Padding and margin are very similar; the primary difference is that the padding is inside the border.

When determining the space used, remember to include the border width. For example, if the padding is set to 10px, the margin set to 5px, and the border-width set to 3px, the space used (in addition to the actual element content) will be (2 * 10) + (2 * 5) + (2 * 3) = 36px.

Vendor Prefixes

Oh, the joys of living on the edge! As with other areas of HTML5, browser vendors will have varying support for the CSS specifications. In many cases, however, these vendors implement new properties before they become part of the official recommendation. In fact, much of what is being included in the CSS3 specification has already been available from one or more browsers.

When a browser vendor adds a new feature that is not part of the CSS3 recommendation, the property is given a vendor-specific prefix to indicate this is a nonstandard feature. If this becomes part of the recommendation, the prefix is eventually dropped. To take advantage of some of the newer properties, you may need to use the vendor-specific properties, and since you want your page to work on all vendors, you'll need to add all of them. For example, to specify the border radius, in addition to the standard border-radius property, you may need to set all of the vendor-specific properties as well like this:

```
header
{
    -moz-border-radius: 25px;
    -webkit-border-radius: 25px;
    -ms-border-radius: 25px;
    border-radius: 25px;
}
```

Table 2-1 lists the most common prefixes. There are others, but this table covers the vast majority of browsers.

Table 2-1. *Vendor Prefixes*

Prefix	Browser Vendor
-moz-	Firefox
-webkit-	Chrome, Safari, Opera
-ms-	Internet Explorer

You can't blindly assume that all vendor-prefixed properties have the same name as the standard property, with the prefix added, although that is true most of the time. Here is a good article that lists many of the vendor-specific properties: `http://peter.sh/experiments/vendor-prefixed-css-property-overview`. Unfortunately, this page has not been updated for a while and may be out of date. If you find that a standard property doesn't work in a particular browser, you may need to do some research to see whether there is a prefixed property available from their developer's site. For example, use this link for Webkit extensions: `https://developer.mozilla.org/en-US/docs/Web/CSS/Reference/Webkit_Extensions`.

■ **Caution**   You should always list the standard property last so it will override the vendor-specific version. Some browsers will support both, and while most of the time the implementation is identical, sometimes the vendor-specific version behaves differently.

Style Attribute

The `style` attribute is not part of a style sheet but is used for a similar purpose so I will explain it here. The `style` attribute is one of the global attributes that is supported by every element. It allows you to set one or more declarations on a single element. While a normal style rule includes a selector that determines which elements the rule applies to, since the `style` attribute is included in an element, no selector is needed. Using a `style` attribute is referred to as inline styles. A sample element using inline styles might look like this:

```
<p style="font-size: 1.5rem; color: hsla(175, 80%, 60%, .8);">
    Hello World!
</p>
```

■ **Tip**   In the above example I used the `rem` unit that I explained earlier, so the font will be 50% larger than the root font size. The color is defined by a hue of 175°, which is somewhere between green and blue, a saturation of 80%, a lightness of 60%, and an opacity of 80%.

Just like other attributes, the value is specified inside double quotes. The value consists of one or more declarations. These are formatted just like declarations in a style sheet would be: a name/value pair separated by a colon and terminated with a semicolon. You can set any property in a style attribute that you could with an external style sheet.

■ **Caution**   I saved the style attribute for last because I'm hoping that you never use it. By including inline styles, you no longer have a separation of content and style. If you later decide that the blue-green font doesn't look good, you can't fix it with merely a CSS change. Remember, inline styles take precedence over any CSS-based rule.

Summary

In this chapter, I explained some of the basic concepts used when creating style sheets. We'll apply this by creating a couple of external style sheets that you can include in your web page.

First, we'll start with a very simple style sheet shown in Listing 2-1. This is in a file named Initial.css.

Listing 2-1. The Initial.css file

```css
/* Make sure the non-content elements are hidden */
head, title, meta, script, link, style, base {
    display: none;
}

/* Default styling for emphasis and strong elements */
em {
    font-style: italic;
}
strong {
    font-weight: bold;
}

/* Style the text */
body>h1 {
    font-size: 1.5rem;
    color: hsla(175, 80%, 60%, .8);
}
```

The first rule makes sure that the non-content elements that you learned about in Chapter 1 are not displayed. The browser default style sheet will set these anyway. The second rule sets the attributes for the emphasis and strong elements as I discussed earlier. Again, these are the default styles. The last rule sets the font size and color of the text using the rem and hsla units that I explained in this chapter.

Next we'll create a second CSS file that will be used for print mode. The file, shown in Listing 2-2 is named Print.css.

Listing 2-2. The Print.css file

```css
body>h1 {
    color: black;
}
```

```
body {
    border: 1px solid;
    border-color: black;
    border-radius: 25px;
    padding: 24px;
}
```

This has two rules: the first sets the color to black and the second adds a border around the entire document.

Finally, modify the MainPage.html file and replace the two style elements with the following link elements. This will reference the new CSS files instead of specifying the style rules in the HTML document.

```
<link rel="stylesheet" href="Initial.css" />
<link rel="stylesheet" href="Print.css" media="print" />
```

The Initial.css was referenced without any media attribute so it will apply to both screen and print modes. The Print.css file will only be used in print mode. Notice that both files use a body>h1 selector, which have an equal specificity since they are identical. This relies on the behavior that rules that are defined later override previous rules.

The Initial.css file includes a font-size declaration and the Print.css file does not, so the font-size will apply to both screen and print modes. Only the color attribute is overridden in print mode.

Now display the web page and you should see the "Hello World!" text in a blue-green font. Then print the document from the browser. The output should look similar to Figure 2-3 depending on the browser you're using.

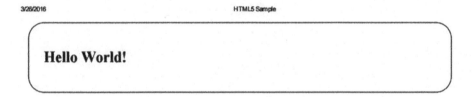

Figure 2-3. *The printed version of the HTML document*

Notice the title (specified in the title element) is shown at the top of the page.

■ **Note**   Each browser handles print mode differently. Some left-justify the title, some put the URL at the top of the page, some include the page number, and some show the print date.

The next chapter will introduce the third main area of this book, JavaScript. This chapter will explain the concepts of the JavaScript language, which is the foundation for the topics explained in sections 4 and 5.

CHAPTER 3

JavaScript Essentials

In this chapter I'll explain the third leg of HTML5 development: JavaScript. In Chapters 16–20 I will demonstrate the many things that you can do with JavaScript within your HTML5 web pages. But in this chapter I must first explain the language itself.

Introducing JavaScript

There's a lot of content here as the JavaScript language is quite powerful. It may seem a bit awkward at first, especially to someone whose background is in compiled languages such as C++ or C#. But it's not hard to learn; I will explain these fundamental concepts here and then you'll apply this in the later chapters.

Objects

The main building block in JavaScript is an *object*. An object is a collection of elements; each element can either be a *property* or a *method*. A property holds a single data value, and a method will perform some action that is defined as a function. Another way of stating this is that a property is simply a variable (note the var keyword) that is defined on an object. Likewise, a method is a function that is defined on an object.

The easiest way to create an object is by specifying the members through a set of name/value pairs like this:

```
var myObject = {
    color: "Red",
    count: 5
};
```

■ **Note**   You may be familiar with formatting data in JavaScript Object Notation (JSON). That's exactly what this is and where JSON came from.

You can also define methods using this notation, like this:

```
var myObject = {
    color: "Red",
    count: 5,
    log: function () {
        console.log("Quantity: " + this.count + ", Color: " + this.color);
    }
};
```

© Mark J. Collins 2017
M. J. Collins, *Pro HTML5 with CSS, JavaScript, and Multimedia*, DOI 10.1007/978-1-4842-2463-2_3

Creating an object in this way is sometimes referred to as *object literal* notation. The object, named myObject contains two properties, color and count and one function, log(). You can then access the properties and functions using the dot notation like this:

```
window.alert(myObject.color);
myObject.log();
```

▪ **Tip**   This code demonstrates two popular ways of debugging. Calling the alert() function on the window object will display a modal dialog containing the text passed into the function. Calling the log() function on the console object will write the specified text to the browser console that you can access through the developer tools provided by the browser. Note that window and console are objects with properties and functions. They will be explained in detail in Chapters 16 and 17.

Another way to create an object is to use an *object constructor*. This uses the new keyword and invokes the default constructor. The following code would create the exact same object:

```
var redObject = new Object();
redObject.color = "Red";
redObject.count = 5;
redObject.log = function() {
    console.log("Quantity: " + this.count + ", Color: " + this.color);
}
```

If you need a simple object, primarily for storing data, the JSON style may be slightly more intuitive and more compact. However, for function-oriented objects, the constructor style provides much more capabilities, which is what I will explain shortly.

If you needed a second instance to count your green items, for example, just repeat the code like this:

```
var greenObject = new Object();
greenObject.color = "Green";
greenObject.count = 7;
greenObject.log = function() {
    console.log("Quantity: " + this.count + ", Color: " + this.color);
}
```

You can then use both objects in your code, for example:

```
if (greenObject.count > redObject.count) {
    console.log("You have more green items than red item");
}
```

Constructors

Notice that you have to define the log() method in both objects. If you're familiar with class-based languages such as C#, this might seem a bit odd. A class is used as a template from which to create each instance of the class. When you use a class to create an object, the definition of all of the properties and methods is copied from the class.

However, JavaScript does not use classes. Instead you can reuse an object definition by creating a *constructor* function. In the previous example you used the generic constructor, Object(), which creates an empty object. However, you could define a custom constructor like this:

```
function Item(){
    this.color = undefined;
    this.count = 0;
    this.log = function() {
        console.log("Quantity: " + this.count + ", Color: " + this.color);
    };
}
```

A constructor is a function that is used to instantiate an object. This one creates a property named color but does not define it. It also creates a property called count and initializes it to zero. The log() method is also defined and uses these two properties. Now you can create an object using this prototype by calling the Item() constructor:

```
var redObject = new Item();
redObject.color = "Red";
redObject.count = 5;
```

You'll need to set the property values for this instance but not the methods. You can then use it like the other objects created earlier. Adding this to the script will write the color and count properties to the console, just like before:

```
redObject.log();
```

Like any other function, a constructor can take parameters, and this is often used to initialize the properties. For example, you can rewrite your constructor to take a color and a count parameter:

```
function Item(color, count){
    this.color = color;
    this.count = count;
    this.log = function () {
        console.log("Quantity: " + this.count + ", Color: " + this.color);
    };
}
```

Then create the greenObject variable like this:

```
var greenObject = new Item("Green", 7);
```

You cannot have multiple constructors with the same name. For example, you cannot define an Item() constructor and an Item(color, count) constructor. If you do, the second definition will replace the first. However, the parameters are optional so you can define a constructor that takes two parameters but you can then call it with no parameters. If you plan to use it this way, the constructor should deal with undefined parameters, such as providing default values like this:

```
function Item(color, count){
    this.color = color;
    this.count = count;
```

```
    // Handle missing parameters
    if (color == undefined){this.color = "Black";}
    if (count == undefined){this.count = 0;}

    this.log = function () {
        console.log("Quantity: " + this.count + ", Color: " + this.color);
    };
}
```

Prototypes

All objects have a *prototype*. A prototype is a model or blueprint from which actual objects are instantiated. What if you needed an additional property? You can add a property to an existing object like this:

```
greenObject.isAvailable = true;
```

This would add the isAvailable property to the greenObject only; however, if you add this to the Item prototype then the new property would be available for all instances. You can modify the prototype by accessing it with the prototype property of the constructor function:

```
Item.prototype.isAvailable = true;
```

This defines the new property on the prototype and initializes it to true. Now all objects created with the Item() constructor will have the isAvailable property:

```
var blueObject = new Item("Blue", 3);
if (blueObject.isAvailable){
    console.log("The blue object is available");
}
```

You can add methods to a prototype in the same way:

```
Item.prototype.add = function(n){this.count += n;};
```

Inheritance

Let's dive in a little deeper. Consider the following JavaScript:

```
var blueObject = new Item("Blue", 3);
console.log(blueObject);
```

This creates a blueObject using the Item() constructor and outputs the result to the console. The console window, after expanding the entries some, will look like Figure 3-1.

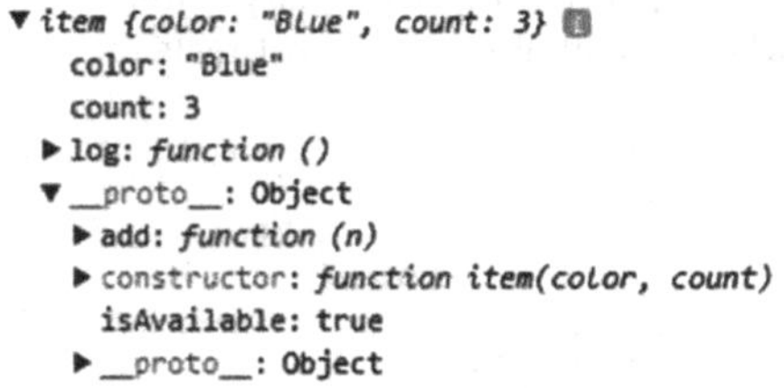

```
▼ item {color: "Blue", count: 3} 🔳
    color: "Blue"
    count: 3
  ▶ log: function ()
  ▼ __proto__: Object
    ▶ add: function (n)
    ▶ constructor: function item(color, count)
      isAvailable: true
    ▶ __proto__: Object
```

Figure 3-1. *Displaying the objects in the console window*

The values of the color and count properties are displayed and the log() method is listed as expected. Notice the __proto__ property, which is defined as type Object. This is the prototype property. If you expand this, you'll see the isAvailable property and the add() method listed as well as the Item() constructor.

■ **Tip**   You can add properties and methods to an object by simply defining them like o.newProperty = 5;. You can also add them to a prototype by defining them on the constructor prototype like Item.prototype. newProperty = 5;. Adding them to the object only affects that object, but adding them to the prototype makes the new property available to objects using that constructor.

As I stated at the beginning of the chapter, an object is a collection of properties and/or methods. These are referred to as its *own* members. The term *own* indicates the members are directly owned by the object and not inherited. Each object also has a prototype, which is also an object and has its own members as well.

When accessing a member from an object, like o.someProperty, JavaScript will first look for the someProperty in the o object's own member collection. If not found there, the search will then look in the object's prototype.

Using Prototypes

JavaScript supports inheritance using an approach known as *prototypal inheritance*. The means that a prototype, being an object itself, will also have a prototype property. This, of course, can also have a prototype, and so on. This is referred to as the *prototype chain*.

Notice there is another __proto__ property listed as a member of the Item prototype. This is the Object prototype that all objects are derived from. If you expand this in the console window, you'll find numerous methods listed such as the Object() constructor that you used earlier and the toString() method. But it does not have a __proto__ property; this is the end of the prototype chain.

■ **Tip**   In some browsers, such as IE, the __proto__ property of the Object prototype is listed with a null value. This is actually more accurate; all objects have a prototype property, but it will be null if there is no further inheritance.

With this in mind, you can establish inheritance by simply assigning the prototype property to the parent class constructor. Suppose you wanted a new object SpecialItem, to inherit from Item. Create the SpecialItem() constructor:

```
function SpecialItem(name) {
    this.name = name;
    this.describe = function() {
        console.log(this.name + ": color=" + this.color);
    };
}
```

This creates a name property that is initialized by the constructor. It also creates a describe() method that writes the name as well as the color properties to the console. To set up the inheritance, set the prototype property like this:

```
// Setup the inheritance using prototypal inheritance
SpecialItem.prototype = new Item();
```

Because the color and count properties were not specified in the constructor, the default values were used. You can fix that by adding color and count parameters in the SpecialItem() constructor and pass these to the Item() constructor. Modify the SpecialItem() constructor by adding the code in bold:

```
function SpecialItem(name, color, count) {
    Item.call(this, color, count);
    this.name = name;
    this.describe = function () {
        console.log(this.name + ": color=" + this.color);
    };
}
```

This uses the parent object's call() method, which I will explain later in this chapter. When you create an object using the SpecialItem() constructor, you can then access both the log() method and the describe() method. To verify this, add the following code:

```
var special = new SpecialItem("Widget", "Purple", 4);
special.log();
special.describe();
console.log(special);
```

The console window will look similar to Figure 3-2.

```
Quantity: 4, Color: Purple
Widget: color=Purple
▼ SpecialItem {color: "Purple", count: 4, name: "Widget"} 🔓
    color: "Purple"
    count: 4
  ▶ describe: function ()
  ▶ log: function ()
    name: "Widget"
  ▼ __proto__: Item
      color: "Black"
      count: 0
    ▶ log: function ()
    ▼ __proto__: Object
      ▶ add: function (n)
      ▶ constructor: function Item(color, count)
        isAvailable: true
      ▶ __proto__: Object
```

Figure 3-2. *Testing the specialItem() constructor*

Using Create

There is another technique for implementing inheritance, which is called *classical inheritance*. It uses the Object.create() function to set up the relationship between the parent and child objects.

To use this approach, you need to define the child object's prototype using the create() method. For example, replace the previous statement that set the SpecialItem.prototype with the following code:

```
// Setup the inheritance using classical inheritance
SpecialItem.prototype = Object.create(Item.prototype);
SpecialItem.prototype.constructor = SpecialItem;
```

You can test the new implementation of SpecialItem() using the same code as before:

```
var special = new SpecialItem("Widget", "Purple", 4);
special.log();
special.describe();
console.log(special);
```

The new object will function like it did before, but the way the elements are inherited is different. Notice that most of the properties and methods are shown in the child class instead of the parent prototype as shown in Figure 3-3.

```
Quantity: 4, Color: Purple
Widget: color=Purple
▼ SpecialItem {color: "Purple", count: 4, name: "Widget"} 🔳
    color: "Purple"
    count: 4
  ▶ describe: function ()
  ▶ log: function ()
    name: "Widget"
  ▼ __proto__: Item
    ▶ constructor: function SpecialItem(name, color, count)
    ▼ __proto__: Object
      ▶ add: function (n)
      ▶ constructor: function Item(color, count)
        isAvailable: true
      ▶ __proto__: Object
```

Figure 3-3. *The SpecialItem object using classical inheritance*

Using the Class Keyword

The ECMAScript version 6 introduced some new keywords, which makes inheritance in JavaScript more palatable for developers who are familiar with class-based inheritance. These include class, constructor, extends, and super. The underlying implementation of this approach is identical to the previous one using the Object.create() method. It uses some new keywords and minor syntax changes but accomplishes the same thing.

■ **Caution**   While support is growing fast, not all browsers support all of the ECMAScript version 6 features. Here's a link that shows what features are currently available: http://kangax.github.io/compat-table/es6

The complete implementation of the Item() and SpecialItem() functions is shown in Listing 3-1.

Listing 3-1. Demonstrating the class keyword

```
class Item {
    constructor(color, count) {
        this.color = color;
        this.count = count;
        this.log = function () {
            console.log("Quantity: " + this.count + ", Color: " + this.color);
        };
    }
}

class SpecialItem extends Item {
    constructor(name, color, count) {
        super(color, count);
        this.name = name;
        this.describe = function () {
```

```
        console.log(this.name + ": color=" + this.color);
      }
    }
};
```

To keep the solution equivalent between each approach, add the following code to define the isAvailable and add() members. This is the exact same code used earlier.

```
Item.prototype.isAvailable = true;
Item.prototype.add = function(n){this.count += n;};
```

While this code uses the new class keyword, it is defining the same constructor functions created earlier. The extends keyword defines the parent constructor name and the super keyword replaces the Item.call(this); statement that calls the parent constructor.

To test this, use the same calls as before. After running this, the console window will be identical to the one shown in Figure 3-3.

```
var special = new SpecialItem("Widget", "Purple", 4);
special.log();
special.describe();
console.log(special);
```

■ **Caution**   When calling an inherited method, the value of this will be the object being invoked, which is not necessarily the same object where the method is defined. In the previous example, when calling special. log(), this points to the SpecialItem object, even though the log() method was defined on the Item() constructor. This is important to remember when a child class overrides any of its parent's members.

Overriding Members

Regardless of which syntax is used to implement inheritance, the way overridden members are handled is the same. As I mentioned earlier, each object has a collection of members, which are called own properties (or members). There are no restrictions on having own members with the same names as the members in the inherited object.

When accessing a property or invoking a method, JavaScript will first look for an own member with the name specified. If not found there, it will search up the prototype chain. For methods, this works much like you probably expect it to. If the method is defined in the child object, the child's implementation will be used. If not, the parent's method will be called.

For properties, if the same name exists in both the parent and child objects, there will be two instances that can have separate values. Which one is used will depend on the scope, which I will explain later.

Properties

I glossed over the concept of properties rather quickly because I wanted to first focus on objects, prototypes, and inheritance. But let me back up a little and explain properties in more detail.

As you have already seen, properties can be one of the simple data types (string, number, and Boolean). You don't explicitly declare the data type; instead, it is inferred based on the value it is assigned. The data type can change as new values are assigned. For example:

```
var test = "Some string";
test = 5;
test = true;
```

This code first creates a string and then changes it to a number and finally, to a Boolean. To verify the data type actually changes, you can run the following code:

```
var test = "Some string";
console.log(test + ': ' + isNaN(test));
test = 5;
console.log(test + ': ' + isNaN(test));
```

The isNaN() function returns true if the value passed in is not a number data type. If you ran this, you would see something like this in the console:

```
Some string: true
5: false
```

Arrays

An array in JavaScript is simply a collection of properties. The array itself has a name and can be a member of an object or a variable. The items in the array are accessed by a numerical index. An array is created using a literal notation, for example:

```
var colors = ["red", "green", "blue", "yellow", "purple", "orange"];
```

You can also create an empty array and add items to it using the push() method:

```
var colors = [];
colors.push("red");
colors.push("green");
```

To access an item in an array you specify its index. For example, colors[0] will return the string "red." The length property indicates how many elements there are in an array. Since the index is 0-based, the length property will always reference the element after the last one. So you can also add to the end of an array by using the following:

```
colors[colors.length] = "blue";
```

■ **Tip**   Items in an array are accessed through a numerical index starting with 0. Arrays do not support named indices or keys. If you need to access an item by name, you should create it as a named property or variable instead of an array element.

An array can contain elements of different types. It is perfectly acceptable to include numbers, strings, and object references in a single array. That may not be logically correct depending on how you will be using the array, but JavaScript does not prevent you from doing it.

You can iterate through the elements of an array using a for loop:

```
for (var i=0; i < colors.length; i++) {
    console.log(colors[i]);
}
```

Attributes

All properties have a set of attributes that can be read and updated. These attributes are the following:

- value - the value of the property; this is the default property.

- writable - set to true if the property can be updated.

- enumerable - set to true if this property should be included when enumerating the object members.

- configurable - set to true if the property can be deleted and if the attributes can be modified.

You can access the *property descriptor* using the getOwnPropertyDescriptor() method. The property descriptor is a set of named values that specify the values of these attributes. For example, consider the following:

```
function Item(color, count){
    this.color = color;
    this.count = count;
}

var redObject = new Item("Red", 5);
console.log(Object.getOwnPropertyDescriptor(redObject, "color"));
```

This will output the attributes of the color property of the redObject. The console would look like this:

```
Object {value: "Red", writable: true, enumerable: true, configurable: true}
```

The getOwnPropertyDescriptor() method takes two parameters: the first is the object that contains the property; the second is the name of the property. It returns a property descriptor.

You can update these attributes using the Object.defineProperty() method. The first two parameters of this method are an object and the name of a property, just like with the getOwnPropertyDescriptor() method. You then pass in a property descriptor for the third parameter. You only need to specify the values that you want changed. For example, if you want the color property to be read-only, call this:

```
Object.defineProperty(redObject, "color", { writable: false });
```

You can also use the defineProperty() method to create new properties, which gives you the ability to set these attributes when the property is first created. If you pass in a name of a property that does not exist, a new one will be created. The code shown in bold adds the size property in the Item() constructor:

```
function Item(color, count){
    this.color = color;
    this.count = count;

    Object.defineProperty(this, "size",
        {value: 7, writable: true, enumerable: false, configurable: "true"});

}
```

You can also determine if a property is enumerable by calling its `propertyIsEnumerable()` method.

Special Types

In addition to the three simple types, there are also two special data types: `null` and `undefined`. The `null` data type is typically used when property is an object reference but the object has not been created yet (or the reference has not been set). You can set a property to null by using the `null` keyword (`test = null;`).

The `undefined` data type indicates that the value has not been defined. Consider the following:

```
var x = null;
var y;
console.log(typeof x);
console.log(typeof y);
```

The variable x has been set to `null` and the `typeof` operator will return "object." In contrast, the y variable has not been defined and the `typeof` operator will return "undefined."

You can use numbers for property names; however, you'll access the property using square brackets like you would an array index. For example:

```
var myEnum = {1: "Red", 2: "Green", 3: "Blue"};
console.log(myEnum[2]);
```

Miscellaneous Topics

There are a few behaviors of JavaScript that are peculiar to JavaScript, or at least not well understood by someone new to JavaScript. I will describe them here briefly.

Comparison Operators

JavaScript supports the typical comparison operators such as less than, greater than, etc. I won't go into much detail as this is mostly self-explanatory. Mozilla has a good article on this topic (`https://developer.mozilla.org/en-US/docs/Web/JavaScript/Reference/Operators/Comparison_Operators`) if you want to explore further.

However, there is one area that I need to elaborate on. JavaScript distinguishes between equality and equivalence. For example, the number 12 and the string "12" are considered equivalent but they are not equal. Equivalence, in this context, means that if the two objects were converted to the same data type they would have the same value. Equality means that the two objects have both the same type and value. This is sometimes referred to as *strict equality*.

The standard operators such as equal (==), less than (<), greater than or equal (>=), use the concept of equivalence. To test for strict equality, JavaScript provides the === and !== operators. For example, a === b will compare objects a and b using strict equality. In the same way you can use !== to test for inequality.

■ **Tip**   I'm using the terms equivalence and equality as they convey a more accurate picture of these concepts. However, you will often see the term "equality" to refer to equivalence and "strict equality" to mean equality. The === and !== operators are a relatively new addition to JavaScript. Prior to that, all of the comparison operators were based on equivalence and we used the equal operator (==) and called it equal. Now we have an operator that really does mean equal (===).

Variable Scope

A variable's *scope* determines where it can be accessed. If a variable is declared outside of a function body it will have *global scope*, which simply means that all functions will have access to it. Further, a single instance is shared by all; if one function modifies its value, it will have the new value wherever it is used. Also, the variable will be available until the browser is closed.

Variables declared inside a function are considered to have *local scope*. The variable is only available to the code within the function. The variable is no longer available once the function returns. Every time the function is called, a new instance of the variable is created so values are not shared between calls. Function parameters always have local scope.

The final type of scope, *block scope*, restricts access to a variable to the *block* that it was declared in. A block is defined by the curly braces {} that surround it, such as in an if or for statement. Block scope is a relatively new feature in JavaScript (introduced with ECMA Script version 6). Because JavaScript did not initially support block scope, variables declared in an if statement, for example, were available to the entire function. If JavaScript suddenly started to enforce block scope, existing applications would fail.

Instead, block scope is selectively applied by using the let keyword instead of var. Consider the following function definition:

```
function testScope(){
    var localScope = 5;
    if (localScope > 3){
        var localScope2 = 7;
        let blockScope = 4;
        console.log(localScope2 + blockScope); // logs 11
    }
    console.log(localScope2); // logs 7
    console.log(blockScope);  // this will fail
}

testScope();
```

The localScope variable is declared using the traditional var keyword and it is available outside of the if block. However, the blockScope variable was declared with the let keyword and it is not. Regardless, none of the local-scoped or block-scoped variables are available to code outside of the testScope() function.

The tricky part about variable scope is when multiple variables are declared with the same name. This will not generate an error but you may not get the result you were expecting. For example, look at the following code:

```
var x = 1; // global scope

function testX(x1){
    var x = 2;   // local scope
    console.log("original x value passed in: " + x1);
    console.log("local-scoped x: " + x);
}

testX(x);
console.log("global-scoped x: " + x);
```

A variable named x is created both in both the global scope and local scope. These are actually two different objects and each has their own value. The value of the global-scoped object is passed into the function and is available within the function as the x1 parameter.

The function declares a variable named x; this is a new object, unrelated to the first one, except they have the same name. Any code that references x will use the local object; it is not possible for the function to access the global-scoped variable. This is referred to as *hiding* the object. Setting the value of x within the function changes only the local variable. When this code is executed, the following will be written to the console.

```
original x value passed in: 1
local-scoped x: 2
global-scoped x: 1
```

■ **Caution**   If you use a variable inside a function without declaring it with either the var or let keyword, it will be created as a global-scoped variable. For example, if you add the statement x=5; in a function, the x variable will be global. You should use always declare a variable using var or let so your intentions are clear.

Strict Mode

When using *strict mode*, undeclared variables are not allowed and will cause an error. Otherwise, if not in strict mode, JavaScript will declare the variable for you. While this may seem like a good idea, it can lead to unexpected results. For example, consider the following code:

```
var myIntervalCounter = 0;

for (var i=0; i < 10; i++)
{
    if (i % 2 == 0) { myInterbalCounter = i * 2; }
}

console.log(myIntervalCounter);
```

Notice the myIntervalCounter variable was misspelled in the for loop. When not in strict mode, a second variable will be created and its value set instead of updating the original variable. The intended variable does not ever get set and its value remains 0.

You can turn on strict mode by adding the following to the top of the script:

```
"use strict";
```

This will turn on strict mode for the entire file. Alternatively, you can apply it to specific functions by adding this to the first line of the function definition. In strict mode, the previous code will generate an error as shown in Figure 3-4.

```
● ▼ Uncaught ReferenceError: myInterbalCounter is not defined
      (anonymous function) @ SampleScript.js:272
```

Figure 3-4. *Strict mode error*

■ **Tip**   There are several other nuances to strict mode such as not allowing you to name a variable using a reserved keyword. Mozilla has a good article that explains exactly what strict mode does at https:// developer.mozilla.org/en-US/docs/Web/JavaScript/Reference/Strict_mode.

Functions

We've looked at functions earlier, using a function to create an object. A function is also an object and can be added as object members just like properties. This satisfies the object-oriented requirement of encapsulation.

A function can also be defined just like any other type of variable. So a function can be defined in global scope (outside of a function body) but it can also be defined within another function. Consider the following code:

```
var functionA = function(){
    var x = 1;
    var functionB = function(){
        var y = 2;
        var functionC = function(){
            var z = 3;
            console.log(x+y+z);
        }
    }
}
```

Here functionA() declares functionB() in local scope, which in turn creates functionC() also in local scope. This is referred to as *lexical scope*, when you define a function within another function.

Each function defines a new scope. The functionA() is in the global scope. Between the curly braces a new local scope is defined; let's call it scope A and it contains the variable x and functionB(). Inside the curly braces of functionB() another scope if defined; we'll call it scope B. It contains the variable y and functionC(). Similarly, inside functionC() there is a third local scope that contains the variable z.

At this point, nothing is calling any of the functions; you're simply defining them. Only functionA() has global scope and it is the only function you can call. Let's rewrite this with some function calls so we can see this in action. The inner function, functionB() can call functionC() because it is scoped within functionB(). Similarly, functionA() can call functionB(). Because functionA() is global scope, you can call it directly.

```
var functionA = function(){
    var x = 1;
    var functionB = function(){
        var y = 2;
        var functionC = function(){
            var z = 3;
            console.log(x+y+z);
        }
        functionC();
    }
    functionB();
}

functionA();
```

Notice that functionC() has access to the local-scoped variables in functionA() and functionB(). This is known as *closure*. Closure happens when an inner function accesses variables in its outer (enclosing) functions. An inner function also has access to the local-scoped functions as well variables. So functionC() could call functionB(). It could also call functionA() as this is global scoped. But if it does either, in this case, you'll end up in an infinite loop.

■ **Note**   Keep in mind that functionA() cannot call functionC(). A function has access to its local scope as well and anything backwards in the scope chain; but it cannot access anything that is further down the chain.

So you can't call functionC() directly. Or can you? Actually, you can call it if a reference to it is returned; this is a common use of closure. Only functionB() has access to functionC() but a function is an object just like any other variable and can be provided to the caller as a return value. I'll rewrite this slightly to demonstrate this.

```
var functionA = function(){
    var x = 1;
    var functionB = function(){
        var y = 2;
        var functionC = function(){
            var z = 3;
            console.log(x+y+z);
        }
        return functionC;
    }
    return functionB();
}

var closure = functionA();
closure();
```

Inside of functionB(), instead of calling functionC(), the function is returned. Notice there are no parentheses in the return statement. This is simply returning the variable named functionC, which happens to be a function, without actually executing it. Inside functionA() it does call functionB() and returns the value returned by functionB(), which is the reference to functionC().

Calling functionA() simply returns a function reference that is stored in the closure variable. The closure variable now has a reference to functionC(). Anytime you want to call functionC(), just call closure().

Context

The this keyword refers to the current execution context, but sometimes it's not clear what *this* is. It's like going to a restaurant and telling your server that "you want some more of *this.*" Hopefully you've indicated what *this* is or you may not get what you expected. JavaScript can be a bit like that.

The this keyword refers to a single object. Inside a function, for example, this refers to the object that invoked the function. In a typical object with properties and methods, inside a method, this usually points to the containing object. For example:

```
var myObject = {
    color: "Red",
    count: 5,
    log: function () {
        console.log("Quantity: " + this.count + ", Color: " + this.color);
    }
};
```

Here the log() function uses this.count to access a property in the containing object. However, and this is a really important point, the value of this is not defined until the function is called... and the value is normally set as the object that invoked the function, although this can be overridden. So, in this example, we're expecting the log() function to be called by something like myObject.log();, in which case myObject will be the invoking object.

If you use a function as a callback, such as an event handler, the invoking object will likely not be the containing object. For example, if the function handles the onclick event for a button, the invoking object will be the button.

The call() function allows you to call a function and specify the this value. I'll demonstrate this with the following code:

```
function Vehicle(weight, cost) {
    this.weight = weight;
    this.cost = cost;
}

function Truck(weight, cost, axles, length) {
    Vehicle.call(this, weight, cost)
    this.axles = axles;
    this.length = length;
}

var tonka = new Truck(5, 25, 3, 15);
console.log(tonka);
```

You might recognize the Vehicle() function; it's a typical way of creating an object and is usually invoked with a statement like:

```
var v = new Vehicle(5, 25);
```

That would create an object with two properties (weight and cost) and initialize them with the values supplied. The Truck() function is similar, initializing the axles and length properties. Notice, however, the first line of the function:

```
Vehicle.call(this, weight, cost);
```

This uses the call() function to invoke Vehicle(), passing in the current this value, which is a reference to the Truck object. When the Vehicle() function is invoked this way, the weight and cost properties are added to the Truck object instead of the Vehicle object. Sending the new tonka variable to the console log will verify this. You should see the following:

```
Truck {weight: 5, cost: 25, axles: 3, length: 15}
```

Notice that there were three parameters passed in the call() function. The first is used as the this value inside the function. The remaining ones are passed along to the function being invoked. The apply() function works exactly the same way as the call() function, except the extra parameters are passed in as an array. The following lines of code will accomplish the same thing:

```
Vehicle.call(this, weight, cost);
// or
Vehicle.apply(this, [weight, cost]);
```

You can use either; it's just a matter of preference. However, the apply() can be used with a variable parameter list. You can build the array dynamically and then pass it to apply() as the second parameter.

Both the call() and apply() function invoke the functions they are called on. So, when you execute Vehicle.call(...), the Vehicle() function is invoked. What if you just wanted to set up the call but not actually invoke it? An example is if you're setting up a callback function to be executed when the click event occurs. This might look like this:

```
myButton.click(myHandler);
```

As I mentioned earlier, when myHandler() is called, this will be the button object. If you wanted a different this value, you can't use call() or apply() because you're not calling the handler yet; you're just setting up the call for when the event is raised. To do this use the bind() function like this:

```
myButton.click(myHandler.bind(newThis));
```

Now, when the event occurs, the myHandler() function will be called and its this value will be the value passed in, newThis. You can pass additional parameters to the function by listing them after the this reference, just like with the call() function.

Immediately-Invoked Functions

Normally when you define a function in JavaScript you simply define it; it is not yet invoked. If you want it to run you have to then call it. For example:

```
var myFunction = function() {
    doSomething();
}
```

Now, if you want to call it, you would then need to add a statement like `myFunction();`. Alternatively, you could define the function as an immediately-invoked function expression (IIFE), which is pronounced "iffy."

You can turn a function into an IFFE by putting it inside a set of parentheses and then adding an open and close parenthesis, like this:

```
(function() {
    doSomething();
})();
```

If this is defined in the global scope, the `doSomething()` function will be executed as soon as the script is parsed.

Namespaces

In JavaScript all objects in the global scope need to have unique names to avoid name collisions. Keep in mind that all scripts running on a browser share the global scope. So even if your code is free of any collisions, other third-party scripts also have objects in the global scope. If you put all of your objects in the global scope, there's a much greater chance of a collision of using the same names as other objects. To write good defensive code, you should organize your code using namespaces.

A namespace is a technique for organizing code in a hierarchical fashion. An object's fully qualified name includes the path in the hierarchy where it is defined. So even if you have two classes both named Item, if they are found in different paths (namespaces), their fully qualified names are unique.

While JavaScript does not support a namespace keyword, the concept of namespaces can be easily implemented with nested objects. The basic principle here is to create a single object in the global scope, and then add everything else as members of the global object. For example, the following code creates a single object in global scope and then creates some nested objects to define a hierarchy.

```
var mySample = {}; // global object

// Define the namespace hierarchy
mySample.things = {};
mySample.things.helpers = {};
mySample.otherThings = {};

// Add stuff to the namespaces
mySample.things.count = 0;
mySample.things.helpers.logger = function (msg) {
    console.log(msg);
}
```

Now if your code was split across multiple files or you needed this code in multiple places, you would need to make sure the objects were not created twice. You can accomplish this by using the OR operator:

```
this.mySample = this.mySample || {};
```

An undefined object will return a falsy value so the OR operator will proceed to the next part of the statement, which will create the object. If the object had already been created, this would return true and the remaining code would be skipped.

All of your code then uses objects within the `mySample` object so it's pretty important that this object be created before any other code executes. The easiest way to do this is to include it in an IIFE at the top of your script, so let's rewrite that as an IIFE:

```javascript
(function () {
    window.mySample = window.mySample || {};

    // Add some other nodes in the hierarchy
    window.mySample.things = window.mySample.things || {};
    window.mySample.things.helpers = window.mySample.things.helpers || {};
    window.mySample.otherThings = window.mySample.otherThings || {};

    // Setup a shortcut
    window.helpers = window.mySample.things.helpers;

    // Now add some members
    window.mySample.things.count = window.mySample.things.count || 0;
    window.mySample.things.helpers.logger = function (msg) {
        console.log(msg);
    }
})();
```

Notice that the var keyword is removed and replaced with the window object; this refers to global scope. By defining mySample on the window object, you make it available everywhere.

Finally, I snuck in a shortcut so I can use shorter references to the namespaces. You can access the logger() method by following the namespace hierarchy (mySample, things, helpers). But you can also access it directly from the helpers shortcut:

```javascript
mySample.things.helpers.logger("some text");
helpers.logger("some more text");
```

■ **Tip**   There are other ways to implement the concept of namespaces. For some examples of these variations, check out the article at https://addyosmani.com/blog/essential-js-namespacing. This also assumes there are no other global objects named mySample or helpers. You might want to prefix these names with something like your company name or acronym to ensure uniqueness.

Exceptions

JavaScript supports a try/catch/finally pattern that is similar to what you'll find in other languages such as C#. Code that can potentially fail should be put into a try block. If an exception is raised within the try block, the catch block will be executed. The finally block is always executed, whether an error occurs or not.

You can also generate an exception in your code using the throw() function. This allows you to put the error handling in the catch block and keep your main code cleaner. Here is a simple example of these constructs:

```javascript
try {
    var x = 5;
    var y = 0;
    if (y == 0) {
        throw("Can't divide by zero")
    }
```

```
        console.log(x/y);
}
catch(e) {
    console.log("Error: " + e);
}
finally {
    console.log("Finally block executed");
}
```

The finally block is a great place to put any necessary clean-up code that needs to run even when an error occurs. Both the catch and finally blocks are optional but you need to have at least one of them.

Promises

A *promise* is a standardized way of dealing with asynchronous function calls. In practice, it is simply a callback function with two parameters: one function to be called on success and a second to be called on a failure. A promise can be in one of three states:

- Pending - the operation has not completed

- Fulfilled - the operation completed successfully

- Rejected - an error occurred during processing

Sometimes fulfilled and rejected are collectively referred to as settled. Let's look at a simple example that uses a promise. The getNumber() function waits 2 seconds and then generates a random number between 0 and 100. If you requested an even number and the random number is even, the function returns success.

```
function getNumber(bEven) {
    return new Promise(function (fulfill, reject) {
        // perform some long running task
        window.setTimeout(
            function () {
                var i = Math.round((Math.random() * 100),0);
                if ((i % 2 != 0 && bEven) ||
                    (i % 2 == 0 && !bEven)) {
                    reject(i);
                }
                else {
                    fulfill(i);
                }
            }, 2000);
    });
}
```

The getNumber() function returns a Promise object, which is a function with two parameters. The work is done inside this inner function. Because the code is inside the getNumber() function, it has access to its variables such as the bEven parameter. The fulfill() and reject() function references are passed into the inner function and one of the two is called when the inner function completes.

To invoke this code, add the following:

```
var p = getNumber(true);

p.then
    (
    function (i) { console.log("Promise fulfilled, i = " + i); },
    function (i) { console.log("Promise rejected, i = " + i);  }
    );

console.log("Promise made...");
```

This calls the getNumber() function requesting an even number. This returns immediately with a Promise object. The then() member of the Promise object is then called, passing in two anonymous function. The first will be called upon success and the second on failure. At this point, the getNumber() function has not completed; it is in a pending state. One of the anonymous callback functions is then executed by the Promise object.

You can also catch the error callback instead of passing it in to the Promise object. For example, this will accomplish the same thing:

```
p.then
    (
    function (i) { console.log("Promise fulfilled, i = " + i);}
    )
.catch
    (
    function (i) { console.log("Promise rejected, i = " + i); }
    );
```

Array Methods

There is quite a lot of built-in functionality when working with arrays. I will explain the more common methods here and a complete list is provided in the reference section in Appendix C.

Accessing Elements

As I mentioned earlier, the simplest way to populate an array is using the literal notation. For example, this will create an array with six string elements:

```
var arr = ["red", "green", "blue", "yellow", "orange", "purple"];
```

The first element has an index of 0 and index of the remaining elements is assigned sequentially. Elements are accessed by their index. To get the value of the second element, use arr[1];, which will return the string "green." You can update a value by setting it directly like arr[2] = "azure";. This will replace the "blue" element with "azure." You can also delete an element using the delete keyword: delete arr[3];. This will delete the value at index 3 ("yellow") but leave an empty element in the array.

JavaScript is very forgiving when it comes to out-of-bound errors. For example, in the above array, there are six elements, each referenced by index 0-5. Calling arr[8]; will not cause an error, instead it will return undefined. Likewise, you can call arr[8] = "brown"; and the array will grow automatically to hold nine elements, the ninth having the value "brown." This will leave some holes in the array; arr[6] and arr[7] will be undefined, but arr[8]; will return "brown."

50

There are two methods for adding a new element: unshift() adds an element to the beginning of the array, and push() adds an element to the end of the array:

```
arr.unshift("white");
arr.push("black");
```

After executing this, "white" will be at the beginning of the list and "black" will be at the end. The original six elements will be in between in their original order. Both of these methods return the new size of the array after adding the element. You can also get the size through the length property:

```
var numberOfElements = arr.length;
```

There are also corresponding methods to remove the first and last elements. The pop() method returns the last element and also removes it from the array. Likewise, the shift() method returns the first element while simultaneously removing it from the array.

The shift() and unshift() methods get their names from needing to adjust the element indices. The first element in an array has an index of 0. When adding a new element as the beginning, it will be at index 0, which means the index of each of the existing elements needs to incremented, or shifted up. Likewise, removing the first elements requires the indices to be shifted down.

■ **Tip** You can implement the functionality of a stack by using the push() and pop() methods. A stack uses Last In, First Out (LIFO) meaning the last element added is the first to be removed. Use push() to add an element to the end and then pop() will remove the element last added. To implement a queue, which uses First In First Out (FIFO), use unshift() to add new elements and use pop() to remove the oldest element in the queue.

Outputting an Array

The valueOf() method will return the array as a collection of values. This is the default method of an array object; this method is called if you access an array without calling one of its methods.

Also, you can easily output the content of an array as a set of comma-separated values by calling the toString() method. If you need to output the elements with a different separator string, use the join() method. This takes a single parameter that specifies the string that will be placed between each element. If you don't pass any parameter to the join() method, it will use the comma character. For example, if you have an array named arr, the following four statements will output its contents: the first two as a collection of strings, the last two as a single string with comma-separated values.

```
console.log(arr);
console.log(arr.valueOf());
console.log(arr.toString());
console.log(arr.join());
```

Manipulating Elements

There are several methods available for manipulating arrays, which I'll briefly explain here. Some of these methods modify the existing array while others do not but return a new array. Pay close attention to this detail.

The concat() method combines two or more arrays and returns the elements in a new array. The existing arrays are not modified. The concat() method is called on the first array and the additional arrays are passed as parameters. For example,

```
var arr1 = ["a", "b", "c"];
var arr2 = ["x", "y", "z"];
var combined = arr1.concat(arr2);
```

The resulting array, combined, will have a, b, c, x, y, and z elements. If you need to combine more than two arrays, just pass the other arrays as additional parameters.

Use the slice() method to create a new array that contains a subset of an existing array without changing the existing array. Pass in a starting and ending index to specify which elements to return. Note that the starting index is inclusive but the ending index is not. So calling arr.slice(2, 4); will return elements 2 and 3. The end parameter is optional; if omitted all elements from the starting index are returned.

You can also use negative values when calling slice, which will count from the right. For example arr.slice(-3, -1); will return the next-to-last element and the one just before it. This syntax might not seem very intuitive; however, it's easier to understand if you think of adding the array length to these parameters. For example, the following two statements will return the exact same results:

```
arr.slice(-3, -1);
arr.slice(arr.length-3, arr.length-1);
```

■ **Tip**   If you want to get the last n elements, use -n for the first parameter and length as the second parameter. For example, to get the last 5 elements, use arr.slice(-5, length);.

The splice() method performs both a removal of elements within an array as well as inserting new elements at a specified location. The first parameter specifies the index where the removal starts and also where the new items are inserted. The second parameter indicates how many elements should be removed. Enter 0 if you do not want to remove any elements. To insert elements, include them as additional parameters.

You can use the splice() method to just remove elements, and you can use it to only insert elements, and you can use it to do both. For example:

```
arr.splice(2, 1);                    // removes one element at index 2
arr.splice(2, 0, "teal", "pink"); // adds two elements at index 2
arr.splice(2, 1, "teal", "pink"); // removes 1 element and inserts 2
```

■ **Caution**   The splice() method returns an array that contains the elements that were removed. In this way, it works just like the slice() method. In fact, arr.splice(2,1); and arr.slice(2,1); will return the same results. However, unlike slice(), the splice() method modifies the array that it is called on. Calling slice() will leave the original array unchanged, but calling splice() will remove the items from the array. Of course if you use splice() to insert elements, the array will be updated as well.

The sort() method modifies the existing array. It takes an optional parameter that specifies a callback function to be used in the sorting process. If not supplied, the sort() method will convert each element to a string, if necessary, and then sort the strings alphabetically. Consider the following code:

```
var numbers = [1, 33, 7, 12, 5];
numbers.sort();
```

After executing the sort() method, the elements will be [1, 12, 33, 5, 7], which is probably not what you want. To correct this, you need to supply a comparison function. This function is passed to two parameters, which will be two elements of the array. It should return 0 if the elements are equal (in terms of how they should be sorted), -1 if the first element should be sort before the second, or 1 if the first element should be sorted after the second.

The following code defines a numericSort() function and passes it to the sort() method. After calling this, the elements will then be sorted in numeric order [1, 5, 7, 12, 33].

```
function numericSort(a, b){
    if(isNaN(a) || isNaN(b)) return 0; // Can't compare if not numeric
    if(a == b) return 0;
    if(a < b) return -1;
    if(a > b) return 1;
}

var numbers = [1, 33, 7, 12, 5];
numbers.sort(numericSort);
```

The reverse() method modifies the existing array by reversing the order of its elements. It does not take any parameters and it returns the modified array. The following code will output the elements as [3, 2, 1].

```
var numbers = [1, 2, 3];
numbers.reverse();
console.log(numbers);
```

Searching

The array object provides several methods for finding an element in an array. The indexOf() method returns the index of the first occurrence of the specified element. For example, arr.indexOf("red"); will return the first element whose value is "red." Similarly, arr.lastIndexOf("red"); will return the last occurrence.

Both of these methods perform the search using strict equality, which means that if you are looking for "12" and the array contains the number 12, it will not find it. The indexOf() method starts at the beginning of the array and searches forward until it finds the first match. The lastIndexOf() methods starts from the end of the array and scans backwards.

Both methods support a fromIndex parameter that specifies where the search should start from. If not specified, the search starts at the beginning (or the end for lastIndexOf()). Negative values are also supported, which indicate the search should start from this number of elements from the end of the array. If a negative number is used to define the starting position of the search, the search is still forward for indexOf() and backwards for lastIndexOf().

```
var arr = ["red", "green", "blue", "yellow", "blue", "purple"];
arr.indexOf("blue");         // return 2
arr.lastIndexOf("blue");     // returns 4
arr.indexOf("blue", 3);      // returns 4
arr.lastIndexOf("blue", -3); // returns 2
```

The find() and findIndex() methods will search for an element in the array using a callback function that you define. This will allow you full control of the search logic. The find() method returns the element and findIndex() returns the index of the element. Both of these methods iterate through the elements in the array, executing the specified callback function. The search stops when the callback function returns true, and the current element, or its index, is returned.

The callback function can have three input parameters, although only the first one is required:

- element - the current array element being evaluated

- index - the index of the current element

- array - the array object that is being searched in

For example, if you want to find the first primary color from the array, implement the callback function as:

```javascript
function isPrimary(color, index, array) {
    if (color == "red" || color == "blue" || color == "yellow"){
        return true;
    }
    return false;
}
```

Then call the find() method, passing in the isPrimary() function:

```javascript
console.log(arr.find(isPrimary));
```

Both the find() and findIndex() methods support a second, optional parameter. This allows the caller to define the value of this when the callback function is invoked.

Creating Subsets

The filter() function does not modify the array but returns a new array, which is a subset of the original array. To implement the filtering logic, you must specify a callback function that will be called for each element in the array. The function returns true if the element should be included in the subset or false if not.

The callback function works just like the one used by the find() method. In fact, you can use the same function for both:

```javascript
var subset = arr.filter(isPrimary);
console.log(subset);
```

This will not affect the existing array but will return a new array containing ["red," "blue," "yellow," "blue"].

The map() method will create a new array that contains an element for every element in the original array. It iterates through the elements in the array, calling the specified callback function. This function will return a new element that is some sort of transformation of the original. For example, you might want to convert an array of strings to be uppercase.

To test this using the previous numbers array, we can implement the isOdd() function:

```javascript
function isOdd(element, index, array){
    if (isNaN(element)) {return false;}
    if (element % 2 != 0) {return true;}
    return false;
}
```

This returns a Boolean value; true if the number is odd and false if not. When you pass this to the map() method, you'll get back a new array of Boolean values:

```
var boolArray = numbers.map(isOdd);
console.log(boolArray);
```

The every() and some() methods are similar to the find() and filter() methods in that you provide a callback function that returns a Boolean, which is called on each element in the array. The find() method returns the first element where the function returns true, and the filter() method returns all elements where the function returns true.

The every() method returns true if the function returns true for every element in the array. The some() method returns true if the function returns true for any (some) of the elements in the array. To test this out, try the following:

```
console.log(numbers.some(isOdd));  // returns true
console.log(numbers.every(isOdd)); // returns false
```

Processing

There are several useful methods that you can call to implement some processing across the elements of an array. Let's start with the simplest, forEach().

The forEach() method will iterate through all of the elements in the array, calling the specified function. You must define the function that will be executed and the function is passed as a parameter to the forEach() method. Like the other callback functions we've looked at, this function has one required parameter, which is the specific element that it is being executed on. In addition, there are two optional parameters, the index of the element and the array being processed. The function might look like this:

```
function process(item, index, array) {
    console.log("[" + index + "]: " + item + ", in array ", array.toString());
}
```

Then to call the forEach() method, add the following:

```
arr.forEach(process);
```

The console entries should look like this:

```
[0]: white, in array  white,red,green,blue,yellow,orange,purple,black
[1]: red, in array  white,red,green,blue,yellow,orange,purple,black
[2]: green, in array  white,red,green,blue,yellow,orange,purple,black
[3]: blue, in array  white,red,green,blue,yellow,orange,purple,black
[4]: yellow, in array  white,red,green,blue,yellow,orange,purple,black
[5]: orange, in array  white,red,green,blue,yellow,orange,purple,black
[6]: purple, in array  white,red,green,blue,yellow,orange,purple,black
[7]: black, in array  white,red,green,blue,yellow,orange,purple,black
```

The reduce() method and its reduceRight() counterpart convert the array into a single value. The best way to explain this how this method works is to describe a specific use case. For example, you have an array of numeric values and you want to get the sum of these values. To do this, you'll need to iterate through all of the elements accumulating the element values.

Like the forEach() method, you'll need to supply a function to the reduce() method. This has two required parameters. The first parameter is an accumulator that holds the interim results as of the last element processed, or an initial value if this is the first element. The second parameter is the element that the function is being called for. This function also has the same two optional parameters as the forEach() method, which are the index and the array reference. This function combines the current element to the accumulator and returns the results. Here's how you would implement the summation use case:

```
function sumArray(total, item, index, array) {
    return total + item;
}

var arr = [1, 3, 5, 2, 8, 1];
console.log(numbers);
var sum = arr.reduce(sumArray, 0);
console.log(sum);
```

Notice that the reduce() method includes a second parameter, which is the initial value of the accumulator. So the total parameter will have a value of 0 on the first call to the sumArray() function.

The reduceRight() does the same thing as reduce(), except the elements are iterated in reverse order, starting from the end of the array. When the order does not matter, as is the case with summing the values, reduce() or reduceRight() will produce identical results.

Summary

I've covered a lot of material in this chapter. While certainly not a comprehensive coverage of every feature, this provides a good introduction of the basics that you'll need to know. If you're fairly new to JavaScript, I recommend working through the SampleScript.js file in the download code and make sure you understand what the code is doing.

In Chapters 16-20, you'll use JavaScript extensively to enhance your HTML5 application. The advanced chapters, 21–26 will also make significant use of these JavaScript features.

In the next chapter, I'll demonstrate the HTML elements used to provide structure to your HTML document.

PART II

■ ■ ■

HTML

In this section, I'll explain the HTML elements that are available and how and when to use them. I covered a few of them in Chapter 1: those used for providing document structure and metadata. Now, I'll get into the real meat of the HTML elements.

HTML5 is all about semantics; you'll read that over and over again in this section. The choice of which element to use is an important one. It conveys the meaning or purpose of the content. In the next five chapters, I will try to drive home *why* each element should be used. And, of course, I'll provide demonstrations and examples of *how* they are used.

Each of the five chapters in this section, describe a set of elements that are organized as follows:

- 4) Structural elements, such as header, footer, section, aside, and div. These create a skeleton that will support the remaining content.

- 5) Text elements – there is a large set of elements that contain primarily text content, and each provides a specific semantic meaning.

- 6) Table elements – these elements are used to arrange tabular data that logically belongs in rows and columns.

- 7) Embedded elements, such as img, audio, and video.

- 8) Form elements, including input, button, label, and other elements used to create data entry forms.

■ ■ ■

CHAPTER 4

Structural HTML Elements

I briefly introduced the basic HTML syntax in Chapter 1 and then explained the information inside the head element. There is no displayable content in the head element; the data there is intended for applications to use such as browsers, screen readers, or search engines. Now we turn our attention to the body element; this is where the content goes.

Content Categories

There are over 100 elements defined in HTML5. I've explained a few of them in Chapter 1 and over the next 5 chapters I'll demonstrate the remaining ones. Elements are organized into content categories and there are general rules, based on these categories, which define where an element can be used and what it can contain. An element can be in more than one category and there are a few elements that don't belong in any category.

- *Metadata* - These were explained in Chapter 1; they have no real content but provide metadata about the HTML document and information to applications that will process the document.

- *Sectioning* - These elements are used to organize a page into sections, and are also used to construct a document outline.

- *Heading* - These elements are used within sections to define the title and subtitles of a section.

- *Embedded* - Embedded elements are used to insert non-HTML content, such as images, within the document. These will be described in Chapter 7.

- *Interactive* - These elements provide for user interaction. A button or an input field are common examples of this.

- *Form* - Form elements are used for capturing user input and are further divided into several subcategories. I will explain these in Chapter 8.

- *Phrasing* - These elements are used to mark up text, or rather phrases, which are combined to form paragraphs. These elements will be demonstrated in Chapter 5.

- *Flow* - The vast majority of elements will fall into this category. These are elements that have actual content such as text or some embedded content like images or video. The term "flow" is used because these elements take up space and generally flow from one element to the next, across, or down the page.

The reference material in Appendix C includes an alphabetical list of all of the HTML5 elements that indicates which categories each is in.

© Mark J. Collins 2017

M. J. Collins, *Pro HTML5 with CSS, JavaScript, and Multimedia*, DOI 10.1007/978-1-4842-2463-2_4

■ **Note**   Most of the elements that are not in any content category are used only as child elements for a specific element. For example, the `table` element is in the flow category, but the child elements such as `tr` and `td` are not assigned a category as they are only used within a `table`.

This chapter will explain the use of sectioning and header elements to organize your HTML document.

Sectioning Content

It's a good idea to organize your HTML document into logical sections, especially for larger documents. Prior to HTML5 the division (`div`) element was used to group content and they can be nested like this:

```
<div>
    <div>
        <div>
        </div>
    </div>
</div>
```

Unfortunately, a `div` can be used to group content for a lot of different reasons, which are not obvious to the reader. HTML5 introduces several new elements that provide more specific semantic groupings. Each of these elements are used to group content into a larger unit. Each one, however, groups the content for a different reason. You could accomplish the grouping with the generic `div` element; the reason to use the more specific element is to make it clear *why* the group is being made. So pay close attention to the specific purpose of each element and use the correct one depending on what you're trying to accomplish.

Section

The `section` element is used to organize content into logical sections. Think back to an essay you may have written for a school assignment where you'd have an introduction, three main points, and a conclusion. Each of these would be represented in HTML as a `section`. Also, `section` elements can be nested just like `div` elements. If each of your main points have subpoints, you can use a `section` for each subpoint.

There are two guiding principles in choosing your `section` elements. First, sections should be topical; you're organizing content based on the material being presented. Second, sections should flow linearly. For example, the introduction flows into the first main point, and so on. The antithesis of this will be more apparent when I discuss the `aside` element.

Article

An `article` element is used to group content that can stand on its own. This is typically used when the content is being reused. If you pick up your local Sunday newspaper and read your favorite comic strip, you may not be aware of this, but the same comic strip is included in newspapers all over the world. The same concept is true of web sites, where syndicated content is included in multiple pages. These should be placed in an `article` element because the content is independent of the rest of the page.

However, one of the most common uses of the `article` element is on blogs. Each post on a blog is generally stand-alone content and is often grouped into an `article` element. Also, comments that are posted to a blog are also typically placed in an `article` element.

You can use an article element anywhere you would use a section element, if the content is independent and reusable. An article, especially a larger one, will often use the section element to organize the article topically as I described previously. Also, an article element can include other article elements, as would be the case with a blog post including comments.

Aside

An aside element is used to group content that does not belong in the normal flow of your document. This could be supporting information provided for reference purposes, or perhaps information about the author. It could also be unrelated information such as advertising space or a calendar of events.

The aside element is often presented as a sidebar so it doesn't interrupt the flow of the other content. However, the CSS will determine that; the job of a content author is to indicate that a group of content is not part of the normal content flow. And this is done with the aside element.

Nav

The nav element is used to group a set of links. A typical example is where you have some sort of menu on the page to jump to internal bookmarks or other related pages. Another example is where you provide links for more information or related material.

You don't have to put every link into a nav element. But if you do have content that is comprised primarily of links, put this in a nav element. This will indicate that this section of content provides navigation.

Address

The address element is not included in the sectioning content. I am describing it here because it is used to provide contact information for either the entire document or for a specific article. To use it for a single article it should be placed somewhere inside the article element. If it applied to the document, it must be inside the body element; this is often placed in the footer element.

■ **Tip** The address element is intended for providing contact information related to a document or article. This can include an email address, URL, phone number, mailing address, or any other method of communicating with the author. It may have been better named **contact** because that is what it should be used for. You should not use it to describe an address unless the address is provided as contact information.

Here is an example of including an address element in a footer:

```
<footer>
    <p>Closing content</p>
    <address>
        <p>Provided by
            <a href="mailto:mcollins@theCreativePeople.com">Mark J. Collins</a>
        </p>
        <p>For more information
            <a href="www.theCreativePeople.com">visit his website</a>
        </p>
    </address>
</footer>
```

The default style for an address element is to display the text in italics. The default styling of this footer will look like Figure 4-1.

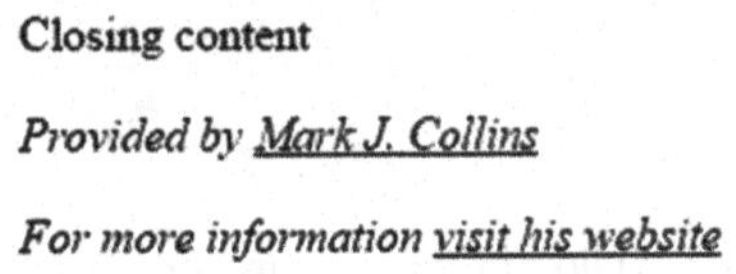

Closing content

Provided by <u>Mark J. Collins</u>

For more information <u>visit his website</u>

Figure 4-1. *The default address style*

Outlines

There is a notion in the HTML5 specifications regarding document outlines that is referred to as the outline algorithm. The body element, which is the root element for your content, creates a topmost node in the document outline. Adding any of the sectioning elements, section, article, aside, or nav, will create a new section in the outline. Embedding additional sectioning elements will add more nodes to the outline. The idea here is that by simply nesting sectioning elements, an explicit outline is created for your document.

Explicit Sections

Let's test this out by creating an HTML document with some nested sections. Creating an outline without any labels is not very interesting. So we'll add an h1 element within each section to give it a name. A sample document is shown in Listing 4-1.

Listing 4-1. Creating a document outline using sections

```
<body>
    <h1>My Sample Page</h1>
    <nav>
        <h1>Navigation</h1>
    </nav>
    <section>
        <h1>Top-level</h1>
        <section>
            <h1>Main content</h1>
            <section>
                <h1>Featured content</h1>
            </section>
            <section>
                <h1>Articles</h1>
                <article>
                    <h1>Article 1</h1>
                </article>
            </section>
        </section>
        <aside>
            <h1>Related content</h1>
```

```
        <section>
            <h1>HTML Reference</h1>
        </section>
        <section>
            <h1>Book list</h1>
            <article>
                <h1>Book 1</h1>
            </article>
        </section>
    </aside>
  </section>
</body>
```

If you render this in a browser using only the default styles, the page would look like Figure 4-2.

My Sample Page

Navigation

Top-level

Main content

Featured content

Articles

Article 1

Related content

HTML Reference

Book list

Book 1

Figure 4-2. *Sample document with default styles*

Notice the font for each of the labels is different, even though the same h1 element was used for all of them. The style is automatically updated based on where the element is in the document outline.

■ **Note** The aside element is below the main section rather than to the side. The alignment of the sections will be controlled through CSS. I will explain this in Chapter 13.

To further illustrate this, there is a handy web page that will read your HTML document and display the outline for it. You can find the site at https://gsnedders.html5.org/outliner. Paste in your HTML document and click the "Outline this" button. The outline that is displayed will be similar to Figure 4-3.

1. My Sample Page
    1. Navigation
    2. Top-level
        1. Main content
            1. Featured content
            2. Articles
                1. Article 1
        2. Related content
            1. HTML Reference
            2. Book list
                1. Book 1

Figure 4-3. *Viewing the document outline*

Document Headings

HTML5 supports document heading elements. In addition to the h1 element that I used in this example, there are also h2, h3, h4, h5, and h6 elements. Each of these is used to indicate that the heading belongs at the specified level in the document outline. The default styling of the h1-h6 elements is the same that was used with the explicit outline document.

Prior to HTML5, the sectioning elements did not exist. However, using the h1-h6 elements, you could provide implicit sections. If the previous heading used an h2 element and the current heading uses h3, a new section is implicitly defined. Similarly, going from h3 to h2 closes the current section.

To create a document with a similar outline, you can create implicit sections using the h1-h6 elements. Instead of using an h1 element everywhere, you would use a different element to indicate its level in the hierarchy. The following HTML will generate the exact same outline (and output in the browser):

```
<body>
    <h1>My Sample Page</h1>
    <h2>Navigation</h2>
    <h2>Top-level</h2>
    <h3>Main content</h3>
    <h4>Featured content</h4>
    <h4>Articles</h4>
```

```
    <h5>Article 1</h5>
    <h3>Related content</h3>
    <h4>HTML Reference</h4>
    <h4>Book list</h4>
    <h5>Book 1</h5>
</body>
```

The official W3C recommendation, however, is to not rely on the outlining of the sectioning elements. Figure 4-4 shows the warning displayed in the W3C documentation (http://www.w3.org/TR/html5/sections.html).

⚠**Warning!** There are currently no known implementations of the outline algorithm in graphical browsers or assistive technology user agents, although the algorithm is implemented in other software such as conformance checkers. Therefore the <u>outline</u> algorithm cannot be relied upon to convey document structure to users. Authors are advised to use heading <u>rank</u> (<u>h1</u>-<u>h6</u>) to convey document structure.

Figure 4-4. *Warning about outline algorithm*

You should definitely use the sectioning elements to organize your HTML document into sections. This warning is recommending that you also use the corresponding h1–h6 element depending on the document hierarchy where this is feasible.

The article element is appropriate for reusable content. In this case, the content is usually not in the same file as the main HTML document. It may be read from a database, provided in some sort of content feed, or extracted from a separate file. It will probably have no knowledge of the document outline in which it will be inserted. The article should start at the h1 level, and include additional sectioning elements as needed. When the article is included in a document, the actual outline level will be adjusted depending on the current level where it is inserted.

■ **Note** The specific algorithm for creating an outline is explained in the W3C recommendation, which you can find at this address: http://www.w3.org/TR/html5/sections.html#outlines

---

Header and Footer

While organizing your page, you should also consider adding a header element at the top and a footer element at the bottom. These elements allow you to group introductory or concluding content for a section of the document.

Unlike the sectioning elements such as article or section, the header and footer elements do not create a new section in the document outline. Rather they are used to group content for the section that they are placed in. You will typically use a header and a footer element in the body element to define the page header and footer. They can also be placed inside a child section such as a section element. In this case, they will group introductory content for the section only.

Planning the Page Layout

Before creating a new web page, it's a good idea to sketch out the basic page structure. This will help you visualize the overall layout and see how the elements are nested together.

The page that I will demonstrate in this chapter will use header and nav elements at the top and a footer element at the bottom. The main area in the middle will use a section element and have two side-by-side areas, each with a series of article tags. The larger area will be enclosed within another section element and provide the primary content, which is organized into article elements. The smaller area, on the right, will use an aside element and will contain a section element. This will contain a series of article elements that will present related information. Figure 4-5 illustrates the page layout.

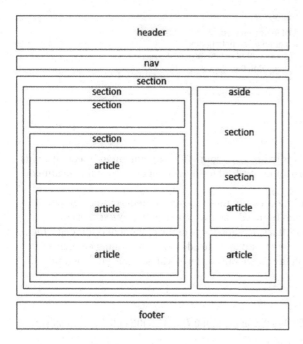

Figure 4-5. *Planning the page layout*

▓ **Note**   This diagram shows spaces between each of the elements to make it easier to understand. In the actual web page, in most cases this space is removed by setting the margin attribute to 0.

Sectioning Roots

There are a few HTML elements that are called sectioning roots, which have their own outline that does not contribute to the outline of the rest of the document. The body element is one of these elements, although this is arguably a special case; the outline of the body element is the document's outline. The other elements in this category include blockquote, details, fieldset, figure, and td. I'll explain the fieldset element in Chapter 8 and the td element in Chapter 6.

Blockquote

The blockquote element is used when you need to include a long quotation in a document. The contents of the quote are placed inside the blockquote element and can consist of multiple elements including header text, paragraphs, and embedded content. A simple quotation might look like this:

```
<blockquote cite="www.apress.com">
    <h1>Quotation</h1>
    <p>This is a quotation</p>
</blockquote>
```

The header text (h1-h6) will define sections within the quotation, but these will not be part of the document outline. You can verify this yourself by adding a blockquote element to your document and running it through the outlining tool I mentioned earlier.

In addition to the global attributes, the blockquote element supports the cite attribute. Use this to identify the URL of the source of the quote or a resource containing information about the quote.

■ **Tip**   The cite *attribute* provides details about the quote but it is not displayed, at least not normally. The browser could use this information but it's basically provided as metadata. To display the source or a citation you should use the cite *element*, which will be explained in the next chapter.

Details

The details element allows you to create collapsible sections of content. Inside the details element you can include an optional summary element that will contain the content that is displayed when the element is collapsed. If no summary element is used, the collapsed text will be "Details."

The remaining content of the details element will be hidden when collapsed. The initial state of the details element will be collapsed. If you want the contents to be displayed when the page is loaded, add the open Boolean attribute.

```
<details open>
    <summary>This is the collapsed text</summary>
    <h1>Details</h1>
    <p>These are collapsable details</p>
</details>
```

Again, like the other sectioning root elements, you can include h1-h6 elements in the details element, which will define an outline for the details. However, these sections are not included in the document outline.

■ **Caution**   As of this writing, the details element is not supported by Internet Explorer or Edge and is not fully supported by Firefox.

Figure

The figure element is used to group content that is self-contained and can be logically moved to a different location without affecting the main flow of the document. A unique feature of the figure element is the ability to include a caption within the content.

A figure element is typically used to group an image or some other embedded content along with a caption. It can also be used to group text, such as a code listing along with a caption.

To add a caption, include the figcaption element within the figure element. The figcaption element must be the first or last child element in the figure element. The caption will be above the content if the figcaption element is the first child element. Otherwise, it will be below the content.

Here's a simple example of a figure that includes an embedded image. This is rendered in Chrome as shown in Figure 4-6.

```
<figure>
    <h1>Figure</h1>
    <img src="HTML5Badge.png" alt="HTML5" />
    <figcaption>Official HTML5 Logo</figcaption>
</figure>
```

Figure

Official HTML5 Logo

Figure 4-6. *Using figure/figcaption elements*

Grouping Elements

The preceding section described the elements used for organizing an HTML document into smaller sections and those elements related to the document outline. Now I'll explain the remaining grouping elements. These elements are used for primarily semantic purposes and do not affect the outline.

Paragraph

The paragraph (p) element is used to define a paragraph, which is a section of text that contains a single thought or idea. It is normally visually distinct from other paragraphs. For example, in this book the first line of most paragraphs is indented so that paragraphs stand out. The default style of the p element will set the margin so there is some extra white space between paragraphs.

The p element is probably one of the most overused elements. I can't stress this enough - the element that is chosen should be based on its semantic meaning. A paragraph is a distinct portion of a document that contains a single thought or idea. If that describes the content you are adding, use a p element. If not, keep looking. The next chapter will describe the phrasing elements and one of these may be more appropriate.

If you use the appropriate element, the default styling will usually make sense as well. But you're not selecting the element based on the style that it is given. The styles can be easily changed through CSS as long as the appropriate elements are consistently used.

Horizontal Rule

In HTML4, the hr element was used to create a horizontal rule, or line. Since HTML5 provides more semantic definition to its elements, this has been redefined as a thematic break. This is usually placed between paragraphs when there is a change of topic.

The hr element is still rendered as a horizontal line for backward compatibility. Of course this can be modified through CSS. There is no content within the hr element and the closing tag is not needed. Add an hr element like this:

```
<p>paragraph 1</p>
<hr />
<p>paragraph 2</p>
```

Preformatted

Content placed inside a preformatted (pre) element will be rendered just like it is entered, including white space. As I explained in Chapter 1, white space, including carriage returns, tabs, and extra spaces, are normally ignored by the browser. Use the pre element to tell the browser to include them. The default style will use a fixed-spaced font, which also aids in preserving the format.

■ **Note** The pre element is one of the rare exceptions where its use is not primarily for semantic reasons.

The pre element is used to include content that is already formatted and you want to maintain that format. Including a snippet of code is a good example. Another common use of the pre element is when including poetry. For example:

```
<pre>I heard the bells on Christmas Day
Their old, familiar carols play,
    And wild and sweet
    The words repeat
Of peace on earth, good-will to men!</pre>
<cite>Henry Wadsworth Longfellow - 1863, public domain</cite>
```

This is rendered in the browser as shown in Figure 4-7.

```
I heard the bells on Christmas Day
Their old, familiar carols play,
    And wild and sweet
    The words repeat
Of peace on earth, good-will to men!
```

Henry Wadsworth Longfellow - 1863, public domain

Figure 4-7. *Using the pre element*

Try replacing the pre element with a standard paragraph (p) element. The content will be displayed on one line, wrapping as necessary based on the page width.

■ **Note**   One bit of trivia here, but this poem was written by Henry Wadsworth Longfellow during the American Civil War. After recently losing his wife, he then learned that his son Charles was wounded in battle. It was during the Christmas season and hearing the church bells playing carols he began to wonder if there really was any peace or goodwill. This poem reflects the author's struggle with this, concluding in the end, that as long as the church bells keep playing, there was still hope.

Main

The main element is used to indicate that its contents present the primary purpose or topic of the document. This identifies the core, the central theme of the document. As such, the main element cannot be inside an article, aside, footer, header, or nav elements, since these are used for ancillary content. Also you can only have one main element per document, which should be fairly obvious. The content in the main element should be unique to the document and not shared by other documents.

Of course, the main element can be divided into sections as appropriate. Although there is no restriction on including an article, aside, or nav element within a main element, this is generally considered poor form. An article contains reusable or stand-alone material so it will seldom be unique to the document. An aside element is used for content that is not part of the main flow and is likely not part of the central theme that the main element is reserved for. However, if the content of aside or article elements satisfies the criteria of a main element, you can use them as well.

There is no default styling for a main element; its use is purely semantic. Using it helps applications such as screen readers or search engines go straight to the core content of your document.

Division

I saved the div element for last. As I mentioned earlier, prior to HTML5, the div element was used for all types of groupings. Now we have new elements to use for specific purposes: topically (section), independent or reusable content (article), outside of normal flow (aside), and navigation (nav). There are also several elements that are available for semantic grouping such as the main, figure, and blockquote elements. The div element is used for all other grouping reasons.

One common use of the div element is to apply styles to all of its child elements. Most style attributes are inherited from the parent element. So setting an attribute on a div element will propagate down to all the elements within the div. For example, you may need to hide or show some content based on user input or the state of the web page. By putting all of this content in a single div, you can simply update the div attributes.

Listing Elements

Now we'll look elements that are used for listing contents, such as a bulleted list. However, lists in HTML5 are not limited to just a series of bullets or numbered items. Any time you have a list of things, even if the "things" are large blocks of content, you should consider creating them inside one of these list elements. Again, it's all about semantics; placing content in a list makes it clear that you are enumerating a list.

List

HTML5 supports both an *ordered list* using the ol element as well as an *unordered list* using the ul element. They work pretty much the same except for a few additional attributes that are available with an ordered list.

With either list, the order of the elements is fixed and defined by the order that the items are included in the list. The appropriate type is chosen based on semantics. If the order of the list is not meaningful, use the unordered list. For example, if you're listing some popular sports such as Football, Baseball, and Basketball, use an unordered list. In contrast, if you are specifying the top three most popular sports, you might want to list them in order of popularity. In this case the order is meaningful and you should use an ordered list.

The default style of an unordered list is to prefix each item with a bullet of some type and the same bullet is used for all of the items. For an ordered list, the default style will use a number, and the numbers will be assigned sequentially.

The items within a list (either ordered or unordered) are represented by a *list item* (li) element. The only elements that can be included inside either a ul or ol element are li elements. However, you can put any flow element inside an li element. Listing 4-2 demonstrates a simple unordered list and an ordered list. With default styling, this will be rendered as shown in Figure 4-8.

Listing 4-2. Sample unordered and ordered lists

```
<h2>Book Topics</h2>
<ul>
    <li>HTML</li>
    <li>CSS</li>
    <li>JavaScript</li>
</ul>
<h2>HTML Chapters</h2>
<ol start="4">
    <li>Structural Elements</li>
    <li>Text Elements</li>
    <li>Table Elements</li>
    <li>Embedded Elements</li>
    <li>Form Elements</li>
</ol>
```

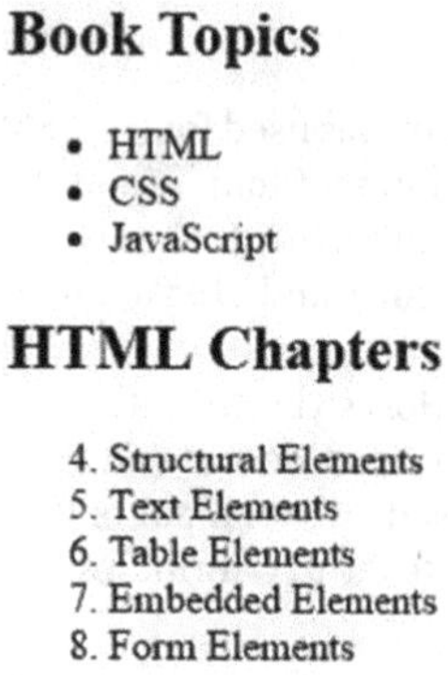

Book Topics

- HTML
- CSS
- JavaScript

HTML Chapters

4. Structural Elements
5. Text Elements
6. Table Elements
7. Embedded Elements
8. Form Elements

Figure 4-8. Sample unordered and ordered list

As I mentioned, the ordered list supports a few additional attributes. The most common one is the start attribute, which I used in the previous example. In this example, I'm listing the chapters of this book that cover the HTML elements. The first three chapters contained introductory material so the first chapter on HTML is this chapter, Chapter 4. The start attribute indicates the number to use for the first li element; in this case 4. If omitted, the numbering will start with 1.

The reversed attribute is a Boolean attribute that is used to assign the numbers in reverse order. You would use this, for example, if you were listing the top three most popular sports and wanted to leave the most popular for last. The numbering would be in reverse order, 3, 2, 1. If you do not specify the start attribute, the number of the first item is set so that the last element will be 1. If you put ten items in a list and specify the reversed attribute with no start attribute, the items will be numbered from 10 to 1. If you do specify start along with reversed, the first item will use whatever was specified in the start attribute and the rest will go down from there, so you could end up with negative numbers.

▪ **Tip** The reversed attribute does not change the order of the li elements. They are always rendered in the order they are included in the list. The reversed attribute only affects the numbering of the items.

The type attribute specifies what type of "numbering" to use. Here are the supported values:

- 1 - Use numbers (this is the default value if not specified)

- A - Use uppercase letters (e.g., A, B, C, D)

- a - Use lowercase letters

- I - Use Roman numerals with uppercase letters (e.g., I, II, III, IV)

- i - Use lowercase Roman numerals

The start attribute is always numeric regardless of what value is specified for type. It will be converted to the appropriate type representation. For example, if you specify 4 and the type is I, the first element will use IV.

▪ **Caution**   Letters or Roman numerals do not support zero or negative numbers. If these values are needed, they will be displayed as numbers. For example, if you have five items in the list and specify the ol element as `<ol start="3" type="a" reversed>`, the numbering will be c, b, a, 0, -1.

You can use a list to present a series of links such as a menu. For example:

```
<nav>
    <h1>Navigation</h1>
    <ul>
        <li><a href="/">Home</a></li>
        <li><a href="http://www.apress.com">Apress</a></li>
        <li><a href="http://www.theCreativePeople.com">My Site</a></li>
    </ul>
</nav>
```

This will display a bulleted list of links. However, with CSS you can render this in a variety of ways including buttons or horizontally arrayed links. I will demonstrate this in Chapter 13.

Description List

The *description list* (dl) element is used define a list of terms. It is implemented as a set of name/value pairs. It is often used to create a glossary. In this case the names are the terms being defined and the values are the definition or description of those terms. You can put series of term (dt) elements and description (dd) elements inside the dl element.

For example, a simple dl element might be used like this:

```
<dl>
    <dt>Term1</dt>
    <dd>Definition</dd>
    <dt>Term2</dt>
    <dd>Definition</dd>
</dl>
```

▪ **Note**   In HTML4, the dl element was called a definition list and was intended to define a list of terms. The syntax has not changed in HTML5, but the name was changed to description list to convey a broader use of the element. In HTML5 it is used to provide a grouping of term/description pairs.

Listing 4-3 illustrates how this pattern can be used to list a series of books along with a description of each. Figure 4-9 shows how this would be displayed in a browser using only default formatting.

Listing 4-3. Using dl, dt, and dd elements

```
<dl>
    <dt>Beginning WF</dt>
    <dd>
Indexed by feature so you can find answers easily and written in an accessible style,
Beginning WF shows how Microsoft's Workflow Foundation (WF) technology can be used in a wide
variety of applications.
    </dd>
    <dt>Office 2010 Workflow</dt>
    <dd>
Workflow is the glue that binds information worker processes, users, and artifacts—
without it, information workers are just islands of data and potential. Office 2010 Workflow
walks you through implementing workflow solutions.
    </dd>
    <dt>Pro Access 2010 Development</dt>
    <dd>
Pro Access 2010 Development is a fundamental resource for developing business
applications that take advantage of the features of Access 2010. You'll learn how to build
database applications, create Web-based databases, develop macros and VBA tools for Access
applications, integrate Access with SharePoint, and much more.
    </dd>
</dl>
```

Beginning WF
> Indexed by feature so you can find answers easily and written in an accessible style,
> Beginning WF shows how Microsoft's Workflow Foundation (WF) technology can be
> used in a wide variety of applications.

Office 2010 Workflow
> Workflow is the glue that binds information worker processes, users, and artifacts—
> without it, information workers are just islands of data and potential. Office 2010
> Workflow walks you through implementing workflow solutions.

Pro Access 2010 Development
> Pro Access 2010 Development is a fundamental resource for developing business
> applications that take advantage of the features of Access 2010. You'll learn how to build
> database applications, create Web-based databases, develop macros and VBA tools for
> Access applications, integrate Access with SharePoint, and much more.

Figure 4-9. *Rendering a description list*

However, you're not restricted to this one-to-one mapping. Another use of the dl element is to list groups of things with a group header. You accomplish this by using the dt element as the group header and the dd elements as the group members. For example, Listing 4-4 contains the starting lineup for the New York Yankees, organized by position categories. Figure 4-10 shows the default rendering of this content.

Listing 4-4. Using multiple description elements for each term

```
<h2>New York Yankees Starting Lineup</h2>
<dl>
    <dt>Infielders</dt>
    <dd>Teixeira, 1B</dd>
    <dd>Castro, 2B</dd>
    <dd>Gregorius, SS</dd>
    <dd>Torreyes, 3B</dd>
    <dd>McCann, C</dd>
    <dt>Outfielders</dt>
    <dd>Hicks, LF</dd>
    <dd>Ellsbury, CF</dd>
    <dd>Ackley, RF</dd>
    <dt>Designated Hitter</dt>
    <dd>Rodriguez, DH</dd>
    <dt>Pitchers</dt>
    <dd>Gausman, R</dd>
    <dd>Wilson, R</dd>
    <dd>Tillman, R</dd>
    <dd>Price, L</dd>
    <dd>Porcello, R</dd>
</dl>
```

New York Yankees Starting Lineup

Infielders
    Teixeira, 1B
    Castro, 2B
    Gregorius, SS
    Torreyes, 3B
    McCann, C
Outfielders
    Hicks, LF
    Ellsbury, CF
    Ackley, RF
Designated Hitter
    Rodriguez, DH
Pitchers
    Gausman, R
    Wilson, R
    Tillman, R
    Price, L
    Porcello, R

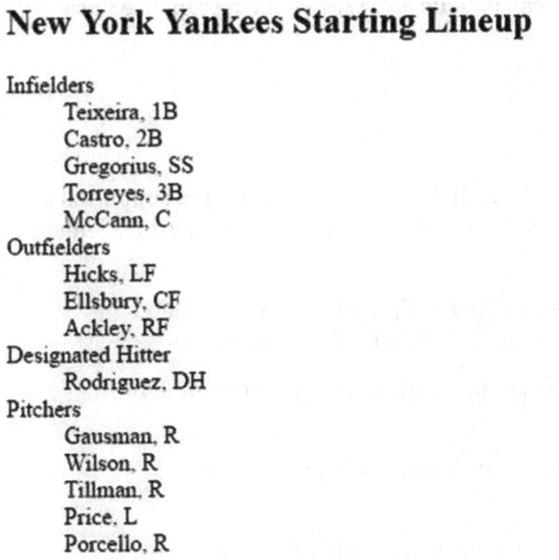

Figure 4-10. *The New York Yankees Starting Lineup*

The other possibility is to have multiple terms refer to the same description. You can do this as well but you need to keep the like terms together. For example:

```
<dl>
    <dt>Hicks, LF</dt>
    <dt>Ellsbury, CF</dt>
    <dt>Ackley, RF</dt>
    <dd>Outfielders - the positions in baseball that are played in the grassy area behind
the diamond, known as the outfield. These positions include the Left Fielder, Center
Fielder, and Right Fielder.</dd>
</dl>
```

The term element is intended to be relatively short such as a word or phrase. There are specific limitations as what kind of elements can be included in a dt element. You cannot use a header, footer, or any sectioning content inside a dt element. Even at that, there's nothing to prevent you from including paragraphs of content inside a dt element. That is inappropriate, however, when you consider the semantic rules. A dl element is used to describe a list of terms, and a paragraph of text is not a term.

There are no such restrictions on the definition element. You can place any flow content inside a dd element, including sectioning and embedded content.

Inline Frames

The iframe element is used to embed another web page within the current document. I'll explain it here briefly, and we'll look at it more closely in Chapter 17. You can include an iframe with markup like this:

```
<iframe src="http://www.apress.com" width="100%" height="400">
    <p>Your browser does not support iframes</p>
</iframe>
```

The content inside the iframe element will be rendered only if the iframe element is not supported by the browser. The iframe element supports several attributes that you can use to configure how the element is rendered and what options it will allow.

- allowfullscreen - If this Boolean attribute is specified, scripts within the embedded page may switch to fullscreen mode using the requestFullScreen() method call.

- height - The height of the iframe element in pixels or a percentage of the parent page.

- name - The name attribute can be used when providing a link to the iframe from within the parent document.

- sandbox - This can be used to restrict what can be done in the embedded page. This will be covered in Chapter 17.

- src - This is used to specify the URL of the page that should be embedded.

- srcdoc - If specified and supported, the srcdoc attribute will override the value of the src attribute. This is normally used in conjunction with the sandbox attribute.

- width - The width of the iframe element in pixels or a percentage of the parent page.

Deprecated Elements

Some grouping elements have been dropped from the HTML5 specification. I will describe them here briefly. These are likely to be supported for some time to ensure backward compatibility. However, you should not use these for any new development.

hgroup

The hgroup element was used to group the h1–h6 elements and hide all but the first one from the document outline. If you wanted a title for a section as well as a subtitle, for example, you might use an h1 element for the title and h2 for the subtitle. However, the h2 element would start a new section in the document outline. Putting them both into an hgroup element would create only a single section, using the h1 title.

Instead of using a hgroup element, the recommendation is to put the title and subtitle(s) into a header element. The title should be in an h1–h6 element to define the section and be added to the document outline. The remaining header content such as subtitles or taglines should be placed in p or span tags and then styled appropriately using CSS. For more information and examples, see the W3C specification at http://www.w3.org/TR/html5/common-idioms.html#sub-head.

dir

The directory list (dir) element was used to present a directory listing. The items within this list are included in an li element. The dir element has been deprecated in HTML5. You should use the unordered list (ul) instead.

frame and frameset

The frame and frameset elements were used to organize a page into sections. This includes both logical sections as well as page layout. The logical sectioning is now accomplished using the sectioning content that I described earlier such as section, aside, and article. The layout is configured through CSS, which I will demonstrate in Chapter 13.

Summary

In this chapter I demonstrated all of the HTML elements that are used to organize content. These provide semantics meaning to the content groupings.

A document is organized using sectioning content to define the larger sections of the document. These along with the heading elements (h1–h6) define the document outline. The header and footer elements are used to identify introductory and concluding content both at the document level as well as within a section. Sectioning roots including blockquote, details, and figure elements have their own sections that do not affect the document outline.

There are several other grouping elements that do not affect the outline but provide semantic grouping at a lower level. These include the main, paragraph (p), horizontal rule (hr), and division (div) elements. The preformatted (pre) element is used primarily to preserve the formatting of the content, rather than for semantic reasons. Finally, ordered lists (ol), unordered lists (ul), and description lists (dl) provide ways to present a list of things.

By using these elements, you provide semantic details about your content, which will make it easier to apply consistent styling rules. Even without any custom CSS, the document begins to take "shape" as the default styling renders the content consistently with the semantic purposes of each element.

The HTML document shown in Listing 4-5 demonstrates all of the techniques described in this chapter. This is also available in the source code download. In the next chapter, I'll start to put some actual content onto this structure. I'll explain the various elements that will provide semantic meaning to the textual content.

Listing 4-5. The complete HTML document for Chapter 4

```
<!DOCTYPE html>

<html lang="en">
    <head>
        <meta charset="utf-8" />
        <meta name="author" content="Mark J Collins" />
        <meta name="description" content="Sample HTML document" />
        <title>HTML5 Sample</title>
        <link rel="stylesheet" href="Initial.css" />
        <link rel="stylesheet" href="Print.css" media="print" />
        <link rel="icon" type="image/x-icon" href="HTMLBadge.ico" />
        <link rel="alternate" type="application/pdf" href="MainPage.pdf" />
        <link rel="author" href="mailto:markc@thecreativepeople.com" />
        <link rel="author" type="text/html" href="http://www.thecreativepeople.com" />
    </head>
    <body>
        <h1>My Sample Page</h1>
        <header>
            <p>Heading</p>
        </header>
        <nav>
            <h1>Navigation</h1>
            <ul>
                <li><a href="/">Home</a></li>
                <li><a href="http://www.apress.com">Apress</a></li>
                <li><a href="http://www.theCreativePeople.com">My Site</a></li>
            </ul>
        </nav>
        <section>
            <h1>Top-level</h1>
            <section>
                <h2>New York Yankees Starting Lineup</h2>
                <details>
                    <summary>This content is collapsed</summary>
                    <dl>
                        <dt>Infielders</dt>
                        <dd>Teixeira, 1B</dd>
                        <dd>Castro, 2B</dd>
                        <dd>Gregorius, SS</dd>
                        <dd>Torreyes, 3B</dd>
                        <dd>McCann, C</dd>
                        <dt>Outfielders</dt>
                        <dd>Hicks, LF</dd>
                        <dd>Ellsbury, CF</dd>
                        <dd>Ackley, RF</dd>
                        <dt>Designated Hitter</dt>
                        <dd>Rodriguez, DH</dd>
                        <dt>Pitchers</dt>
                        <dd>Gausman, R</dd>
                        <dd>Wilson, R</dd>
                        <dd>Tillman, R</dd>
```

```
                            <dd>Price, L</dd>
                            <dd>Porcello, R</dd>
                        </dl>
                        <dl>
                            <dt>Hicks, LF</dt>
                            <dt>Ellsbury, CF</dt>
                            <dt>Ackley, RF</dt>
                            <dd>Outfielders - the positions in baseball that are played in the
grassy area behind the diamond, known as the outfield. These positions include the Left
Fielder, Center Fielder, and Right Fielder.</dd>
                        </dl>
                    </details>
                    <main>
                        <h1>Main content</h1>
                        <section>
                            <h1>Featured content</h1>
                            <blockquote cite="www.apress.com">
                                <h1>Quotation</h1>
                                <p>This is a quotation</p>
                            </blockquote>
                            <p>paragraph 1</p>
                            <hr />
                            <p>paragraph 2</p>
                        </section>
                    </main>
                    <section>
                        <h1>Articles</h1>
                        <article>
                            <h1>Article 1</h1>
                            <pre>I heard the bells on Christmas Day
Their old, familiar carols play,
    And wild and sweet
    The words repeat
Of peace on earth, good-will to men!</pre>
                            <cite>Henry Wadsworth Longfellow - 1863, public domain</cite>
                            <figure>
                                <h1>Figure</h1>
                                <img src="HTML5Badge.png" alt="HTML5" />
                                <figcaption>Official HTML5 Logo</figcaption>
                            </figure>
                        </article>
                    </section>
                </section>
                <aside>
                    <h1>Related content</h1>
                    <section>
                        <h1>HTML Reference</h1>
                        <h2>Book Topics</h2>
                        <ul>
                            <li>HTML</li>
                            <li>CSS</li>
                            <li>JavaScript</li>
                        </ul>
```

```
        <h2>HTML Chapters</h2>
        <ol start="3" type="I" reversed>
            <li>Structural Elements</li>
            <li>Text Elements</li>
            <li>Table Elements</li>
            <li>Embedded Elements</li>
            <li>Form Elements</li>
        </ol>
    </section>
    <section>
        <h1>Book list</h1>
        <dl>
            <dt>Beginning WF</dt>
            <dd>Indexed by feature so you can find answers easily and written in
an accessible style, Beginning WF shows how Microsoft's Workflow Foundation (WF) technology
can be used in a wide variety of applications.</dd>
            <dt>Office 2010 Workflow</dt>
            <dd>Workflow is the glue that binds information worker processes,
users, and artifacts—without it, information workers are just islands of data and potential.
Office 2010 Workflow walks you through implementing workflow solutions.</dd>
            <dt>Pro Access 2010 Development</dt>
            <dd>Pro Access 2010 Development is a fundamental resource for
developing business applications that take advantage of the features of Access 2010. You'll
learn how to build database applications, create Web-based databases, develop macros and VBA
tools for Access applications, integrate Access with SharePoint, and much more.</dd>
        </dl>
        <article>
            <h1>Book 1</h1>
            <iframe src="http://www.apress.com" width="100%" height="400">
                <p>Your browser does not support iframes</p>
            </iframe>
        </article>
    </section>
</aside>
</section>
<footer>
    <p>Closing content</p>
    <address>
        <p>Provided by
            <a href="mailto:mcollins@theCreativePeople.com">Mark J. Collins</a>
        </p>
        <p>For more information
            <a href="www.theCreativePeople.com">visit his website</a>
        </p>
    </address>
</footer>
</body>
</html>
```

CHAPTER 5

■ ■ ■

Phrasing HTML Elements

In the previous chapter we looked at the elements that are used to organize an HTML document into sections and lower-level groupings. Each of these elements is used for a specific semantic purpose. In this chapter I'll demonstrate the HTML elements that are used to mark up the actual text content. When creating your content, these should also be chosen for semantic reasons.

■ **Note**   Embedded elements such as images (`img`), `audio`, `video`, and `canvas` are also considered phrasing content. However, these will be covered by themselves in Chapter 7.

Highlighting Text

■ **Caution**   In HTML4 there were several elements that were purely presentational, that is, they were used solely to define how they were to be rendered. These include bold (`b`), italic (`i`), underline (`u`), and strikethrough (`s` or `strike`). As HTML5 is all about semantics, these have been replaced with more semantic-based elements. The `strike` element has been removed from HTML5. The `b`, `i`, `u`, and `s` elements have been given new names and semantic definitions to go with them.

HTML5 provides several elements that are used to provide stylistic emphasis to a section of text. Each of these has a semantic purpose for using it; some are more specific while others are a little more generic. I will explain each of them and their intended use. You should always use the most specific element that fits your situation and use a more generic one only when a more specific element in not appropriate.

■ **Note**   I will call these elements by a name that describes their intended use, rather than the actual HTML tag that is used to create it. This may seem a little confusing to readers who are already familiar with tags such as `b`, `i`, `em`, and `strong`. However, I'm trying to drive home the appropriate usage of each and in most cases, the tags do not communicate that very well, if at all.

© Mark J. Collins 2017
M. J. Collins, *Pro HTML5 with CSS, JavaScript, and Multimedia*, DOI 10.1007/978-1-4842-2463-2_5

Importance (strong)

The W3C reference says "The strong element represents a span of text with strong importance." The key word here is *importance*. The strong element is used to indicate the text has a higher importance than the surrounding text. This could be a word, phrase, sentence, or even paragraph that is critical.

You can also nest the strong element to indicate extra importance. For example:

```
<strong>
    <strong>Warning!</strong> Be sure to <strong>extinguish</strong> all fires!
</strong>
```

This identifies important words within an important sentence.

Emphasis (em)

In everyday speech, emphasis is often used to alter the meaning of a sentence. Consider the sentence, "Boys like chocolate donuts," and how the meaning changes when different words are emphasized. For example, "*Boys* like chocolate donuts" adds the implication that girls don't. Similarly, "Boys like chocolate *donuts*" will leave you wondering what chocolate items they don't like.

The above paragraph is a perfect illustration of how the emphasis (em) element should be used. Text placed within an em element should be read with emphasis. Even though you may not be reading the text out loud, in your mind you're still hearing the emphasis and catching the nuances implied by it.

Another good example is when introducing new terms or concepts. You may have already noticed that, in this book, whenever a new term is introduced it is given emphasis. It's like I'm talking to you and the first time I use a new word I say it a little louder, perhaps with a slight pause before and after it, because I want you to hear it. I'll then follow this with an explanation of what the term means. The emphasis helps you tie the new term with the definition that follows.

Relevance (mark)

The relevance element (mark) is used to indicate text that is particularly relevant in the current context. Here's what the specification states:

> *The mark element represents a run of text in one document marked or highlighted for reference purposes, due to its relevance in another context.*

The idea here is that you're including content from another source and adding emphasis that was not there originally because of its relevance in the current context. The key point here, and what differentiates this from the importance and emphasis elements, is that the emphasis was not in the original content. It is being added later, because of its relevance in the current context.

There are two common applications of this. First, you can use the relevance element to highlight a portion of a quote that is particularly relevant to the current usage. For example:

```
<p>
    "Read my lips: <mark>no new taxes</mark>", declared presidential candidate George H. W. Bush
    in 1988. However, the 1990 budget agreement increased taxes in several areas.
</p>
```

The default styling will set the background color to yellow as shown in Figure 5-1.

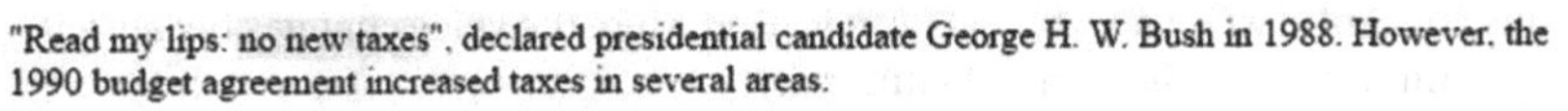

"Read my lips: no new taxes", declared presidential candidate George H. W. Bush in 1988. However, the 1990 budget agreement increased taxes in several areas.

Figure 5-1. *Using the relevance element to highlight text*

A second common use of the relevance element is when displaying search results. It is used to highlight words or phrases that were included in the specified search criteria. For example, if someone was searching for the text "HTML" and the page displays articles containing that text. In this case you might want to highlight every place the HTML text appears. The relevance (mark) element is used to accomplish this.

▪ **Tip**   Remember, the relevance (mark) element is used to highlight text that is being quoted from another source, where the emphasis was not in the original content. Don't use it to emphasize original text; instead use one of the other elements such as importance or emphasis.

Alternative Voice (i)

The i element was used to indicate italic presentation in HTML4 but in HTML5 has been given semantic meaning. This is how the W3C reference describes it:

> *The i element represents a span of text offset from its surrounding content without conveying any extra emphasis or importance, and for which the conventional typographic presentation is italic text; for example, a taxonomic designation, a technical term, an idiomatic phrase from another language, a thought, or a ship name.*

Essentially, the i element should be used when the text needs to be styled differently from the surrounding text but you don't need to imply any greater importance or emphasis. Unfortunately, that is not very specific and tends to overlap with the b element that I'll describe shortly.

However, the specification goes on to provide examples where the i element is appropriate. These scenarios can be summarized as using an *alternate voice* and I think this helps to understand when this element is appropriate.

If the text is quoting someone speaking and you want to interject a thought in the middle, use this, for example:

```
<p>
    "Class, pay attention!" <i>I wonder if they're even listening to me.</i> "Who's ready
    for tomorrow's exam?"
</p>
```

The thought is a different voice because it's in their head instead of coming out of their mouth. Another example is when someone is speaking in English and they quote a foreign word or phrase. It is a different voice from the rest of the text because it is in a different language.

```
<p>
    "This needs some... <i>je ne sais quoi</i>."
</p>
```

Another application of this concept is when a technical term is used. Here the voice changes because it goes from everyday English to terminology that has limited familiarity.

```
<p>
    "He's not really bald, he just has a severe shortage of <i>folliculus pili</i> on his
head."
</p>
```

In all of these examples, the text is identified by the alternate voice (i) element, to indicate a change in voice or mood: whether it is changing from one language to another, from spoken words to unspoken, or from everyday speech to technical jargon. The default style will render this in italic as demonstrated in Figure 5-2.

"Class, pay attention!" *I wonder if they're even listening to me.* "Who's ready for tomorrow's exam?"

"This needs some... *je ne sais quoi.*"

"He's not really bald, he just has a severe shortage of *folliculus pili* on his head."

Figure 5-2. *The rendering of alternate voice elements*

Small (small)

Ever heard the expression, "read the small print"? This generally refers to the legalese that is important, although sometimes overlooked. HTML5 defines the small element where you can put this type of content. The small element is intended for short runs of text that provide details that are typically outside of the primary content.

Use the small element for copyright information, disclaimers, or other legal information. You can also use it for including disclosures, licensing details, or for attributing material to its source. Don't use the small element for large blocks of content that is outside of the main document flow. Use the aside element for this purpose.

■ **Note**   In HTML4, the small element was used to make the font smaller. This has been repurposed in HTML to provide semantic meaning, specifically for legal details. Don't use the small element just to make the font smaller. This should be done in CSS.

The small element does not imply any lesser importance. In fact, the details in a small element are often very important. If the content is legal details that are outside of the main flow, put it in a small element. If it is also important information, put it inside an importance (strong) element as well.

Strikethrough (s)

The strikethrough element (s) is used to indicate content that is no longer *relevant* or *accurate*. The terms relevant and accurate come from the HTML5 specification and are the key concepts you should consider when deciding if the strikethrough element is the semantically correct one to use.

■ **Caution**   In HTML4 both s and strike elements were supported to render text with a strikethrough font. However, in HTML5 the strike element is obsolete.

In most situations, if you have inaccurate information you would just simply correct it; irrelevant data would be removed or replaced. However, if you want to highlight that a change has been made, you can leave the old text but wrap it in a strikethrough element like this:

```
<p>
    For a limited time only <s>$9.95</s> $7.99 will get you a...
</p>
```

In this case, the $9.95 price is no longer accurate; the price has been updated to $7.99. However, the previous price is being displayed to demonstrate the price reduction.

■ **Tip**   Do not use the strikethrough element to indicate text that has been deleted. The deleted (del) and inserted (ins) element are used for this purpose and I will explain them later in this chapter.

Suppose you had a page that listed the date and time of all of the home games for a particular sports team. Each of these might be a link to a page where you could reserve seats for the game. You can then put all of the games that are in the past or that have sold out inside a strikethrough element. You leave these games listed as that could be useful information, but they are not relevant for the current purpose of reserving seats.

In the examples I've given, the content inside the strikethrough element has been text and the default style will render this with the strikethrough font. However, the strikethrough element is used for its semantic meaning, and as such, it applies equally well to other types of content such as images, audio/video, and input controls. You'll have to define how an inaccurate or irrelevant image should be rendered in the CSS, but it is certainly semantically valid to include it in HTML inside a strikethrough element.

Stylistically Offset (b)

The old bold element (b) from HTML4 has been redefined in HTML5 as stylistically offset content without conveying importance. I'm calling it by the wonderfully clear name of *stylistically offset*. Here is how the HTML5 specification defines it:

> *The b element represents a span of text to which attention is being drawn for utilitarian purposes without conveying any extra importance and with no implication of an alternate voice or mood, such as key words in a document abstract, product names in a review, actionable words in interactive text-driven software, or an article lede.*

In other words, you should use this element when the text needs to stand out in some way and none of the other elements that I've previously described are appropriate. It's not important, requires any emphasis, or reflects an alternate voice or mood. However, you want to draw attention to this text for some other reason.

The specification goes on to list some examples where the stylistically offset element should be used:

- Keywords
- Product names

- Actionable words

- Article lead (opening paragraph)

Since this element is purposely generic, it's a good idea to include a `class` attribute that indicates why this element needs to stand out. This not only clarifies the semantic meaning but also enables the CSS to style these differently depending on why it is being used. For example:

```
<p>
    The text highlighting elements include <b class="keyword">importance</b>,
    <b class="keyword">emphasis</b>, and <b class="keyword">alternate voice</b>.
</p>
```

■ **Tip**   The stylistically offset element (b) is the most generic element that should only be used when none of the more specific elements are appropriate.

Unarticulated (u)

The underline (u) element was used in HTML4 to specify text that should be underlined. Apart from being purely presentational like the b and i elements, the u element was also avoided because underlined text is often mistaken for a hyperlink. However, the u element has been included in HTML5 with the semantic meaning of *unarticulated* content.

The specification is not very clear about when this element should be used, citing only two examples: misspelled words and Chinese proper names. The actual definition from the specification is "an unarticulated, though explicitly rendered, non-textual annotation." Essentially, this is saying to use the unarticulated element when you need to annotate text (format it differently) but there is not another element that clearly defines your reason for doing so.

The specification goes on to say that there is probably a different element that is more appropriate:

> In most cases, another element is likely to be more appropriate: for marking stress emphasis, the em element should be used; for marking key words or phrases either the b element or the mark element should be used, depending on the context; for marking book titles, the cite element should be used; for labeling text with explicit textual annotations, the ruby element should be used; for technical terms, taxonomic designation, transliteration, a thought, or for labeling ship names in Western texts, the i element should be used.

In other words, use this as a last resort. So when should you use the unarticulated element? Let's look at the two examples given. When indicating a misspelled word, the standard convention is to underline it. Similarly, underlining Chinese proper names is a standard practice. In Western languages, a proper noun is indicated by capitalizing the first character. In Chinese, however, the method of indicating a proper noun is to underline it. So, if you're including Chinese content, proper nouns should be included in the unarticulated element.

For both of the stated examples, you have text that should be annotated in some way; none of the other elements have an appropriate semantic meaning, and the accepted convention is to underline them. However, in general, you can use the unarticulated element whenever none of the more specific elements are appropriate.

As with the stylistically offset (b) element, you should include a `class` attribute to indicate the reason why the text is being annotated, since the element by itself does not make that clear. For example, this content highlights spelling, grammar, and word usage errors in the text:

```
<p>
    Please be sure to <u class="spelling">chek</u> <u class="usage">four</u> spelling
    <u class="grammar">mistake</u>.
</p>
```

You could use the class attribute in CSS to change the color of the underline. For example, you could use a red underline for spelling mistakes and use green for the grammar errors.

■ **Tip** If you want to simply underline some text without indicating the semantic meaning of being an unarticulated notation, put the text in a span tag and use CSS to apply the underline style.

Element Review

I'm writing this book in English and presumably most of you are reasonably fluent in reading English. However, HTML is used to render any language in the world. These semantic concepts such as importance and emphasis are universal, but the way they are physically represented on a web page can vary from one language or culture to another. This is another reason why content authors should focus on the semantic meanings of these elements and not on their default representations.

- importance - `<strong>` - key point or critical concept that should not be missed
- emphasis - `<em>` - read with emphasis, something that is pronounced differently
- relevance - `<mark>` - text that is highlighted for reference purposes
- alternative voice - `<i>` - foreign word, technical terms, etc.
- small - `<small>` - short runs of legal details outside of the main flow
- strikethrough - `<s>` - no longer accurate or relevant
- stylistically offset - `<b>` - keywords or other phrases that need to stand out
- unarticulated - `<u>` - indicates spelling or grammatical errors, proper nouns, or family names

---

■ **Tip** The W3C provides a short but useful article that explains when and how the more generic elements, b and i, should be used. It can be found at `http://www.w3.org/International/questions/qa-b-and-i-tags`. I recommend reading through this and the examples are quite helpful.

Other Semantic Phrasing

HTML5 provides several elements that have a very specific purpose. If these fit the content that you're adding, use them to provide the appropriate semantic information.

Code, Sample, Keyboard, and Variable

If you are documenting a computer application, the code, keyboard (kbd), and sample (samp) elements are helpful in distinguishing these types of content. The variable (var) element is also useful in this and other scenarios, such as including formulas. These are all inline phrasing elements that do not usually span paragraphs.

The code element represents a portion of some type of computer code, typically source code or some type of computer script. It can also be used for a file name, a database table, or a server name. Basically the code element is used for any text that is recognizable by a computer program.

■ **Tip**   There is no explicit mechanism for indicating the computer language of the source code. The recommendation, however, is to use the class attribute and prefix the value with **language-**. For example: <code **class="language-javascript"**>Item.prototype.isAvailable = true;</code>.

The next two elements, keyboard and sample, are poorly named, in my opinion. The keyboard element identifies content that is input into a computer, such as keyboard input. Inversely, the sample element is used to indicate content that is some sort of computer output, such as a prompt on a screen or text that is written to a console window or log file. The specification sometimes refers to this as sample output, which is where the name samp is derived from.

The key point here is that kbd is used for input and samp is used for output. They could also be used in a code element as they are recognizable by a computer program. However, kbd and samp are more specific and should be preferred over code when appropriate.

If the code snippet is longer than one line, you should include the code element inside a preformatted (pre) element. As I explained in the previous chapter, the preformatted element maintains the white space characters and renders the content exactly how it was entered.

Inside a code snippet, the variable element can be used to identify variables. This can be used to make the code more readable. The default styling of the variable element is to use an italic font.

The following HTML includes a snippet of JavaScript code. The default rendering is shown in Figure 5-3.

```
<pre>
    <code class="language-javascript">
this.log = function () {
    console.log("Quantity: " + <var>this.count</var> + ", Color: " + <var>this.color</var>);
};
    </code>
</pre>
```

```
this.log = function () {
    console.log("Quantity: " + this.count + ", Color: " + this.color);
};
```

Figure 5-3. *Using the code, pre, and var elements*

■ **Tip**   The keyboard and sample elements are used for semantic purposes; to indicate the content is input or output to/from a computer program. It is possible to nest them as well. For example, if part of the output is input that is echoed to the screen. In this case, the input should be inside a keyboard element, while the entire output is inside a sample element.

The variable element can also be used in other contexts as well. For example:

```
<p>
    The area of a rectangle with length <var>l</var> and width <var>w</var> is
    <var>l</var> * <var>w</var>.
</p>
```

Abbreviations and Definitions

The abbreviation (abbr) element is used to include the expanded version of an abbreviation or acronym. The abbreviated form is provided as the content of the element (between the opening and closing tags). The title property contains the full version of the abbreviation, which is not displayed until the mouse is moved over the abbreviation.

For example, this code uses the term HTML in an abbreviation element and is rendered as shown in Figure 5-4.

```
<p>
    The use of <abbr title="Hypertext Markup Language">HTML</abbr> has contributed greatly to
    the popularity of web-based applications. <br />
</p>
```

The use of HTML has contributed greatly to the popularity of web-based applications.

Hypertext Markup Language

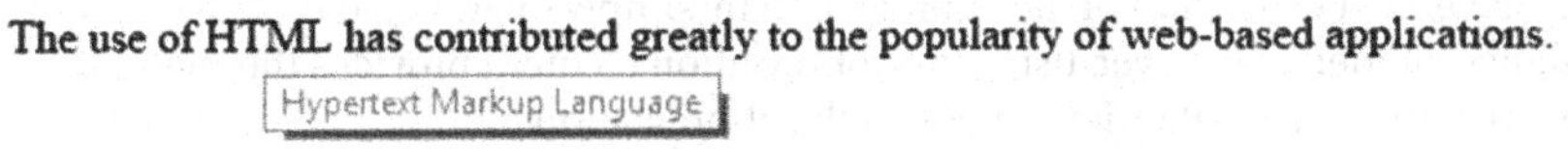

Figure 5-4. *Displaying an abbreviation*

The title property is optional. Without a title property, the abbreviation element simply indicates that the enclosed text is an abbreviation or acronym. This could be useful, especially if you want to apply a different style. If you specify the title property, it should contain only the expanded version. The sentence should read correctly if the abbreviation was replaced with the expanded version.

The defining instance (dfn) element is used to identify a term that is being defined. Put the term inside the defining instance element and the actual definition outside of it, typically after it. For example, the following code indicates that the term HTML is being defined.

```
<p>
    <dfn>HTML</dfn> is a standardized way of adding semantic information to support rich
    formatting of content.
</p>
```

The W3C specification states that if a dfn element is used, the nearest parent element must contain the definition of the term inside the dfn element. In this example, the paragraph element containing the dfn element also contains the definition of the term.

The default styling of the defining instance element is to show the text in italics. In this book, the first time a term is used, it is shown in italics and followed by its definition. The defining instance element provides the semantic framework for this technique.

Just like the abbreviation element, you can also include a title attribute, which will be displayed when the mouse is placed over the element. Also, if you want to be able to reference this definition when the term is used later in the document, include an id attribute. For example, this markup demonstrates using both the title and id attributes. There is a link in the second paragraph where the HTML term is used that will go back to the initial definition.

```
<p>
    <dfn id="htmlDef" title="HyperText Markup Language">HTML</dfn> is a standardized way of
    adding semantic information to support rich formatting of content. <br />
</p>
<p>
    Learning <a href="#htmlDef">HTML</a> is certainly worthwhile and rewarding.
</p>
```

When the term being defined is also an abbreviation or acronym, you can combine both the abbreviation and defining instance elements like this:

```
<p>
    <dfn><abbr title="Hypertext Markup Language">HTML</abbr></dfn> is a standardized way of
    adding semantic information to support rich formatting of content.
</p>
```

You can accomplish the hover text expansion of the abbreviation by simply including the title attribute in the defining instance element. However, using the abbreviation element provides the semantic meaning, making it clear that the title is the expanded version of the abbreviation.

Subscripts and Superscripts

Use the subscript (sub) element if you need to show text as subscript. This will render the character(s) slightly lower than the other characters. Similarly, use the superscript (sup) element to render the text higher. For example, the following code is rendered as displayed in Figure 5-5.

```
<p>
    H<sub>2</sub>O is the chemical formula for water.<br />
    e=mc<sup>2</sup> is the formula for mass-energy equivalence.
</p>
```

H_2O is the chemical formula for water.

$e=mc^2$ is the formula for mass-energy equivalence.

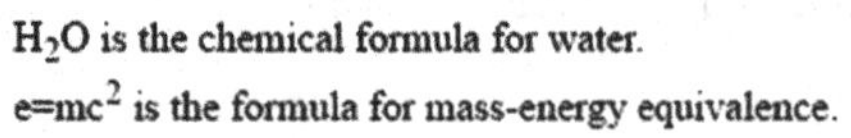

Figure 5-5. *Using subscripts and superscripts*

■ **Caution** The use of the subscript and superscript elements should not be used for purely presentational reasons. They should only be used when their absence would change the meaning of the content. For example, e=mc2 without the superscript has a different meaning; the character 2 in superscript means the variable should be squared. Similarly, in some languages, superscripting or subscripting characters can change the meaning of a word.

The subscript element can also be used as part of a variable (var) element, which I demonstrated previously.

Time

The time element allows you to provide semantic meaning around text that refers to a point in time. You can then use the datetime attribute to include a machine readable version as well. For example:

```
<p>
    Your follow-up appointment will be a week from <time datetime="2016-06-28">Tuesday</time>.
</p>
```

The datetime attribute is not displayed; it is provided only for scripts and other applications that may need to access this information. If you want the actual date displayed, put it in the content portion of the time element.

The datetime attribute can contain a specific date as demonstrated in this example. It can also specify the time as well as the date, or just a time by itself. There are quite a few different ways of formatting the datetime attribute. The W3C specification provides lot of details with examples, which can be found at http://www.w3.org/TR/html5/text-level-semantics.html#the-time-element .

Edits

If you want to show changes that have been made to a document, you can include them in insert (ins) and delete (del) elements. Put the content that has been removed from the original version in a delete element and put the added content in an insert (ins) element. If text has changed, put the original version in a delete element and the new version in an insert element.

For example, this HTML indicates how the original draft of the Declaration of Independence was edited before the final version was published.

```
<p>
    We hold these truths to be
    <del cite="https://www.loc.gov/exhibits/declara/ruffdrft.html" datetime="1776-06-28">sacred
    & undeniable;</del><ins>self-evident,</ins> that all men are created equal<del> &
    independant</del>, that <del>from that equal creation they derive rights inherent &
    inalienable</del><ins>they are endowed by their Creator with certain unalienable
    Rights</ins>, <del>among which are the preservation of life, & liberty, & the pursuit
    of happiness;</del><ins>that among these are Life, Liberty and the pursuit of
    Happiness.</ins>
</p>
```

The default styling of these elements is to underline the new text and strike through the deleted text as shown in in Figure 5-6.

We hold these truths to be ~~sacred & undeniable:~~self-evident, that all men are created equal ~~& independant,~~ that ~~from that equal creation they derive rights inherent & inalienable~~they are endowed by their Creator with certain unalienable Rights. ~~among which are the preservation of life, & liberty, & the pursuit of happiness:~~that among these are Life, Liberty and the pursuit of Happiness.

Figure 5-6. Illustration of default edit rendering

In addition to the global attributes, both the insert and delete elements support two specific attributes:

- `cite` - Use this attribute to indicate the source of the change. If used, this is expected to be a reference to an online resource. This is not displayed but could be used by search engines as well as scripts.

- `datetime` - This indicates the date/time when the change was made. The standard format is `YYYY-MM-DDThh:mm:ss`*(time zone)*.

■ **Tip**   Of course, you can always change the default styling through CSS and through JavaScript. For example, you could provide an option on the page to show only the final version. To do that, set the style to `display: none` for delete elements and use the standard styling for the insert elements. And you can show the original version by hiding the insert elements and using the standard style for the delete elements.

Quoting

In the previous chapter I introduced the `blockquote` element as a structural element that contains a large quotation and other elements related to it. Now I'll explain the recommended techniques for using quotations, including the `blockquote`, inline quote (q), and citation (`cite`) elements.

Use the inline quote (q) element when you want to include a short quote inside the current sentence or paragraph. For example:

```
<p>
    As Abraham Lincoln once said, <q>Whatever you are, be a good one</q>.
</p>
```

An inline quote does not start a new paragraph, rather the content flows from the previous element just like any other phrasing element such as strong or emphasis. Also, an inline quote should not span paragraphs.

In contrast, the `blockquote` element defines a new section just like a `div` or the more semantic elements such as `aside` and `section`. It can contain multiple paragraphs as well as other elements including heading text and footers. For example, this HTML is rendered as shown in Figure 5-7.

```
<blockquote>
    <h1>Gettysburg Address</h1>
    <p>
        Four score and seven years ago our fathers brought forth, upon this continent, a new
        nation, conceived in Liberty, and dedicated to the proposition that all men are
        created equal.
    </p>
```

```
<p>
    Now we are engaged in a great civil war, testing whether that nation, or any nation so
    conceived, and so dedicated, can long endure. We are met here on a great battlefield
    of that war. We have come to dedicate a portion of it, as a final resting place for
    those who here gave their lives that that nation might live. It is altogether fitting
    and proper that we should do this.
</p>
<footer>
    <small>Abraham Lincoln, 1864</small>
</footer>
<cite>
    <a href="http://www.abrahamlincolnonline.org/lincoln/speeches/gettysburg.htm">
        Gettysburg Address
    </a>
</cite>
</blockquote>
```

Gettysburg Address

Four score and seven years ago our fathers brought forth, upon this continent, a new nation, conceived in Liberty, and dedicated to the proposition that all men are created equal.

Now we are engaged in a great civil war, testing whether that nation, or any nation so conceived, and so dedicated, can long endure. We are met here on a great battlefield of that war. We have come to dedicate a portion of it, as a final resting place for those who here gave their lives that that nation might live. It is altogether fitting and proper that we should do this.

Abraham Lincoln, 1864
Gettysburg Address

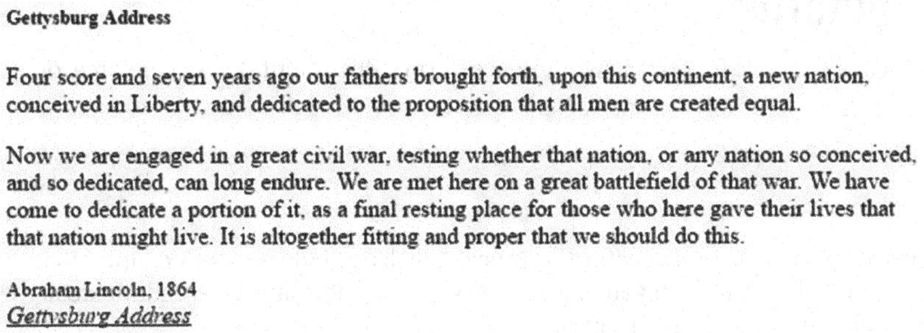

Figure 5-7. *Default rendering of a block quote*

All quotations should be cited to give credit to the source. Since an inline quote cannot include other elements except other phrasing element, the citation is entered using the cite attribute that was explained earlier. The value of the cite attribute should be a URL to a location providing more information about the quote. This information is not usually displayed by the browser. To provide a visual citation, you'll need to include additional text outside of the inline quote element, such as "As Abraham Lincoln once said" in this example.

For block quotes, the citation is made through the cite element. The name of the quoted source, for example, Gettysburg Address, should be inside the cite element. If you want to include a link as well, include an anchor (a) tag for that purpose. By putting this inside the cite element, the semantic meaning of the link becomes more obvious.

■ **Tip** Since a blockquote is a flow element, you can include just about anything in it. For example, you can include an image, or an audio or video clip. If you wanted to include a picture of the Mona Lisa, putting it in a blockquote element makes it clear that you are quoting someone else's work. Also include a cite element in the blockquote to name the work, "Mona Lisa," and add other content to indicate it was painted by Leonardo da Vinci, circa 1506.

Span

The span element is a generic container that provides no semantic meaning. However, you can use attributes on the span element to indicate the semantic information. The class attribute is the most commonly used attribute for this purpose, but there are others such as lang and dir that may useful as well.

Consider the following HTML:

```
<p>
    The primary colors are <span class="red">red</span>, <span class="blue">blue</span>,
    and <span class="yellow">yellow</span>.
</p>
```

The span element has no semantic meaning; it also has no default styling. Without any CSS rules, this span element in this content has no affect. However, you could use CSS to change the font color or perhaps the background color of these portions of text.

Adding Carriage Returns

There are a few techniques that are available for adding white space in your document. These can force, or suggest, line breaks within the text.

Line Break

The line break element (br) inserts a carriage return within your text. Recall from the previous chapter that browsers ignore white space characters in HTML. If you need text to start on a new line, insert a line break element before the text or after the previous text. For example:

```
<p>
    Fourscore and seven years ago, <br />
    our fathers brought forth to this continent <br />
    a new nation, conceived in liberty <br />
    and dedicated to the proposition <br />
    that all men are created equal. <br />
</p>
```

The line break element is an *empty* element, meaning that it has no content between the opening and closing tags. In fact, HTML5 does not distinguish between an opening tag (<br>) and a closing tag (</br>). If you entered

```
One <br> Two </br> Three
```

each word would be rendered on a separate line because both the opening and closing tags would generate a line break. HTML5 is pretty lenient, allowing <br>, </br>, <br/>, and <br /> as all valid syntax. I will be using the <br /> formatting convention consistently for all self-closing tags throughout this book.

■ **Caution**   Don't use the line break element merely to add vertical spacing between elements. This should be done using CSS styles. The line break element should only be used when you need to force text to a new line. A good example of this is when formatting an address block.

Word Break Opportunity

The browser will automatically wrap text to fit within the horizontal space defined for an element. There are several ways to control the rules used to wrap text and I'll cover that in Chapter 10. Wrapping normally occurs where there is white space or punctuation between words. However, if you have a rather long word, this may not work as well as you would like.

If you don't allow words to be broken, you may end up with a lot of white space on one line as the long word must start the next line. Worse, if the word by itself won't fit, it will spill over the allotted area. If you allow words to be broken, it may break at an undesirable place.

The word break opportunity element (wbr) is used to indicate where a word could be broken if the wrapping logic needed to. For example, consider the following HTML:

```
<p style="width: 70px; word-wrap: break-word">
    Supercalifragilisticexpialidocious<br />
    --<br />
    Super<wbr />cali<wbr />fragilistic<wbr />expiali<wbr />docious
</p>
```

The inline style sets the width for the paragraph to 70 pixels and then enables the word wrapping to break words, if necessary. The longest word in the English language, supercalifragilisticexpialidocious, is then included twice. The second instance contains the wbr element at logical places, where wrapping would still make the word readable. This is rendered as shown in Figure 5-8. As you can see, the second instance wraps in more logical places.

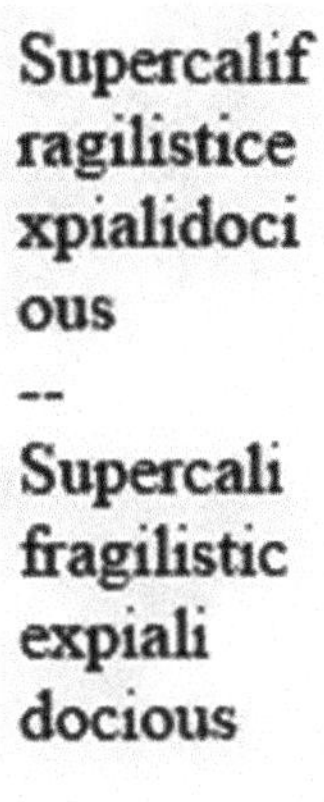

**Supercalif
ragilistice
xpialidoci
ous
--
Supercali
fragilistic
expiali
docious**

Figure 5-8. Demonstrating the word break opportunity element

■ **Note**   OK, maybe supercalifragilisticexpialidocious is not a real word. But it is listed in both Webster's and Oxford dictionaries. Variants of the nonsense word have been around for a while. This particular version was made famous in Disney's 1964 movie, *Mary Poppins*.

You will likely never have to break a word as long as this. However, one useful application of this is when displaying a URL, which can be rather long and does not usually include any white space characters. You can place the word break opportunity element in carefully chosen places so if the URL needs to be wrapped, it will still render it in a reasonable fashion.

Hyphens

The word break opportunity element identifies logical places where a word can be broken and wrapped to the next line, if necessary. You can also accomplish this using a hyphen or a *soft hyphen*.

A hyphen character (-) will be displayed even if the word does not need to be wrapped. However, a soft hyphen is an invisible character inserted in a word. It is entered as ­. Both hyphens and soft hyphens will also tell the browser where a break can occur. A soft hyphen is only displayed if the word is actually wrapped at that location.

■ **Tip** You can also specify a soft hyphen using the Unicode notation, ­.

To try this out, let's change our sample HTML to include a third instance of supercalifragilisticexpialidocious, using soft hyphens instead.

```
<p style="width: 70px; word-wrap: break-word">
    Supercalifragilisticexpialidocious<br />
    --<br />
    Super<wbr />cali<wbr />fragilistic<wbr />expiali<wbr />docious<br />
    --<br />
    Super&shy;cali&shy;fragilistic&shy;expiali&shy;docious
</p>
```

When rendered this will look like Figure 5-9.

**Supercalif
ragilistice
xpialidoci
ous
--
Supercali
fragilistic
expiali
docious
--
Supercali-
fragilistic-
expiali-
docious**

Figure 5-9. *Using soft hyphens*

When wrapping a URL, you don't want to include hyphens because when the lines are assembled together you'll end up with extra characters, making the URL incorrect. In this case, use the word break opportunity element. However, for a word like supercalifragilisticexpialidocious, you should use a soft hyphen (­) because you'll want a hyphen displayed to indicate that the word continues on the next line.

Bidirectional Text

In some languages, such as Hebrew and Arabic, the text flows from right-to-left. Browsers are generally pretty good about dealing with right-to-left languages. Simply setting the dir attribute on the html element to **rtl** will render things correctly, for the most part. There are, of course, situations that you'll need to deal with, and to do that you must first understand the *Unicode Bidirectional (bidi) algorithm*, which I'll explain now.

Text Direction

A string is simply an array of characters. The logical order refers to how they are sequenced in memory. For example, the Hebrew word for happy contains four characters:

1. א
2. שׁ
3. ר
4. י

This is the logical order. However, because Hebrew is a right-to-left language, the visual order, or how it is rendered is:

אשׁרי

■ **Note**   In fact, if you paste these characters, one at a time, into Microsoft Word, or even Notepad, the order will be reversed automatically. After pasting the characters, try navigating with the left and right arrows and you'll see that it does some interesting things. The Home key moves the cursor to the right of the word, and the right arrow key actually moves left.

Each Unicode character has a direction property that indicates the ordering (left-to-right or right-to-left). As you type characters, the cursor automatically moves past the current character (to the right of it) indicating where the next character will go. If you are using a character set for a right-to-left language, as you type, the cursor will move to the left of the character. This happens automatically based on the characters that are being entered.

However, while using a right-to-left character set, if you enter a number, the cursor will go to the right of it. This is because numbers are always left-to-right, even when included in a right-to-left language. This is why the *bidirectional* term is used. Within a block of text, there is a mixture of left-to-right and right-to-left. Each section is referred to a *directional run*, which is a string of text that flows in a single direction.

Flow Direction

Generally, each portion of inline content flows from left-to-right because this is the default direction. The direction is set using the dir attribute, which is a global attribute that can be placed on any element. If the entire page is using a right-to-left language, set the direction on the html element:

```
<html dir="rtl">
```

If only a portion of the text is right-to-left, set the `dir` attribute on the appropriate containing element such as a div, p, or span tag. The `dir` attribute is inherited from the parent element, and the default value for the html element, if not specified otherwise, is `ltr`. In the bidi algorithm, this is referred to as the *base direction*.

Spaces and punctuation characters are considered neutral, since they can be used in both left-to-right and right-to-left languages. If one or more neutral characters are between two characters of the same direction, they will be assumed to have the same direction and will be included in the same directional run. Neutral characters between runs of different directions will use the base direction. This means that they will be included in one of the direction runs, whichever one has the same direction as the base direction. Likewise, neutral characters at the beginning or end of a block of text will also use the base direction. If that matches the direction of the adjoining run, they will be included; otherwise they will be in their own directional run.

For example, consider the following markup. Figure 5-10 illustrates each of the directional runs.

```
<p>
    In Hebrew, this אַשְׁרֵי means happy.
</p>
```

In Hebrew, this אַשְׁרֵי means happy.

Figure 5-10. *Illustration of directional runs*

The short, thicker underlines in Figure 5-5 indicate content where the direction is determined by the base direction. If this is `ltr`, these characters will also be `ltr` and there will be three directional runs, with only the four Hebrew characters being in a separate run.

However, if the base direction is `rtl`, there will be four directional runs since the period at the end of the sentence will be `rtl` and must be in its own run. Each of these directional runs will also flow from right-to-left. So reading from left-to-right as we are used to, there would be a period, followed by "means happy," followed by a Hebrew word, and finally "In Hebrew, this."

Numeric characters are weakly typed and are handled a little differently. A string of numeric characters is always rendered left-to-right; however, they are considered part of the direction run of the previous text, even if that is right-to-left. For example, consider the following:

```
<p>
    <span>!123</span> <span>אַשְׁרֵי</span> <span>456!</span><br />
</p>
```

The 456 text will be rendered left-to-right but will be considered part of the Hebrew text direction run, which is right-to-left. The 456 text will come after the Hebrew text, which means that it will be to the left of it. The 123 text will be in its own left-to-right directional run, which means if the base direction is `ltr`, it will be to the left of 456. This paragraph will be rendered as !123 456 אַשְׁרֵי! If the base direction is `rtl`, however, all the directional runs will be right-to-left. Each span will be rendered in reverse order (from our left-to-right perspective), with the Hebrew text in the middle and the 123 text to its right and 456 to its left.

Tightly Wrapping

Now that I have explained what the bidi algorithm does, let's look at some ways to manipulate it to ensure we get what we're expecting. The first approach is to *tightly wrap* each phrase. This means that each part of the text that could use a different direction is in its own element and the dir attribute is used on each to explicitly set the direction.

For example, the previous HTML with the 123 and 456 phrases presented an unexpected issue when the base direction was ltr. I had already put each phrase in its own span element for illustration purposes. To fix the issue, you just need to set the dir attribute like this:

```
<p>
    <span dir="ltr">!123</span> <span dir="rtl">אֲשֶׁרֵי</span> <span dir="ltr">456!</span>
</p>
```

Now the text will be rendered as expected in both left-to-right as well as right-to-left modes.

■ **Tip**   You don't have to use a span element when tightly wrapping directional phrases. If that text is already in a separate element for semantic reasons, you can add the dir attribute to the existing element.

Using Isolation

Sometimes you need to insert dynamic text that comes from a database or from user input and you don't know the direction of the text. In this case, put the dynamic text inside a bidirectional isolation (bdi) element like this:

```
<p>
    The user entered <mark><bdi>user input</bdi></mark> on this form.
</p>
```

If the dynamic text is already in its own element, nest the bdi element inside of it as shown in the previous example. The bdi element defaults the dir attribute to auto. This allows the direction of the dynamic text to be determined based on its contents. It also tells the browser to ignore the direction of this text when rendering the adjoining text. This is done by setting the CSS attribute unicode-bidi: isolate on this element.

■ **Note**   You can accomplish this yourself without using the bdi element by setting dir="auto" and applying the CSS unicode-bidi: isolate rule. However, using the bdi element provides the semantic meaning and is the best way to do this.

Whenever you use the dir attribute on an element, the unicode-bidi: isolate rule is automatically applied. The tightly wrapping approach described earlier is also establishing the isolation. Also, the previous issue with the 123 and 456 text could also be solved by simply placing the right-to-left text inside a bdi element:

```
!123 <bdi>אֲשֶׁרֵי</bdi> 456!
```

Overriding the Direction

You can also override the text direction by using the bidirectional override (bdo) element. For example:

```
<p>
    <bdo>אֶשְׁרֵי</bdo><br />
    <bdo dir="rtl">Supercalifragilisticexpialidocious</bdo>
</p>
```

In the first line, the dir attribute was not set and will be inherited from the parent element. In the second line, the dir attribute is explicitly set to rtl so the word will be spelled backward, regardless of the previous base direction.

If the base direction is the default, ltr, this will be rendered as shown in Figure 5-11.

אֶשְׁרֵי

suoicodilaipxecitsiligarfilacrepuS

Figure 5-11. *Overriding the text direction*

■ **Caution**   There is seldom any valid reason for using the bdo element, except just for fun. You may be curious to see what supercalifragilisticexpialidocious looks like spelled backward. For someone who reads Hebrew, the preceding example looks just as odd.

In all other elements, the dir attribute defines the flow direction of its child elements. The bdo element is a special case; when the dir attribute is used in the bdo element it affects the text direction.

■ **Tip**   For more information regarding bidirectional text, the W3C provides several useful articles, which you can find at http://www.w3.org/International/tutorials/bidi-xhtml.

Ruby

The ruby element is used to annotate content with small text, which is known as ruby annotations. Ruby annotations are used in East Asian typography, primarily for Japanese, Chinese, and Korean languages, to aid in pronunciation. The content that is being annotated is included within the ruby element.

Also inside a ruby element are one or more rt elements. These are the actual annotations. Ruby annotations get their name from a typography term for a very small font (typically 5.5 points). This text is usually displayed above the main content. If there are more than one, additional annotations are displayed to the side.

The following content displays some common currency symbols and annotates them with their name and currency code:

```
<p>
    <ruby>$<rp>(</rp><rt>Dollar</rt><rt>USD</rt><rp>)</rp></ruby><br />
    <ruby>€<rt>Euro</rt><rt>EUR</rt></ruby><br />
    <ruby>£<rt>Pound Sterling<rt>GBP</ruby><br />
    <ruby>¥<rt>Japanese Yen</rt><rt>YEN</rt></ruby><br />
</p>
```

The rt element does not require a closing tag if it is followed by another rt element, an rp element, or the closing ruby tag. To demonstrate this, the code above for the Pound symbol does not use end tags.

If a browser does not support ruby, the annotations are simply displayed inline, following the main content. For fallback functionality, you should wrap them with parentheses to make is clear that the annotations are not part of the main content flow. To do that, use the rp element. The rp element is hidden when ruby is supported. The entry for USD currency demonstrates the use of rp elements.

This previous HTML is rendered as shown in Figure 5-12 (I have zoomed in quite a bit in this screenshot as the annotations use very small font).

Dollar

$ USD

Euro

€ EUR

Pound Sterling

£ GBP

Japanese Yen

¥ YEN

Figure 5-12. *Rendering ruby annotations*

■ **Tip** These ruby annotations are similar to the abbr and small elements that I described earlier in this chapter. While you can certainly use ruby annotations in other scenarios, they were intended primarily for East Asian languages. For other scenarios consider using the abbr or small instead. For some background on ruby, see the article at http://html5doctor.com/ruby-rt-rp-element.

Summary

Make a careful choice when selecting an element to use when including content in your HTML document. Sure, you can put everything in a paragraph or span tag and it will "work." But each element provides semantic meaning to your content. This will ultimately make your document more maintainable, and when it comes time to write the CSS, you'll be glad you did.

In the next chapter, I will demonstrate how to organize tabular data in an HTML document. Putting content into rows and columns is a great way to present certain types of data.

CHAPTER 6

■ ■ ■

Table HTML Elements

In this chapter, I'll show you how to organize contents into a table of rows and columns. There are a lot of scenarios where you need to display a list of things, and tables are the perfect solution. In Chapter 4, I demonstrated using ordered and unordered list (ol, ul) elements. These support multiple rows but only a single column, however. If you need to organize a row into multiple columns, tables are the way to go.

■ **Caution**   Tables should only be used when presenting tabular data, such as a phone list, or team standings. Do not use tables to define the layout of multiple sections of a document. For example, if you want an aside element to be aligned to the right of the main section, use CSS instead of tables. I'll explain how to do this in Chapter 13.

Simple Table

I'll start with a very simple table that has three rows and three columns. Use the table element to define a table. Inside the table element, use the table row (tr) element to define each row. Within each row, use the table cell (td) element to define contents of each cell within the row. For example, the HTML in Listing 6-1 will be rendered as shown in Figure 6-1.

Listing 6-1. Creating a simple table

```
<table>
    <tr>
        <td>One</td>
        <td>Two</td>
        <td>Three</td>
    </tr>
    <tr>
        <td>Four</td>
        <td>Five</td>
        <td>Six</td>
    </tr>
    <tr>
        <td>Seven</td>
        <td>Eight</td>
        <td>Nine</td>
    </tr>
</table>
```

© Mark J. Collins 2017
M. J. Collins, *Pro HTML5 with CSS, JavaScript, and Multimedia*, DOI 10.1007/978-1-4842-2463-2_6

One   Two   Three
Four Five Six
Seven Eight Nine

Figure 6-1. *A simple table*

■ **Note**   HTML4 supported a number of attributes on the `table`, `tr`, and `td` elements such as `border`, `bgcolor`, `width`, and `align` that were used for defining the table format. In HTML5, these have all been deprecated in favor of using CSS for this purpose. In Chapter 13, I will explain how to style tables using the capabilities in CSS.

If you want to include a caption for the table, add a `caption` element as the first child element with the table element (before the first row). For example:

```
<table>
    <caption>Simple Table</caption>
    <tr>
```

Even though the caption is before the row details, using CSS you can place the caption, visually, anywhere relative to the actual table.

Column and Row Headings

If you want to place a column or row heading in one of the cells, you should use a table header cell (`th`) element instead of the `td` element. The default styling of the table header cell element is to make the text bold. More importantly, using this element provides the semantic information that its contents describe a set of cells.

When using the table header cell element, you should specify its `scope` attribute. This defines the set of cells that the header content describes. For column headings, use `scope="col"` and for row headings, use `scope="row"`. The other possible values are `colgroup` and `rowgroup`, which I'll explain later in this chapter. The `scope` attribute does not affect how the content is rendered in most browsers. However, this information may be useful in certain applications such as screen readers.

Listing 6-2 demonstrates a table that uses column and row headings. The table lists three numbers (2, 3, and 4) along with the squared and cubed values of these numbers. The first row contains the column headings, and the first cell in each row includes the row heading. This is rendered as shown in Figure 6-2.

Listing 6-2. Using column and row headings

```
<table>
    <caption>Squares and Cubes</caption>
    <tr>
        <td></td> <!-- empty cell -->
        <th scope="col">Number</th>
        <th scope="col">Squared</th>
        <th scope="col">Cubed</th>
    </tr>
    <tr>
        <th scope="row">Two</th>
        <td>2</td>
```

```
        <td>4</td>
        <td>8</td>
    </tr>
    <tr>
        <th scope="row">Three</th>
        <td>3</td>
        <td>9</td>
        <td>27</td>
    </tr>
    <tr>
        <th scope="row">Four</th>
        <td>4</td>
        <td>16</td>
        <td>64</td>
    </tr>
</table>
```

	Number	Squared	Cubed
Two	2	4	8
Three	3	9	27
Four	4	16	64

Figure 6-2. Using column and row headings

■ **Tip** Notice the empty cell in the first row. Even though there is no content in this cell, it must be defined to keep the other cells aligned properly. You should have the same number of cells in each row. If a cell is omitted from a row, the last cell in the row will be empty.

Column Groups

By using the table header cell element for headings and table cell element for normal content, you can easily style them differently. However, you may want to style some columns of normal cells differently from other columns. For example, in the previous example, you might want the Squared and Cubed columns to be formatted differently than the Number column. You can do that by including those columns in a column group (colgroup) element and then apply styles to the column group element.

There are two ways to use the column group element. First, use the span attribute to specify how many columns the group will include. Columns are assigned to groups sequentially. If the first group spans two columns, it will contain the first two columns. If the next group spans a single column, it will be the third column in the table. To put the last two columns from the previous example in their own group, just add the following bolded code before the first row:

```
<table>
    <caption>Squares and Cubes</caption>
    <colgroup span="1"></colgroup>
    <colgroup span="1"></colgroup>
    <colgroup span="2" style="background-color: #b6ff00"></colgroup>
    <tr>
```

The first two groups span one column each: the row headings and the Number column. The default value for the span attribute is 1 so you could also omit the span attribute on these column group elements. The last group spans the remaining two columns, which are the Squared and Cubed values. I have added a style attribute on this group so you can see how the group can be used, but this should normally be handled in CSS. With these additions, the table is now rendered as shown in Figure 6-3.

	Number	Squared	Cubed
Two	2	4	8
Three	3	9	27
Four	4	16	64

Figure 6-3. Adding column groups with styling

The other approach is to use column (col) elements within the column group element instead of using the span attribute. Include a column element in the group for each column that should be included. Columns are assigned sequentially just like they were with the first approach. You also can use the span attribute on the column element.

■ **Caution**   In a column group (colgroup) element, you cannot include both a span attribute and one or more column (col) elements. You can use either approach but not both in the same group.

To demonstrate the second approach, the following bolded code can replace the previous column group elements. In this example, I'm putting the first two columns in one group instead of separate groups. In the first group, there are two column elements to indicate there are two columns in this group. In the second group, a single column element is used with a span attribute to indicate that two columns are included.

```
<table>
    <caption>Squares and Cubes</caption>
    <colgroup>
        <col style="background-color: #f00"/>
        <col />
    </colgroup>
    <colgroup style="background-color: #b6ff00" >
        <col span="2" />
    </colgroup>
    <tr>
```

One advantage of the second approach is that you can define styles on both the column and column group elements. You can apply a style to a group of columns through the column group element or to a specific column using the column element as demonstrated in the previous example. This table is rendered with a red background on the first column as shown in Figure 6-4.

	Number	Squared	Cubed
Two	2	4	8
Three	3	9	27
Four	4	16	64

Figure 6-4. *Using both col and colgroup elements*

If you have defined column groups using either approach, you can use them when defining the scope of a table head cell (th) element. Setting the scope attribute to **colgroup** will indicate that the heading text applies to the columns in the current column group.

Table Heading and Footer

Quite often a table will have one or more rows with column headings at the top, followed by rows of data and then one or more rows of summary data at the bottom. You can implement this using the elements already discussed. As HTML5 is all about semantics, additional elements are available to distinguish rows that belong in the header or footer from rows that form the main body of the table. In general, it's a good idea to provide as much information in the HTML as possible. This will also allow more options later when applying the styles.

You should put the column headings, if any, in a table head (thead) element. If there is summary information, these rows should be inside a table footer (tfoot) element. The remaining rows that form the main part of the table should be in a table body (tbody) element. A simple example is shown in Listing 6-3.

Listing 6-3. A table with header and footer

```
<table>
    <caption>Scoreboard</caption>
    <thead>
        <tr>
            <th>Inning</th>
            <th>Runs</th>
            <th>Hits</th>
            <th>Errors</th>
        </tr>
    </thead>
    <tbody>
        <tr><td>1</td><td>0</td><td>1</td><td>0</td></tr>
        <tr><td>2</td><td>2</td><td>5</td><td>0</td></tr>
        <tr><td>3</td><td>0</td><td>1</td><td>1</td></tr>
        <tr><td>4</td><td>0</td><td>0</td><td>0</td></tr>
        <tr><td>5</td><td>1</td><td>2</td><td>0</td></tr>
        <tr><td>6</td><td>0</td><td>1</td><td>0</td></tr>
        <tr><td>7</td><td>0</td><td>0</td><td>0</td></tr>
        <tr><td>8</td><td>1</td><td>3</td><td>1</td></tr>
        <tr><td>9</td><td>1</td><td>2</td><td>0</td></tr>
    </tbody>
    <tfoot>
        <tr><td>Final</td><td>5</td><td>15</td><td>2</td></tr>
    </tfoot>
</table>
```

■ **Caution**   In HTML4 the table footer element needed to be specified before any body elements. In HTML5 this restriction has been removed so you can put the footer after the body where it logically belongs. Regardless of where the footer element is placed, however, it will be rendered at the end of the table. For this reason, including multiple table footer elements does not make any sense. This does not cause an error, but all footer elements will be combined at the bottom of the table.

The table head, body, and footer elements, by themselves, do not affect the way the table is rendered. With the default styling, this sample table is formatted as shown in Figure 6-5. All three of these elements are optional, and you can include any combination of them.

Inning	Runs	Hits	Errors
1	0	1	0
2	2	5	0
3	0	1	1
4	0	0	0
5	1	2	0
6	0	1	0
7	0	0	0
8	1	3	1
9	1	2	0
Final	5	15	2

Figure 6-5. *Using a table head and footer element*

The rows within a head, body or footer element are considered a *row group*. When defining the scope attribute of a table head cell element, using the **rowgroup** value indicates that the heading text applies to the current row group.

You can have multiple table body sections within a table. This is especially useful if you have a large table and want to divide it into sections. You can also have multiple table head elements so you can place different heading text before each body element. As I mentioned earlier, there will only be one footer element and it will be at the end of the table.

Spanning Cells

When working with tables in HTML5, you can make a single cell out of several adjoining cells. This works much like merging cells in a spreadsheet. The cells of an HTML table are comprised by the table cell (td) and table head cell (th) elements as I explained earlier. Each one of these elements occupies a single cell in the table grid. However, both of these elements support the colspan and rowspan attributes. The default value of both attributes is 1, so each element takes up exactly one space.

Suppose you have a table with five columns. Each table row element would contain a total of five table cell or table head cell elements (td and th elements can be used interchangeably). If you set the colspan attribute on one of these elements to 2, it would occupy the space of two cells and you would only need four elements in that row. This is illustrated in Figure 6-6.

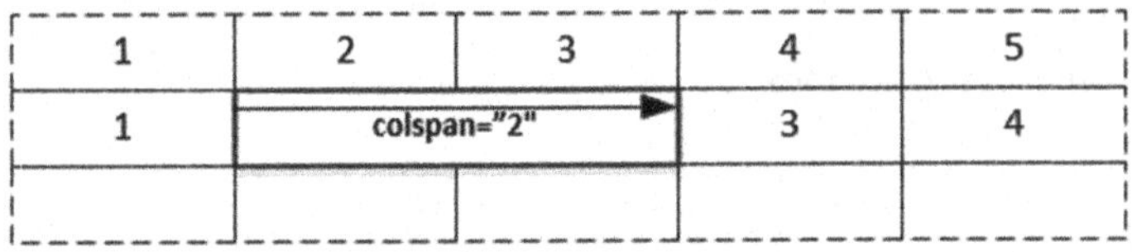

Figure 6-6. *Using the colspan attribute*

The first row contains five elements. However, in the second row there are only four elements because one element occupies two cells. This is similar to how the span attribute works in the column group or column element that I explained earlier.

The rowspan attribute works the same way except that the cell is expanded to include the cells below it instead of to the right. Of course, you can include both the colspan and rowspan attributes. In this case, the merged cell will be both wider and taller as illustrated in Figure 6-7.

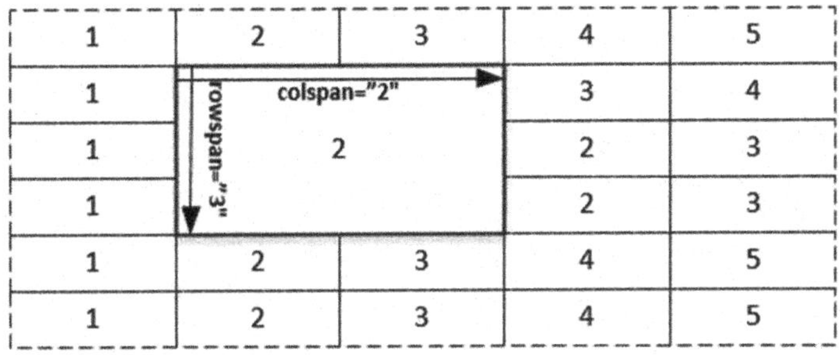

Figure 6-7. *Using the colspan and rowspan attributes*

This introduces some interesting side effects on the subsequent row elements. In the table shown in Figure 6-7, the second row has only four elements because one element takes up two cells. In the third row, however, cells 2 and 3 were already allocated to the merged cell in the previous row. There are only three available cells left so the third row will only add three elements. The same is true for the fourth row.

Now let's apply this concept to construct the Periodic Table of the Elements. You've probably seen a version of this if you've ever taken a basic Chemistry class. It lists all of the elements in a table. The columns and rows have special meanings that have to do with their atomic structure. For example, all of the elements in the last column are knows as noble gases; the column to its left contain all of the halogen elements. Because of this table layout, there will be gaps in the grid, especially in the first few rows. While we could just create a lot of empty cells, instead we'll merge these empty cells into a single cell.

A portion of the HTML for this table is shown in Listing 6-4. I have removed the last four rows of the table for brevity. The downloaded code will have the complete source. The complete table has eighteen columns, seven rows of data, and two header rows.

Listing 6-4. Source for Periodic Table

```
<table id="Periodic">
    <caption>Periodic Table of the Elements</caption>
    <tr>
        <th>I</th>
        <th>II</th>
        <th colspan="10" rowspan="4"></th>
        <th>III</th>
        <th>IV</th>
        <th>V</th>
        <th>VI</th>
        <th>VII</th>
        <th>VIII</th>
    </tr>
    <tr>
        <th>1</th>
        <th>2</th>
        <!-- Skipping 10 cells-->
        <th>13</th>
        <th>14</th>
        <th>15</th>
        <th>16</th>
        <th>17</th>
        <th>18</th>
    </tr>
    <tr>
        <td>H</td>
        <th></th> <!-- empty cell -->
        <!-- Skipping 10 cells-->
        <th colspan="5"></th>
        <td>He</td>
    </tr>
    <tr>
        <td>Li</td>
        <td>Be</td>
        <!-- Skipping 10 cells-->
        <td>B</td>
        <td>C</td>
        <td>N</td>
        <td>O</td>
        <td>F</td>
        <td>Ne</td>
    </tr>
    <tr>
```

```
            <td>Na</td>
            <td>Mg</td>
            <th>3</th>
            <th>4</th>
            <th>5</th>
            <th>6</th>
            <th>7</th>
            <th>8</th>
            <th>9</th>
            <th>10</th>
            <th>11</th>
            <th>12</th>
            <td>Al</td>
            <td>Si</td>
            <td>P</td>
            <td>S</td>
            <td>Cl</td>
            <td>Ar</td>
        </tr>
        <!-- Last four rows omitted for brevity -->
</table>
```

The first row has an element that spans ten columns and four rows. In the three subsequent rows, I have included a comment to show where the skipped cells are. The space for these is taken up by the large merged cell. I am using the table head cell (th) element for all of the heading data as well as the empty cells in the first four rows.

I will explain how to use CSS to format a table in Chapter 13. However, for now, in order to make this table look familiar, I'll we'll add some really simple CSS. Because there are so many elements, adding inline styling is not practical. In the head element I'll add the following style element:

```
<style>
    #Periodic td {
        width: 35px;
        border: 1px solid black;
        padding: 1px;
        margin: 1px;
        text-align: center;
    }
</style>
```

This selector will find all table cell elements that are within an element with the id of "Periodic," which is the id assigned to this table element. The declarations set the width of each element as well as centering the text and adding a border. The periodic table will be rendered as shown in Figure 6-8.

Periodic Table of the Elements

I	II											III	IV	V	VI	VII	VIII
1	2											13	14	15	16	17	18
H																	He
Li	Be											B	C	N	O	F	Ne
Na	Mg	3	4	5	6	7	8	9	10	11	12	Al	Si	P	S	Cl	Ar
K	Ca	Sc	Ti	V	Cr	Mn	Fe	Co	Ni	Cu	Zn	Ga	Ge	As	Se	Br	Kr
Rb	Sr	Y	Zr	Nb	Mo	Tc	Ru	Rh	Pd	Ag	Cd	In	Sn	Sb	Te	I	Xe
Cs	Ba		Hf	Ta	W	Re	Os	Ir	Pt	Au	Hg	Tl	Pb	Bi	Po	At	Rn
Fr	Ra		Rf	Db	Sg	Bh	Hs	Mt	Ds	Rg	Cn	Uut	Fl	Uup	Lv	Uus	Uuo

Figure 6-8. The Periodic Table of the Elements

To be able to see the merged cells, add the following CSS rule shown in bold to the style element. This will put a border around the table head cell elements as well as setting a background color.

```
<style>
    #Periodic td {
        width: 35px;
        border: 1px solid black;
        padding: 1px;
        margin: 1px;
        text-align: center;
    }
    #Periodic th {
        border: 1px solid black;
        background-color: #0ff;
        padding: 1px;
        margin: 1px;
        text-align: center;
    }
</style>
```

Now the table will be rendered as shown in Figure 6-9.

Periodic Table of the Elements

I	II											III	IV	V	VI	VII	VIII
1	2											13	14	15	16	17	18
H																		He
Li	Be											B	C	N	O	F	Ne
Na	Mg	3	4	5	6	7	8	9	10	11	12	Al	Si	P	S	Cl	Ar
K	Ca	Sc	Ti	V	Cr	Mn	Fe	Co	Ni	Cu	Zn	Ga	Ge	As	Se	Br	Kr
Rb	Sr	Y	Zr	Nb	Mo	Tc	Ru	Rh	Pd	Ag	Cd	In	Sn	Sb	Te	I	Xe
Cs	Ba		Hf	Ta	W	Re	Os	Ir	Pt	Au	Hg	Tl	Pb	Bi	Po	At	Rn
Fr	Ra		Rf	Db	Sg	Bh	Hs	Mt	Ds	Rg	Cn	Uut	Fl	Uup	Lv	Uus	Uuo

Figure 6-9. Styling the table head elements

Notice the large block in the middle of the table. It is four rows high and ten columns wide. There is a border around the entire area because this is being treated as a single cell.

Summary

In this chapter I explained how to use the `table` element to present tabular data. A table consists of rows that are represented by the table row (`tr`) element. Each row contains a collection of table cells (`td`) and/or table head cell (`th`) elements. Columns are not explicitly defined but are inferred based on the existence of `td` or `th` elements. For example, the first element of each row is considered the first column.

You can define columns using the `colgroup` and/or `col` element. This does not actually create or define any table cells but allows you to apply styles to a specific column or group of columns. You can also group table rows into a header (`thead`), body (`tbody`), and footer (`tfoot`) elements for semantic purposes.

Finally, you can merge cells into a single cell by using the `colspan` and `rowspan` attributes. Since the merged cell will take up more space, you will need fewer elements in a row that contains a merged cell. Using the `rowspan` attribute is particularly interesting, requiring you to skip cells in subsequent rows. I recommend you add comments to your table to indicate skipped cells.

In the next chapter, I'll explain how to included embedded content, such as images, in your document. I'll also demonstrate using the native audio and video elements.

CHAPTER 7

■ ■ ■

Embedded HTML Elements

In this chapter I'll demonstrate the embedded elements that are available in an HTML5 document. The content I have examined so far, which is mostly text, was provided in the HTML document. However, with embedded elements, the content is provided by an external file such as an image or a video clip. The HTML document provides a reference to that file through one of the embedded elements. I will first demonstrate the anchor element that is used to provide a hyperlink to other resources. Then I'll explain the three most common embedded elements: images (img), audio, and video; most of this chapter will explain the capabilities of these three elements.

Both audio and video elements are also considered interactive elements because a user will often manipulate them through the UI. For example, they may want to play, pause, rewind, or adjust the volume. I'll describe the native controls for these interactions in this chapter. In Chapter 21 I'll demonstrate how to implement your own custom controls using JavaScript.

HTML5 also supports the embedded (embed) and object elements that allow you to reference custom plug-ins that will render this content. The other embedded elements, scalar-vector graphics (svg) and canvas, require their own chapter to fully describe, which I will do in Chapters 22 and 23 respectively.

Anchor

The anchor (a) element is not technically categorized as embedded content. I'm including it here because it doesn't fit well in any other chapter. However, the understanding of anchor elements (and navigating to other resources in general) is needed for this and future chapters.

The anchor element is used to turn content into a hyperlink. The content inside the anchor element can be any type of flow or phrasing context except interactive content. The anchor element supports the href attribute, which defines the URL that the link will navigate to. For example:

```
<a href="http://www.apress.com">
    Apress
</a>
```

The content inside the element, "Apress" in this case, will be rendered and when that content is clicked, the browser will render the URL specified in the href attribute. Textual content inside an anchor element is normally underlined. The content inside the anchor element could also be an image as I will explain later in this chapter.

© Mark J. Collins 2017
M. J. Collins, *Pro HTML5 with CSS, JavaScript, and Multimedia*, DOI 10.1007/978-1-4842-2463-2_7

The href attribute can also provide a link to a specific element on the current page. For example, setting href="#Chapter5" will scroll the current document so the element that has the id attribute set to Chapter5 will be in view. Also, the linked resource does not have to be a web resource. The first part of a URL specifies the protocol (e.g., http:) but there are other types of resources that you can link to. Here are some of the more common types that are used:

- http: - web resource

- ftp: - file transfer

- mailto: - send an email

- tel: - dial a phone number (particularly useful for mobile devices)

- file: - open a file

The target attribute is used to specify where the linked resource should be displayed. The attribute value indicates the browsing context that should be used. I explained browsing contexts in Chapter 4. There are several values that can be used, but the most commonly used are _self (which is the default value) and _blank. Using _self, or not specifying the target attribute, will cause the linked resource to be displayed in the current context. Generally, this means that the browser will navigate away from the current page and load a new one. If you specify _blank, the linked resource will be displayed in a new tab or window.

If the linked resource is a file that should be downloaded rather than rendered by the browser, use the download attribute. Include the default name that the file should be saved as: for example, download="MyPicture.png". When the user clicks the link, the file save dialog will display and this filename will be set as the default. The / and \ characters are not allowed so you cannot default the file path, however.

There are several other attributes that can be included, which provide purely semantic information about the linked resource:

- hreflang - indicates the language of the linked resource

- rel - defines the relationship with the linked resource (see Chapter 1 for more information)

- type - indicates the MIME type of the resource

Images

The most commonly used embedded elements are images. In our visually oriented world, you can scarcely find a web page without images; a lot of web pages are mostly images (or video). The image element has no content, that is, content between the open and closing tags. In fact, it is one of the self-closing tags that I listed in Chapter 1. These are sometimes referred to as *empty* elements since their "content" is configured solely through its attributes.

The image element is formatted like this:

```
<img src="Media/HTML5.jpg" alt="The HTML5 Badge logo" />
```

The image has two required attributes, src and alt. The src attribute specifies the URL of the image file that is being referenced. Provide a textual description of the image in the alt attribute. This will be displayed if the image cannot be downloaded or the file format is not supported. Non-visual browsers such as screen readers will also use this information.

There are several file formats that images can be stored in. The differences in these formats are primarily due to how the data is compressed and the number of colors that are supported. Each format works better for some scenarios. The reality is that we will continue to have multiple formats, and the HTML5 specification does not specify which file formats must be supported.

▪ **Tip** If you stick to the top three formats, – JPEG, GIF, and PNG – you should be safe for the foreseeable future. These are support by all browsers and should be around for a long time. TIFF and BMP are also fairly well supported but not considered web friendly because their relative file size will slow downloads. Here is a good article that describes all five file types and where they are best suited: `http://1stwebdesigner.com/image-file-types`. Here is another article with similar information from a photographer's perspective: `http://users.wfu.edu/matthews/misc/graphics/formats/formats.html`.

The image element also supports the `height` and `width` attributes. If used, the units must be set in pixels; these cannot be set using relative units. If not supplied, the intrinsic dimension of the image file will be used. One advantage to specifying these attributes is that the space can be allocated prior to the download completing. If not specified, the page layout may change once the images become available.

Multiple Sources

The image element includes the `srcset` and `sizes` attributes that allow you to specify a set of image files with information about them so the browser can choose the most appropriate one to download and render. I'll explain these attributes by demonstrating the use cases they were intended to solve.

Pixel Ratio Selection

On a typical mobile or tablet device, you will usually have a lot more pixels in the same amount of space. For example, my 24" flat screen monitor has a resolution of 1920 x 1200 pixels. My 5" Lumia phone has nearly as many, 1280 x 720. The monitor has a pixel density of 93 pixels/inch (PPI); the phone is 294 PPI, roughly three times the pixel density.

Considering this, you may want to provide one or more scaled-down versions of the same image depending on the pixel density. This is done using the `srcset` attribute and providing a comma-separated list of image sources along with an x descriptor. A 1x descriptor corresponds to the typical desktop resolution; a 2x descriptor is for devices with twice the pixel density. For example, the following defines two additional versions of the image file:

```
<img src="Media/HTML5.jpg" alt="The HTML5 Badge logo"
     srcset="Media/HTML5_2.jpg 2x, Media/HTML5_3.jpg 3x"/>
```

You should still include the `src` attribute in case the browser doesn't support the `srcset` attribute. Also, the image in the `src` attribute will have the 1x descriptor by default, so you don't need to include a 1x option in the `srcset` attribute.

▪ **Tip** When you are specifying multiple files in the image element, you need to provide multiple file versions in your web site. However, the browser will pick only one to download. Not only do these solutions improve the user experience, they should also improve performance.

Viewport Selection

Suppose you had an image that you wanted to span the entire width of the screen (or window). You can accomplish that in CSS by setting the width to 100%. If you have a very wide screen, like my 24" monitor, the image will be stretched as necessary to fit. The image can also be stretched vertically to maintain the aspect ratio, or the height can be fixed and the image will be distorted. Neither of these options may be what you're expecting.

To help deal with this scenario, you can use a combination of the srcset and the sizes attribute to specify a different image file based on the width of the *viewport*. The viewport is simply the visible area of a web page. On a mobile device this is the size of the device; on a desktop, this is controlled by the size of the window that the browser is running in.

To address this use case, from an author's perspective, the solution is quite simple actually. You tell the browser how wide each of the images are and tell the browser how much space, width wise, it should use. The browser figures out from this, which file to download. In all of these decisions, we're only addressing the width of the image and the width of the viewport.

The first part is to define the width of each image. To do that, you'll use the srcset attribute but instead of an x descriptor, you'll use a w descriptor. If the image is 300 pixels wide, for example, set the descriptor to **300w**.

```
srcset="Media/HTML5.jpg 300w, Media/HTML5_2.jpg 150w"
```

When using the w descriptor, the src attribute is ignored by browsers that support the srcset attribute. With the x descriptor, the src attribute has a default value of 1x, but there is no such default for the w descriptor. You should still supply the src attribute, but it is only used by older browsers that do not support srcset attribute.

Now for the second part, let me provide a little background here. The browser will know, eventually, how wide the image should be, after the document has been parsed, the CSS file(s) downloaded, and all of the CSS rules applied. However, to speed up the rendering process, the images are preloaded, before the CSS is applied. So the browser will need some hints as to which files to download and this is where the sizes attribute comes in.

The sizes attribute is a hint that specifies the expected width of the rendered image. I explained in Chapter 2 how the distance units can be specified in both fixed units, such as pixels or relative units. The sizes attribute can be supplied with any of these. Although, specifying this relative to the viewport width is most useful in this scenario. If the image will take the full width, for example, set sizes="100vw"; if it's only half of the width, set it to 50vw.

If the web page is organized into columns, the number of columns may be determined by the viewport site. On a large screen, you may have four columns, in which case the sizes attribute would be 25vw. But as the viewport shrinks, the number of columns may drop to three and then two and eventually one. To support this, the value of the sizes attribute needs to change based on the viewport.

Now you may already be wondering why the sizes attribute is plural. It actually supports a comma-separated list, allowing you to specify multiple values. Each value can be qualified using a media query to indicate when the value should be used. I will explain media queries in more detail in Chapter 9. The following sets the sizes attribute to either 25%, 33%, 50%, or 100% depending on the width of the viewport:

```
sizes="(max-width: 600px) 25vw, (max-width: 400px) 33vw, (max-width: 200px) 50vw, 100vw"/>
```

If the viewport is at least 600 pixels wide, there will be four columns so the sizes is set to 25vw. As the viewport gets smaller, the number of columns decreases, and the relative size of a single image increases.

Another useful application of this is to select an appropriate image based on the device size. For example, suppose you want to show Arnold Friberg's famous painting *The Prayer at Valley Forge*. On a widescreen device, you would want to show the entire painting shown in Figure 7-1.

Figure 7-1. *Arnold Friberg's The Prayer at Valley Forge*

However, if your web page is being rendered on a mobile device in portrait mode, you might want to display a cropped version of it like the one shown in Figure 7-2.

Figure 7-2. *A cropped version*

You can accomplish this using the srcset attribute like this:

```
<figure>
    <img src="Media/G_Wash_Wide.jpg" alt="The Prayer at Valley Forge"
            srcset="Media/G_Wash_Narrow.jpg 422w, Media/G_Wash_Wide.jpg 885w"
            width="100%"/>
    <footer><small>Copyright©Friberg Fine Art</small></footer>
    <figcaption>Arnold Friberg's The Prayer at Valley Forge</figcaption>
</figure>
```

■ **Note** A new picture element is being proposed to further assist with the image file selection. As of this writing it is only supported by the Chrome browser so I'm not covering it in this book. But if you're interested, you may want to follow this feature. Here is a link to the current specification: https://html.spec.whatwg.org/multipage/embedded-content.html#the-picture-element.

Image Map

You can easily turn an image into a hyperlink by placing inside an anchor tag like this:

```
<a href="https://html.spec.whatwg.org/multipage/embedded-content.html">
    <img src="Media/HTML5.jpg" alt="The HTML5 Badge logo" />
</a>
```

You insert an image for the content instead of text. Clicking anywhere on the image will navigate to the address in the href attribute. If the image cannot be loaded, the text in the alt attribute will be displayed as the hyperlink.

However, if you want to follow the link only when a specific part of the image is clicked you'll need to set up an image map. You can also define multiple areas on a single image, each navigating to a different link. To demonstrate this, I have created an image that contains a red square, a green circle, and a blue triangle. The image is 50 pixels high and 150 pixels wide and is shown in Figure 7-3.

Figure 7-3. *A sample image with three shapes*

The image map (map) element can be placed anywhere in the HTML document, before or after the image that uses it. You set the name attribute and reference it by this name when using it in an image. You can create multiple maps but they each need a unique name.

The map element contains one or more area elements. Each area element defines an area of the image and the href that is followed when this area is clicked. Here is the map element that will define a link for each of the shapes shown in Figure 7-3.

```
<map name="shapeMap">
    <area shape="rect" coords="0,0,50,50" alt="square" title="Square"
        href="https://en.wikipedia.org/wiki/Square" />
    <area shape="circle" coords="75,25,25" alt="circle" title="Circle"
        href="https://en.wikipedia.org/wiki/Circle" />
    <area shape="poly" coords="101,50,126,0,150,50" alt="triangle" title="Triangle"
        href="https://en.wikipedia.org/wiki/Triangle" />
</map>
```

The area is defined by a shape attribute and a set of coordinates that are in a comma-separated list in the coords attribute. There are three supported shapes: rectangle (rect), circle, and polygon (poly). For rectangles, there should be four values in the coords attribute; the x and y coordinates of the upper-left corner and the x and y coordinates of the lower-right corner. There should be three values for a circle; the x and y coordinates of the center and the radius. For polygons, the coords attribute will have a variable number of pairs of values. Each pair specifies the x and y coordinates of a point; the set of points define the polygon. In this example, there are three points: the lower-left corner, the top of the triangle, and the lower-right corner.

■ **Tip** You can define an area with no href attribute. This is referred to as a dead area: an area that is not clickable. Also, if you want to define an area that covers the entire image, set the shape="default" and do not specify the coords attribute.

The area element also supports the target, rel, and download attributes that work just like other hyperlinks. The alt attribute is used as the hyperlink text if the image cannot be displayed. You can also specify the title attribute. This is displayed as hover text when the mouse is over the clickable area as demonstrated in Figure 7-4.

Figure 7-4. *Displaying hover text*

To link the map to an image, you need to set the usemap attribute on the image element. The value of this attribute will be the name of the map element prefixed with a hashtag. For example:

```
<img src="Media/Shapes.png" alt="Shapes" width="150" height="50" usemap="#shapeMap" />
```

■ **Tip** This example is somewhat contrived to demonstrate the image map capability. If you really wanted to link to a page based on the shape that was clicked, it would be preferable to create a separate image for each shape and include them in their own anchor tag.

Audio

The audio element in HTML5 makes it extremely easy to embed audio to your HTML document. This is made even easier now that the major browsers have now settled on standard file formats. I like to put embedded files such as audio and video clips into a separate folder in my web applications. That provides a clean separation between the HTML files that I develop and maintain from the content that is not created through HTML. I have created a Media folder in my web project and put all embedded content there.

■ **Note**   If you're using the source code download, the actual audio files have been removed to avoid any copyright infringements. To try out the sample in the rest of this chapter you'll need at least one audio clip. You should be able to get an audio clip by ripping an audio CD. The video file that is included with the download is licensed through the Creative Commons Attribution license, which allows free reuse and distribution.

Adding audio is as simple as adding an audio element and setting the src attribute to the location of the audio clip. For example:

```
<audio src="Media/Linus and Lucy.mp3" >
    <p>HTML5 audio is not supported on your browser</p>
</audio>
```

The content between the open and closing tags is only used when the audio element is not supported or the file cannot be loaded or played. There are several Boolean attributes that can be used with the audio element:

- preload - if exists, the audio content is preloaded when the page is rendered

- autoplay - if exists, the audio clip is started as soon as the content has been loaded

- muted - when set, the audio is muted; no sound is generated

- loop - if set, the audio clip will automatically start back at the beginning when it is finished

- controls - if exists, the native controls are provided to the user to interact with the audio clip

If you add the autoplay attribute, the music will start as soon as the page is loaded. However, there are no controls to stop it from playing. As of this writing, Chrome, Firefox, and Opera include an icon in the browser tab to indicate that an audio clip is playing. Firefox and Opera allow you to click on this icon to mute or unmute the sound. For example, the Firefox tab icon is shown in Figure 7-5.

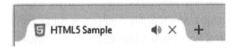

Figure 7-5. *Displaying the audio icon in the tab*

The audio element supports the volume attribute where you can preset the volume level when playing the audio clip. This is specified as a number between 0 and 1, with the default value being 1. Essentially, 1 means the volume should be 100% of the volume the device is set to.

Using the Native Controls

In terms of the UI, there are basically three options:

- No controls: The audio plays, but there are no controls available to the user. The clip can be started automatically when the page is loaded using the autoplay attribute. You can also start, pause, and stop the audio clip using JavaScript.

- Native controls: The browser provides the native controls for the user to play, pause, and stop the audio clip and control the volume.

- Custom controls: The page provides custom controls that interact with the audio element through JavaScript.

To enable the native controls, simply add the controls attribute like this:

```
<audio src="Media/Linus and Lucy.mp3" autoplay controls>
```

The native controls should appear in Internet Explorer like the image shown in Figure 7-6. In the Edge browser they look similar but smaller.

Figure 7-6. *Displaying the native audio controls in Internet Explorer*

In Opera and Chrome, the controls look like Figure 7-7.

Figure 7-7. *The audio controls in Opera*

In Firefox, the controls look like Figure 7-8.

Figure 7-8. *The audio controls in Firefox*

In Safari, the audio controls look like Figure 7-9.

Figure 7-9. *The audio control in Safari*

■ **Tip**   Safari on Windows 7 requires that QuickTime be installed in order to support the audio element. You can download it from this site: https://support.apple.com/kb/DL837?locale=en_US. You may need to reboot your PC after installing QuickTime before Safari will be able to work.

As you can see, the controls are styled differently in each browser. With native controls you have little control over how the audio controls are displayed. You can change the width by setting the style attribute, which will stretch the progress bar. Extending the height beyond the normal height will only add white space on top of the control. In IE, decreasing the height, however, will shrink the control; in Chrome, it will clip it.

File Formats

In HTML5 you can specify multiple sources for an audio clip. This allows you to provide an audio clip in different file formats, letting the browser choose the format that it supports. While all major browsers support the audio element, they don't all support the same audio formats. However, most current browsers now support MP3, as well as MP4 for videos.

■ **Tip**   I'm providing this information to explain the capability provided in HTML5. However, you should rarely need to use this. In the early days of HTML5, this was an important feature as browsers did not all support the same file types. Fortunately, all major browsers now support MP3 audio and MP4 video.

The audio element allows you to specify multiple sources, and the browser will iterate through the sources until it finds one that it supports. Instead of using a src attribute, you can provide one or more source elements within the audio element, like this:

```
<audio autoplay controls>
    <source src="Media/Linus and Lucy.ogg" />
    <source src="Media/Linus and Lucy.mp3" />
    <p>HTML5 audio is not supported on your browser</p>
</audio>
```

The browser will use the first source that it supports, so if it matters to you, you should list the preferred file first. For example, Chrome supports both MP3 and Vorbis formats. If you prefer that the MP3 file be used, you should list it before the .ogg file.

While just listing the sources like this will work, the browser must download the file and open it to see whether it is able to play it. It's not very efficient to download a fairly large file only to find out it can't be used. You should also include the type attribute, which specifies the type of resource this is. The browser can then determine whether the file is supported by looking at the markup. The type attribute specifies the MIME format like this:

```
<source src="Media/Linus and Lucy.ogg" type="audio/ogg" />
<source src="Media/Linus and Lucy.mp3" type="audio/mp3" />
```

You can also specify the codecs in the type attribute like this:

```
<source src="Media/Linus and Lucy.ogg" type='audio/ogg; codecs="vorbis"'/>
```

This will help the browser choose a compatible media file more efficiently. Notice that the codecs values are included within double quotes, so you'll need to use single quotes around the type attribute value.

■ **Tip** Here's a handy page that tests browser support for the audio and video elements: http://hpr. dogphilosophy.net/test/. It also provides an overview of the support for various browsers.

Video

For this section, I'll be using a demo video that is provided with the download source code. This is a trailer from the *Big Buck Bunny* movie. This video is provided by Creative Commons and is freely redistributable (copyright 2008, Blender Foundation / www.bigbuckbunny.org). You can certainly use your own video, however, if you prefer. It should be in MP4 format to be compatible with all major browsers.

The video element is nearly identical to the audio element. You can provide fallback content inside the element, which is only displayed when the video element or the file type is not supported. Simply set the src attribute to the URL of the video file like this:

```
<video src="Media/BigBuckBunny.mp4" autoplay>
    <p> HTML5 video is not supported on your browser</p>
</video>
```

The autoplay attribute will start the video when the page loads, but without the native controls, you won't be able to pause or restart the clip. However, if you right-click on the video you'll get a menu of options to interact with the video, including showing the native controls. The options you will have might vary from one browser to another. The menu in Chrome is shown in Figure 7-10. Firefox also lets you adjust the playback speed, as well as pausing, muting, and switching to full-screen mode.

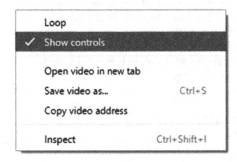

Figure 7-10. Video menu in Chrome

Adding the controls attribute will provide the controls that are similar to the audio clip as demonstrated in Figure 7-11. The controls are usually hidden unless the mouse is hovering over the video element.

Figure 7-11. *Displaying a video with native controls*

The video element also allows you to specify multiple sources through the source element just like with the audio element. You should not need to use that feature, if you provide the video in an MP4 format.

The poster attribute is supported by the video element (but not the audio element). Before the video is started, you can use the poster attribute to specify the image that is displayed. If this is not specified, the browser will usually open the video and display the first frame. To add a poster, just include the image in your project and reference it in the poster attribute. You would not usually set the autoplay attribute when using a poster as the poster would never be seen.

There's one thing to be careful about, however. If you define a poster, the initial size of the video element will be the size of the poster image. If this is not the same as the video, the size will change when the video starts playing. You should either ensure the image is the same size as the video or explicitly size the video element, which will stretch (or shrink) the poster image to fit.

Here's an example of using a poster image. This is rendered in Firefox as shown in Figure 7-12. Notice that the poster is dimed and the play button is shown in the center of the video.

```
<video src="Media/BigBuckBunny.mp4" controls
       poster="Media/BBB_Poster.png" width="852" height="480">
    <p> HTML5 video is not supported on your browser</p>
</video>
```

Figure 7-12. *Displaying a video poster in Firefox*

Tracks

Both the audio and video elements support the track element, which is used to provide text-based contents that are time-synchronized with the media clip. For example, you can display the lyrics to a song while the audio is playing. For videos, you might want to include closed captioning or subtitles.

The track element is an empty element; it uses a self-closing tag and is configured solely through its attributes. The track element can only be used inside an audio or video element. If you're using the source element to provide multiple file types, the track element should come after the source elements.

The kind attribute specifies the purpose of the track details. The allowed values are:

- captions - used for closed captioning, the track provides a transcription of the spoken words as well as pertinent sounds effects such as "laughing" or "phone ringing," etc. This is used for hearing impaired users or when the audio is muted.

- chapters - for longer clips, this provides chapter titles when a user if navigating through the media file.

- descriptions - a textual description of the content of the audio or video file. Used for visually impaired users or when the video is not available.

- metadata - provides data to be used by scripts; this is not normally displayed to the user.

- subtitles - this is the default value, if the kind attribute is not specified. Subtitles provide a translation of the spoken text in a different language. This can also provide additional information such as the date and location of an event being portrayed.

The src attribute is required and it specifies the URL of the file that contains the track details. This is usually a WebVTT file but other formats may be supported as well. This file contains a series of cues, each of which has a start and end time (relative to the start of the file) and the text that should be displayed during this interval. The time element is specified in hours, minutes, seconds, and milliseconds, for example, "00:02:15:420," which is 2 minutes, 15 seconds, and 420 ms into the clip. A sample WebVTT file is shown in Listing 7-1.

Listing 7-1. bbb.vtt, a sample track file

```
WEBVTT - For Big Buck Bunny trailer.

NOTE This is for demonstrational purposes

00:00:09.231 --> 00:00:11.121
- [Bunny looks around]

00:00:15.712 --> 00:00:16.892
- [Rodents snickering]

00:00:25.528 --> 00:00:27.631
- [ Squirrel takes aim ]
```

Mozilla has some helpful examples of WebVTT files that can be found at https://developer.mozilla.org/en-US/docs/Web/API/Web_Video_Text_Tracks_Format. Track files can be created in other formats as well. The following article provides more details on optional formats: http://www.miracletutorials.com/how-to-create-captionssubtitles-for-video-and-audio-in-webtvv-srt-dfxp-format/.

■ **Caution**   Track files must be provided through a web server such as Apache or IIS. You can't simply access the WebVTT files from a local file folder like you can with HTML documents. You may need to also define the MIME type of **text/ttt**.

The srclang attribute specifies the language of the text content. This attribute is required if the kind attribute is set to **subtitles**. The label attribute defines the text that is displayed when the user is selecting the appropriate track. To add a track to the Big Buck Bunny video, add the track element like this:

```
<video src="Media/BigBuckBunny.mp4" controls
       poster="Media/BBB_Poster.png" width="852" height="480">
    <track kind="captions" src="bbb.vtt" srclang="en" label="English" />
    <p> HTML5 video is not supported on your browser</p>
</video>
```

Since the video element includes a track element that contains captions, the native controls will include an extra button that enables the user to control the captioning. The label attribute is displayed in the closed captioning menu as demonstrated in Figure 7-13. If you had included multiple track elements, this allows the user to choose from the available tracks.

Figure 7-13. *The closed-caption menu in the Edge browser*

■ **Tip** There's a simple demo on using tracks to implement subtitles that was developed by Google. You can try it out at `http://html5-demos.appspot.com/static/video/track/index.html`. This uses a webm video format, which is not supported by all browsers, particularly IE or Edge. Open this in Chrome to view the demo.

HTML5 Plug-Ins

So far, I have explained how images, audio, and video can be embedded in an HTML document using the appropriate elements. This type of content is so prevalent that specific elements are provided to access the built-in capability of the browsers. In this final section, I'll cover how you can embed just about anything using the object element.

The object element is a generic container for any external content. The actual type of object is defined by the type attribute, which is provided as a MIME type. For example, if you're embedding a flash video, use application/x-shockwave-flash; if you're embedding a PDF file, use application/pdf. Of course, the browser may need an appropriate plug-in to be able to render the content, but using the object element provides a standard way of working with custom embedded content.

The object element has two required attributes: the type attribute that I've already mentioned and the data attribute that specifies the URL to the embedded content. The data attribute defines the external resource and the type attribute specifies what application (or plug-in) should be used to render the content. You can also specify the height and width attributes to allocate the desired space for this content.

For example, to embed a PDF file in the HTML document, add the following, which will be rendered as demonstrated in Figure 7-14.

```
<object data="MainPage.pdf" type="application/pdf" width="850" height="200">
    <a href="MainPage.pdf">MainPage</a>
</object>
```

Figure 7-14. *Embedding a PDF document*

Notice the alternate content inside the object element. This is a hyperlink to the same PDF file. If the object element is not supported or the particular type is not supported, the user will see a link to the file instead of the embedded file. If you're using a custom plug-in, you might want to put instructions on how to install the plug-in here. If the plug-in is not installed, they'll see those instructions instead of the embedded content.

The object element also allows you to pass parameters to the plug-in using the param element. The param element has two attributes, name and value. You use the param element to provide a set of name/value pairs. The param element uses a self-closing tag, can only be used inside an object element, and should come before any fallback content. For example:

```
<object data="some file" type="application/some plug in">
    <param name="paramName" value="paramValue" />
    <p>fallback content</p>
</object>
```

■ **Tip** Not all plug-ins will support parameters using the param element. Case in point, passing options to the PDF viewer need to be included in the URL. For example, using data="MainPage.pdf#zoom=50 will set the initial zoom to 50%. You'll need to check on the plug-in you're using to see what features it supports.

HTML5 also supports the embedded (embed) element, which is similar to the object element. The embed element was supported in HTML4 while the object element is relatively new. A number of articles suggest that the embed element has been deprecated, but as of this writing, it is still included in the HTML5 specification. However, the general consensus is that the object element is preferred over embed.

The embed element is an empty element, meaning that it uses a self-closing tag. This also means that it does not support fallback content or param elements. Other than that, is works much like the object element except the URL to the resource is provided in the src attribute. You can embed a PDF document using the embed element like this:

```
<embed src="MainPage.pdf" type="application/pdf" width="850" height="150"/>
```

Summary

In this chapter, I explained how to embed external content into an HTML5 document. The primary types of embedded content are images, audio, and video and HTML5 supports specific elements for each of these types. You can provide multiple image files and let the browser choose the most appropriate one to download and render based on the device characteristics. You can also define clickable areas on an image that can be used as links.

The major browsers have all standardized on MP3 for audio and MP4 for video, making it pretty easy to include either in an HTML document. For both audio and video, you can also include time-synchronized text that will appear as subtitles, captions, or other details.

For other types of embedded content, the object element provides a standardized way of including it. This may require custom browser plug-ins but the object element is a consistent way for referencing them. You can also provide fallback content for when the plug-in is not supported.

In the next chapter, I'll demonstrate the HTML elements that support user input. Whether you're creating a full-blown input form, or just a simple search field, these elements provide the ability for a user to interact with your web page.

■ ■ ■

CHAPTER 8

HTML Form Elements

In traditional web applications, a form is a web page or a part of one that contains places for a user to enter information. Once the data has been entered, the form is then submitted to the server, along with the input data. This is processed by the server, and the new page is returned and rendered by the client.

In this chapter I'll explain how to create forms in HTML5. I'll also demonstrate the HTML elements that are typically associated with forms, such as the label, input, and button elements. Many of these elements can also be used in an HTML5 document without actually being on a form.

Overview

When you navigate to a web page in a browser, the URL of the page is sent to the appropriate web server as an HTTP request (or HTTPS if using a secure transport). The web server responds with an HTML document that is rendered by the browser. This is illustrated in Figure 8-1.

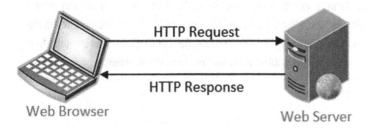

Figure 8-1. *Client/Server Architecture*

If the web page contains a form, when the form is submitted, another HTTP request is sent to the server. The request contains a URL just like the first one, but also includes the data from the input fields. This data can either be included in the body of the request or in the URL itself as query string parameters. I'll explain this later in the chapter. The response is either a new web page or an update to the existing one.

Form Element

Submitting input data through these server requests is a fundamental capability of web sites and HTML. The form element is used to group one or more input elements for the purpose of sending this information to a web server. You can also configure where (and how) the data is submitted in the form element.

A form element will contain one or more input elements, which are the fields where the user can enter data. A form will usually also contain label elements, which are simple text blocks that describe the input elements. A simple form is defined like this:

```
<form action="" method="get">
    <label for="iFirstName">First Name:</label>
    <input id="iFirstName" type="text" />
    <label for="iLastName">Last Name:</label>
    <input id="iLastName" type="text" />
    <input type="submit" value="Submit" />
</form>
```

This form contains two input fields (first and last name) and a label element for each one. The final input element has type="submit", which will render this as a button, by default. More importantly, when this button is clicked, the form will be submitted to the server. This form is rendered as shown in Figure 8-2.

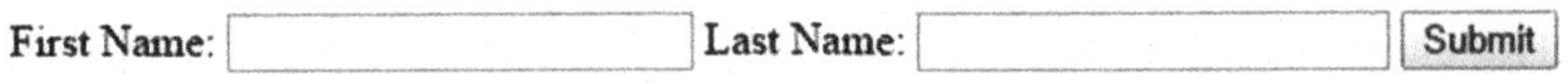

First Name: [   ]   Last Name: [   ]   [Submit]

Figure 8-2. *A simple form rendering*

▪ **Tip** As I demonstrated in this sample form, input elements are associated with a form by placing them inside the form element. However, you can also include an input element in a form by referencing it using the form attribute. This allows you put an input element anywhere in the document and set its form attribute to the id attribute of a form element. The input value will be submitted when the form is submitted.

Form Action

If you enter data into these fields and click the submit button, an HTML request similar to this will be sent:

http://localhost:5266/?FirstName=Mark&LastName=Collins

You'll also probably notice a flicker as the page is refreshed. The web server will respond to this request with a new HTML document. The action attribute specifies the URL of the request. Since this was left blank, the address of the current page is used. In my case, this is http://localhost:5266. So the same page is returned and re-rendered by the browser.

In many cases, the action attribute will specify a different page. Suppose, for example, the initial page provided a form to enter search criteria. Upon submitting this data, you would them want to return a result page, based on the user input. The action attribute in this case would be the address of the results page. When the initial form is submitted, you're actually requesting the results page to be rendered and providing the search details as part of the request.

In other scenarios, you'll want the existing page to be rendered. More accurately, you want it to be *re-rendered* based on the information that was just entered. This is referred to as a *postback*. This is where a web page submits a request to have itself refreshed from the server, usually passing data to the server. For example, if you present a series of questions on a page, but the answer of one question may make some other questions non-applicable. Once the question is answered, a simple postback can re-render the page with only the applicable questions.

■ **Note**   In current web designs postbacks are generally frowned upon as a round trip to the server and re-rendering an entire page can be slow. If this example, it would be better to handle this in JavaScript on the client.

Form Method

So by now you're probably figured out, correctly, that the form element is all about defining the HTTP request when the form is submitted. I've already explained the action attribute, which specifies the URL that the request is sent to. The method attribute indicates which HTTP verb should be used. Only two are supported currently: GET and POST.

The GET verb does not support a message body so all of the form data must be passed in the URL as I've already demonstrated. If you set the method attribute to post, the form data will be in the body of the request. To demonstrate that, I have intercepted the request using Fiddler and the raw request is shown below:

```
POST http://localhost:5266/ HTTP/1.1
Host: localhost:5266
Connection: keep-alive
Content-Length: 31
Cache-Control: max-age=0
Origin: http://localhost:5266
Upgrade-Insecure-Requests: 1
User-Agent: Mozilla/5.0 (Windows NT 10.0; WOW64) AppleWebKit/537.36 (KHTML, like Gecko)
Chrome/51.0.2704.103 Safari/537.36
Content-Type: application/x-www-form-urlencoded
Accept: text/html,application/xhtml+xml,application/xml;q=0.9,image/webp,*/*;q=0.8
Referer: http://localhost:5266/
Accept-Encoding: gzip, deflate
Accept-Language: en-US,en;q=0.8

FirstName=Mark&LastName=Collins
```

The first line indicates the URL being requested and the subsequent lines list all of the headers included with the HTTP request. Some of these headers can be adjusted using additional attributes, which I will explain later. The last line is the body of the message and includes the form data.

■ **Tip** Representational State Transfer (REST) is an architectural style for communicating with web sites and web services. In a RESTful application, the HTTP verb is an important part of the request. You can use the exact same URL with different verbs and get very different results. In my opinion, it's very unfortunate that the other verbs such as PUT and DELETE are not supported by HTML5. There has been some movement to add these but it seems to lack any traction. If you're interested, check out this article: `http://programmers.stackexchange.com/questions/114156/why-are-there-are-no-put-and-delete-methods-on-html-forms`

Additional Attributes

The enctype attribute is available to control how the data should be formatted; however, there are not a lot of options here. The default value is `application/x-www-form-urlencoded`, which is a long way of saying that the input data is URL encoded. Essentially, spaces and special characters are encoded to satisfy URL formatting rules. If the method attribute is get, this is the only option you can use. In fact, the enctype attribute is only allowed when the method attribute is set to post.

If you're using the post method, URL encoding is still available and is the default option. Notice the message body in the previous example is formatted exactly as it was when passed in the URL. There are two other options available as well. When using text/plain, spaces are converted to "+" but other special characters are not encoded. The other option is multipart/form-data. Again, the name is not very intuitive, but this value must be used when uploading one or more files in the request.

You can use the accept-charset to specify the character sets that the server will support. If not specified, the character set of the document will be used (see Chapter 1 for details). Since this is user-entered data, you may need to support additional character set(s) depending on the expected audience. You can include multiple sets by separating them with spaces. For example, accept-charset="UTF-8 ISO-8859-1" includes the two most common character sets. The browser will choose one based on what sets it supports.

Client-side validation of the input fields is performed by the browser when the form is submitted. I will explain this validation later. However, you can disable validation by including the novalidate attribute in the form element. This is a Boolean attribute.

Input Elements

The most interesting part of a form are the input elements, which the user interacts with to enter information into the form. HTML5 defines an impressive set of input types to choose from. They all use the same input element but are distinguished by the type attribute that is assigned. The available types are listed in the reference data in Appendix C.

Textual Form Data

Much of the form data that is entered will be textual; however there are several elements and element types that deal with special types of text. These have some common functionality so I will describe them as a group.

Text Values

There are several input types that are basically text boxes that provide data validation based on the specified type attribute. These types are:

- **text** - this is the default if the type attribute is not specified. If line breaks are entered into the text field, they will be removed before the form is submitted. Use the textarea element if you want multiple lines. The single line constraint also applies the remaining text value types.

- **email** - this works like a normal text field except there is built-in validation to verify the format of the text conforms to a standard email address. Keep in mind that this only validates the format; this does not ensure that this is an actual, valid email address, or even verify that the domain exists. You can also include the multiple attribute to allow more than one email address to be entered.

- **password** - this simply displays the entered characters as asterisks or some other method of obscuring the input. This is only a UI feature; the data still exists in the form as clear text and will be sent that way when the form is submitted.

- **search** - this type doesn't function differently from a normal text type but there may be styling differences applied to search fields. You can add the autosave attribute so the data entered can be used in an auto complete list in other pages.

- **tel** - use this for entering phone numbers; however, it is used for semantic purposes only. It provides no built-in validation due to the wide variety of formats used internationally. You can provide your own validation rule using the pattern attribute.

- **url** - like the email type, this validates that the enter text is a well-formed URL. It does not verify that the resource actually exists. A well-formed URL includes the protocol so apress.com or even www.apress.com are not valid URLs, however, http://www.apress.com is valid.

Textarea

The textarea element is a separate HTML element, not a type of input element. However, it functions much like an input element with type text, except it allows CR/LF characters. It supports a few specific attributes, including:

- **cols** - specifies the number of characters that should be displayed on a single line, similar to the size attribute described later.

- **rows** - specifies the number of rows that should be visible. The actual data can have more rows than that but the user will need to scroll to see them.

- **wrap** - specifies how the text should be wrapped; the allows values are hard and soft. The default value is soft, which means that the text is only wrapped when the data contains a CR/LF character. The user may need to scroll horizontally to see all of the data. The value of hard indicates that the text is always wrapped to fit in the width of the element.

Each of the text-based input elements and the textarea element support several common attributes. These attributes are:

- **inputmode** - for email, password, text, or url – this can be provided as a hint as to which keyboard to display. This is important for touch-enabled devices where a keyboard is displayed for user input. The supported values are verbatim, latin, latin-name, latin-prose, full-width-latin, kana, katakana. The other supported types (email, numeric, tel, or url) should be set using the appropriate type attribute rather than using inputmode, however, they are supported here as well.

- **maxlength** - specifies the maximum number of characters that can be entered into the field.

- **minlength** - specifies the minimum number of characters required for this field.

- **pattern** - this specifies a regular expression that is used to validate the input data. Some of the text value types have built-in validation logic. Using the pattern attribute will provide additional validation. This attribute is not supported on the textarea element.

- **placeholder** - text that is placed inside the element where the actual input is keyed, which explains what data is expected in the field. It's a hint about the format of the data, often being a sample of the expected input. For example, if the field is expecting a phone number, the placeholder may contain a phone number formatted the way the form is expecting it. The placeholder text is only shown when the field is empty and is hidden when the field is selected or as soon as the first character is typed.

- **size** - specifies the physical size of the input element entered as a number of characters. The default value, if size not specified, is 20. This means that the element should be large enough to display at least 20 characters. This is guideline, not an absolute requirement, however, as characters can have different widths. If you were to enter twenty W's, they may not all fit. For example, I tested this in Chrome and I could enter 64 lowercase i's but only 13 uppercase W's in a default sized input element. Note, this is different from the maxlength attribute, which limits the number of characters in the data. You could set the size attribute to 10 and roughly 10 characters would be visible. The maxlength attribute can be set to a much higher value, but not all of the characters would be visible. For textarea elements this attribute is not supported; use the cols and rows attributes instead.

- **spellcheck** - a Boolean attribute that indicates if the input data should have the spelling and grammar checked.

Autofill

Autofill is a really handy feature where the browser can fill the input field based on previous entries that were made. As you type, the list is filtered to only show the entries matching the characters entered so far. Generally, after only typing a character or two, the choice can be made without further typing. The autocomplete attribute determines if this feature is used and controls the available selections.

The autofill feature can be turned on or off at either the form or field level. If the autocomplete attribute is set to off on the form element, it will be off for all fields unless explicitly turned on in one or more input elements. Similarly, it can be set to on in the form element, and it will be on for all fields unless set to off in the input element.

However, simply turning on autofill is not enough information. If I'm entering an email address, for example, I don't want to see names, addresses, or phone numbers showing up in the autofill list. Instead of setting the `autocomplete` attribute to the value on, you should set it to a specific autofill detail token, `email` in this case. Then the autofill list will only include values that were entered in other fields that had the same autofill detail token.

There is a fairly long list of autofill detail tokens that have been defined including the individual parts of a phone number, address, or payment information, along with many other types of information. Rather than repeating all of the information here, it's best to just consult the specification, which can be found at `https://html.spec.whatwg.org/multipage/forms.html#autofill`. This will also give you the most up-to-date information.

You can also supply a custom autofill list using the `datalist` element. A `datalist` element contains a set of `option` elements. You can then assign the `datalist` to an input element using the `list` attribute. Whatever values you have included in the `datalist` will now be included in your autofill suggestions. Here's a simple example:

```
<datalist id="sports">
    <option value="Baseball" />
    <option value="Basketball" />
    <option value="Hockey" />
    <option value="Football" />
</datalist>
<label for="iSport">Favorite Sport:</label>
<input type="text" id="iSport" name="Sport" list="sports" />
```

The `datalist` element contains four values that are the names of four popular sports. A `datalist` is referenced by its `id` attribute and I've specified **sports** as its `id`. Then in the `input` element I've added the `list` attribute: `list="sports"`.

A text box with a prefilled `datalist` is not the same thing as a drop-down list that you create with the `select` element, which I'll explain later. The user is not limited to only those choices; they can type in anything they want. This just makes it a little easier if one of the more common values are needed. The suggestions are automatically filtered as you type. After entering the letter "b," for example, only Baseball and Basketball will be left to choose from. Also, if autocomplete is enabled, additional entries will be added to the suggested list based on a previous entry. For example, I had entered **tennis** earlier and now the text box looks like Figure 8-3.

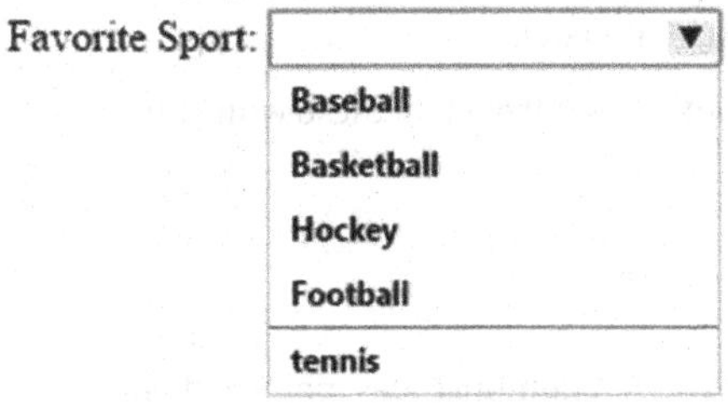

Figure 8-3. *Using a prefilled datalist*

Attributes

Before I continue describing the remaining input types I want to cover the other attributes supported by the input element that are mostly available for all types. (There are a couple that have a few restrictions). This will give you a complete view of the textual elements.

- **name** - When a form is submitted, the input fields are sent to the server as a set of name/value pairs, either in the body of the message or in the URL as I demonstrated earlier. The name portion comes from the name attribute and the value comes from the value attribute, which I'll explain next. If the name attribute is not supplied, the data will not be sent to the server.

- **value** - As I said, the value attribute provides the data that is passed to the server. When you enter data into an input element, such as a text box, this is stored in the value attribute of that element. This value attribute is displayed in the input field and submitted when the form is submitted. You can also set the value attribute in the HTML, which will prefill the field with the specified value. The value attribute is required for checkbox and radio types but is optional on all other types. For button types, the value attribute provides the display text on the button.

- **disabled** - This is a Boolean attribute that will, when true, disable any user interaction with the input element. Also, disabled fields are not submitted with the form data.

- **readonly** - a Boolean attribute that prevents the user from changing the value of an input element. This is subtly different from the disabled attribute, where the user can interact with the element but can't change the value. Elements marked readonly are also submitted when the form is submitted. However, the readonly attribute is ignored by several input types, including checkbox, color, file, hidden, radio, range, or one of the button types (button, image, reset, submit).

- **required** - a Boolean attribute that indicates the user must enter (or select) a value for this element. Page validation will enforce this setting when the form is submitted. You can apply styling for required or optional elements using the pseudo classes, :optional and :required. I'll cover these in Chapter 9. The required attribute is not allowed on a hidden type or one of the button types.

- **autofocus** - a Boolean attribute that indicates the input element should have the focus when the page is loaded. Only one element can have this attribute set and this attribute is not allowed on the hidden type, which I'll explain later.

There are a few more attributes that are specific to certain input types. I'll explain these while I'm demonstrating those types.

Review

For a quick review of the textual input types, here is snippet of HTML that demonstrates many of them:

```
<input type="email" name="Email" size="100"
        placeholder="enter 1 or more email addresses" multiple required />
<input type="password" name="Password" maxlength="12" minlength="6" size="12" />
<input type="search" name="Search" placeholder="search criteria..." autofocus />
<input type="tel" name="Phone" placeholder="(800) 555-1212"
        pattern="^(\+\d{1,2}\s)?\(?\d{3}\)?[\s.-]\d{3}[\s.-]\d{4}$" />
```

```
<input type="url" name="Website" placeholder="http://www.apress.com" size="50" />
<input type="text" value="Read-only text" readonly name="ReadOnly" />
<input type="text" value="Disabled text" disabled />
<label for="iComments">Comments:</label>
<textarea id="iComments" rows="3" cols="50" wrap="hard" maxlength="250" name="Comments">
</textarea>
```

On the email field, this sets the size to 100 to make it large enough to hold an email address or two. This also has the multiple attribute to allow for more than one to be entered. The password field uses the minlength and maxlength attribute to provide client-side length validations. The phone number field includes a regex pattern that supports U.S. phone numbers. A placeholder attribute also provides a hint for how the number should be formatted.

This includes both a disabled and a read-only textbox so you can see the difference in how they work. For both of these the value is set using the value attribute since it cannot be entered on the form. You can highlight the text on the read-only field and copy it, put you can't on the disabled field. Finally, the comments field uses a textarea element that shows three rows of text. This has a maximum length of 250 characters.

If you add these input elements to the initial form shown at the beginning of this chapter, it would look something like Figure 8-4.

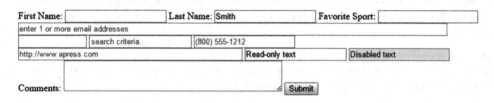

Figure 8-4. *Adding sample text fields*

The cursor should be in the search box since this element had the autofocus attribute. When you submit the form, if any of the validations fail, the form will display an error as demonstrated in Figure 8-5.

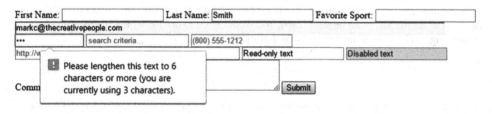

Figure 8-5. *Displaying a validation error*

Selection Elements

There are several constructs that allow you to present a fixed set of choices on a form. Checkboxes and radio buttons can be created using the type attribute of the input element. Drop-down lists are created using the select and option elements.

Checkbox

Checkboxes are used when representing a Boolean value such as "Available?" or "Can call?" A true value is checked and a false value is unchecked. A checkbox is created by using an input element with the type set to checkbox.

You can also use checkboxes when you want to allow multiple selections from a set of choices. For example, if you're ordering a pizza and selecting toppings, you might want to list all of the available items such as Mushrooms, Sausage, Olives, etc. with a checkbox next to each. Technically, each of these is a separate field with a Boolean value: Do you want mushrooms? Do you want sausage?

To indicate that a checkbox has been checked, use the Boolean checked attribute. If this attribute exists, the box is checked; otherwise it in not. When the form is submitted, only checked elements are included with the form data and the value attribute determines what is actually submitted. If you want the data to be CanCall=true, then set the name attribute to **CanCall** and the value attribute to **true**. In the pizza example, you can set the name attribute on all of the checkboxes to **Topping** and set the value attribute to **Mushrooms**, **Sausage**, or **Olives**. When the form is submitted, you'll have a Topping field submitted for each one that was checked, with its corresponding value.

■ **Tip** Checkboxes are either checked or unchecked; there is no indeterminate value. HTML5 does not support a tri-state checkbox (checked, unchecked, not specified), although there are some JavaScript solutions that will provide this capability. For example, see `http://jquer.in/jquery-plugins-for-html5-forms/tristate/`

The input element does not display any text. The name and value attributes are only used when submitting data. You can use a label element for each input element or simply embed content around the checkboxes. For example, the selected toppings can be presented like this:

```
<p>Toppings:
    <input type="checkbox" name="Topping" value="Mushrooms" />Mushrooms?
    <input type="checkbox" name="Topping" value="Sausage" />Sausage?
    <input type="checkbox" name="Topping" value="Olives" />Olives?
</p>
```

The required property, when used on an input element with type="checkbox," indicates that the box must be checked before the form can be submitted. You would want to do this where the user needs to acknowledge something, such as terms and conditions, before proceeding.

Radio

You create a radio button by using an input element and setting the type attribute to radio. A radio button works very much like a checkbox: the checked attribute indicates if it was selected; only checked values are submitted; and the value attribute specifies the text that should be submitted.

The main difference is that radio buttons are usually provided as a group of buttons and only one radio button in a group can be selected. When a radio button is checked, the checked attribute in all of the other elements in the group is removed. A radio button group is determined by the name attribute. All elements with the same name attribute value are considered in the same group.

Back to our pizza example. Suppose you offered three types of crust: thin, thick, and deep dish. You can add three radio buttons all with the name attribute set to **Crust**. Each one would have a different value, **Thin**, **Thick**, or **DeepDish**. When the form is submitted, if the Thick option was selected, for example, the field would be posted as Crust="Thick." You can define additional text around the radio button just like for checkboxes:

```
<p>Crust:
    <input type="radio" name="Crust" value="Thin" />Thin
    <input type="radio" name="Crust" value="Thick" />Thick
    <input type="radio" name="Crust" value="DeepDish" />Deep Dish
</p>
```

You can default a selection by adding a checked attribute on one of them. If you want to require a selection, add the required attribute to one of the radio buttons; it doesn't matter which one has the attribute. Adding the required attribute to more than one has no effect. If the required attribute is present, the browser will not submit the form until one of the radio buttons is checked as demonstrated in Figure 8-6.

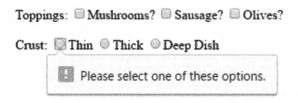

Figure 8-6. *Validating the required radio button*

Drop-Down Lists

With the last two input types, all of the options are always shown. With checkboxes, multiple selections can be made; with radio buttons only one per group can be selected. With a drop-down list however, only the selected option is shown until the user clicks the drop-down and then the available choices are displayed.

Use the select element to create a drop-down list. Within the select element, include an option element for each of the available choices. Set the name attribute on the select element to specify the field name that will be posted when the form is submitted. Use the value attribute on the option element to indicate the field value that will be submitted when that option is selected.

The option elements can be organized into groups by nesting them inside an optgroup element. This is used for purely visual purposes and has no effect on the data that is submitted or the selecting and unselecting of options. The optgroup element is helpful when there is a relatively long list of options. The optgroup element has a label attribute that is required. This is where you specify the group text that is displayed before the options. Options in an optgroup element are also indented.

By default, the first option will be selected and submitted when the form is submitted. You can choose a different option to be the default choice by adding the selected attribute to the desired option element. Only one option should have the selected attribute; if more than one has the selected attribute, all but the last one are ignored.

You unselect an option by selecting a different one. There's no way to unselect an option so that none are selected. To work around this, you can include an *unselected* option that has a `value` attribute set to an empty string. You would typically give this a display string such as **Please select**. If this `option` was chosen, an empty string is posted to the server. You can add the `required` attribute on the `select` element to require some other `option` (that has a non-empty `value` attribute) is chosen.

A drop-down list with groups can be created like this. This will be rendered as shown in Figure 8-7.

```
<p>Addons:
    <select name="Addons" required>
        <option value="">Please select...</option>
        <option value="None">Pizza only</option>
        <optgroup label="Addons">
            <option value="Wings">Side of Buffalo Wings</option>
            <option value="GarlicBread">Add Garlic Bread</option>
        </optgroup>
    </select>
</p>
```

Figure 8-7. *A select option with grouping*

In this example, the initial `option` has an empty `value` attribute and the `select` element has the `required` attribute. The user will need to make a choice in this drop-down before submitting the form.

Multi-Select Lists

The `select` element allows you to choose more than one option if you add the `multiple` attribute. With the `multiple` attribute, the UI changes significantly. This is no longer a drop-down list with only the selected option displayed. Instead, this is more like a simple list where all of the options are shown. You can control how may options are visible by setting the `size` attribute. If there are more options than that, the user can scroll through the list to see them.

To select multiple options, you need to hold down the Ctrl key while clicking the desired options. You can also select one option, hold down the Shift key, and select another. This will select all of the options between the two. Clicking an option without either the Ctrl or Shift keys will unselect all options first.

To demonstrate this, let's reimplement the Toppings field using a multi-select list box like this. After selecting a couple of options, this will be rendered as demonstrated in Figure 8-8.

```
<select name="Toppings" multiple size="4">
    <option label="Mushrooms?" value="Mushrooms" />
    <option label="Sausage?" value="Sausage" />
    <option label="Olives?" value="Olives" />
</select>
```

Figure 8-8. Using a multi-select list box

■ **Note**   The size attribute is also supported for a drop-down list (where the multiple attribute is not included). This will show the specified number of options all the time. However, from a UI perspective this rarely makes sense to do so.

When the form is submitted, the data that is posted will be identical to the initial implementation using checkboxes. The name attribute defines the field name that is used, and the value attribute specifies the string that is posted. A separate field is submitted for each option that is selected.

Miscellaneous Types

There are several miscellaneous input types that are used for special purposes. Each has specific attributes to control the unique aspects of these elements.

Number

The number input type is fairly straightforward. It acts much like a textbox except that it only allows numeric input. It will allow decimal values to be entered but does not enforce any particular formatting or type of number, such as whole numbers only. If you need that, you can use the pattern attribute as described earlier.

Use can use the min and max attributes to specify the allowed range for this field. The browser will ensure the number entered is within this range. Most browsers also provide up and down arrows that can be used to increment or decrement the current value. This only works with whole numbers and won't help if decimal values are expected.

Here is a typical implementation of a numeric input field:

```
<p>Number of utensils:
    <input type="number" min="1" max="4" value="1" name="Utensils" />
</p>
```

Color

The color input type will display a sample of the selected color. When this is clicked, the browser will display a color picker like the one shown in Figure 8-9.

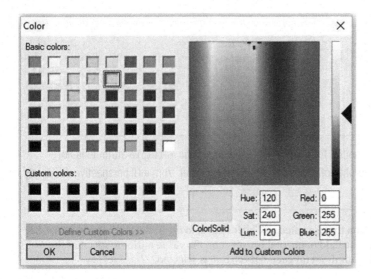

Figure 8-9. *A sample color picker*

The selected color will be provided in RGB notation when the form is submitted. For example, the color green is specified as #00ff00. However, if this is URL encoded, the hashtag is replaced with %23.

■ **Caution**   As of this writing, only Chrome, Firefox, and Opera support the color input type.

File

Selecting one or more files is easy with the file input type. Add the multiple attribute if you want to allow more than one file to be selected. You can also provide a hint to the type of file that is needed by using the accepts attribute. This takes a comma-separated list of MIME type such as text/css. You can use a wildcard such as one of the following popular values:

- text/* - text files
- image/* - images files
- audio/* - audio files
- video/* - video files

You can also list one or more file extensions, for example, accepts=".jpg, .gif". Here is a simple example with two input fields. The first can select a single audio file: the second one or more images with .jpg or .png extensions:

```
<p>Select file(s) to upload:
    <input type="file" name="music" accept="audio/*" />
    <input type="file" name="pictures" multiple accept=".jpg, .png" />
</p>
```

■ **Caution**   The accepts attribute is useful for guiding the user to select an appropriate file type. However, they can easily override this and select a different type of file. The server-side code should always validate that the file is the correct type.

Figures 8-10 and 8-11 demonstrate the input buttons and the file dialog used in Chrome and Firefox, respectively.

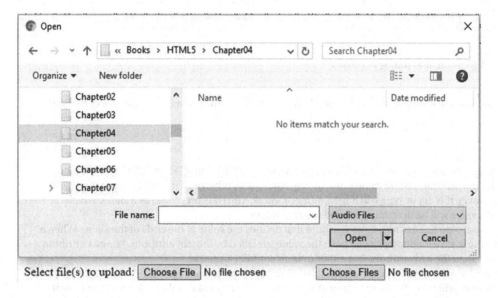

Figure 8-10. *A file input and dialog in Chrome*

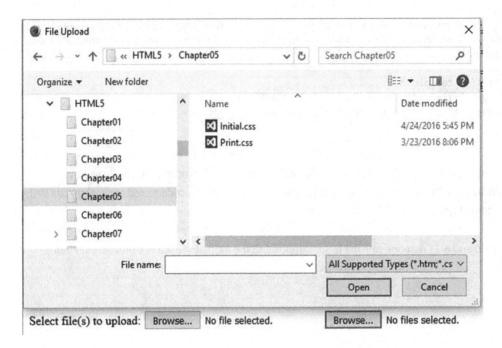

Figure 8-11. A file input and dialog in Firefox

As you can see, the format and specific functionality may very but the basic capability is consistent.

Range

The range input type is also known as the "imprecise number-input control" in the W3C specification. It is generally used when the specific value is not as important as its relative value along some sort of scale. Ultimately however, this input type will have a numeric value. The UI is presented as a slider, which the user can drag, and a value will be determined based on its position.

A range input type has a min and max attribute that defines the value at the ends of the slider. When at the left end of the scale (or bottom), it will have the value specified by the min attribute. The max attribute must be greater than the min attribute, but either or both could be negative.

You can also specify the step attribute, which defines the stops along the slider. For example, setting the step attribute to **10** will only allow you to stop at intervals of 10. The default value is 1, which will ensure the user can only select whole numbers. If you set the value to any, there will be no preset stops and the user can stop anywhere.

■ **Caution**   Be careful when setting step="any" because the value will be a floating-point number such as 44.9814126394052 (I just happened to get this value when testing). As this is known as the "imprecise number-input control," that is probably more detail than you want. If you need finer granularity than 1, use can use decimal values, such as .1 for the step attribute.

You can display tick marks above the slider to indicate where the stops are. To do that, however, you have to define them using a `datalist` element. Add an `option` element with a `value` attribute for each place where a tick mark should be. Then reference the `datalist` in the `input` element using the `list` attribute. For example:

```
<datalist id="SurveyStops">
    <option value="0" />
    <option value="10" />
    <option value="20" />
    <option value="30" />
    <option value="40" />
    <option value="50" />
</datalist>
<p>How satisfied were you with the ordering process?
    <input type="range" name="Survey" min="0" max="50" step="10" list="SurveyStops" />
</p>
```

The UI varies greatly between browser implementation. For example, the rendering of this markup for Chrome, Firefox, IE, and Opera is shown in Figures 8-12, 8-13, 8-14, and 8-15, respectively.

Figure 8-12. *The range input type in Chrome*

Figure 8-13. *The range input type in Firefox*

Figure 8-14. *The range input type in IE*

Figure 8-15. *The range input type in Opera*

Because the stops and the tick marks are defined independently, they don't have to be the same. You could have stops at intervals of 5 but tick marks at intervals of 10. Of course they can be completely out-of-sync, such as tick marks every 7 and `step` set to 10. However, this would be confusing to the user and should be avoided.

As of this writing, Firefox does not support the tick marks as you can see from Figure 8-13. Also, in IE 11, if you don't specify the tick marks through a `datalist` element, it will automatically display them using the `step` attribute. In both IE and Edge, the selected numeric value is displayed above the slider while the user has clicked on the input field.

Hidden Input

The `input` element also supports the `hidden` type. This, as you might expect, has no UI; the user cannot see or modify its value. However, it is submitted along with the other elements when the form is submitted. This allows you to include some hard-coded content in the data that is submitted. Suppose, for example, that you had several forms that submit to the same server address. You could include which page was used in the `hidden` input field. To do this, simply set the `value` attribute in the markup.

Another more probable application of this is to capture data collected in JavaScript. For example, you could use JavaScript to get the user's location and include that in the form data. In this case, the `value` attribute is set through JavaScript.

Date and Time Data

The HTML5 specification defines a number of input types related to date/time values. There are five that are supported by most major browsers, Firefox being the most significant exception. These are also not supported by IE but they do work in the Edge browser. If not supported, these `input` elements will be displayed as a simple text box. You should include the `placeholder` attribute to indicate the format that is expected. The `placeholder` is ignored in browsers that support the input type.

The five types are:

- `date` - a date without any time portion

- `datetime-local` - a date and a time; the time being the local time (of the browser) - there is no support for universal time or time zones

- `time` - a local time; again no time zone support

- `month` - a single specific year and month

- `week` - a single specific week, expressed as year and week number (1-53)

■ **Note**   Yes, there are only 52 weeks in a year, normally. However, 52 * 7 is only 364 days, so every year there is an extra day, and every four years, roughly, there will be two extra days. So every five or six years, we get a 53rd week.

Each of these types allow a `min` and `max` attribute to define the boundaries of the allowed input values. However, the browser support for these attributes is mixed. They are not supported by any browsers for the `month` and `week` types. For the other three types they are honored, for the most part, but not consistently. However, you should always provide additional client or server-side validation and not rely on the browser. You should define these attributes as appropriate because where they are supported, the browser provides a better user experience.

The `step` attribute is also defined for these types. However, this is only supported, currently, for the `time` and `datetime-local` types. The UI generally provides up/down arrows to allow the user to scroll through allowed values. The specification is not clear how the `step` attribute is to be used. The browsers that support this use it primarily for the seconds. For example, if you set `step="15"`, clicking the up arrow will increment the selected time by 15 seconds.

As with other input types, you can set the initial value by adding the `value` attribute. If not specified, the field will generally use the current date (or time). This may be affected by the `min` and `max` attributes. For example, if the `min` attribute is in the future, this will usually be the initial value. The initial value only affects the date picker and the scrolling feature. The actual `value` of the field will be null until a value is entered by the user (unless provided in the markup).

The following markup will create one of each of the supported types:

```
<p>
    Date:
    <input type="date" name="Date" min="2016-08-06" max="2016-08-11"
        placeholder="mm/dd/yy" />
    Date/Time:
    <input type="datetime-local" name="DateTime" step="30"
        placeholder="mm/dd/yy hh:mm:ss AM" />
    Time:
    <input type="time" name="Time" min="10:00:00" max="17:00:00" step="15"
        placeholder="hh:mm:ss AM" />
    Month:
    <input type="month" name="Month" min="2016-01-01" max="2017-12-31"
        placeholder="yyyy-mm" />
    Week:
    <input type="week" name="Week" min="2016-01-01" max="2017-12-31"
        placeholder="yyyy-W##" />
</p>
```

The UI presented by each of the browsers varies widely. The date picker in Chrome and Opera is probably the most natural. It shows a monthly calendar that you can scroll through. Since I used the min and max attributes to set a date range of August 6-11, all the other dates are grayed out as demonstrated in Figure 8-16. The month scrolling is also disabled since they are outside of the allowed range.

Figure 8-16. *The date picker in Chrome*

Most browsers support a scrolling feature to select the individual date/time elements. In the datetime-local type, for example, there are seven parts: month, day, year, hour, minute, second, AM/PM as shown in Figure 8-17. You can click each of these and then use the up/down arrows to select a value for that part. I set the step attribute to **30** so there are only two values when scrolling through the seconds, 0 and 30. If the min and max attributes are set, the scrolling feature will generally honor this. For example, scrolling up when at the maximum date will change the value to the minimum.

Date/Time: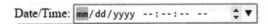

Figure 8-17. *The datetime-local input type in Chrome*

As of this writing, only the Edge browser supports a time picker. To see the time picker, click anywhere on the `time` field or on the time portion of the `datetime-local` field. The UI is a bit different for a desktop browser but similar to what you would expect on a mobile device. The hour, minute, second, and AM/PM values are displayed in columns. You hover in one of the columns and scroll that column using the mouse wheel as shown in Figure 8-18.

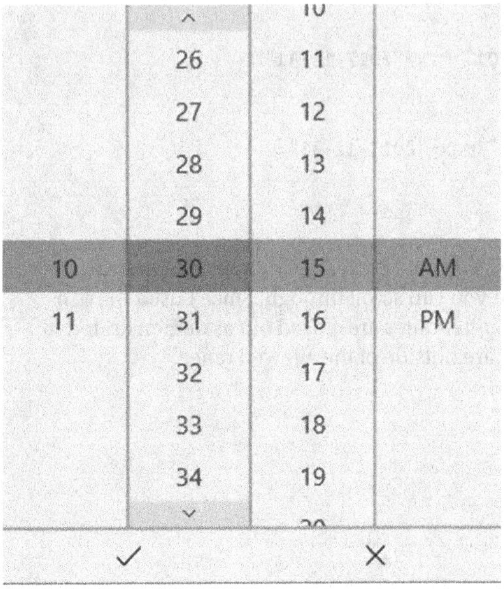

		10	
	26	11	
	27	12	
	28	13	
	29	14	
10	30	15	AM
11	31	16	PM
	32	17	
	33	18	
	34	19	
		~~20~~	

Figure 8-18. *The time picker in Edge*

As you can see from Figure 8-18, the available hours are restricted to only 10 and 11 because of the `min` attribute was set to 10:00 a.m. To select a value past noon, change the AM/PM column to PM and you'll see hours 12-5 since the `max` attribute was set to 5:00 p.m. If you select the 5 hour, the only available minute value is 00.

The date picker in Edge works the same way. You can scroll through the month, day, and year columns individually to select the desired date. This also honors the `min` and `max` attributes as demonstrated in Figure 8-19.

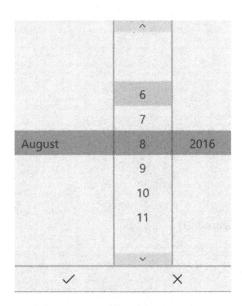

Figure 8-19. *The date picker in Edge*

The biggest disadvantage of the Edge date picker is that is doesn't show the day of week. If you want to select next Monday, for example, you would have to know the specific date. With Chrome's date picker, you can easily see that since it shows the monthly calendar.

Safari does not provide any date or time pickers. Also, you can't select an individual portion and scroll to select its values. There is a scroll feature but it is for the entire field. For a date type, this will scroll one day at a time. For the datetime-local or time types, it will scroll one second at a time, unless you set the step attribute.

When using the week input type, you're selecting a year and the week number (1-53). The UI in Chrome and Opera shows a monthly calendar where you can select a specific week. The actual week number is also displayed as well as shown in Figure 8-20.

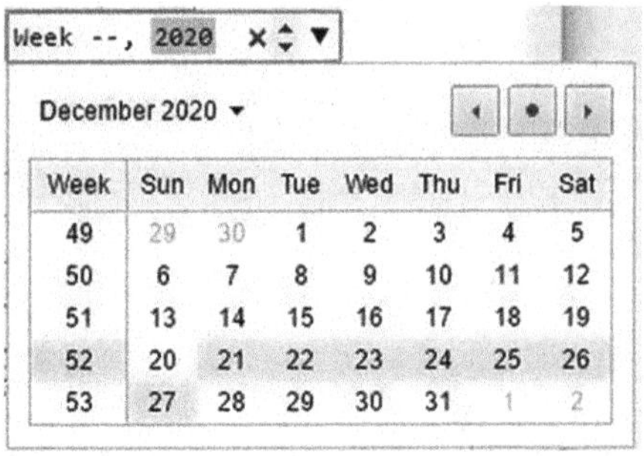

Figure 8-20. *The week picker in Chrome*

In Edge, only the year and week number are displayed (see Figure 8-21)

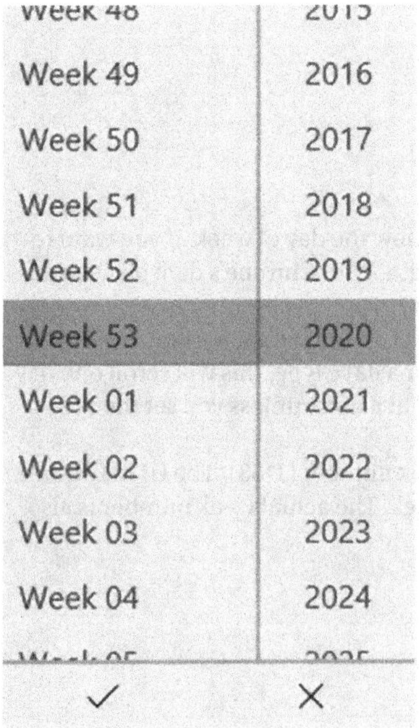

Figure 8-21. *The week picker in Edge*

Other Visual Elements

There are several elements that provide visual information to the form rather than accepting input from the user. You have undoubtedly seen the label element as it is used on almost every form. The others, output, meter, and progress have more specialized usages but can be quite helpful.

Labels

I introduced the label element at the beginning of this chapter without saying much about it. You need to add captions to the fields in a form so the user will know what needs to be entered into each. However, as I've demonstrated through much of this chapter, you can include content within a form, without using the label element. Since HTML5 is all about semantics, content that is a caption (or label) should be called a label by placing it in a label element.

The label element should be associated with the input element that it describes and there are two ways to do that. My personal preference is to simply embed the input element inside the label element. The other option is to use the for attribute of the label element. The for attribute specifies the id of the input type. Of course, this requires you to assign a unique id to the input element. Both of these techniques are shown here:

```
<p>Deliver to: <br />
    <label>
        Address:
        <input type="text" size="30" name="Address" />
    </label>
    <label>
        ZipCode:
        <input type="text" maxlength="5" size="5" name="Zip" />
    </label>
    <label for="telephone">Phone #:</label>
    <input type="tel" id="telephone" name="Phone" />
</p>
```

There is one advantage for using linked label elements (beyond better semantics). If you click a label element, the associated input element will be given the focus and the user can start entering data into it. In the previous example, if you click the **Deliver to:** text, nothing happens. But if you click the **Address:**, **ZipCode:**, or **Phone #:** text, the associated input element is selected.

Output Element

If forms have inputs then it seems reasonable that they can also have outputs, right? Well, prior to HTML5 that answer was no, but now we have the output element. This is used for calculated data that is generally based on the user's input but is not entered directly. For example, after choosing all of the pizza options, you would want to display the total amount due. This is precisely what the output element is for.

When the page is first loaded, you will probably not know the value of the output element. You can either use a default value like 0, or add the hidden attribute so it will not be displayed. Once the necessary inputs have been entered, you can perform the calculation on the client side and update the output element. In our pizza order example, however, you will probably need to submit the form to the server and the postback response will have set the contents of the output element.

You should add a label for the calculated value and you can nest this inside a `label` element like this:

```
<p>
    <label>Total due:
        <output id="total" name="Total">$0.00</output>
    </label>
</p>
```

The `output` element supports a `for` attribute where you can specify the `input` elements that were used to calculate this value. The `id` of each `input` element should be included in the `for` attribute, separated by a space.

Meter Element

The `meter` element is similar to the `range` element that I described earlier in that is displays a value, not as a specific number, but by its location along a scale. The value of a `meter` element cannot be changed by the user, however.

The `meter` element is analogous to the temperature gauge in a car. I don't really care if the temperature is 205° or 210°, I just want to know that it's *OK*. I was driving to work one day, and after driving for a while happened to notice that the temperature gauge was in the cool area. I thought that was interesting but was not too alarmed. Sometime later I saw that it was showing the engine was running hotter than normal; I thought that was even more interesting. Before long, it was off the scale and I knew I was in trouble. As you might have guessed, I had a stuck thermostat. At first it was stuck open and then it was stuck closed. The gauge told me everything I needed by presenting the value as simply cool, normal, hot, or pull over now!

The `meter` element works the same way. You specify the `min` and `max` attributes, which define the scale, and the `value` attribute is then displayed somewhere along that continuum. Like the temperature gauge, you can define ranges within that scale to indicate where the optimal values are. The `meter` element supports the `low`, `high`, and `optimum` attributes that define these ranges.

This can be a bit tricky to sort out, however, because the optimal range could be at the low or high end of the scale, or somewhere in the middle. How you set these attributes changes depending on each scenario. Figure 8-22 demonstrates each scenario and indicates how the attributes should be set for each.

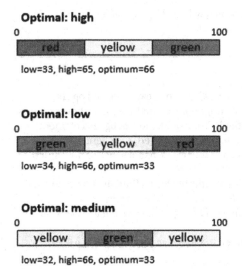

Optimal: high

0   100

low=33, high=65, optimum=66

Optimal: low

0   100

low=34, high=66, optimum=33

Optimal: medium

0   100

low=32, high=66, optimum=33

Figure 8-22. *Defining the optimal range*

To test this out, the following markup will create three meter elements for each scenario, setting the value attribute on each to test all three ranges. The resulting content as rendered in Chrome is shown in Figure 8-23.

```
<p>Meter examples:<br />
    <meter min="0" max="100" low="33" high="65" optimum="66" value="25"></meter>
    <meter min="0" max="100" low="33" high="65" optimum="66" value="50"></meter>
    <meter min="0" max="100" low="33" high="65" optimum="66" value="75"></meter>
    Optimal: high<br />
    <meter min="0" max="100" low="34" high="66" optimum="33" value="25"></meter>
    <meter min="0" max="100" low="34" high="66" optimum="33" value="50"></meter>
    <meter min="0" max="100" low="34" high="66" optimum="33" value="75"></meter>
    Optimal: low<br />
    <meter min="0" max="100" low="32" high="66" optimum="33" value="25"></meter>
    <meter min="0" max="100" low="32" high="66" optimum="33" value="50"></meter>
    <meter min="0" max="100" low="32" high="66" optimum="33" value="75"></meter>
    Optimal: medium<br />
</p>
```

Meter examples:

Optimal: high
Optimal: low
Optimal: medium

Figure 8-23. *The meter element in Chrome*

155

You can provide fallback content inside the meter element, which will be displayed if the browser doesn't support the meter element.

Progress Element

The progress element is similar to the meter element except you don't have the low, high, and optimum attributes. It also has a very specific semantic purpose - to display progress. You might want to show progress on a single form, for example. Suppose there were seven input fields. You could add a progress element with a min attribute set to 0 and a max attribute set to 7. As each input field is entered, the client-side code could increment the value of the progress element by one. This gives the user a visual sense of how much work is left.

Another example that is perhaps more useful, is when there are multiple forms that must be submitted. If you're applying for a job, for example, there could be different forms to enter such as education, experience, contact details, etc. Providing a progress element on each form provides visual feedback on where they are in the overall process.

A simple progress element is created like this. This is rendered in Firefox as shown in Figure 8-24.

```
<p>Progress example:
    <progress min="0" max="7" value="3">
        Your browser does not support the progress element! Value is 3 of 7.
    </progress>
</p>
```

Progress example: ▓▓▓▓▓░░░░░░░░

Figure 8-24. *The progress bar in Firefox*

You should include fallback text if the information in the element is important in case the browser doesn't support it. For example, since Safari does not support the progress element, this is rendered as shown in Figure 8-25.

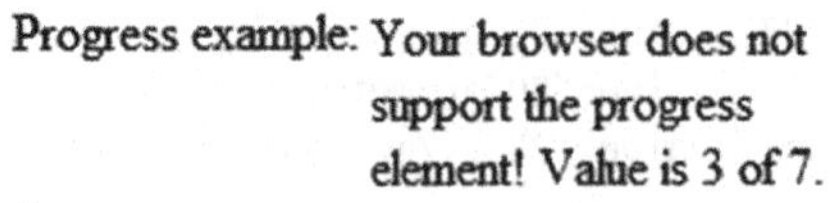

Progress example: Your browser does not support the progress element! Value is 3 of 7.

Figure 8-25. *The progress bar in Safari*

Button Types

In a typical form you will have content that provides information to the user, input elements where users enter information, and buttons that initiate actions. I've already demonstrated a submit button using an input element with the type attribute set to submit. There are actually two ways to create form buttons; the first, as I've already demonstrated, is to use the input element with an appropriate type (there are four types that will generate a button). The second approach is to use the button element, which also supports the type attribute and there are three different types that are essentially equivalent to the input types.

The input element supports the following button types:

- submit - when clicked, this will submit the form.

- reset - when clicked, this will clear the input elements and return the form to its original values.

- image - functions like the submit type but supports a src attribute to specify an image to be used for the button.

- button - this creates a button with no default action. You can use this to implement custom actions using JavaScript.

The button element supports the following type values:

- submit - submits a form, just like the submit input type.

- reset - resets a form, just like the reset input type.

- button - a button with no defined action, just like the button input type.

Using the input types has been the long-time standard for web forms, the button element being somewhat newer. There were some issues with older browsers not handling the button element properly but this is not a significant consideration anymore.

The input element as I explained earlier, has no content. The text of the button is set through the value attribute and the src attribute can be used to specify an image (for the image type only). However, the button element does have content inside it so you have more flexibility; you can use any type of phrasing content. For this reason, there is no need for a separate image type with the button element; all button elements can include images. Also, since the button element uses regular content (not through attributes), you have more styling options, including the ::before and ::after pseudo elements.

Changing the input element to a button element has no effect on the page:

```
<!--<input type="submit" value="Submit" />-->
<button type="submit">Submit</button>
```

Organizing a Form

A well laid-out form will have groups of related information organized into logical sections. In our pizza order, for example, the user will pick the crust, choose the toppings, select additional side dishes, enter the delivery details, etc. Grouping the various input elements along these lines will make the ordering process easier to follow.

This is certainly true with checkboxes and especially radio buttons. In our crust example, there were three radio buttons, each selecting a different type of crust. By setting the name attribute to the same value on all of them, the browser can automatically deselect the others when one is selected. But the name attribute is not visible to the user, and there is no visual clue that these three input elements go together.

The fieldset element is used to provide the visual grouping of these input elements. It will cause a box to be drawn around the input elements. You can also include a legend element inside the fieldset element to define the text that is displayed with the box. For example, the toppings and crust selections from our previous example, can use the fieldset and legend elements like this:

```
<fieldset>
    <legend>Toppings:</legend>
    <input type="checkbox" name="Topping" value="Mushrooms" />Mushrooms?
    <input type="checkbox" name="Topping" value="Sausage" />Sausage?
```

```
        <input type="checkbox" name="Topping" value="Olives" />Olives?
</fieldset>
<fieldset>
    <legend>Crust:</legend>
    <input type="radio" name="Crust" value="Thin" required />Thin
    <input type="radio" name="Crust" value="Thick" />Thick
    <input type="radio" name="Crust" value="DeepDish" />Deep Dish
</fieldset>
```

The page is then rendered as shown in Figure 8-26.

Figure 8-26. *Using fieldset and legend elements*

The fieldset element supports a disabled attribute. If this is included, all the input elements within the fieldset will be disabled.

■ **Caution**   The fieldset element supports a name attribute; this does not replace the name attribute on the individual input elements. The name attribute on the input element is used when submitting the form and is also used in grouping radio buttons.

Validation

You should always provide server-side validation when a form is submitted and not rely on the client-side validation. However, that is outside the scope of this book. You should also provide as much client-side validation as practical. Finding validation errors on the client side will generally provide a better user experience.

The first step is to use the most appropriate input type. You can use a standard textbox for every input field, but using a more specific one will often enable some built-in validation. For example, using a date picker is much better that having to verify a valid date string was entered.

The next step is to define all applicable constraint validation. For example, you can set the maxlength attribute on all textual input types. If your database column only holds 30 characters, you should set the maxlength attribute on the input element to **30** to prevent truncation errors. Where applicable, use the pattern attribute to ensure the data is valid. If you have a field that should not have any spaces in it, set the pattern attribute to check that before the form is submitted.

Provide hints in the placeholder attribute so the user knows what is expected. This will not ensure the data is entered this way, but it will help clarify the field format to the user and will likely minimize validation errors. Use the required attribute to specify which fields must be filled in. In addition to providing validation when submitted, you can also style these fields to make it clear to the user that they are required.

■ **Tip** Mozilla provides a good article on client-side form validation: `https://developer.mozilla.org/en-US/docs/Web/Guide/HTML/Forms/Data_form_validation`. I recommend reviewing this and applying any of the techniques that are applicable. Some of these require JavaScript and I will cover some of them in Section 4.

Summary

In this chapter I explained how forms are submitted and the `input` element that is used to collect this information. The same `input` element is used for almost every type of information. The `type` attribute is used to indicate the specific data input and validation that should be used. These types are listed in the reference information in Appendix C.

In this chapter I explained the capabilities that are provided by most major browsers. There are a few that have somewhat limited support, as of this writing, which I have pointed out. You should be able to use everything I have demonstrated with confidence that most of your users will have a good experience. Check with sites such as `html5test.com`, to see the latest browser support, as new capabilities are released periodically.

This concludes the section on HTML markup elements. The next section, which includes Chapters 9–15, will explore the capabilities of CSS that allow you to style the content. The next chapter will demonstrate the CSS selectors that define the elements a style rule is applied to.

PART III

CSS

Once you have the HTML content created, you'll use CSS to define the style rules used to format the content. As you'll see, there is a lot that you can do with CSS. This is actually the longest of the three sections because of the variety of features available to dramatically alter the presentation of the HTML document.

This section contains the following chapters:

- 9) Selectors – each CSS rule includes a selector that determines which elements it should be applied to; this chapter describes the capabilities that exist to build these selectors.

- 10) Layout and positioning – this chapter explains how elements are positioned relative to the other elements and the various methods available for controlling their arrangement.

- 11) Text – this chapter demonstrates how to select the font and the font characteristics, text alignment, and spacing, as well as numerous special effects, including shadows and decorations.

- 12) Borders and background – this chapter shows you how colors, images, gradients, and various styles can be used to configure the background and borders of elements.

- 13) Tables – this chapter covers both styling tabular data as well as using table constructs to arrange non-tabular elements.

- 14) Flex – this chapter demonstrates how the flexbox model is used to define dynamic page layouts.

- 15) Animation – this chapter explains how you can create animations using CSS as well as transformation and transitions.

CHAPTER 9

CSS Selectors

In Chapter 2 I presented an overview of how HTML is styled using cascading style sheets. A style sheet is a set of styling rules, and each rule consists of a selector and one or more declarations. A selector determines what elements the rule should apply to; the declaration specifies a style attribute that is being set. In this chapter I will demonstrate the capabilities that are available when constructing the selectors. The remaining chapters in this section will explain all the wonderful things you can do with CSS once you've selected the appropriate elements.

For a quick review, if you wanted all the paragraph elements to use a green 12px font, the style rule would look like this:

```
p {
    color:green;
    font-size:12px;
}
```

The first part, p, is the selector. This simply selects all paragraph (p) elements. There are two declarations inside the curly braces: one sets the color attribute, the other sets the font-size.

Selector Overview

A selector will choose zero or more elements from the HTML document based on some aspect of the elements. There are six types of selectors, each one using different information in the element to make the selection. These selector types are:

- Element selectors (sometimes called type selectors)
- Class selectors
- ID selectors
- Attribute selectors
- Pseudo-class selectors
- Pseudo-elements

Element Selectors

The first one that I just showed you is an element selector, which is also known as a type selector. To use this, simply specify the element type such as p, h1, input, ol, div, and so on. In the previous section of this book, I demonstrated all of the available HTML elements.

As I stressed numerous times, choosing the appropriate element provides rich semantic information. If you have been careful to choose the elements correctly and consistently, you will have a great advantage when applying styles. These context-specific elements communicate their purpose more clearly and therefore make it more likely that consistent formatting will be applied to all content.

Class Selectors

Of course, it would be naïve to think that all styling could be done through element selectors alone. You will likely have content that needs to have unique styles applied. This is where the class selector comes in.

All HTML elements support the class attribute; it's one of the global attributes. The class attribute can contain a space-separated list of classes. For example:

```
<p class="featured new">some text...</p>
```

This element has two classes, featured and new. The class selector allows you to select elements with a specific class attribute. For this reason, the class attribute is often referred to as the CSS class. A class selector is created by prefixing the class name with a dot (.) like this:

```
.featured {
    background-color:yellow;
}
```

This will apply the background-color attribute for all elements that have the featured class. The class selector looks for whole words that match the selector value.

ID Selectors

An ID selector works just like a class selector except that it uses the id attribute instead of class and you prefix it with a hash symbol (#) like this:

```
#Submit {
    color:blue;
}
```

An ID selector specifies a single element based on its unique ID, so, by definition, the style will not be reused. It is better to define styles based on elements or classes so similar elements can be styled the same way. ID selectors should be used sparingly and only for unique situations where the style does not need to be reused.

Attribute Selectors

Attribute selectors give you a great deal of flexibility, allowing you to select elements based on any of the element's attributes. These are specified as [attribute=value] like this:

```
 [class="book"] {
    background-color:yellow;
}
```

This is functionally equivalent to using the `.book` class selector; however, the attribute selector allows you to perform the match using only portions of the attribute's value. To do that, prefix the equal sign (`=`) with one of the following:

- ~ (for example, `[class~="book"]`): The attribute value must include the word indicated by the selector value (for example, `class="some book titles"`). This is exactly how the class selector works.

- | (for example, `[class|="book"]`): The attribute value must begin with a word that matches the selector value (for example, `class="book titles"`)

- ^= (for example, `[class^="book"]`): The attribute value must begin with the selector value (for example, `class="books"`)

- $ (for example, `[class$="book"]`): The attribute value must end with the selector value (for example, `class="checkbook"`)

- * (for example, `[class*="book"]`): The attribute value must contain the selector value (for example, `class="overbooked"`)

You can specify the attribute without a value, which will return all elements that have the attribute. A good example of this is the `[href]` selector, which will select all elements that have the `href` attribute, regardless of its value. You can also include an element selector before an attribute selector to further restrict the selected elements. For example, this will return all `img` elements whose `src` attribute begin with `https`:

```
img[src^="https"] {
    color:blue;
}
```

This example is combining an element selector with an attribute selector. When combined like that, they form a logical AND operation. It will select elements that are images AND the `src` attribute begins with `https`. Similarly, you can combine multiple attribute selectors such as:

```
[src^="https"][target="_self"] {
}
```

This will further restrict the selected elements to only this that have the `_self` target.

Pseudo-Class Selectors

Pseudo-classes are like regular class attributes except they are added automatically by the browser instead of set in the HTML markup. Pseudo-classes are prefixed with a colon (`:`). Many of these are dynamically applied depending on the state of the elements. Consider a hyperlink, for example. If the link has already been navigated, the link is usually displayed with a different color. This is achieved using a CSS rule like this, which will change the color of all elements that have the `:visited` pseudo-class.

```
:visited {
    color: blue;
}
```

Here is the complete list of pseudo-classes:

- `:active` - Selects the link that has just been clicked.

- `:checked` - Selects elements that are checked (applies to checkboxes).

- `:default` - Selects the default element on a form, usually the submit button.

- `:disabled` - Selects elements that are currently disabled (typically used for input elements.)

- `:empty` - Selects elements that have no children (elements that include text are not selected).

- `:enabled` - Selects elements that are enabled (typically used for input elements).

- `:first-child` - Selects the elements that are the first child of its immediate parent.

- `<tag>:first-of-type` - Selects the elements that is the first of the specified type within its parent.

- `:focus` - Selects the element that currently has the focus.

- `:hover` - Selects the element that the mouse is currently hovering over.

- `:in-range` - Selects input elements that have values within the specified range.

- `:indeterminate` - Selects radio buttons where none in a group have been selected. This will also select checkboxes that have the indeterminate state (this must be set through JavaScript).

- `:invalid` - Selects input elements that do not have a valid value.

- `:lang(value)` - Selects the elements that have a `lang` attribute that start with the specified value.

- `:last-child` - Selects the elements that are the last child within its parent.

- `<tag>:last-of-type` - Selects the elements that are the last of the specified type within its parent.

- `:link` - Selects all unvisited links.

- `:nth-child(n)` - Selects the elements that are the nth child within its parent.

- `:nth-last-child(n)` - Selects the elements that are the nth child within its parent, counting in reverse.

- `<tag>:nth-last-of-type(n)` - Selects the nth child of the specified type within its parent, counting in reverse.

- `<tag>:nth-of-type(n)` - Selects the nth child of the specified type within its parent.

- `:only-child` - Selects the elements that are the only child element of its parent.

- `<tag>:only-of-type` - Selects the elements that are the only sibling of the specified type within its parent.

- `:optional` - Selects input elements that are not required (that is, do not have the `required` attribute).

- `:out-of-range` - selects input elements whose value is outside of the allowed range.

- `:read-only` - Selects input elements that have the `readonly` attribute.

- :read-write - Selects input elements that do not have the readonly attribute.

- :required - Selects input elements that have the required attribute.

- :root - Selects the root element of the document.

- :target - Selects the elements with a target attribute where the target is the active element.

- :valid - Selects input elements that have a valid value.

- :visited - Selects all visited links.

■ **Caution** There are four pseudo-classes that can be used with an anchor (a) element (:link, :visited, :hover, and :active). If you use more than one, they should appear in this order in the style rules. For example, :hover must come after :link and :visited if they are used. Likewise, :active must come after :hover. You can use this simple mnemonic to help you remember the correct order: LoVe HAte.

The nth-child(n) selector counts all child elements of the parent, while the nth-of-type(n) counts only child elements of the specified type. The distinction here is subtle but important. The same is true with the only-child and only-of-type selectors.

■ **Tip** There's a really useful article that explains the pseudo-classes with examples that you can find at https://www.smashingmagazine.com/2016/05/an-ultimate-guide-to-css-pseudo-classes-and-pseudo-elements/. Take a look at this if you would like more information and a demonstration of how these work.

Pseudo-Elements

While pseudo-classes provide a mechanism for selecting elements, pseudo-*elements* actually return new, virtual elements that you can style without actually being part of the DOM. These are either empty elements or a portion of an existing element.

Pseudo-elements start with a double colon (::) to distinguish them from pseudo-classes. These are the pseudo-elements that are available:

- ::after - this creates an empty element just after the selected elements.

- ::before - this creates an empty element just before the selected elements.

- ::first-letter: Selects the first character of every selected element.

- ::first-line: Selects the first line of every selected element. The first line is the portion of text up to the point where the text wraps to the next line.

- ::selection : Returns the portion of an element that is selected by the user.

■ **Note** The double-colon syntax was introduced with CSS3; prior to that, a single colon was used for both pseudo-classes and pseudo-elements. For backward compatibility, most browsers will allow a single colon for either.

You can add the ::before or ::after qualifiers to a selector to insert content in the document before or after the selected elements. Use the content: keyword to specify the content and include any desired style commands (the style applies only to the inserted content). For example, to add "Important!" before each p tag that immediately follows a header tag, use the following rule. This will also style the "Important!" text with a bold, red font.

```
header+p:before {
    content:"Important! ";
    font-weight:bold;
    color:red;
}
```

■ **Caution**   Content that is inserted using the ::after or ::before pseudo-elements is generated by CSS and is not part of the DOM. There are a couple of side effects that you should be aware of. First, the text cannot be selected – if you were to copy and paste content from the web page, the extra generated content would be omitted. Second, some screen readers don't support it so the text will not be read. Don't use these for critical information as there are cases when it won't be available.

There are some restrictions on what style attribute can be set using the ::first-letter and ::first-line pseudo-elements. Essentially, you can use any of the font or background attributes. With the ::first-letter pseudo-element you can also include margin, padding, and border attributes.

Also, these pseudo-elements are only supported when block layout is used. I will explain the layout options in Chapter 10.

Using Combinators

The different types of selectors that I just described can also be combined to perform more complex selections.

Combining Element and Class Selectors

You can combine element and class selectors by simply appending the class selectors. For example, this will select all paragraph elements that have the featured class:

```
p.featured {
}
```

Using the same syntax, you can also combine multiple class selectors. These will be processed with the logical AND operator. For example, this selects all paragraph elements that have both the featured and new classes:

```
p.featured.new {
}
```

Pseudo-Selectors

Pseudo-class selectors are often combined with an element selector, for example:

```
a:visited {
}
```

This selects all anchor tags that have been visited already. In this case, the pseudo-class further refines the element selector. They can also be combined with a class selector such as:

```
.featured:focus {
}
```

However, pseudo-classes can also stand on their own. A common example of this is the :default pseudo-class, which selects the default element, which is typically the submit button on a form:

```
:default {
}
```

However, pseudo-elements will always modify either an element or class selector. These don't actually select an element; they either return a portion of a selected element or a new empty element before or after the selected element. Therefore, they must be preceded with some sort of actual selector.

Combinator Operators

You can combine selectors to specify certain element hierarchies. By combining elements with one of the following *combinators*, you can create a more complex selector:

- **Group ,** (for example p, h1): A logical OR operator, selects all p elements as well as all h1 elements.

- **Descendant** space (for example, header p): Selects the second element when it is inside the first element. For example, if you want all p elements that are inside a header element, use header p. The header element does not have to be the immediate parent, just somewhere in the node's ancestry.

- **Child** > (for example header>p): Selects the second element when the first element is the immediate parent. The header>p selector returns all p elements whose immediate parent is a header element.

- **Adjacent Sibling** + (for example header+p): Selects the second element when the first element is the preceding sibling of the second element.

- **Follows** ~ (for example p~header): Selects the second element when it follows the first element (not necessarily immediately).

To illustrate the last two, if your document looks like the following, the h1+p selector will not return any element, but both h2+p and h1~p will both return the p element:

```
<h1>Some header</h1>
<h2>Some sub-header</h2>
<p>Some text</p>
```

The asterisk (*) is used as the universal selector; it is basically a wildcard that will match all elements. Combining it with other selectors generally has no affect. However, it can be useful when combining operators. Consider the following selector:

```
h2 * p {
}
```

Notice the space before and after the asterisk; they are descendant operators. Using just h2* by itself will select all elements that are a descendant of an h2 element. Adding another descendant operator will select elements that are a descendant of a descendant. This, will return all paragraph elements that are a grandchild (or later descendant) of an h2 element.

■ **Tip** Spaces between selectors and operators are ignored. So header>p and header > p are equivalent. However, it important to remember that a space between selectors (including the universal selector, *) indicates the descendant operator. So h2 * p contains three selectors, each combined with the descendant operator.

Similarly, using h2>*>p will return all paragraph elements that are grandchildren of an h2 element. Only grandchildren are selected because the > combinator is specific to a child relationship, not a general descendant like the space combinator.

The Not Selector

You can also prefix any selector with :not to return all the elements not selected. However, the selector cannot start with :not; you must start with another selector. For example, this selects all elements in the body except header elements:

```
body:not(header) {
    color:purple;
}
```

Group Operator

If you want to apply the same declarations to more than one element type, you can group them like this:

```
p, h1, h2
{
    color:green;
    font-size:12px;
}
```

The comma (,) character serves as a logical OR operation, for example, "all elements of type p OR h1 OR h2". You can also combine complex selectors in a logical OR relationship by separating them with commas. Each selector can be any of the more complex types. For example, this is also a valid selector:

```
header+p, .book, a:visited {
}
```

It will return all elements that are either a paragraph element that immediately follows a header element, an element with the book class, or a visited anchor element.

Resolving Conflicts

With all of this ability to write complex selectors, it is inevitable that two or more rules will specify conflicting styles. Having a well-organized HTML document with appropriate element usage will certainly help. Along the same lines, applying consistent and well-named class attributes will also minimize conflicts.

To troubleshoot issues that do arise, you'll need to understand how the CSS rules are applied. The order that styles are applied is based on where they are defined. The rule specificity is also a significant factor. I covered both of these topics in Chapter 2.

Media Queries

CSS 2.1 introduced the `media` keyword, allowing you to define a printer-friendly style sheet. For example, you can use something like this:

```
<link rel="stylesheet" href="Initial.css" />
<link rel="stylesheet" href="Print.css" media="print" />
```

You can then define one style sheet for browsers (screen) and a different style sheet for the print version of your web page. Alternatively, you can embed media-specific style rules within a single style sheet. For example, this will change the font size when printed:

```
@media print
{
    h1, h2, h3
    {
        font-size: 14px;
    }
}
```

■ **Tip**   There are other media types that are supported including `aural`, `braille`, `handheld`, `projection`, `tty`, and `tv`. As you can see, the media type was initially used to represent the type of device that is rendering the page. Also, the `all` type is supported but is also implied if no media type is specified. Styles with the `all` type are applied for every device.

Media Attributes

With CSS3, this has been enhanced significantly to allow you to query various attributes to determine the appropriate styles. For example, you can apply a style when the width of the window is 600px or smaller like this:

```
@media (max-width:600px)
{
    h1
    {
        font-size: 12px;
    }
}
```

The features that can be selected in a media query are as follows:

- width
- height
- device-width
- device-height
- orientation
- aspect-ratio
- device-aspect-ratio
- color (0 if monochrome or number of bits used to specify a color)
- color-index (number of colors available)
- monochrome (0 if color, or number of bits for grayscale)
- resolution (specified in dpi or dpcm)
- scan (for TV, specifies scanning mode)
- grid (1 if a grid device such as TTY display, 0 if bitmap)

Most of these support min- and max- prefixes, which means you don't have to use a greater-than or lesser-than operator. For example, if you wanted a style for windows between 500px and 700px, inclusive, you would specify this as follows:

@media screen and (min-width: 500px) and (max-width: 700px)

Notice in this example I also included the screen media type. In this case, this style is ignored for all other types such as print.

■ **Tip**   For a complete definition on each of these features, see the W3 specification at www.w3.org/TR/css3-mediaqueries/#media1.

Using Media Queries

There is a lot that you can do with media queries to dynamically style your web page. For example, you could use the color and monochrome features to apply more appropriate styles when displayed on a monochrome device. The color feature returns the number of colors supported, so (min-color: 2) will select all color devices. You can also use (orientation: portrait) and (orientation: landscape) to arrange the elements based on the device's orientation.

One of the most common use of media queries is to determine the width of the window. As the width of the window shrinks, the styles will gradually adjust to accommodate the size while retaining as much of the original layout as possible. This is known as a *responsive* web design.

A typical approach is to plan for three different styles: large, medium, and small. The large style is probably how the site is initially designed for desktop users. There may be sidebars and multiple columns of content. The medium style will keep the same basic layout but start to shrink areas as needed. A useful technique is to use relative sizing so as the window shrinks, each element gradually shrinks as well. The small style will be used for handheld devices, and you'll generally keep the layout to a single column. Since the page will tend to be longer now, links to bookmarks on the page become more important.

Summary

In this chapter, I have explained the various ways to select elements from your HTML document. Element selectors will be of great use, especially if the HTML was marked up consistently with the appropriate elements. Class selectors will give you even finer control of how styles are applied. The pseudo-class and pseudo-element selectors provide an impressive suite of capabilities, allowing dynamic styling of your document.

Each of these selectors can be combined using several combinators that allow you to select elements based on where they are in the document relative to other elements. The grouping combinator allows you to apply a set of declarations to multiple selectors.

Finally, you can use media queries to adjust your styles based on the device that is being used. This will enable you to build a responsive web page that renders well on any device.

In the next chapter, I'll demonstrate the CSS techniques available for controlling the layout and positioning the content.

CHAPTER 10

■ ■ ■

Positioning Content

In Chapter 2 I explained the basic box model, and in this chapter I'll demonstrate how each "box" is positioned relative to the other content on the page. Each HTML element takes up a certain amount of space, which is defined as a rectangle; it has a height and a width. In addition, the padding, border, and margin contributes to the space that must be allocated.

So an HTML document can be thought of a series of boxes. In Chapter 4 I explained the structural elements that define the larger boxes, such as the header, section, and article elements. These define the structure of your document. Within these you'll place smaller elements such as paragraph and image elements. And within the paragraph elements you include lots of small boxes using the phrasing elements I described in Chapter 5, such as strong, emphasis, and span elements.

In the previous chapters I told you not to worry about how all of this content would be arranged. The focus of the HTML document is to organize the content in a logical fashion, in a - this belongs to that - line of reasoning. Now it's time to worry! There are several concepts that you need to understand to effectively lay out the content of an HTML document, which I will explain in this chapter.

Display

The most fundamental attribute regarding layout in CSS is the display attribute. There are two basic options: block and inline. There are other supported values, which I'll explain later. But for now, I'll focus on these two (and the none option).

- block - the element uses the entire width of its parent element. Additional blocked elements are then stacked vertically, just below the previous element.

- inline - the element is arranged horizontally. Each inline element is placed to the right of the previous elements (assuming left-to-right direction is used). If there is not enough room for the element, some or all of the element content is wrapped to the next row.

- none - the element is not rendered at all. Not only is the content hidden, but it doesn't take up any space on the screen.

Browsers do a great job defaulting CSS properties so elements are rendered in a reasonable fashion without needing to add any CSS rules. Each element has a default value for the display attribute, for example. The structural elements such as section, article, and div are all block elements (by default). Phrasing content such as strong and emphasis are inline elements. The paragraph element, being the notable exception, is a blocked element because a paragraph normally takes up the entire width of a page or section.

© Mark J. Collins 2017
M. J. Collins, *Pro HTML5 with CSS, JavaScript, and Multimedia*, DOI 10.1007/978-1-4842-2463-2_10

The following HTML provides a simple demonstration of this. This contains five div elements and five span elements with simple text content.

```
<div>div 1</div>
<div>div 2</div>
<div>div 3</div>
<div>div 4</div>
<div>div 5</div>
<span>span 1 - blah blah</span>
<span>span 2 - blah blah</span>
<span>span 3 - blah blah</span>
<span>span 4 - blah blah</span>
<span>span 5 - blah blah</span>
```

To make the layout easier to visualize, I'll add the following CSS rule. This will put a thin border around each div or span element and a small space between the borders.

```
div, span {
    border: 1px solid black;
    margin: 1px;
}
```

This will be rendered as shown in Figure 10-1.

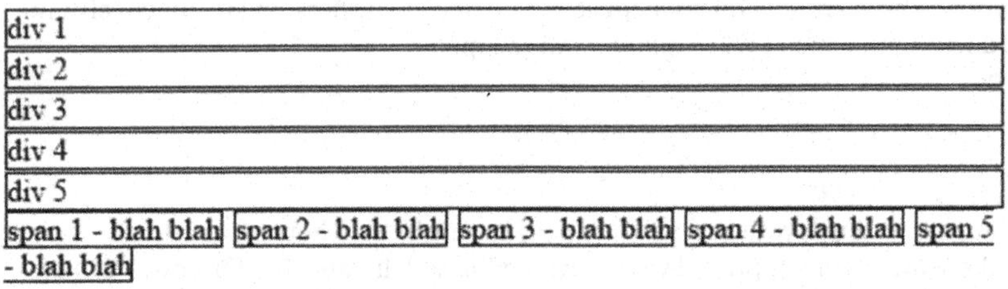

Figure 10-1. *Default display alignment*

You can see that the div elements are stacked vertically, while the span elements are arranged horizontally. Of course, you can override the default settings. Adding display: inline; to the CSS rule, will cause both elements to be arranged horizontally as shown in Figure 10-2.

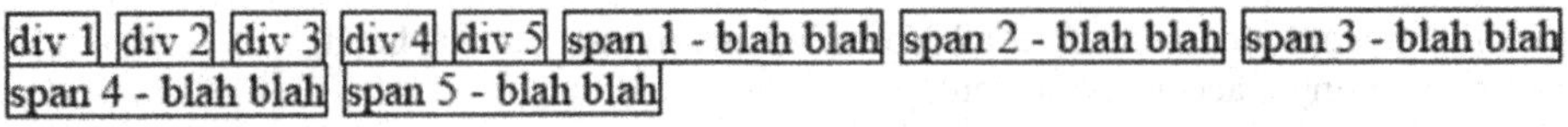

Figure 10-2. *Using inline formatting*

■ **Tip**   Regarding the display: none; setting, as I mentioned this causes the page to be rendered as if the element were not there. Alternatively, you could set the visibility attribute to hidden (visibility: hidden;), which would also hide the content, but it would leave an empty space on the page where the element would be shown if it were not hidden. There are important applications of both approaches and it's important to know how each works.

A block element takes up the entire width of its container. In the previous example, this was the width of the browser window. If nested inside another element, it will only use the space available within its parent. To demonstrate that, this markup creates three div elements inside a parent element:

```
<div class="container">container
    <div>div a</div>
    <div>div b</div>
    <div>div c</div>
</div>
```

Notice that I've given the parent element a class attribute. This will allow me to set its width attribute using a class selector like this:

```
.container {
    width: 150px;
}
```

These div elements are then rendered as shown in Figure 10-3.

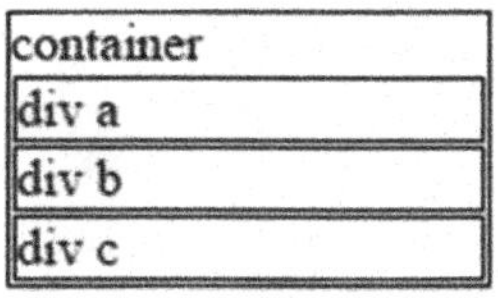

Figure 10-3. *Including div elements in a parent div*

Defining Sizes

There are numerous ways to define the size of an element and there are consequences with each of these methods.

Absolute Size

In the previous example, I set the width attribute, giving it an absolute width of 150 pixels. You can also set the height attribute as well. This will force that much space to be allocated whether it is needed or not, and whether it is available or not – the latter being somewhat more problematic.

If the space is not available, the element will overrun its container. If the outer container is the browser window and the element size exceeds the window size, a scroll bar will appear so you can scroll to see the missing content. While horizontal scrolling should be avoided, this is not terribly bad, as the content is still viewable.

Consider, however, if the container is just a portion of the document and there is other content around it. To demonstrate what happens, in the previous example, we can set the height attribute also, like this:

```
.container {
    width: 150px;
    height: 100px;
}
```

This fixes the height at 100px. There is a little extra space in the container. However, if you add a couple more div elements inside this container and some additional content afterwards, you'll see the overrun issue, which is shown in Figure 10-4. In the screenshot I have zoomed in to make it easier to see.

```
<div class="container">container
    <div>div a</div>
    <div>div b</div>
    <div>div c</div>
    <div>div d</div>
    <div>div e</div>
</div>
<div>More content</div>
```

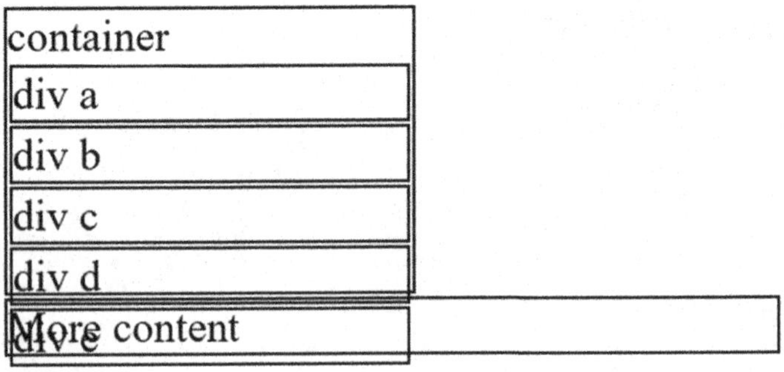

Figure 10-4. *Demonstrating the overrun issue*

Part of div d and all of div e is outside of the container element and superimposed on top of the more content div. Hopefully by now you see the fallacy of setting absolute sizes, especially when setting the height. This really boxes you in (pun intended) and makes your page susceptible to numerous scenarios that can break the layout. Consider, for example, if the page is translated and the translation uses more characters than the original text. Also, if the user-specified CSS increases the font size, your layout could break.

Relative Size

I mentioned briefly in Chapter 2 that distance units can also be expressed as a percentage. Instead of specifying the width as a fixed size, say 300px, you can specify it as a percentage. This will be a percentage of the element's immediate parent:

```
.container {
    width: 70%;
}
```

Using relative sizing is helpful when creating responsive web pages as the size will automatically adjust based on the available space.

Setting Maximum Values

If you're primarily dealing with text, defining the width of a container is useful to constrain the area that will contain the text. The text will be wrapped as needed to fit within the specified area. However, if the available space is less than that, the content will overrun this area as I illustrated previously.

A simple improvement to deal with this is to use the max-width attribute instead of width. Replace both declarations in the CSS rule with max-width:

```
.container {
    max-width: 300px;
}
```

By removing the height attribute, the vertical overrun is solved. By replacing width with max-width, if the window size is reduced, the container will shrink as needed to fit into the current window. To better demonstrate these, let put some additional text in these div elements. Replace the container div and all of its child elements with the following content. Each element will be wrapped, as necessary, to fit into a 300px div as shown in Figure 10-5.

```
<div class="container">container
    <div>Fourscore and 20 years ago,</div>
    <div>our fathers brought forth to this continent</div>
    <div>a new nation, conceived in liberty</div>
    <div>and dedicated to the proposition</div>
    <div>that all men are created equal</div>
    <div>Now we are engaged in a great civil war, testing where that nation, or any</div>
    <div>nation, so conceived, so dedicated, can long endure.</div>
</div>
```

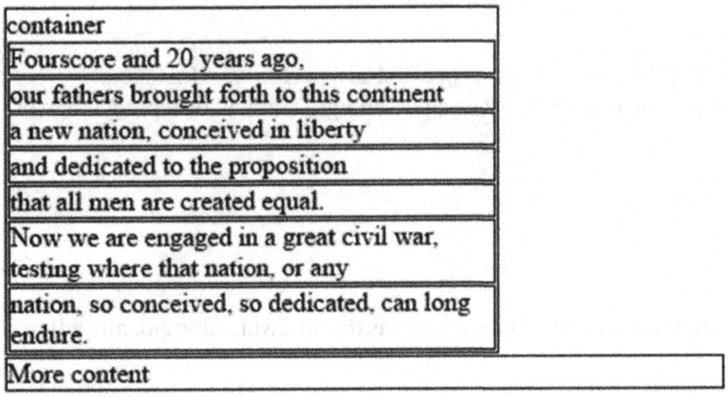

Figure 10-5. *Wrapping using the max-width attribute*

Content-Based

There are two settings that you can use to define the width of an element based on its contents:

- min-content - uses the smallest possible area that will fit the content after taking advantage of all of the wrapping opportunities.

- max-content - uses the smallest space needed without wrapping any content.

To demonstrate this, set the height and width attributes using max-content. This will be rendered in most browsers as shown in Figure 10-6. The width of the container will be based on the width of the widest element inside it. The height is based on the total size of all child elements.

```
.container {
    width: -moz-max-content;
    height: -moz-max-content;
    width: max-content;
    height: max-content;
}
```

■ **Note**   Firefox requires the prefixed versions, as of this writing.

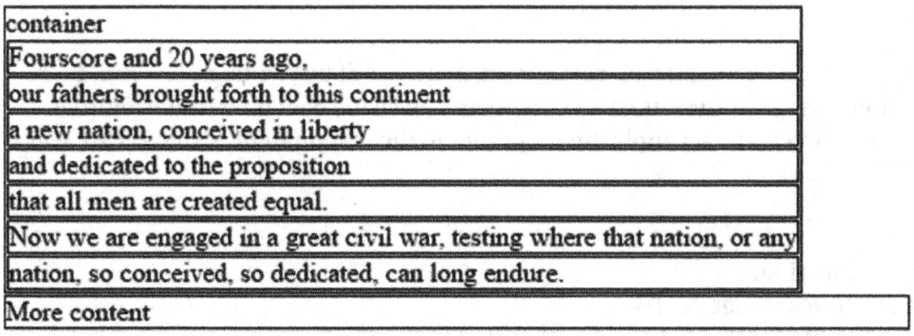

container
Fourscore and 20 years ago,
our fathers brought forth to this continent
a new nation, conceived in liberty
and dedicated to the proposition
that all men are created equal.
Now we are engaged in a great civil war, testing where that nation, or any
nation, so conceived, so dedicated, can long endure.
More content

Figure 10-6. *Using max-content*

If you use min-content instead of max-content, the content will be rendered as shown in Figure 10-7. The width is now based on the largest non-wrappable content, which happens to be the word "proposition." If there were other types of content such as images, the widest one would determine the container width.

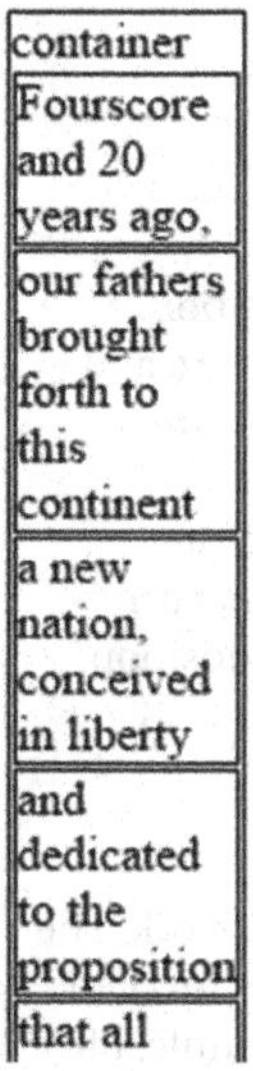

container
Fourscore and 20 years ago,
our fathers brought forth to this continent
a new nation, conceived in liberty
and dedicated to the proposition
that all

Figure 10-7. *Using min-content*

IE Work Around

Neither IE nor Edge support the min-content and max-content attributes, as of this writing. However, there is a workaround using the custom -ms-grid attribute. You have to first place the container inside another parent element (grandparent, actually) and then apply the properties to the grandparent. So the HTML will look like this:

```
<div class="grandParent">
    <div class="container">container
        <div>Fourscore and 20 years ago,</div>
        <div>our fathers brought forth to this continent</div>
        ...
    </div>
</div>
```

I set the class attribute so it can be styled using this additional rule:

```
.grandParent {
    border: none;
    margin: 0px;
    display:  -ms-grid;
    -ms-grid-columns: max-content;
}
```

The new grandparent div, is only used to assign the styling attributes; we don't want an extra box drawn. So the border and margin attributes are cleared. Then the display attribute is set to -ms-grid and the custom -ms-grid-columns attribute is set. Because these are prefixed attributes or values, they are ignored by all other browsers except IE and Edge.

With these changes in place, the page will be rendered in all other browsers just like it was before. However, IE9 and above and Edge browsers will also display the content the same way. You can also use min-content instead of max-content and the size of the container will be based on the word "proposition."

Min-Content Example

The previous example is somewhat contrived to demonstrate how min-content and max-content work. The min-content attribute is most useful when you have a mixture of content such as images and text. Text can be wrapped to fit almost any size container but images cannot. To demonstrate a more useful example, I'll use a figure element with a rather long caption. Here is the markup:

```
<figure>
    <img src="HTML5Badge.png" alt="HTML5 Badge" />
    <figcaption>
        The HTML5 badge is a well-recognized symbol in the web design community.
    </figcaption>
</figure>
```

The figure element has two child elements, an image and a caption. I explained this in Chapter 4 as the preferred method including a caption with an image.

By default, this uses block layout so the caption will be below the image and will take the entire width of its container, the figure element. The figure element is also a block element so it takes up the entire width of the window. If the window is wide enough, the rather long caption will be displayed on a single line.

Ideally, you would like the caption to be wrapped as needed so it stays under the image. Here's where the min-content attribute is really helpful. Adding the following CSS rule will do exactly that.

```
figure {
    border: 1px solid black;
    margin: 1px;
    width: -moz-max-content;
    width: min-content;
}
```

This also sets the border and margin so you can more easily visualize the layout. This is rendered in most browsers as shown in Figure 10-8.

Figure 10-8. *Using min-content in a figure*

Box Sizing

As I explained in Chapter 2, the space allocated to an element also includes the padding, border, and margin in addition to the actual element content. It's important to remember that the size settings that I've explained so far apply only to the actual content. The actual space used can be more than that, sometimes significantly more, depending on these other settings.

This can lead to problems when you're trying to align elements that have different attributes. To demonstrate this, consider the following markup:

```
<section>
    <article class="bigBorder">I am really padded!</article>
    <article class="smallBorder">Me, not so much.</article>
</section>
```

The section element contains two article elements with some simple text content. Each article has different class attributes. Now apply the following CSS rules:

```
article {
    width: 300px;
    height: 60px;
    margin: 1px;
}
.bigBorder {
    padding: 30px;
    border:  10px solid olive;
}
.smallBorder {
    padding: 5px;
    border:  2px solid olive;
}
```

First, this sets the article element to have a fixed size, 300px by 60px. Then it applies different padding and border settings using class selectors. The content is rendered as shown in Figure 10-9.

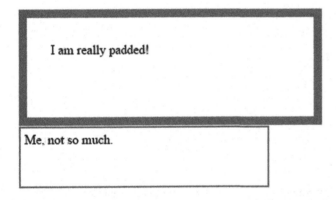

Figure 10-9. *Different size elements*

The result may be somewhat surprising, considering that both elements were set to the same size. Well, they actually are the same size, but the padding and border around them is different. You can address this by compensating for the extra padding and border and set the first element to a smaller width (66px smaller to be exact).

However, there is an easier way due to the new box-sizing attribute. This attribute specifies how the height and width attributes are applied. The default value, content-box, indicates the size applies only to the actual element content. Alternatively, you can set it to border-box, and the size attribute will apply after the padding and border have been added. We can fix this up by adding the following CSS rule:

```
* {
    box-sizing: border-box;
}
```

Remember from Chapter 9 that the asterisk is the universal selector, meaning that this applies to every element. With this rule, all sizing attributes will include the `padding` and `border`. With this adjustment, the content is now rendered as shown in Figure 10-10.

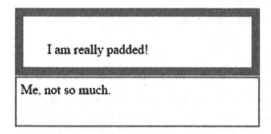

Figure 10-10. *Elements sized identically*

■ **Note** There are a few other `width` settings that have been defined but the browser support for these is sketchy. This Mozilla site provides more information if you want to try them: `https://developer.mozilla.org/en-US/docs/Web/CSS/width`

Float

The `float` attribute is used to cause block content to be aligned to either the left or right edges of its containing element. For example, adding `float: left;` to an element will cause it to be left-aligned. Subsequent content in the container is then wrapped around the floating content. For example, this markup has a `div` element followed by a paragraph of text content.

```
<header>
    <div>div</div>
    <p>Lorem ipsum dolor sit amet, consectetur adipiscing elit, sed do eiusmod ...</p>
</header>
```

Adding the following CSS rule will add some space around the `div` element and cause it to be floated to the left, allowing the text to wrap around it. This is rendered as shown in Figure 10-11.

```
header>div {
    padding: 25px;
    float: left;
}
```

```
┌──────┐  Lorem ipsum dolor sit amet, consectetur adipiscing elit, sed do
│      │  eiusmod tempor incididunt ut labore et dolore magna aliqua. Ut enim
│ div  │  ad minim veniam, quis nostrud exercitation ullamco laboris nisi ut
│      │  aliquip ex ea commodo consequat. Duis aute irure dolor in
└──────┘
```
reprehenderit in voluptate velit esse cillum dolore eu fugiat nulla pariatur.
Excepteur sint occaecat cupidatat non proident, sunt in culpa qui officia deserunt
mollit anim id est laborum.

Figure 10-11. *Using float: left*

Remember that block content normally takes up the entire width of its container. Setting the `float` attribute on an element allows subsequent content to be positioned as if it were inline. Additional elements will be positioned to the right of the floated content. If they also have `float: left`, subsequent content will continue to be positioned to the right. To demonstrate that I'll add a few more div elements The previous CSS rule will set these all to float:left and this will be rendered as shown in Figure 10-12.

```
<header>
    <div>div 1</div>
    <div>div 2</div>
    <div>div 3</div>
    <div>div 4</div>
    <div>div 5</div>
    <div>div 6</div>
    <p>Lorem ipsum dolor sit amet, consectetur adipiscing elit, sed do eiusmod ...</p>
</header>
```

```
┌────────┬────────┬────────┬────────┬─────────
│        │        │        │        │ Lorem
│        │        │        │        │ ipsum
│ div 1  │ div 2  │ div 3  │ div 4  │ dolor sit
│        │        │        │        │ amet,
├────────┼────────┼────────┴────────┴─────────
│        │        │ consectetur adipiscing elit, sed do
│        │        │ eiusmod tempor incididunt ut labore
│ div 5  │ div 6  │ et dolore magna aliqua. Ut enim ad
│        │        │ minim veniam, quis nostrud
└────────┴────────┴───────────────────────────
```
exercitation ullamco laboris nisi ut aliquip ex ea commodo
consequat. Duis aute irure dolor in reprehenderit in voluptate

Figure 10-12. *Multiple floated div elements*

■ **Tip**   Using `float: right;` will align the content to the right side of the container. Subsequent floated blocks will be positioned to the left of the first block. This will essentially render them in reverse order.

Clearing Floats

The float attribute also affects how subsequent content is positioned. The floated element is aligned to the left or right, but also, subsequent content can continue inline instead of starting a new row like normal blocked content. To illustrate that, the following markup creates four div elements and using inline styling to explicitly set the float attribute.

```
<section>
    <div style="float: left; padding: 25px">div 1</div>
    <div style="padding: 25px">div 2</div>
    <div style="float: right; padding: 25px">div 3</div>
    <div style="padding: 25px">div 4</div>
</section>
```

The first element is floated to the left. The second element is not floated but continues on the same row because the previous element is floated. Because this element is not floated, it takes up the remainder of the current row. The third element is floated to the right and the final element is positioned to the left and takes up the remainder of the row. This is shown in Figure 10-13.

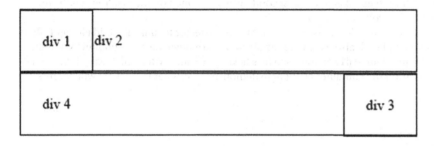

Figure 10-13. *Demonstrating floated and non-floated content*

If you wanted to cancel the effect of a previous float on a subsequent element, use the clear attribute. This does not affect how the previous element is positioned but it neutralizes the float effect on the subsequent element. The clear attribute can be set to left, right, or both. So you can remove the effect of all previous floats or just left or right floats. To demonstrate this, I'll add the clear attribute to the previous markup, which is rendered as shown in Figure 10-14.

```
<section>
    <div style="float: left; padding: 25px">div 1</div>
    <div style="clear: left; padding: 25px">div 2</div>
    <div style="float: right; padding: 25px">div 3</div>
    <div style="clear: right; padding: 25px">div 4</div>
</section>
```

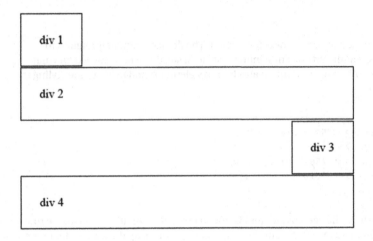

Figure 10-14. Using the clear attribute

The first div is aligned to the left as expected. The second div is positioned on the next row, taking up the entire row like normal blocked content.

For a little more complicated example, I'll use the :nth-of-type selector to make the odd elements float left and the even elements float right. I'll also use the clear attribute to remove the effect on previous floats. This will cause the left- and right-aligned div elements to be stacked vertically instead of flowing inline. This also sets the background-color on the container element to demonstrate another issue that I will address next.

```
header {
    background-color: #f3f3f3;
}
header>div {
    padding: 25px;
}
header>div:nth-of-type(odd) {
    float: left;
    clear: left;
}
header>div:nth-of-type(even) {
    float: right;
    clear: right;
}
```

This removes the float: left; declaration from the header>div selector and creates new selectors using the :nth-of-type pseudo-class that was described in Chapter 9. These use the even and odd keywords. This is rendered as shown in Figure 10-15.

	Lorem ipsum dolor sit amet, consectetur adipiscing elit, sed do eiusmod tempor incididunt ut labore et dolore magna aliqua. Ut enim ad minim veniam, quis nostrud exercitation ullamco laboris nisi ut aliquip ex ea commodo consequat. Duis aute irure dolor in reprehenderit in voluptate velit esse cillum dolore eu fugiat nulla pariatur. Excepteur sint occaecat cupidatat non proident, sunt in culpa qui officia deserunt mollit anim id est laborum.	
div 1		div 2
div 3		div 4
div 5		div 6

Figure 10-15. *Using left and right floats*

Containing Floats

Figure 10-15 demonstrates a common problem with floats. Basically, the floated content is not considered when calculating the height of a container. To see this more clearly, I'll remove the text using the following CSS rule, which sets the display attribute to none.

```
header>p {
    display: none;
}
```

When this is rendered, you'll see the odd div elements on the left and the even on the right with no text in between. If you inspect the header element using the browsers tools, you'll see that the element's height is set to 0 as illustrated in Figure 10-16.

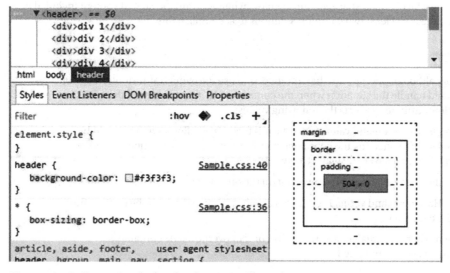

Figure 10-16. *Inspecting the header element in Chrome*

I set a gray background color for the header element, and since the div elements are inside the header element, I expect them to have a gray background. However, since the computed height of the header element is 0, there is no gray area. Similarly, in Figure 10-15, you can see that only part of the div elements have a gray background because the text is not as large as the floated content.

At first glance this might seem like a bug in the browser; the size of a parent element is not considering its child elements. However, there is an important reason for this behavior. Floated content is intended to be able to span multiple blocks. For example, the layout shown in Figure 10-17 has three div elements with textual content. The floated content spans two of these.

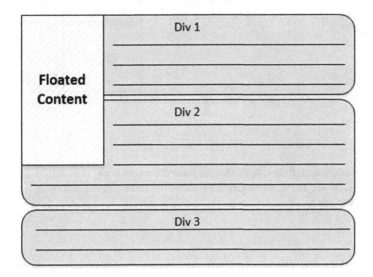

Figure 10-17. *Floated content spanning blocks*

If the size of the first div includes the floated content, then the second div would not start until after the floated content, leaving a lot of empty space. In our scenario, when we want the floated content included in the size calculation; there are at least two common solutions to accomplish this.

Setting Overflow

The simplest solution, although perhaps not that intuitive, is to use the overflow attribute. This specifies how the browser should handle the situation when the contents of an element exceed the area of its container. The overflow attribute supports the following values:

- visible - this is the default value and indicates that the overflow content should be displayed without affecting the container. As I showed, the container height was zero but all of its contents were displayed anyway.

- hidden - the content is clipped so any content outside of the container is not visible.

- scroll - Horizontal and vertical scroll bars are always created even if the content fits inside the container.

- auto - Scroll bars are created only when the content overflows the container; otherwise they are suppressed.

In this scenario, however, with any value other than visible, the browser will calculate the size of the container taking into account the floated content. This solves the issue with the background color not covering all of the div elements. Using scroll, you will also get scroll bars, which is probably not what you want. I recommend using overflow: auto; for any container that has floated content to resolve this issue.

Using a Pseudo-Element

Another solution for this is to use the ::after pseudo-element to create additional content after the container and use the clear attribute on this content. For example, adding this CSS rule, will add content after the floated content.

```
header::after {
    content: "";
    display: block;
    clear: both;
}
```

The content declaration, which is required, is set to an empty string so this doesn't add any actual content. However, the pseudo-element will have the clear: both; declaration. This causes the content to "appear" after the floated content but still be part of the container. This also forces the floated content to be included in the container size.

Inline Block

In the beginning of the chapter I told you that there were two basic values for the display attribute: block and inline, and I demonstrated how these work. There are actually quite a few available values for the display attribute. Most of these are related to tables, which I'll cover in Chapter 13. But I'll explain the inline-block value here.

So block elements, as I've explained, use the entire width of their parent element and each block element creates a new row. In contrast, inline elements use only the horizontal space needed and subsequent elements continue on the existing row, wrapping to the next when necessary.

There are some limitations when using inline elements, such as not being able to set the height and width attributes. In some of the previous examples, where there was a row of boxes, these had to be created as block content and use the float attribute to allow them to flow horizontally.

The following markup creates six div elements inside a navigation element:

```
<nav>
    <div>div a</div>
    <div>div b</div>
    <div>div c</div>
    <div>div d</div>
    <div>div e</div>
    <div>div f</div>
</nav>
```

By default, each div element would be displayed as blocked content and be on a separate row. However, we can use inline-block to allow these to flow on a single row (or wrap, if necessary). This is applied through a CSS rule like this:

```
nav>div {
    display: inline-block;
    width: 75px;
    height: 25px;
    vertical-align: bottom;
    clear: both;
}
```

This also sets the height and width of the div elements. The clear attribute is needed to clear the float from the previous example. (If you're using floats, you will find yourself using clear a lot as well).

The CSS rule also sets the vertical-align property so all the bottom edges of the elements will be aligned. Since these are all the same size, alignment is not really an issue. To make this more interesting, I'll adjust the height on some of the elements using this CSS rule, which will make every other one larger. The result is shown in Figure 10-18.

```
nav>div:nth-of-type(even) {
    height: 35px;
}
```

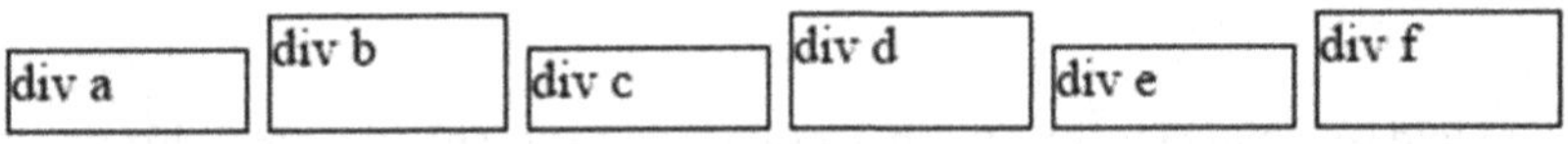

Figure 10-18. *Using inline-block with alignment*

Position

So far, all of the elements we have worked with in this chapter have been positioned statically. This is the default behavior where elements flow from one to the next using either block or inline layout. This is defined by setting position: static; but since this is the default value it's not necessary to actually add this to your CSS.

There are several values for the position attribute and I'll explain each of these:

- static - this is the default value; the content is positioned based on its location in the document and the flow properties that are assigned.

- relative - the element position is offset from where its normal flow position would be.

- absolute - the element is positioned at a specific location; no space is allocated for it.

- fixed - the element is positioned relative to the viewport; its position on the screen does not change when the document is scrolled.

> **▪ Tip** Non-statically positioned content is sometimes referred to as *positioned* content. That's not a very insightful term as all content is positioned; it just differs in how it is positioned. However, if you see that term, it generally applies to content that uses either the `relative`, `absolute`, or `fixed` position values.

Relative Positioning

With relative positioning, the content is positioned just like with static positioning except it is then offset from its original, calculated position. The shifting of the element does not affect the position of other elements. The space assigned to the element based on its original position is still honored. This will usually lead to some overlapping content as well as blank spaces.

After setting the `position` attribute to `relative`, you can then specify the offset using the `top`, `bottom`, `left`, or `right` attributes. If you want the element shifted down, set the `top` attribute to the distance that it should be adjusted. Similarly, to shift the position up, use the `bottom` attribute. To shift the element to the right, use the `left` attribute. This may seem backward at first, but it is similar to increasing the left margin, which will push the element to the right.

> **▪ Tip** Setting the `top` attribute to a positive value will shift the element down; using a negative value will shift the element up. So `top: -20px;` and `bottom: 20px;` are equivalent. Likewise, setting the `left` attribute to a negative value accomplishes the same thing as setting the `right` property to a positive value.

To demonstrate relative positioning, I'll use the following markup, which creates four `div` elements.

```
<header>
    <div class="square red">div 1</div>
    <div class="square yellow">div 2</div>
    <div class="square blue">div 3</div>
    <div class="square green">div 4</div>
</header>
```

I'll also set the background color for each of these squares using the following CSS rules. (In case you're wondering about my choice of colors here, I'm purposely using lighter colors because they show up better in print, especially when using greyscale for black and white printing).

```
.red {
    background-color: pink;
}
.yellow {
    background-color: yellow;
}
.blue {
    background-color: cyan;
}
.green {
    background-color: chartreuse;
}
```

Each of the div elements has the square class assigned and each has a different color class as well. The positioning is then accomplished using a pair of class selectors:

```
header>div.square {
    padding: 0px;
    float: left;
    clear: none;
    width: 100px;
    height: 100px;
}

.blue {
    position: relative;
    top: 20px;
    left: 20px;
}
```

I'm adding the markup and CSS rules for this example to the same files used for the previous examples where I already had a header>div selector. This new selector, header>div.square, is more specific and will therefore override any conflicting declarations. I explained the specificity rules in Chapter 2. The previous declarations set the padding, float, and clear attributes; however, I want these new square div elements to be styled differently so these specific declarations are overridden.

■ **Tip** Notice that this is setting clear: none; and that is the default value for this attribute. Sometimes you have to set default values when you're overriding a less-specific rule.

The blue class selector sets the relative position and specifies the offset amount. Only one of the div elements has this class so only the div with the blue class will be offset. The is rendered as shown in Figure 10-19.

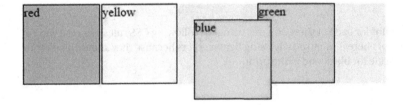

Figure 10-19. *Demonstrating relative positioning*

Notice that there is now extra space near the top and left edges of the blue div and the blue div overlaps the green div. Also notice that the background for the header element does not cover all of the blue div. As I said, the offset is performed on the element with making any adjustments to the other elements. All the other content is positioned based on the element's original position, before the offset was applied.

■ Tip   If you want to shift an element and have the new position honored as well as the original in the normal (static) content flow, use the `margin` attribute instead. This adds extra space to the element giving an appearance of being shifted. However, the remaining content is adjusted based on the new increase in size of the element.

Absolute Positioning

Absolute positioning is similar to relative positioning except the element is completely removed from the content flow. The original position is not honored; it's like the element was never there. It uses the same `top`, `bottom`, `left`, and `right` attributes to specify the position. However, the tricky part of using absolute positioning is determining the positioning context.

To be clear, both the `relative` or `absolute` values for `position` attribute will position the element relative to something. With both, you specify an offset using the `top`, `bottom`, `left`, or `right` attributes. Setting `position: relative;` will position the element relative to its original position. Using `position: absolute;` will position the element relative to its positioning context.

A positioning context is created whenever relative or absolute positioning is used. When absolute positioning is used, the browser will look through the element's ancestry to find the nearest ancestor that has the `position` attribute set to either `absolute` or `relative`. If none is found, the document is used as the default positioning context.

To demonstrate this, I'll add the following CSS rule:

```
header {
    position: relative;
}
```

This will make every header element a positioning context. Notice, however, that I did not specify an offset. This will not affect the `header` element; it will be positioned as if static positioning was used. However, if any of its children use absolute positioning, they will be positioned based on the location of the `header` element.

With the `header` change in place, I'll then create the blue class selector. The blue `div` should now be positioned based on the header element, the top edge is 10 pixels above it and the right edge is 50 pixels from the right edge of the `header`, as shown in Figure 10-20.

```
.blue {
    position: absolute;
    top: -10px;
    right: 50px;
}
```

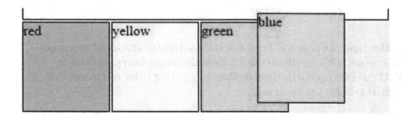

Figure 10-20. *Absolution positioning based on parent position*

Fixed Positioning

Fixed positioning is identical to absolute positioning except that the positioning context is always the viewport. The content will always stay in the same place on the screen regardless of how the document is scrolled – horizontally or vertically. To demonstrate this, I'll change the position of the blue div by replacing the previous CSS rule with this:

```
.blue {
    position: fixed;
    top: 50px;
    left: 0px;
}
```

The top or bottom attribute is required; otherwise the content will not be displayed. In this example, I set it so the top edge of the content will start 50px from the top of the window. The left or right attributes are optional; if omitted, left: 0px; will be used. This is rendered as shown in Figure 10-21.

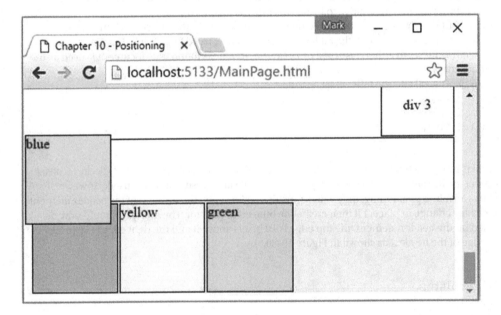

Figure 10-21. *Using fixed positioning*

Z-Index

The x-axis refers to the horizontal direction on a page and the y-axis is the vertical direction. As web pages are 2-dimensional, there is not really z-axis, although this is used to describe how overlapping content is stacked on top of other content. The z-index property then, defines the stacking order, in a manner of speaking. The content with the highest z-index will be on top.

With statically positioned content, you don't have to be concerned with the z-index. In fact, the z-index only applies to non-statically positioned content. However, with the other position values, relative, absolute, and fixed, you will need to consider the "stacking order."

The z-index has a default value of 0. So if everything has the same z-index, how does the browser know which to put on top? There are a couple of rules that are followed.

First, all non-statically positioned content will be on top of the other content. Go back and look at Figures 10-19, 10-20, and 10-21 and notice that the blue div is always on top of the others. If you don't want that behavior, set the z-index to -1 and that content will appear underneath the statically positioned content.

Secondly, content that comes later in the document will be on top of the previous content. To test this out, I'll add the following rule to make the green div used fixed positioning:

```
.green {
    position: fixed;
    top: 70px;
    left: 20px;
}
```

The green div will now be fixed near the blue div but will appear on top of it since it comes after it in the document, as demonstrated in Figure 10-22. You can try the same thing with the yellow div and you'll see that it will be under the blue div, since it comes before it.

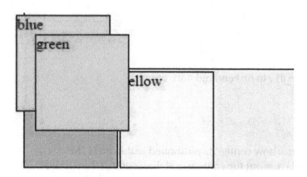

Figure 10-22. *Displaying two fixed elements*

When determining the display order, the browser uses *stacking contexts*. A stacking context is created at the document level, for all statically positioned content. Whenever relative, absolute, or fixed positioning is used, a new stacking context is created. All the child elements within this element use the same stacking context.

Child elements can also use one of the positioning values and create a new stacking context. This can cause some confusion because these contexts are hierarchical. For example, suppose there are two stacking contexts, the first with a z-index of 1 and a the second with a z-index of 2. Then you add a child element with relative positioning inside the first stacking context and set its z-index to 3. However, everything in the second context (z-index of 2) will be on top of the first (z-index of 1). The subcontext (z-index of 3) only affects the ordering of elements in the first context.

■ **Caution**   Setting the opacity attribute to less than 1 will also create a new stacking context. Child elements that then create a new stacking context will actually be subcontexts and the ordering may not happen as expected. There's an article that explains this in more detail if you're interested: https://philipwalton. com/articles/what-no-one-told-you-about-z-index.

Centering Content

Before we leave this chapter on positioning, I need to explain a simple trick for centering content. The margin attribute defines the space between an element and the elements next to it. If this is set to auto, the left and right margins will be calculated to center the content within its parent elements.

To try this out, I'll create a single div element with the class attribute set to center:

```
<div class="center"></div>
```

Then I'll use the following CSS rule to center it. This will set the width and height attributes as well as the background color.

```
.center {
    width: 100px;
    height: 30px;
    background-color: teal;
    margin: 0 auto;
}
```

The margin is set to 0 auto, which will cause the div to be centered horizontally.

Summary

In this chapter I covered a number of topics that control how content is positioned within an HTML document. There are a lot of options available when laying out the content and this is one of the trickiest concepts in CSS. When deciding how to arrange your content, consider these techniques and choose the one that fits best:

- Block layout - takes up the entire width of its parent and always starts a new row.
- Inline layout - designed to flow horizontally from one element to another.
- Specifying size - using absolute, relative, or max sizes and setting the size based on content.
- Box sizing - automatically considers padding and border in sizing.
- Floats - float content left or right and let other content wrap around.
- Inline block - allows normally blocked content to flow horizontally.
- Relative position - offset content from its calculated position.
- Absolute or fixed positioning - positioned independent of the DOM.
- Centering - using the margin attribute.

In the next chapter, I'll explain the CSS features that you can use to format primarily textual content.

CHAPTER 11

Text Styles

In this Chapter I'll demonstrate the CSS attributes that are available for styling the text portions of an HTML document. I'll start with choosing the font and the various font characteristics and then the text formatting capabilities that you can use. I'll cover spacing and alignment and ways to control line and page breaks. I'll also explain a few miscellaneous topics such as color, opacity, and cursor, which are not specific to text formatting.

Fonts

The most basic factor when formatting text is choosing the font. There is a seemingly endless collection of available fonts, and a simple change in the font can have a dramatic effect on your web page. A font is a set of symbols, known as *glyphs* in typography, which are mapped to a character set. The browser will display the letter "A," for example, based on what glyph it is mapped to in the current font.

Obtaining Fonts

There are three ways that a browser can get a font definition so it can be rendered.

Web-Safe Fonts

The first is known as *web-safe fonts*, which is somewhat of a misnomer. All operating systems have built-in fonts; in order to display text on a screen a font is needed to map each character code to a glyph. The browsers can use any of these built-in fonts. The problem, however, is that operating systems do not all support the same set of fonts. A web-safe font is one that is generally supported by most devices. This is more art than science and there are no fonts that have 100% support across every OS. There are a few such as Arial, Verdana, Times New Roman, and Courier New that are pretty safe bets. There is an article at http://www.cssfontstack.com/ that shows the font availability for Windows and Mac (unfortunately, it does not show Android or iOS coverage).

Web Fonts

As you can probably tell, with web-safe fonts, your choices are somewhat limited. The second approach, which significantly increases your options, is to use *web fonts*. A web font is downloaded by the browser just like other resources such as CSS and image files. There are two drawbacks to this approach:

- Older browsers don't support web fonts; however, that only effects a small and shrinking population of users.

© Mark J. Collins 2017
M. J. Collins, *Pro HTML5 with CSS, JavaScript, and Multimedia*, DOI 10.1007/978-1-4842-2463-2_11

- The additional download can slow the page's load time, especially if you're using several web fonts. These are generally cached by the browser so only the initial load is normally affected.

If you're interested in using web fonts, go to https://fonts.google.com/. As of this writing, this site provides 808 font families and an impressive UI for previewing and selecting a font. After selecting a font, the site provides instructions on how to include it in your HTML document. To include a web font, you can use a link element like this:

```
<link href="https://fonts.googleapis.com/css?family=Cabin" rel="stylesheet">
```

Alternatively, you can use the @import rule to include the font in the CSS file like this:

```
@import url(//fonts.googleapis.com/css?family=Cabin);
```

Either way accomplishes the same thing. Using a link element puts this in the markup and the @import rule is done in the CSS. I recommend using @import so that all styling changes are contained in the CSS file. If you later decide to change the font, you should be able to do that without modifying the HTML markup.

The CSS font stack site previously referenced also provides a nice UI for selecting fonts as well as configuring the CSS and previewing the font definitions. This references the same fonts.googleapis.com site for the actual font resources.

Custom Fonts

The third approach is to embed your own font definitions in the CSS file. Just like with images, there are several formats for defining a font. True Type Fonts (TTF) have been around for about 30 years now and this along with Open Type Fonts (OTF) are the standard for installing fonts on a desktop computer. These formats are also supported by the major web browsers. However, the Web Open Font Format (WOFF) is the W3C recommendation and is also supported by most browsers. Also WOFF 2.0 is growing in popularity and support.

Creating a font definition is beyond the scope of this book. However, once you have created or purchased a font definition file, you can copy it to your web server. You then need to reference it in the CSS file using the @font-face rule. Just like with audio and video files, you can supply multiple file formats so the browser can choose one based on its supported types. To provide support for TTF, WOFF, and WOFF2.0, for example, include a rule like this. Of course, you'll need to provide each of these file formats on your server.

```
@font-face {
  font-family: 'CustomFont';
  src: url('custom.ttf') format('truetype'),
       url('custom.woff') format('woff'),
       url('custom.woff2') format('woff2');
}
```

There are other sites that provide fonts such as https://www.fontsquirrel.com/ and http://www.fontex.org/. Both of these sites provide a font file download that you'll need to host on your web server and reference as a custom font.

Font Families

Fonts are identified by the term *family*. The terms Arial, Courier New, and Times New Roman are font families. When defining a custom font in the previous example, the font-family attribute was assigned and this is how the CSS will later select it. There are also a set of generic font families, an example of each is shown in Figure 11-1:

- cursive - fonts in this family resemble cursive writing rather than printed text. Sometimes the characters connect from one to another giving the suggestion of being handwritten.

- fantasy - these fonts are more ornamental and have decorations or nonstandard character representations.

- monospace - monospaced characters all have the same width.

- sans-serif - sans means "without" and a serif is an additional stroke, often a tapered end. So sans-serif fonts do not have these extra marks and are usually more plain looking.

- serif - these are the more traditional fonts, especially in printed text. This is what you're reading right now.

cursive

fantasy

monospace

sans-serif

serif

Figure 11-1. *Sample generic font families*

So the browser has a set of fonts available to it, whether native OS fonts, linked web fonts, or embedded custom fonts. You can select which one to use with the font-family attribute like this:

```
p {
    font-family: Cabin;
}
```

However, since you cannot guarantee that every browser will support this font, you should provide some additional options as a fallback. This is referred to as a *font stack*. You can specify more than one family by separating them with commas. For example:

```
p {
    font-family: Cabin, Verdana, sans-serif;
}
```

The browser will process these in order so list your first choice first. You should always end with a generic font, so you will least get something similar to what you intended. The previous example uses a typical approach, which is to put the custom or web font first, followed by a web-safe font that is similar, and lastly a generic font family. You can test this out by changing **Cabin** to **Cabin1** and then **Verdana** to **Verdana1**. With each change notice that the font is different but still similar to the first choice.

■ **Caution**   If the font family contains punctuation or numbers, such as **Modern No. 20**, you'll need to put quotes around the name.

Font Settings

Choosing the font family is just the beginning, however. There are other attributes such as size, weight, and style that will configure the font more precisely. There are quite a few advanced features as well that give you more control to handle special cases.

Style

The font-style attribute is used to select italic font. There are three possible values: normal (the default), italic, and oblique. Oblique means slanted or leaning. The oblique keyword is not very well supported and will usually provide the same effect as italic.

Size

Historically, the font size was measured as the width of the letter "M"; however, it now represents the height of the uppercase letters. Of course, in non-Western character sets this definition may not be applied exactly. There are a surprisingly large number of options when it comes to setting the size of a font. Its value is a distance unit, and I explained all of the units that can be used to define distances in Chapter 2. These units are also summarized in the reference material in Appendix C.

Designers, however, are encouraged to avoid using absolute sizes such as 12px. If a user needs to increase the font size for accessibility reasons, they will not be able to adjust these absolute sizes. Using relative sizing also helps when designing a page, especially when dealing with responsive solutions. For these reasons, there are several ways to set the font size, in addition to the standard distance units.

There are a set of keywords defined that the browser will map to physical units based on the user's font settings:

- xx-small
- x-small
- small

- medium

- large

- x-large

- xx-large

These allow you to set your font size while still allowing the user to increase or decrease this as needed. There are also two keywords that will set the font size relative to the parent element's font size:

- smaller

- larger

These will adjust the font size by approximately the same amount that separates the previous keywords. For example, if the parent element uses small, using larger will be roughly equivalent to choosing medium. You can also express the font size as a percentage of the parent element's font size. Setting font-size: 120%; will make the font 20% larger than the parent element's font.

Some of the distance units that I described in Chapter 2 are relative units. The em unit, for example, is based on the current font size and rem is based on the font size of the root element. There are also viewport-relative units such as vh, which is 1% of the viewport height.

■ **Tip** There's a good article at https://css-tricks.com/almanac/properties/f/font-size/ that provides examples of the various sizing approaches.

Weight

The font-weight attribute is used to set a bold font and it supports the two values, normal (default) and bold. However, you can also set this to one of the specific values: 100, 200, 300, 400, 500, 600, 700, 800, or 900. Most fonts will support a normal and bold type face but they may not support all 9 weight versions. For those that only support normal and bold, values 100 - 500 will map to normal and 600 - 900 will be bold. For those that do support the more precise values, the normal keyword will map to a value of 400 and bold maps to 700.

There are also relative keywords that set the font weight relative to the parent element's font. Using lighter will make the font weight lighter than its parent and bolder will do the opposite. To demonstrate the relative values for both size and weight, consider the following markup:

```
<p class="relative">
    This is going to be big, <strong>big, <strong>big</strong></strong>.
</p>
```

This text includes a strong element nested inside another strong element. I explained in Chapter 5 that this has semantic meaning, that this text is really important. To style this, the following CSS rules take this meaning into account.

```
.relative {
    font-family: Arial;
    font-size: medium;
}
strong {
    font-size: larger;
    font-weight: bolder;
}
```

The first rule simply chooses the font and sets the font size to medium. The next rule uses the relative values for size and weight, larger and bolder. Implemented this way, the nested strong element will have the larger and bolder values applied twice. The result is shown in Figure 11-2.

This is going to be big, **big, big**.

Figure 11-2. *Demonstrating relative size and weight*

Color

The font color is set with the color attribute. I explained the various color units in Chapter 2, and they are also summarized in the reference material in Appendix C. You can also set the opacity attribute, assigning a number from 0 to 1, with 1 meaning completely opaque and 0 being transparent. You can also set both the color and opacity attributes using either the rgba() or hsla() functions.

Kerning

Generally, each character occupies a spaced defined by a rectangle. With proportionally spaced fonts, the width is different for each character. However, some characters are really more like triangles; the capital A and V are the most outstanding examples. If these two characters are together, for example VA, using the rectangular model, there will appear to be extra space between them. Another example is a period or comma next to a top-heavy character like T or Y.

Kerning is a feature that removes this space so that the spacing between characters is more consistent. This is controlled by the font-kerning attribute. This supports the following values:

- auto - this is the default value and allows the browser to determine when this should be used. In most cases, kerning will be on; however, for smaller font sizes the browser will usually turn it off.

- normal - this will force kerning to be always on.

- none - this will turn kerning off.

The best way to explain the effects of kerning is with a demonstration. The following markup includes two paragraphs with the same characters; the first includes the kerning class and the second has the noKerning class.

```
<p class="kerning">T,VAY. - with kerning</p>
<p class="noKerning">T,VAY. - w/o kerning</p>
```

Then the following CSS rules will assign a large serif font to both paragraphs and set the font-kerning attribute based on the class attribute. This will be rendered as shown in Figure 11-3.

```
.kerning, .noKerning {
    font-family: serif;
    font-size: 48px;
}
```

```
.kerning {
    font-kerning: normal;
}
.noKerning {
    font-kerning: none;
}
```

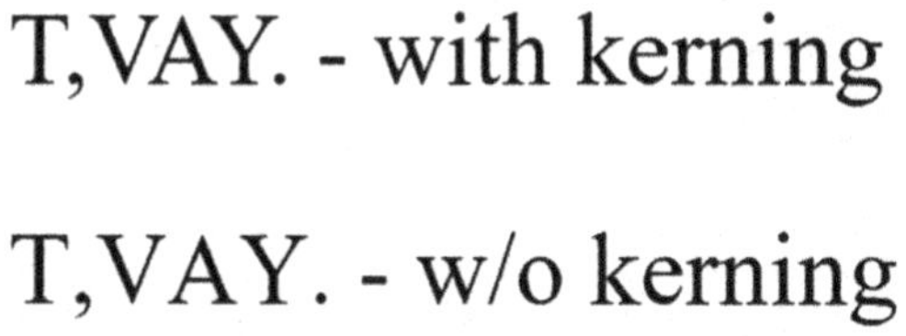

T,VAY. - with kerning

T,VAY. - w/o kerning

Figure 11-3. *Demonstrating kerning*

Notice when kerning is on, the rectangles of the V, A, and Y characters overlap. Also, the period and comma are closer to the T and Y characters.

Stretch

The font size describes the height of a font, not the width. Some fonts provide multiple versions with different character widths. Wider fonts are referred to as *stretched* and narrow fonts are called *condensed*. You can use the font-stretch attribute to control the width. The following values are defined:

- ultra-condensed
- extra-condensed
- condensed
- semi-condensed
- normal
- semi-expanded
- expanded
- extra-expanded
- ultra-expanded

A particular font may not support all of these options, and the browser will choose an available width that is closest to the requested value. This attribute has no effect on fonts that only provide one width. For a demonstration, the following markup has two paragraphs: one with the stretched class and one with the condensed class. The CSS that follows chooses the Arial font and applies the font-stretch attribute to these two classes. The result is shown in Figure 11-4.

```
<p class="stretched">stretched</p>
<p class="condensed">condensed</p>

.stretched, .condensed {
    font-family: arial;
    font-size: 48px;
}
.stretched {
    font-stretch: extra-expanded;
}
.condensed {
    font-stretch: extra-condensed;
}
```

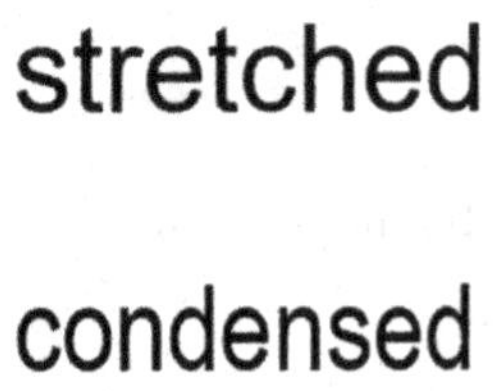

stretched

condensed

Figure 11-4. *Demonstrating font-stretch*

Variant Capitals

The font-variant-caps attribute allows you to use capital glyphs for lowercase characters. This feature is not supported by IE or Edge browsers. It is also limited by the font capabilities. This attribute supports the following values:

- all-petite-caps - both lower and uppercase characters will use the petite capital glyphs, if supported. If not, the small capital glyphs will be used for both.

- all-small-caps - both lower and uppercase characters will use the small capital glyphs.

- normal - this is the default value and will disable the use of the capital glyphs.

- petite-caps - only the lowercase characters will use the petite glyphs; if not supported, the small capital glyphs will be used instead.

- small-caps - the small capital glyphs will be used for the lowercase characters; uppercase characters will use the normal glyphs.

- titling-caps - uses special glyphs for both lower and uppercase characters, which are design to not appear too bold when a long run of text uses the capital glyphs. If these are not supported, this attribute is ignored.

- unicase - uses the small capital glyphs with the uppercase characters only. This will cause the uppercase characters to be the same size as the lowercase characters.

For a quick demonstration, the following markup has a paragraph with the smallCaps class and the CSS sets the font-variant-caps attribute to small-caps. This is rendered in most browsers as shown in Figure 11-5.

```
<p class="smallCaps">Using Small Capitals</p>

.smallCaps {
    font-size: x-large;
    font-variant-caps: small-caps;
}
```

Using Small Capitals

Figure 11-5. Demonstrating small capitals

Numeric

The font-variant-numeric attribute provides the ability to control how certain numerical content is rendered. For example, ordinal numbers such as 1st, 2nd, and 3rd can be displayed with a superscript. Likewise, fractions can be rendered as diagonal (½) or as stacked. This attribute is not currently supported by IE, Edge, or Safari. Also, this requires that the font support these specials glyphs.

I found the diagonal fractions seem to work fairly consistently, but the other features did not work most of the time. Mozilla has a good explanation of the options that are defined by the W3C recommendation at https://developer.mozilla.org/en-US/docs/Web/CSS/font-variant-numeric if you want to investigate further.

The diagonal fractions can be demonstrated with the following markup and CSS. This is rendered as shown in Figure 11-6.

```
<p class="diagonal">1/2 2/3 3/4 4/5</p>

.diagonal {
    font-family: Verdana;
    font-size: xx-large;
    font-variant-numeric: diagonal-fractions;
}
```

½ ⅔ ¾ ⅘

Figure 11-6. Demonstrating diagonal fractions

Feature Settings

The font-feature-settings attribute provides low-level access to control advanced features of a particular font. It can be used to modify OpenType font features by setting font-specific configuration values. It should be used only when the desired effect cannot be achieved through one of the other attributes. There is a good write-up of this at https://css-tricks.com/almanac/properties/f/font-feature-settings/. However, check to see what features the font you're using will support.

Shorthand Notation

I explained in Chapter 2 that you can often set multiple attributes with a single declaration using a shortcut notation. The `font` attribute is a good example of this. Using a single declaration, you can set the following attributes

- `font-family`
- `font-size`
- `font-weight`
- `font-style`
- `font-stretch`
- `font-variant`
- `line-height` (explained later in this chapter)

There are a few restrictions, however. The `font-family` and `font-size` are required; the others are optional. The `font-family` attribute must be listed last. If the `font-weight`, `font-style`, or `font-variant` attributes are specified, they must come before `font-size`. If any of these rules are violated, the entire declaration is ignored. The `line-height` attribute, if specified, must come immediately after the `font-size` attribute and the two should be separated by a slash (/) character.

■ **Caution**   The `font-stretch` attribute is relatively new and may not be supported by some browsers. If not supported and it is included in a shorthand notation, the entire declaration will be ignored. For this reason, you should not include `font-stretch` but this should be specified separately.

When using the shorthand notation, there are a few defined keywords that you can use to set all of the font attributes to match the font used by the OS. These are the supported font values:

- `caption`
- `icon`
- `menu`
- `message-box`
- `small-caption`
- `status-bar`

For example, setting `font: icon;` will use a font that matches the desktop icons.

■ **Tip**   Google provides a nice overview of fonts in this article: `https://developers.google.com/fonts/docs/getting_started`. This also demonstrates some advanced techniques such as font effects. Many of these are only supported by the Chrome browser so beware of that; but it's still useful information.

Text Formatting

There are also CSS attributes that you can use to control how the text is formatted, such as alignment and indentation. You can also decorate the text with shadows and other effects.

Horizontal Alignment

The text-align attribute defines how the text is aligned horizontally within its block. The primary values are left, right, center, and justify, which work just like you would expect. There are two new values, start and end, which are not yet supported by Edge. The start value is the same as left for left-to-right language, but is right-aligned in right-to-left languages. If justify is used, the text-justify attribute specifies the method of justification. The default method is to add spaces between words. There is very little support for the text-justify attribute currently.

Indent

The text-indent attribute specifies how the first line of a block should be indented (or out-dented). This is entered as a distance in either absolute or relative units. A negative value indicates the first line is out-dented. A percentage can also be used, which will be the percentage of the containing block's width.

Overflow

Text can overflow its horizontal space if it is not able to wrap to the next line. I'll explain the wrapping attributes later in this chapter. When that happens, and the overflow attribute is not set to visible, the portion of text that does not fit will be hidden. The text-overflow specifies how the browser should handle this scenario. There are two keywords that can be used, clip and ellipsis. The clip value simply clips the text but the ellipsis value will include an ellipsis (...) inside the block, indicating that there is more text that cannot be displayed. This will also reduce the amount of text that can be displayed.

■ **Note**   This W3C specification for this attribute provides for either one or two parameters. If a single parameter is specified it indicates what to do on the right side of the block. If two parameters are specified, they specify the left and right side, respectively. Currently, however, only Firefox supports the two-value version.

For a demonstration, the following markup includes a rather long word. The CSS rule then sets a fixed width and sets overflow to hidden. Finally, text-overflow: ellipsis; is used to indicate an ellipsis should be displayed. This is rendered as shown in Figure 11-7.

```
<p class="overflow">Supercalifragilisticexpialidocious</p>
```

```
.overflow {
    font-size: large;
    border: 1px solid black;
    width: 150px;
    overflow: hidden;
    text-overflow: ellipsis;
}
```

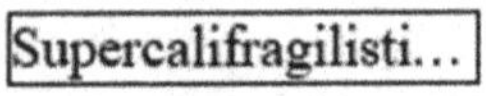

Supercalifragilisti…

Figure 11-7. *Setting the text-overflow attribute*

Quotes

Quotation marks are automatically created by the browser in a couple of scenarios. The most common is when the quote (q) element is used. The browser also detects when there are nested quote elements, for example:

```
<q>What do you mean <q>I can't believe he said <q>No</q></q>?</q>
```

In this case it will put double quotation marks around the outer quote and single quotation marks on the inner quotes. This will be displayed as: "What do you mean 'I can't believe he said 'No"?". However, you can control what characters are used for the quotation marks using the quotes attribute. For example, the following CSS rule will tell the browser to use the curly braces for outer quotes and square brackets for inner quotes. There are four string values supplied with the quotes attribute; the first two are used for the outer quotation marks and the next two are used for the inner quotation marks.

```
* {
    quotes: "{" "}" "[" "]"
}
```

The other scenario where quotation marks are entered is when the ::before and ::after pseudo-element are used. To demonstrate this, the following markup contains a paragraph with an embedded quote:

```
<p class="quote">He said, <q>Eureka!</q></p>
```

Then, these CSS rules use the pseudo-elements to add quotation marks before and after the text. As I explained in Chapter 9, the content attribute is used to specify what content should be appended or prepended to the selected element. In this case, it is set to the open-quote and close-quote keywords.

```
.quote::before {
    content: open-quote;
}
.quote::after {
    content: close-quote;
}
```

With these CSS rules in place, both examples are rendered as shown in Figure 11-8.

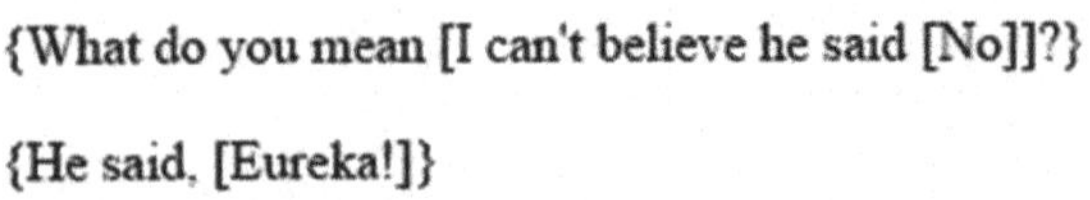

{What do you mean [I can't believe he said [No]]?}

{He said, [Eureka!]}

Figure 11-8. *Demonstrating the quotes attribute*

Notice that the quotation marks around Eureka! are using the inner marks. Because quotation marks were added by the pseudo-elements; the browser treated the quote element as if it were nested inside an outer quote. In the pseudo-elements, if you used the no-open-quote and no-close-quote keywords instead, no outer quotation marks would be rendered, but the quote element would still be treated as if nested as used the inner marks.

Shadow

To provide an interesting effect you can add shadows to your text using the text-shadow attribute. This takes a color value and three distance values. The color value can be either the first or last value. It is technically optional; however, for maximum support, you should always include it. Some browsers, such as Safari, will not display the shadow if the color is not specified. Most browsers will default the color to the text color.

The three distance values are the x offset, y offset, and blur radius, and they must be supplied in this order. The blur radius defines how far the original text image is spread out. The larger the blur radius, the wider and lighter the shadow will be. This is optional and will default to 0. The x and y offset values are required and indicate the position of the shadow relative to the text. Positive values will be shifted right and down; negative values are shifted left and up.

To demonstrate the various effects of text shadows, the following markup contains three paragraphs with the same text and different class values. A different CSS rule is defined for each class with different values for the text-shadow attribute. This is rendered as shown in Figure 11-9.

```
<p class="shadow">This text has shadows</p>
<p class="background">This text has shadows</p>
<p class="blurred">This text has shadows</p>

.shadow {
    font-size: xx-large;
    text-shadow: 10px 5px 1px gray;
}
.background {
    font-size: xx-large;
    text-shadow: 0px 0px 5px gray;
}
.blurred {
    font-size: xx-large;
    text-shadow: 10px 5px 10px gray;
}
```

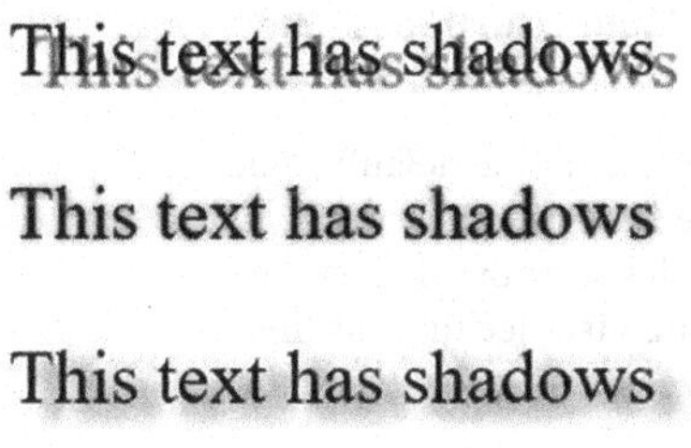

This text has shadows

This text has shadows

This text has shadows

Figure 11-9. *Demonstrating text shadows*

Capitalization

The text-transform attribute can be used to force the capitalization of text. This only effects how characters are rendered in the browser; in the DOM the text retains its original value. The text-transform attribute supports the following values:

- capitalize - the first letter of every word is converted to uppercase. Be aware, however, this does not support title casing where words such as "a" or "the" in the middle of a title are not capitalized.

- uppercase - all characters are changed to uppercase.

- lowercase - all characters are changed to lowercase.

- none - no changes are made (use this to override a previous rule).

■ **Caution**   Some languages have unique capitalization rules and browser support will vary in this regard. There are cases where these are handled properly and some in which they are not.

Spacing and Alignment

You can control the spacing of text in your HTML document using CSS attributes. You can also define how whitespace characters in your content should be handled by the browser. Vertical alignment of inline elements can be accomplished through the vertical-align attribute.

Basic Spacing

There are three simple CSS attributes that allow you to control the space between letters, words, and lines. These don't need much explanation so I'll describe them briefly

- letter-spacing - a positive value will create additional space between characters and a negative value will remove space that can causing overlapping. All distance units except percentages are allowed, including absolute values such as pixels and relative units such as em, rem, and vw. The default value is normal, which allows the font to perform standard spacing, including justification.

- word-spacing - affects the spacing between words and inline elements. Any distance unit is allowed; however, only Firefox supports percentages. Values can be absolute or relative but negative values are not supported. The default value is normal.

- line-height - specifies the vertical space used for each line of text. The default value is normal, which is roughly 20% more than the font size. The line-height can be specified as a number, like 1.2, or a percentage like 120%, which is multiplied by the font size or a distance unit such as 20px or 3em. Avoid absolute distance units as this can produce unexpected results. The line-height attribute can also be set using the font shorthand notation, which I explained earlier.

Handling Whitespace

In Chapter 1 I said that whitespace characters are generally ignored and that is the default behavior unless the content is inside a pre element. However, you can change the way whitespace characters are handled with the white-space attribute. It supports the following values:

- normal - this is the default value. Sequences of whitespace characters are collapsed to a single space and newline characters are treated as a space. Text is only wrapped as needed to fill the block.

- nowrap - whitespaces are collapsed just like with normal ones but text is never wrapped.

- pre - this functions just like the pre element; it preserves the whitespace characters and text is wrapped only at newline characters.

- pre-wrap - functions like the pre value except text is also wrapped as necessary to fill the block.

- pre-line - whitespace characters are collapsed like the normal value except text is wrapped at newline characters as well as when necessary to fill the block.

To demonstrate this, I'll use the poem by Henry Wadsworth Longfellow that I introduced in Chapter 4. This time, it will be inside a normal paragraph element instead of a preformatted element, but I can achieve the same effect using CSS.

```
<p class="whitespace">I heard the bells on Christmas Day
Their old, familiar carols play,
    And wild and sweet
    The words repeat
Of peace on earth, good-will to men!</p>
```

With only the default styles applied, this text would be on a single line, or wrapped where necessary, depending on the width of the window. However, the following CSS rule will treat this a preformatted text, as shown in Figure 11-10.

```
.whitespace {
    font-family: monospace;
    white-space: pre;
}
```

```
I heard the bells on Christmas Day
Their old, familiar carols play,
    And wild and sweet
    The words repeat
Of peace on earth, good-will to men!
```

Figure 11-10. *Handling preformatted text in CSS*

Vertical Alignment

Vertical alignment can be tricky. The vertical-align attribute is used for this but its behavior is not always intuitive. It works great for table cells, which I will cover in Chapter 13. For other content, it only works for inline and inline-block elements. For inline content (including inline-block), the following values are defined:

- baseline - the baseline of the element is aligned with the baseline of the parent element.

- bottom - the bottom of the element is aligned with the bottom of the current line.

- middle - this one is a little different than you might expect; the middle of the element is aligned with the baseline of the parent plus half of the height of the parent's lowercase x character.

- sub - the baseline is aligned with the subscript baseline of the parent element.

- super - the baseline is aligned with the superscript baseline of the parent element.

- text-bottom - the bottom of the element is aligned with the bottom of the parent element.

- text-top - the top of the element is aligned with the top of the parent element.

- top - the top of the element is aligned with the top of the current line.

- You can also enter a distance unit using either absolute or relative units, which will adjust the baseline of this element with the baseline of the parent. A percentage can also be used, which will be multiplied by the line height. Negative values are allowed as well.

Except for the top and bottom values, the alignment is based on the parent element. To demonstrate this, I'll use the following markup that places two span elements inside a paragraph element.

```
<p id="Align">
    X
    <span class="large">Large </span>
    <span class="small">Small</span>
    X
</p>
```

The paragraph is the parent element and I have included an "X" before and after the span elements so you can visualize the location of the parent that the span elements are being aligned to. I'll then create three CSS rules. The first simply defines the font of the parent element.

```
#Align {
    font-family: Verdana;
    font-size: 36px;
}
.large {
    font-size: 48px;
    vertical-align: text-bottom;
}
.small {
    font-size: 24px;
    vertical-align: text-top;
}
```

The next two rules set the font size for the span element and sets the vertical-align attribute. The large font is aligned to the bottom and the small font is aligned to the top. The result is shown in Figure 11-11.

x Large Small x

Figure 11-11. *Demonstrating vertical alignment*

You might have noticed that the text doesn't quite line up like you would expect. This is because of the way the browser computes the baseline and other factors that are used to perform the alignment. If you want to look into this further, there is a good article at http://christopheraue.net/2014/03/05/vertical-align/.

For a second example, I'll align a fixed-size div element next to a text element. Here is the markup; there are two div elements with the align class. Inside of each there is an empty div with the box class and a span element with some text.

```
<div class="align">
    <div class="solid box"></div>
    <span>Solid Box</span>
</div>
<br />
<div class="align">
    <div class="outline box"></div>
    <span>Outline Box</span>
</div>
```

To style this, the following CSS rules will cause the first inner div to have a solid square and the second an outlined square. Both the box div and the span element have the vertical-align attribute set to middle. This is rendered as shown in Figure 11-12.

```
.align {
    display: inline-block;
    font-size: 48px;
}
.box {
    display: inline-block;
    height: 10px;
    width: 10px;
    border: 1px solid black;
    vertical-align: middle;
}
.solid {
    background-color: black;
}
.align>span {
    vertical-align: middle;
}
```

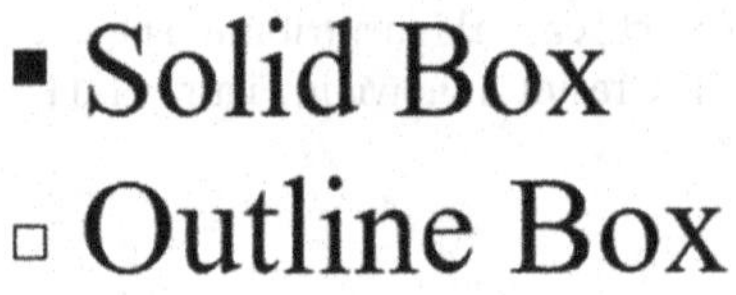

- Solid Box
- Outline Box

Figure 11-12. *Aligning a box with text*

Break

There are CSS attributes that you can use to control when line and page breaks should occur. Page breaks are primarily used when printing a document.

Word Wrap

The overflow-wrap attribute determines where line breaks can be inserted to wrap text to fit the width of its container. The normal value indicates that breaks can only be inserted between words, at word-break opportunity (wbr) elements, or at hard or soft hyphens. These were explained in Chapter 5. The break-word value indicates that a word can be broken at any arbitrary point in order to fit into the allowed space.

■ **Caution**   The word-wrap attribute is supported by most browsers but has been replaced with overflow-wrap. The word-wrap attribute will likely be supported for a long time, but you should use overflow-wrap instead.

There is an additional word-break attribute that is similar to overflow-wrap. It supports a normal and break-all values that are roughly equivalent to the normal and break-word attributes of overflow-wrap. The word-break attribute also supports a keep-all value that applies primarily to Chinese, Japanese, and Korean languages. There are some slight differences in how overflow-wrap: break-word; and word-break: break-all; behave between different browsers and contexts. Unless you're working with these specific languages, I would stick with the overflow-wrap attribute.

When a line break is inserted in the middle of a word, you might want to also include a hyphen at the end of the line to indicate that the word continues. The hyphens attribute controls when this occurs and supports the following values:

- none - hyphens are never used when breaking a word.

- manual - a hyphen is used only when either a hard or soft hyphen character exists where the word was broken.

- auto - the default value. This works like manual except that a hyphen may also be added when determined by a language-specific resource that indicates when a hyphen is appropriate. This, of course, relies on language specific support, which is currently very limited. In most cases, this will function like manual.

Page Break

When rendering an HTML to be printed, you can control how page breaks are generated. There are three attributes that you can apply:

- page-break-after - identifies the rules to be applied at the end of the element.

- page-break-before - specifies any page break rules that should be applied before the element.

- page-break-inside - indicates if page break should be allowed inside of the element.

For each of these attributes, the default value is auto, which doesn't define any rules; the browser will generally break to a new page at the bottom of a page. The page-break-inside attribute supports one other value, avoid. Use this to prevent a page break in the middle of a particular element. For example, if you don't want to break in the middle of header element, create the following rule:

```
header {
    page-break-inside: avoid;
}
```

The other two attributes, page-break-before and page-break-after, support the following values, in addition to auto and avoid:

- always - a page break should always be made before (or after) the element.

- left - works like always except it may generate either one or two page breaks to force the next page to be a left-hand page.

- right - just like left except the next page will be a right-hand page.

You can use the page-break-before attribute to force a new page for each h1 element, for example. You could do the same for each section or article element depending on how the document is structured.

▪ **Caution** These page break attributes are being replaced with generic break attributes. For example, page-break-after will be replaced with break-after. However, as of this writing, there is no support for the new attributes.

Cursor

The shape of the cursor provides important feedback as the mouse is moved over the web page. For example, when hovering over a link, the cursor normally changes to a hand with a pointing finger. It's really easy to set the cursor shape by using the cursor attribute and selecting one of the predefined keywords. For example,

```
a {
    cursor: pointer;
}
```

Rather than listing all of the options here, I'll refer you to the following Mozilla article that lists all of them with sample images: `https://developer.mozilla.org/en-US/docs/Web/CSS/cursor`. You can also hover your mouse over them to see exactly what they will look like in your OS. The cursor is controlled by the OS and the actual shape will vary depending on which OS you are using.

You can also define your own cursors by specifying a URL to an image file. When using a custom cursor, you should also include a predefined keyword as a fallback in case the image file is not supported. Multiple cursors may be defined like this:

```
a {
    cursor: url(custom.png), url(fallback.cur), crosshair;
}
```

Summary

In this chapter I explained how to use both web-safe fonts and web fonts and how to configure the various aspects that can be controlled through CSS. There are quite a few CSS attributes that give you great control over how text is arranged. In the next chapter, I'll demonstrate how to use borders and backgrounds to enhance the content in your HTML document.

■ ■ ■

CHAPTER 12

Borders and Backgrounds

Borders

In some of the examples in previous chapters, I added a border around elements to help visualize the space allocated to them. I used a CSS rule like this:

```
border: 1px solid black;
```

This uses shorthand notation that sets the three primary aspects of a border: width, style, and color. This is equivalent to setting each of the attributes separately:

```
border-width: 1px;
border-style: solid;
border-color: black;
```

Basic Styles

There are eight border styles, which are demonstrated in Figure 12-1. All the major browsers support these, although the implementation varies with each one.

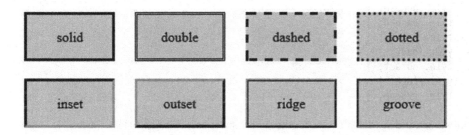

Figure 12-1. *The basic border styles*

© Mark J. Collins 2017

M. J. Collins, *Pro HTML5 with CSS, JavaScript, and Multimedia*, DOI 10.1007/978-1-4842-2463-2_12

To create this demonstration, I used the following markup that creates eight div elements, each with a box class attribute and a specific class for each of the eight styles.

```
<section>
    <div class="box solid">solid</div>
    <div class="box double">double</div>
    <div class="box dashed">dashed</div>
    <div class="box dotted">dotted</div>
    <div class="box inset">inset</div>
    <div class="box outset">outset</div>
    <div class="box ridge">ridge</div>
    <div class="box groove">groove</div>
</section>
```

To make this easier to see, I used the following style rules to give these elements a fixed size, set a background color, and center the text.

```
section {
    background-color: lightyellow;
}

.box {
    display: inline-block;
    width: 100px;
    height: 50px;
    margin: 10px;
    background-color: lightblue;
    text-align: center;
    line-height: 50px;
}
```

The following rules then sets only the border style using a class selector; the width and color are not specified, allowing the browser to use default values.

```
.solid { border-style: solid; }
.double { border-style: double; }
.dashed { border-style: dashed; }
.dotted { border-style: dotted; }
.inset { border-style: inset; }
.outset { border-style: outset; }
.ridge { border-style: ridge; }
.groove { border-style: groove; }
```

The default width is 3px and the default color, for the simple styles, is black. The last four styles, however, use multiple colors to achieve a 3D effect. To make this a little more obvious, I'll make the border wider by adding this to the box selector. The result is shown in Figure 12-2.

```
border-width: 12px;
```

Figure 12-2. *Using a wider border*

You can also adjust the color like this:

```
border-color: green;
```

For the first four styles, since these use a solid color, the border-color attribute works just like you would expect it to. However, the 3D styles use a combination of light and dark to create a shadow effect. When you specify the color, most browsers will honor this color for the light portion, and use black for the shadow areas. For example, Chrome will render this as shown in Figure 12-3.

Figure 12-3. *Using 3D and color in Chrome*

In my opinion, this diminishes the 3D effect and does not look very realistic. In contrast, Firefox uses a light and dark shade of the specified color and has a much better effect as shown in Figure 12-4.

Figure 12-4. *Using 3D and color in Firefox*

Individual Edges

Each of these attributes: border-style, border-width, and border-color are actually shorthand properties as well. You can specify the attribute for each edge independently. For example:

```
.solid {
    border-top-width: 3px;
    border-right-width: 6px;
    border-bottom-width: 9px;
    border-left-width: 12px;
}
```

There is also a shorthand for each edge, allowing you to specify the width, style, and color with a single declaration like this:

```
.double {
    border-top: 3px solid red;
    border-right: 6px dashed blue;
    border-bottom: 9px dotted green;
    border-left: 12px double orange;
}
```

■ **Caution**   Just because you can, doesn't mean you should. The CSS syntax gives you a lot of flexibility to control the border attributes. However, as a general design principle, a border should be consistent around all of the edges. Look at Figure 12-5 to see how bad this looks when mixing border properties. Certainly the 3D effects will completely fail if you don't apply them consistently.

Figure 12-5. *Mixing border attributes*

To demonstrate a more appropriate use of individual border attributes, I'll create a new paragraph element and apply the following CSS rule:

```
<p class="standOut">Make this stand out!</p>

.standOut {
    border-top: 2px solid black;
    border-bottom: 2px solid black;
    display: inline-block;
    text-align: center;
    font-size: xx-large;
}
```

I set only the top and bottom edges with a solid border, which will add a line above and below the text as shown in Figure 12-6.

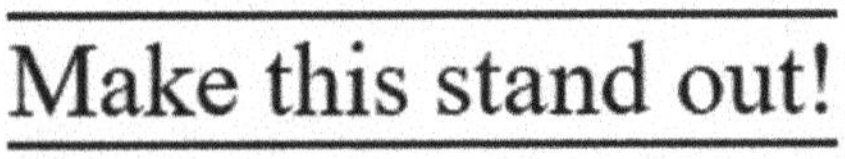

Make this stand out!

Figure 12-6. *Using only a top and bottom border*

Radius

You can easily create rounded corners by setting the border-radius attribute. For example, to set all four corners to be curved with a 5px radius, use the following:

```
border-radius: 5px;
```

Again, this is actually a shorthand property; you can also set individual values. However, the radius applies to corners rather than edges, so the individual attributes are as follows:

- border-top-left-radius
- border-top-right-radius
- border-bottom-right-radius
- border-bottom-left-radius

You can also specify multiple values with a single border-radius declaration. As I've shown, passing a single value will adjust all four corners. If you pass two values, the first will apply to the top-left and bottom-right corners and the second to the top-right and bottom-left corners. If you pass three values, the first will apply to the top-left corner, the second to the top-right and bottom-left corners, and the third to the bottom-right. If you pass four values, each will apply to a different corner, starting with the top left and proceeding in clockwise order.

To demonstrate this, I'll add the following declaration to the box class selector. This will set the top-left and bottom-right corners to have a larger radius than the other two corners. This is rendered as shown in Figure 12-7.

```
border-radius: 20px 10px;
```

Figure 12-7. Applying different corner radii

There are actually two radii for each corner: one in the horizontal direction and one vertical. This is illustrated in Figure 12-8.

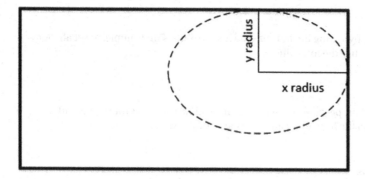

Figure 12-8. *Explaining elliptical corners*

If a single value is supplied, as in the previous example, it will be used for both the x and y radii. In this case, the border shape is a circle. The syntax for entering two values is to separate them with a "/" character. For example:

```
border-radius: 5px / 10px;
```

If you are specifying different radii for each corner, specify the x values first, then add the "/", and then enter the y values. You can supply 1-4 values for the x radius and 1-4 values for the y radius. You don't have to use the same number of values for both x and y. For example, you can supply a single value for x and four values for y; or vice versa. By way of illustration, the following set of declarations are equivalent:

```
border-radius: 20px 10px 5px / 5px 10px;
```

is equivalent to:

```
border-top-left-radius: 20px / 5px;
border-top-right-radius: 10px / 10px;
border-bottom-right-radius: 5px / 5px;
border-bottom-left-radius: 10px / 10px;
```

In the previous example, the radius was specified as an absolute length; however, you can also provide this as a percentage of the element. One particularly interesting application of this is to set the radii like this, which is rendered as shown in Figure 12-9.

```
border-radius: 50% / 50%;
```

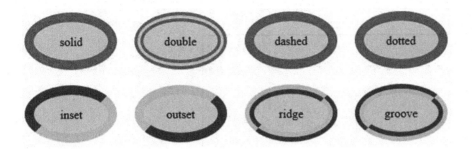

Figure 12-9. *Using elliptical borders*

Using Images

In addition to the eight standard border styles, you can also use an image to give you virtually unlimited flexibility. The image file is specified using the border-image-source attribute:

```
border-image-source: url(pattern.png);
```

Slicing

An image file will have a fixed size but the element that you are bordering may shrink and grow depending on content. You may also apply the image border to elements that have varying shapes and sizes. To deal with this effectively, and avoid distorting the image, the image file is *sliced* into pieces and reassembled. The border image is sliced into nine regions using the specified offset values as illustrated in Figure 12-10.

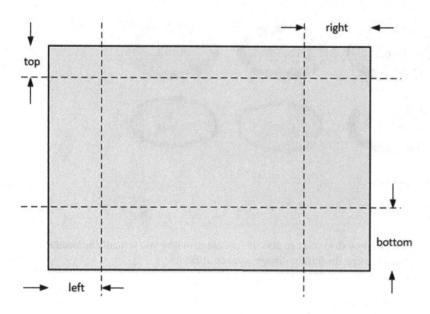

Figure 12-10. *Slicing a border image*

These offsets are specified using the border-image-slice attribute, providing the top, right, bottom, and left values:

```
border-image-slice: 20 25 30 35;
```

The values are specified as numbers with no units; these will be interpreted as pixels for bitmapped images and coordinates for raster images (such as SVG). You can also specify these values as percentages, which will indicate the portion of the overall image width (or height). In typical CSS fashion, you can supply fewer than four values as well. A single value will be used for all four offsets. If two values are provided, the first will be used for the top and bottom and the second for left and right. If three values are supplied, the first will be the top offset, the second will be the left and right, and the third will be the bottom. You can also include the keyword fill anywhere in the value list. If omitted, the center portion of the image will be discarded. If fill is specified, the center will be used as a background.

Allocating

Now that you have your eight (or nine) pieces, you define how they are used to create a border. The first step is to allocate space for the border. The simplest way to do that is to define a normal solid border with a transparent color. For example:

```
border: 35px solid transparent;
```

This does not add a visible border, but will define a space that is 35 pixels wide around the existing element. The subsequent border attributes will then be applied to this space. The alternative is to use the border-image-width attribute:

```
border-image-width: 35px;
```

This will also allocate a space that is 35 pixels wide but with one very important difference. The border attribute will allocate space outside of the element. If the element was a square 100 pixels wide, for example, adding the border will increase the total space used to 170 pixels. However, the border-image-width attribute will allocate the space inside the element. The same 100-pixel square will now only have 30 pixels available to render the actual content. You can adjust for this by using the border-image-outset attribute.

```
border-image-outset: 35px;
```

This will shift the position of each edge toward the outside; the left edge will shift to the left the distance specified, the right edge will shift to the right, etc. Now the actual content of the element will have the original 100-pixel square. However, this introduces another issue; the border-image-outset attribute does not allocate additional space in the DOM; the positioning of the neighboring elements is not changed causing a potential overflow condition. This can be resolved by increasing the margin. So you would need the following declarations:

```
border-image-width: 35px;
border-image-outset: 35px;
margin: 35px;
```

■ **Tip** For simplicity, I'm passing a single value for each of these attributes to define the width, outset, and margin, which will use the same distance for all four edges. You could also specify, two, three, or four values that would be applied as previously described.

As I said, using the border attribute is the simplest approach. In either case, however, you now have a 35-pixel wide strip around the element that will be used to display the image pieces.

Assembling

So back to the eight or nine image pieces; these are now assembled into the allocated space. Figure 12-10 illustrates how the image file is sliced into areas. A similar process also happens to the element that you are now bordering. The width of the narrow strips along the edges is defined by the border width, 35px in the current example. The length of the top and bottom strips is determined by the element width. Likewise, the length of the left and right edges is determined by the height of the element. The corner sections are defined by the border width: in this case a 35-pixel square.

The corresponding slices from the image file are then scaled to fit the spaces of the border. The corners are pretty straightforward. In fact, if you set the offset for the slicing to be the same as the border width, no scaling is needed; the corners are not distorted at all. The edges, however, will often require considerable scaling, especially when you adding a border to elements of different sizes. There are several options to address this using the border-image-repeat attribute.

- stretch - the pieces from the image file are stretched or shrunk as needed to fit the border. This is often only needed in one direction, if the slice offset and border width are the same.

- repeat - the piece is repeated as many times as needed to fill the space, often clipping a partial copy for the last instance.

- round - the pieces are repeated like the repeat option, but only a whole number is used and the individual pieces are scaled to fit the space. This prevents a partial copy from being rendered.

To demonstrate this, I'm using an image file that has an animal print pattern (I think this is a jaguar), which will be used for the border. The markup will create a simple div element:

```
<div class="pattern"></div>
```

The CSS rule will set a fixed width and height and then define a 35-pixel border. I'm also using 35 for the slice offset so the corners will not be scaled. Regardless of the size of the actual element, the edge pieces will only be scaled in one direction. If the image were stretched, it would be somewhat obvious because of the pattern being used, so I'm using the repeat option. The final CSS rule follows and the element is rendered as shown in Figure 12-11.

```
.pattern {
    width: 350px;
    height: 250px;
    margin: 10px;
    border: 35px solid transparent;
    border-image-source: url(pattern.png);
    border-image-slice: 35;
    border-image-repeat: repeat;
}
```

Figure 12-11. *A image border using repeat*

If you look closely at the border, you can see where it has been spliced together because of the repeat option. However, because of the general randomness of the pattern this is not very obvious unless you zoom in. This illustrates the trade-off between the stretch, repeat, and round options. Certain images stretch well and some repeat well.

■ **Caution** Image borders do not support rounded corners. If you apply the border-radius attribute to your border, the element will have rounded corners but the actual visible border around it will have square corners.

For an additional demonstration, I will put a border around an image. The image is a famous painting of George Washington, which I used in Chapter 7. The border uses an image of a picture frame. Here is the markup and CSS rule to accomplish this.

```
<img src="G_Wash.jpg" alt="G. Washington" />
```

```
img {
    margin: 10px;
    width: 350px;
    border: 34px solid transparent;
    border-image-source: url("frame.jpg");
    border-image-slice: 34;
    border-image-repeat: stretch;
}
```

The CSS is similar to the first example; I'm only specifying the width of the image element so the painting will retain its original aspect ratio. The border configuration is basically the same except I'm using the stretch option. The corners are not scaled at all since I'm using 34px for both the slice offset and border with. The edges are mostly straight lines so stretching them along that dimension will not appear distorted. This also avoids the splicing of pieces, which would be more visible with this image. The result is shown in Figure 12-12.

Figure 12-12. *Using the stretch option*

Gradients

For a final border option, you can also use a color gradient. A gradient allows the color to gradually change over an area. They are often used for a background, which I will demonstrate later in this chapter. They can be applied to a border as well. There are two types of gradients:

- linear - the color changes from one edge (or corner) to the opposite.

- radial - the color changes as you move outward from the center.

The result of a gradient is essentially an image. It's not a resource that is downloaded; however, it can be used any place in CSS where an image is expected. To use a gradient border, you'll need to define the gradient as the value for the border-image-source attribute.

Linear Gradients

A linear gradient, as you might expect, is defined by a line, called the gradient line, which passes through the center of the element. This is illustrated in Figure 12-13. The gradient line is defined as an angle measured in clockwise direction from the vertical axis; the gradient line in Figure 12-13 is roughly 130°. The direction of the line is important; if you wanted the starting point to be on the right, add 180° to the angle.

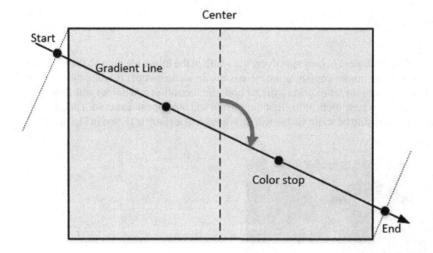

Figure 12-13. *Defining a linear gradient*

The gradient line can also be specified using the to keyword. After the to keyword you then specify one of the sides (top, right, bottom, or left). So to right would create horizontal gradient going from left to right. If you want the gradient to go from corner to corner, specify the ending corner as a pair of sides. For example, to bottom left the gradient will start at the opposite corner, top right and end at the bottom-left corner. The pair of sides can be in either order.

The color is specified at points along this line. At a minimum, the color at the start and end points is required. You can also specify one or more color stops, which are defined as a percentage of the total distance between the start and endpoints. Between these specified points, the color changes gradually. For a simple demonstration, the following markup creates an empty div element and the CSS rule defines the border as a linear gradient.

```
<div class="linear"></div>

.linear {
    width: 350px;
    height: 150px;
    margin: 10px;
    border: 35px solid yellow;
    border-image: linear-gradient(130deg, red, yellow 20%, green 80%, blue);
    border-image-slice: 1;
}
```

This creates a linear gradient that changes gradually from red, yellow, green, and blue. However, since the two color stops were close to the starting and ending point, most of the color will be between yellow and green, with a little bit of red at the start and a little bit of blue at the end. This is rendered as shown in Figure 12-14.

Figure 12-14. *Using a linear gradient for a border*

■ **Caution**   Some browsers may not support gradients, so you should have a fallback to set a solid color. (Currently, Safari does not support border gradients). Instead of setting the solid border to transparent as in the previous examples, set it to a color, which will be used if the gradient can't be used. Also, the border-image-slice attribute is required but you can set this to 1. Since gradients automatically grow and shrink based on the size of the element, there is no need to actually slice the image and reassemble.

Radial Gradients

A radial gradient starts from its center point and the color changes uniformly as it moves outward. This is illustrated in Figure 12-15. The final shape at the end of the gradient can either be a circle or an ellipse. Like linear gradients, you must specify the starting and ending color and you can also define one or more color stops in between.

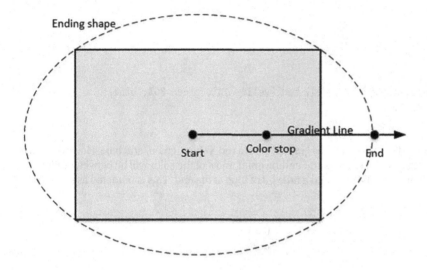

Figure 12-15. *Radial gradients*

To define a radial gradient, you specify the following details:

- Final shape - this can either be `circle` or `ellipse`; the default is `ellipse`.

- Extent - the final size of the gradient is determined by one of the following keywords: (`farthest-corner`, `farthest-side`, `closest-corner`, `closest-side`).

- Starting position - the default, if omitted, is the center of the element. This is specified as an offset from the top-left corner.

- Color stops - 0% indicates the starting point and 100% the ending shape.

For a demonstration, the following markup creates an empty div element and the CSS rules defines a radial gradient to be used with it. This is rendered as shown in Figure 12-16.

```
<div class="radial"></div>

.radial {
    width: 350px;
    height: 150px;
    margin: 20px;
    border: 35px solid yellow;
    border-image: radial-gradient(ellipse farthest-corner at 175px 0px, yellow 0%, orange
75%, green 100%);
    border-image-slice: 1;
}
```

Figure 12-16. *A border with a radial gradient*

Box Shadows

In the last chapter I explained how to configure text shadows. You can accomplish similar effects on almost any element using the box-shadow attribute. This attributes accepts a number of values; some are required but many are optional. If supplied, the values should be in this order:

- inset - (optional) If this value is not included, the shadow will be drawn outside of the element as if the element was above the surrounding area. If inset is specified, the shadow is drawn inside the element, as if the element were sunken below its surroundings.

- x offset - (required) the horizontal offset of the shadow; negative values will cause the shadow to be to the left of the element.

- y offset - (required) the vertical offset of the shadow; negative values will cause the shadow to be above the element.

- blur radius - (optional) specifies how much the shadow diffuses beyond its original size. A larger size will cause a larger, but lighter shadow. Defaults to 0 if not supplied; negative values are not allowed.

- spread radius - (optional) defines the relative size of the shadow. The default value is 0, which means the shadow is the identical size of the element. A negative value will make the shadow smaller and a positive value larger.

- color - (technically optional but should be supplied for maximum support) defines the color of the shadow using any color unit.

The shadow is essentially a new element that sits just below the original element in the z order. Its size and position is relative to the original element. To compute the size and position of the shadow, the original element's shape is shifted based on the x and y offset values. It is then stretched or shrunk as specified by the spread radius. This is illustrated in Figure 12-17. The shadow has a solid fill background using the specified color. If a blur radius is defined, the edges are then stretch beyond the specified size with a blur effect.

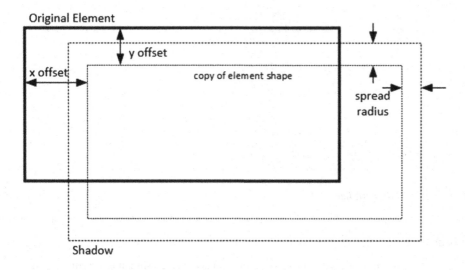

Figure 12-17. Computing the shadow position and size

There are two common uses of box shadows. One is to make an element appear to come off the page. This is accomplished by shifting the shadow slightly, typically down and to the right as illustrated in Figure 12-18. This is accomplished with the following declaration:

```
box-shadow: 10px 10px 5px black;
```

Figure 12-18. *Making an element come off the page*

The other technique is to soften the lines of the element by adding a blur effect on all sides as shown in Figure 12-19. This is done through this declaration, which keeps the same size and position as the original, leaving only the blur visible:

```
box-shadow: 0px 0px 15px black;
```

Figure 12-19. *Adding a blur around an element*

■ **Note**   If a border radius is used, the shadow will also have rounded corners. It follows the same shape as the original element.

Outlines

An outline is a box drawn around an element, like a border. The important difference is that it does not take up any space; it is drawn on top of the space allocated to the existing elements. Because of this, outlines are often used with pseudo-classes such as :hover, since the box can be added or removed without affecting the layout of the page. When defining an outline, you can specify the following attributes:

- outline-color
- outline-style
- outline-width

These attributes can be set individually or with the outline shorthand notation, just like a border is defined. The supported style values are the same eight values supported for border styles (solid, double, dashed, dotted, inset, outset, ridge, and groove). You can also use the value none, which will cause the outline to be hidden.

In addition, the `outline-offset` attribute adds padding between the element and the outline. For example, adding this will shift the outline 5 pixels in all directions. This cannot be done with the `outline` shorthand.

```
outline-offset: 5px;
```

■ **Caution**   The `outline-offset` attribute is not currently supported in IE or Edge.

The following markup creates a div element and the CSS rule adds an outline to it, which is rendered as shown in Figure 12-20.

```
<div class="outline">This is an outline</div>
```

```
.outline {
    outline: 1px solid black;
    outline-offset: 5px;
}
```

This is an outline

Figure 12-20. *Demonstrating an outline*

■ **Note**   The wider the border, the more space the outline will use. It doesn't adjust the position of the elements but superimposes the box on the existing space. The box is always outside of the element that is being outlined so it won't affect the element, but it can overflow the neighboring elements.

Backgrounds

There are basically two options for setting a background to an element; a color or an image. To use a color simply set the `background-color` attribute using any of the color units explained in Chapter 2. These are also summarized in the reference material in Appendix C. When using images there are a few more attributes that control how the image is displayed.

Image Attributes

A background image can be specified for an element using the `background-image` attribute. This is pretty straightforward; just specify the URL for the image file to be used. You can specify multiple images that are stacked on top of each other in the order specified. However, there are a few other attributes that affect how the image is rendered.

Attachment

The background-attachment attribute defines how the image is positioned and supports the following values:

- fixed - the image stays fixed relative to the window; scrolling the window has no effect on the background image.

- local - the image is fixed relative to the element's content. If you scroll the contents, the background image will scroll with it.

- scroll - (this is the default value) the image is fixed relative to the element. It will move with the element but if the contents within the element are scrolled, the background is not.

Also, since multiple images can be specified, multiple values for the background-attachment attribute can be specified as well. Each one is separated with a comma and applied to the corresponding image in the order specified.

Origin

For local and scroll options, the background-origin attribute defines the containing rectangle for the image. The following values are supported:

- border-box - the background extends to the outside edge of the element's border.

- content-box - the background only covers the actual element content area (does not include the padding and border).

- padding-box - the background includes the element content and the padding but not the border.

Repeat

The background-repeat attribute specifies if and how a background image should be repeated to fill the necessary space. The image can be repeated in both the horizontal and vertical directions and you can provide two different values to the background-repeat attribute. The first value applies to the horizontal behavior and the second is used for vertical repeat. The following values are allowed:

- no-repeat - the image is not repeated, possibly leaving areas not covered by the image.

- repeat - (default) the image is repeated as often as necessary, with the last repeat often being clipped.

- round - repeats the image but only whole images are displayed. The displayed images are then stretched uniformly to fill in any remaining gaps.

- space - repeat only whole images similar to the round option. However, instead of stretching the images to fill the gap, it leaves a uniform spacing between them. The first and last images are pinned to the left and right edges (or bottom and top) and the spaces are between the images.

There is also a shorthand where both the horizontal and vertical behaviors can be specified with a single value. If a single value of no-repeat, repeat, round, or space is used, it will be applied for both the horizontal and vertical values. In addition, repeat-x indicates the repeat option is used for horizontal but no-repeat for vertical. Likewise, repeat-y indicates the opposite.

■ **Caution** As of this writing, the round and space values are not supported by Firefox or Safari.

Position

The background-position attribute is used to specify where the image is positioned relative to its origin. The default value is 0 0, indicating the top-left corner. The position can be specified with one of the following keywords: top, right, bottom, left, or center. It can also be specified as a pair of distance values, either relative or absolute, separated with a space. If multiple images are used, multiple positions can be specified as well; these should be separated by a comma.

Size

The size of the image is indicated through the background-size attribute. The size can be specified with one of the following keywords:

- contain - the image is scaled as large as possible while still maintaining the original aspect ratio. This generally means that in one dimension or the other, there will be blank space around the image. It is normally centered unless this is overridden by the background-position attribute.

- cover - the image is scaled as large as possible, maintaining the aspect ratio. However, in order to cover the small dimension, the image is often clipped in the other dimension.

Alternatively, you can specify a single distance value, either relative or absolute, which will define the width of the background. In this case, the height will be set to auto. You can also specify two values, separated by a space: the first defining the width and the second defining the height. The keyword auto can be used with either the single or double value entry. This specifies that this dimension is set based on the intrinsic image size or as needed to maintain the aspect ratio. If there are multiple images, multiple sizes can be supplied as well, separated by a comma.

Clipping

The background-clip attribute specifies where the background should be clipped. This attribute allows you to control whether the background should extend over the padding and border area of an element. The following values are supported:

- border-box - the background extends to the outside edge of the element's border.

- content-box - the background only covers the actual element content area (does not include the padding and border).

- padding-box - the background includes the element content and the padding but not the border.

■ **Note** These values are identical to the background-origin attribute and in fact the background-clip works much like the background-origin. To be clear, background-origin determines the positioning of the image, that is, which rectangle is the image aligned with. The background-clip attribute determines the rectangle where the background ends, either for a color or an image background.

Background Shorthand

It's a fairly common practice to specify several of the background attributes in a single declaration using the background shorthand notation. The following attributes can be set in the background shorthand:

- background-image
- background-position
- background-size
- background-repeat
- background-attachment
- background-origin
- background-clip
- background-color

All of these are optional. Generally, the order doesn't matter except background-size must come directly after background-position, if both are used, and they should be separated with a slash (/). The other attributes are separated by a space.

I mentioned several times that you can define multiple images in a background, which are referred to as layers. When using the shorthand, you should specify all the desired attributes for one layer, then add a comma, and then specify the attributes for the next layer. The attributes for a single layer are declared together and each layer is separated by a comma. The background-color attribute can only be set on the final layer.

When using the background shorthand, any attributes that are not specified will be set to the default value. If you specify a background attribute, background-position for example, in one declaration and then set another using the shorthand, the previous setting for background-position will be undone and revert back to the default value. For example, consider the following. The background will not be centered because the shorthand only supplied the color attribute; the position was reverted to the default value.

```
div {
    background-position: center;
    background: red;
}
```

Examples

For a quick demonstration, I'll go back to the border samples at the beginning of the chapter and replace the background color with an image using the background shortcut. The CSS rule now looks like this:

```
section {
    /*background-color: lightyellow;*/
    background: url(smiley.png) scroll space;
}
```

I used scroll for the background-attachment because I wanted the image fixed to the containing element. Since the image is relatively small I need it to repeat in both directions; however, I don't want any faces clipped leaving only half of a face. The round value would accomplish this but would distort the images by stretching them to fill in the gaps. The space value is the appropriate choice for the background-repeat option. This is rendered as shown in Figure 12-21.

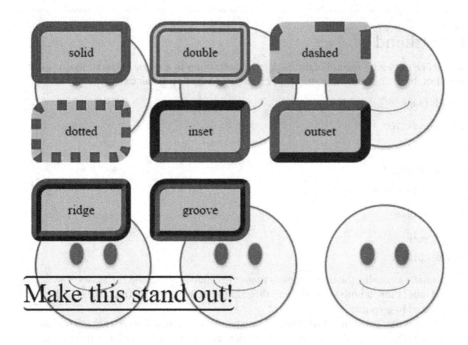

Figure 12-21. *Using a repeated background image*

To demonstrate using a gradient, I'll replace this with a linear gradient, which is set using the background-image attribute. In this example, I'm using the direction keywords instead on an angle to define the gradient line. This is rendered as shown in Figure 12-22.

```
section {
    /*background-color: lightyellow;*/
    /*background: url(smiley.png) scroll space;*/
    background-image: linear-gradient(to right bottom, #FFF, #0EE);
}
```

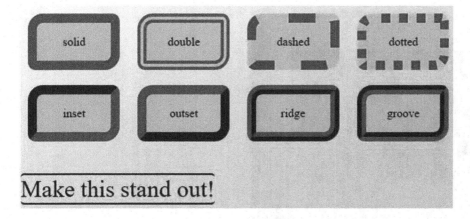

Figure 12-22. *Using a background gradient*

When framing a picture, a mat is often used to provide a border between the picture and the actual frame. You can accomplish the same effect in CSS by combining the background and border attributes. I'll show how this is done using the George Washing painting. I'll add padding and a background color to the previous CSS rule that I demonstrated earlier. The result is shown in Figure 12-23.

```
img {
    margin: 10px;
    width: 350px;
    border: 34px solid transparent;
    border-image-source: url("frame.jpg");
    border-image-slice: 34;
    border-image-repeat: stretch;
    padding: 30px;
    background-color: silver;
}
```

Figure 12-23. *Adding a mat to a picture*

■ **Tip**   If you wanted to create multiple mats, you could accomplish that by putting the image element inside a div element. Set the background of image to be the inner mat and the background of the div to be the outer mat. Then put the border around the div instead of the image.

For a final demonstration, I'll add a fixed background image to the body element:

```
body {
    background: url(smiley.png) fixed no-repeat center;
}
```

This will use the same smiley face image but make it fixed to the window. When you scroll, the background image does not move with the content. The no-repeat value sets the background-repeat attribute so only a single instance will be displayed. The center value sets the background-position attribute and causes the image to be centered, in this case centered on the window. The result is shown in Figure 12-24.

Figure 12-24. *Using a fixed background image*

This works like the `display: fixed;` attribute that I explained in Chapter 10. The difference, however, is that since the background image is behind the foreground elements in the z-order, some or all of the image may be hidden.

■ **Tip** When using a fixed background image, it doesn't matter which element it is assigned to since its position is based on the window, not the element. However, if you added this to a `div` or paragraph element, for example, a separate image would be displayed for each one. They would all be in the same place so it would not change how the page appears, but it is certainly less efficient to have multiple images to render. Since there can only be one `body` element, this is the logical place to put fixed background images.

Summary

In this chapter I explained numerous techniques for enhancing your web page using various types of borders and backgrounds. There are similarities between the two, primarily that they can both be defined with a color, an image, or a gradient. Both are also just below the element in the z-order. Borders take up space in the document while backgrounds do not. I also explained how box shadows and outlines can be used. These are different from borders although they can have a similar effect.

There are a lot of attributes that can be used and many of these can be expressed using shorthand notation. Borders, in particular, have a significant number of attributes because each edge can be defined separately. However, a shorthand can be used to define all of the attributes of a single edge. Similarly, a shorthand can be used to set a single attribute on all of the edges.

Using images for a border can achieve some very interesting effects but require an understanding of how the browser uses them. The image is sliced into parts and each part is applied to a different part of the border. The attributes give you control on how each part is stretched or repeated, as necessary, to fill the space.

Gradients are used to gradually change the color along a particular direction. Linear gradients change the color from one edge or corner to the opposite. Radial gradients change color from the center moving outward. You define the beginning and ending color, and can also define specific color stops along the gradient.

In the next chapter I will explain how tables can be used to arrange and format content.

Styling Tables

In this chapter I will explain two different topics that are largely unrelated except that they both involve tables. First, I will demonstrate how to use CSS to format a `table` element. In Chapter 6 I described all of the various HTML elements that are used to construct a table such as `table`, table row (`tr`), table header cell (`th`), and table cell (`td`). Now I'll show you the CSS attributes that are available to arrange these elements, visually. The second topic is to explain how you can use CSS to turn non-tabular data into table-like elements so you can use similar styling techniques.

Styling Tables

I explained the markup elements used to create a table in Chapter 6. You can refer back to that chapter for more details; however, as a quick review, the following table uses most of the common table elements. This provides a summary of the pieces used in the game of Chess. I will be using this table to demonstrate most of the styling options. The markup is shown in Listing 13-1 and the resulting table is rendered as shown in Figure 13-1.

Listing 13-1. A simple HTML table

```
<table>
    <caption>Chess Pieces</caption>
    <thead>
        <tr>
            <th>Name</th>
            <th>Qty</th>
            <th>Points</th>
            <th>Symbol</th>
            <th>Movement</th>
        </tr>
    </thead>
    <tbody>
        <tr>
            <th>King</th><td>1</td><td>n/a</td>
            <td><img src="king.png" alt="King" /></td>
            <td>1 space in any direction</td>
        </tr>
```

```
        <tr>
            <th>Queen</th><td>1</td><td>10</td>
            <td><img src="queen.png" alt="Queen" /></td>
            <td>any number of spaces in any direction</td>
        </tr>
        <tr>
            <th>Rook</th><td>2</td><td>5</td>
            <td><img src="rook.png" alt="Rook" /></td>
            <td>any number if spaces forward, backwards, or sideways</td>
        </tr>
        <tr>
            <th>Bishop</th><td>2</td><td>3</td>
            <td><img src="bishop.png" alt="Bishop" /></td>
            <td>any number of spaces diagonally</td>
        </tr>
        <tr>
            <th>Knight</th><td>2</td><td>3</td>
            <td><img src="knight.png" alt="Knight" /></td>
            <td>2 spaces up or down and 1 space sideways OR 1 space up or down and 2 spaces
                sideways; can jump pieces</td>
        </tr>
        <tr>
            <th>Pawn</th><td>8</td><td>1</td>
            <td><img src="pawn.png" alt="Pawn" /></td>
            <td>generally 1 space forward; first move can be 2 spaces forward;
                captures 1 space forward diagonally</td>
        </tr>
    </tbody>
    <tfoot>
        <tr>
            <th>Totals</th><td>16</td><td>40</td><td></td><td></td>
        </tr>
    </tfoot>
</table>
```

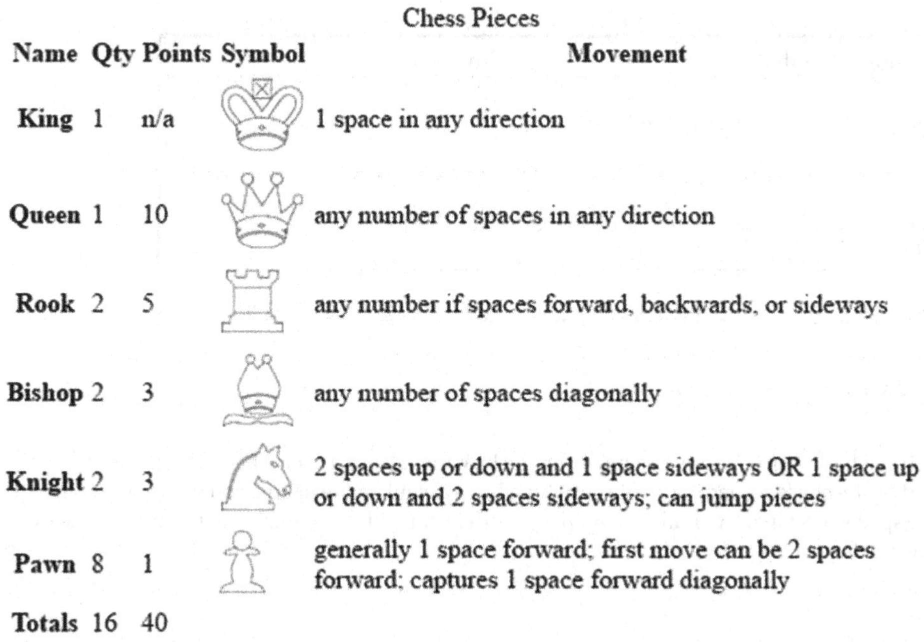

Chess Pieces

Name	Qty	Points	Symbol	Movement
King	1	n/a		1 space in any direction
Queen	1	10		any number of spaces in any direction
Rook	2	5		any number if spaces forward, backwards, or sideways
Bishop	2	3		any number of spaces diagonally
Knight	2	3		2 spaces up or down and 1 space sideways OR 1 space up or down and 2 spaces sideways; can jump pieces
Pawn	8	1		generally 1 space forward; first move can be 2 spaces forward; captures 1 space forward diagonally
Totals	16	40		

Figure 13-1. *The initial, unstyled table*

Basic Table Styling

You can see from Figure 13-1 that we have some work to do as this looks awful. However, applying some simple border, padding, and alignment attributes will do wonders.

Borders

There are four elements that you can place a border around: the entire table (table), the caption (caption), and the cells (th and td). The table row (tr) element is a container element but does not have any visible content of its own. Likewise, thead, tbody, and tfoot are also containers and have no visible content. You can apply styles to these elements and they would be inherited by the child elements. However, border properties are not inherited for good reason. I will come back to row borders later but for now, we'll start with the table and cells. The following CSS rules will add a thick border around the table and a thin border around the cells. This is rendered as shown in Figure 13-2.

```
table {
    border: 3px solid black;
}

th, td {
    border: 1px solid black;
}
```

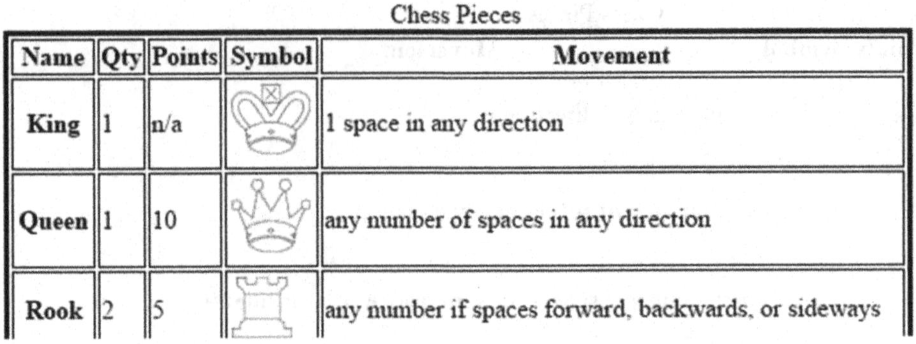

Chess Pieces

Name	Qty	Points	Symbol	Movement
King	1	n/a		1 space in any direction
Queen	1	10		any number of spaces in any direction
Rook	2	5		any number if spaces forward, backwards, or sideways

Figure 13-2. *Add a border to the table and cells*

So now each cell has a border around it; however, the browser has put a space between the borders. This is controlled by the border-spacing attribute, which has a default value of 2px. You can increase this if you want more space or set it to 0 to remove the space entirely. If I add the following to the table selector, the result is shown in Figure 13-3.

```
border-spacing: 0;
```

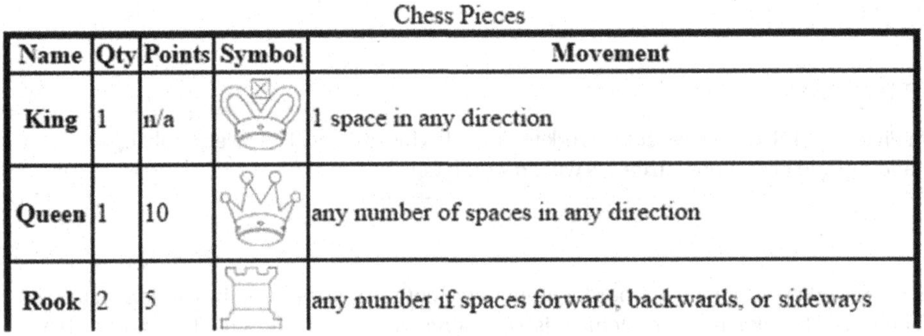

Chess Pieces

Name	Qty	Points	Symbol	Movement
King	1	n/a		1 space in any direction
Queen	1	10		any number of spaces in any direction
Rook	2	5		any number if spaces forward, backwards, or sideways

Figure 13-3. *Removing the border space*

The spaces are gone but the borders are thicker now. They're not actually thicker, but since they are touching, the width of each is combined. If this is not the effect you want, instead of removing the space between the border, you can use the border-collapse attribute to make adjoining cells share a common border. This supports the following values:

- separate - (default) the borders between adjoining cells are drawn separately. The amount of space between them is controlled by the border-spacing property as I've previously explained. This invokes the browser's *separated borders model*.

- collapsed - two adjoining borders are collapsed into a single shared border. This is referred to as the *collapsing border model*.

What happens when adjoining borders have different style attributes: which one is used? The W3C Recommendation provide simple and clear guidelines:

The following rules determine which border style "wins" in case of a conflict:

1. Borders with the 'border-style' of 'hidden' take precedence over all other conflicting borders. Any border with this value suppresses all borders at this location.

2. Borders with a style of 'none' have the lowest priority. Only if the border properties of all the elements meeting at this edge are 'none' will the border be omitted (but note that 'none' is the default value for the border style.)

3. If none of the styles are 'hidden' and at least one of them is not 'none', then narrow borders are discarded in favor of wider ones. If several have the same 'border-width' then styles are preferred in this order: 'double', 'solid', 'dashed', 'dotted', 'ridge', 'outset', 'groove', and the lowest: 'inset'.

4. If border styles differ only in color, then a style set on a cell wins over one on a row, which wins over a row group, column, column group and, lastly, table. When two elements of the same type conflict, then the one further to the left (if the table's 'direction' is 'ltr'; right, if it is 'rtl') and further to the top wins.

Cascading Style Sheets Level 2 Revision 1 (CSS 2.1), paragraph 17.6.2.1, Border conflict resolution

Replacing the border-spacing attribute with the following declaration will cause the table to be rendered as shown in Figure 13-4.

```
border-collapse: collapse;
```

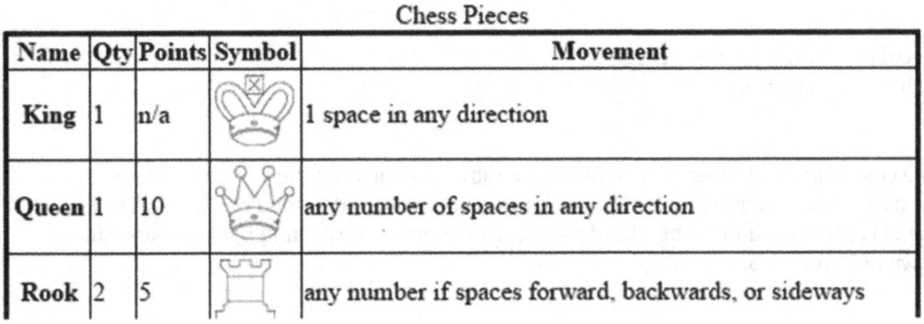

Chess Pieces				
Name	Qty	Points	Symbol	Movement
King	1	n/a		1 space in any direction
Queen	1	10		any number of spaces in any direction
Rook	2	5		any number if spaces forward, backwards, or sideways

Figure 13-4. Using the border-collapse attribute

Empty Cells

If you're using the separated borders model, you can control what happens to an empty cell using the empty-cells attribute. This has two values: show and hide, with show being the default. Obviously, if the cell is empty there is no content to display. However, the border can still be drawn around the cell and whatever background is used can be shown as well.

If this value is set to show, the border and background will be shown; this will appear as an empty cell. If the empty-cells attribute is set to hide, the border and background will be hidden. This will appear as if the cell did not exist.

■ **Note** The empty-cells attribute only works if the separated borders model is used. If you're using the collapsing border model, this attribute is ignored.

Row Borders

Now let's see about adding a row border. As I said, you can't add a border to a row, only the cells within the row. However, as I explained in the last chapter, you can set the border edges individually. For example, you can set a border only for the top and bottom edges. Then you'll need to set the left edge for the first cell and the right edge for the last cell. To illustrate this technique, replace the entire CSS with the following rules to create a border around the rows, not the individual cells.

```
table {
    border: 3px solid black;
    border-collapse: collapse;
}

th, td {
    border-top:  1px solid black;
    border-bottom: 1px solid black;
}

table th:first-child, table td:first-child {
    border-left: 1px solid black;
}

table th:last-child, table td:last-child  {
    border-right: 1px solid black;
}
```

The first rule creates a thick border around the entire table and includes the border-collapse attribute. The next rule creates a thin top and bottom border around all of the cells (th and td). The last two rules use the :first-child and :last-child pseudo-classes to set the left and right borders. This is rendered as shown in Figure 13-5.

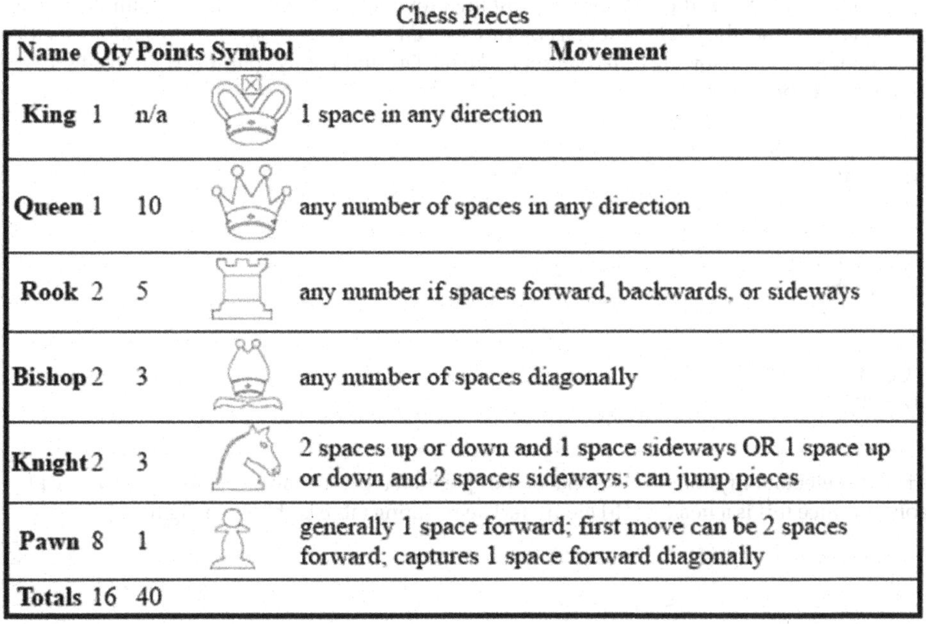

Chess Pieces

Name	Qty	Points	Symbol	Movement
King	1	n/a		1 space in any direction
Queen	1	10		any number of spaces in any direction
Rook	2	5		any number if spaces forward, backwards, or sideways
Bishop	2	3		any number of spaces diagonally
Knight	2	3		2 spaces up or down and 1 space sideways OR 1 space up or down and 2 spaces sideways; can jump pieces
Pawn	8	1		generally 1 space forward; first move can be 2 spaces forward; captures 1 space forward diagonally
Totals	16	40		

Figure 13-5. Creating row borders

Personally, I don't think this looks good for this particular table so I will revert back to the previous CSS for the remaining demonstrations.

Padding and Alignment

I won't say much about padding as I've explained this in the previous chapter. However, one of the issues with the default style is that the borders are too close to the contents. You easily fix this by setting the padding on all of the visible elements using the following rule.

```
th, td, caption {
    padding: 5px;
}
```

■ **Caution** You might be tempted to simply set the padding on the table element; however, the padding attribute is not inherited. So, you'll need to set it on each element.

I explained the alignment attributes in Chapter 11, which also apply to tables. By default, the table header cell (th) elements are centered both horizontally and vertically. The table cell (td) elements are centered vertically but left justified. As a general rule of thumb, text should be left justified and numbers are right justified. While perhaps not as universally accepted, I recommend that images be centered. Certainly, in this table, the images would look better centered. Notice the pawn is smaller than the rest and it appears misaligned.

Table cells are grouped into rows; there is no such container for columns. Column 2, for example, is just the second cell of each row. To set the alignment of a column, we can use the :nth-of-type pseudo-selector that I explained in Chapter 9. The following rules will set make the Qty and Points columns right justified, and the Symbol column will be centered.

```
td:nth-of-type(1) { /*Qty*/
    text-align: right;
    }

td:nth-of-type(2) { /*Points*/
    text-align: right;
    }

td:nth-of-type(3) { /*Symbol*/
    text-align: center;
    }
```

The :nth-of-type selector only counts elements of the specified type: the table cell, in this case. It will skip the Name column since this is a header (th) element. The resulting table is shown in Figure 13-6.

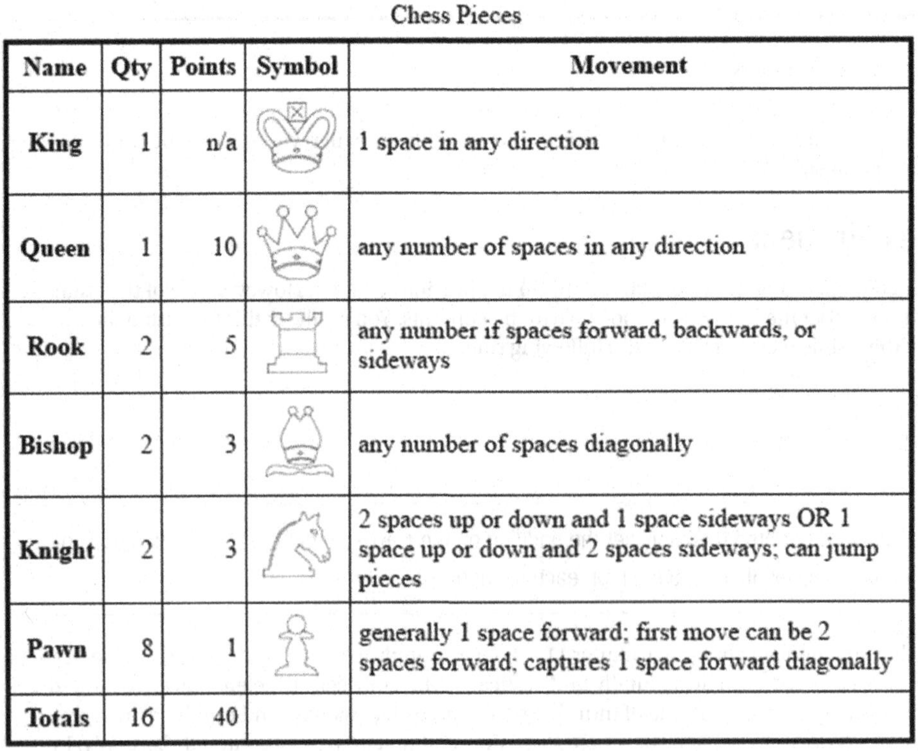

Chess Pieces

Name	Qty	Points	Symbol	Movement
King	1	n/a		1 space in any direction
Queen	1	10		any number of spaces in any direction
Rook	2	5		any number if spaces forward, backwards, or sideways
Bishop	2	3		any number of spaces diagonally
Knight	2	3		2 spaces up or down and 1 space sideways OR 1 space up or down and 2 spaces sideways; can jump pieces
Pawn	8	1		generally 1 space forward; first move can be 2 spaces forward; captures 1 space forward diagonally
Totals	16	40		

Figure 13-6. Adjusting padding and alignment

Caption

Notice that the caption, visually, is outside of the table, by default, just above the table. Even though the caption element is nested inside the table element, in terms of the table layout it is not part of the table. To change the style of the caption you'll need to style it separately. To keep the caption consistent with the table you can add the following CSS rule. This will give the same size border and amount of padding as the table.

```
table caption {
    border: 3px solid black;
}
```

However, the bottom border will be adjacent to the top border of the table, creating a line that is twice as wide as the other borders. The border-collapse attribute won't help in this scenario because the caption is not a table element. Instead, I'll make the width of the bottom edge 0, since it can use the table's top border as its bottom border. The final CSS rule will look like this, and it is rendered as shown in Figure 13-7.

```
table caption {
    /*border: 3px solid black;*/
    border-style: solid;
    border-color: black;
    border-width: 3px 3px 0px 3px;
}
```

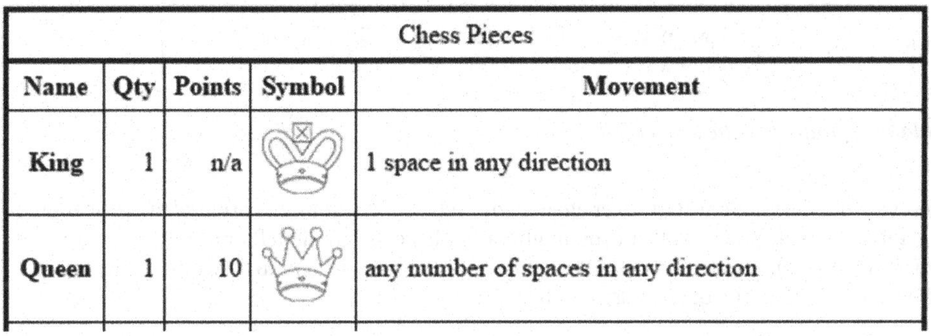

Chess Pieces				
Name	**Qty**	**Points**	**Symbol**	**Movement**
King	1	n/a	♔	1 space in any direction
Queen	1	10	♕	any number of spaces in any direction

Figure 13-7. Styling the caption

With the caption-side attribute, you can move this, although the only supported values are top and bottom. If you choose to move it to below the table, set caption-side: bottom; and don't forget to also fix the border because now you'll need the top edge to be 0 width instead of the bottom.

Additional Table Styling

We now have a decent-looking table; however, I will demonstrate a few more techniques, such as backgrounds and highlighting, that you can use to improve the table layout.

Background

You can set a background color, image, or gradient on any of the table elements. I explained how each of these can be used in the previous chapter so I won't say much about them here. My typical approach is to provide either a background color or gradient to the header cells. You can do this with a simple CSS rule like this; the result is shown in Figure 13-8.

```
th {
    background-color: #DDB;
    background: linear-gradient(to bottom right, #FFF 0%, #DDB 100%);
}
```

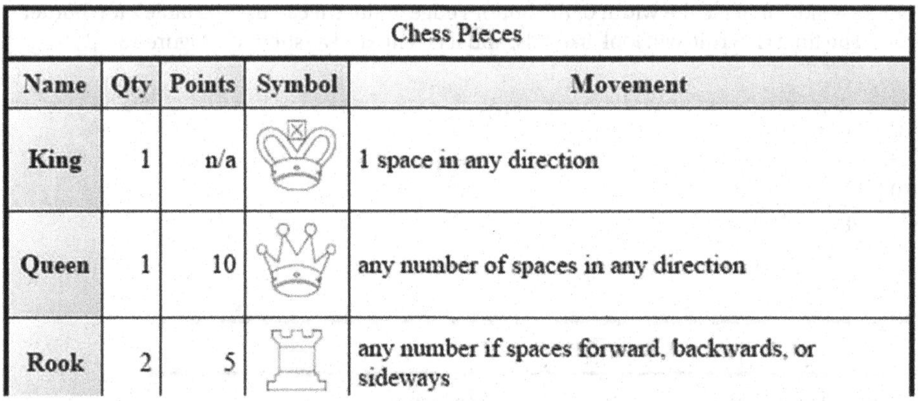

Chess Pieces				
Name	Qty	Points	Symbol	Movement
King	1	n/a	♔	1 space in any direction
Queen	1	10	♕	any number of spaces in any direction
Rook	2	5	♖	any number if spaces forward, backwards, or sideways

Figure 13-8. *Adding a gradient to the header cells*

Notice, however, that the gradient starts over again with each cell. The top-left corner of every header cell is white. You might actually prefer that, but you might rather have the gradient flow evenly across the whole header row (or column). You can accomplish that by applying the gradient to the entire table, and then clearing the background for the other cells, like this:

```
table {
    background-color: #DDB;
    background: linear-gradient(to bottom right, #F4F4F0 0%, #DDB 100%);
}

td {
    background-color: white;
    background-image: none;
}
```

Since the gradient is spread over a larger area, I changed the beginning color to be slightly darker to keep it from looking too washed out in the first few cells. The resulting table is shown in Figure 13-9.

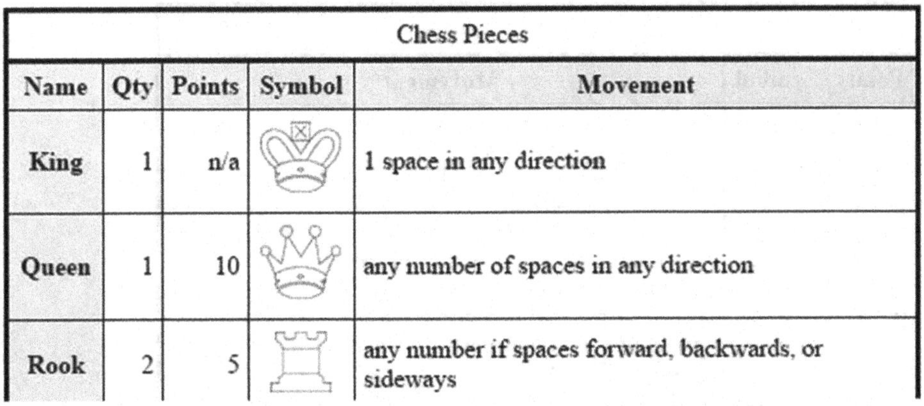

Chess Pieces				
Name	**Qty**	**Points**	**Symbol**	**Movement**
King	1	n/a		1 space in any direction
Queen	1	10		any number of spaces in any direction
Rook	2	5		any number if spaces forward, backwards, or sideways

Figure 13-9. *The revised header gradient*

▤ **Tip**   I am setting both the background-color and background-image in case the browser doesn't support gradients. The border-image attribute is defined last, which will overwrite the color setting if both are supported. This is a good practice to follow.

Zebra Striping

Another simple technique using the :nth-of-type pseudo-selector is to alternate the background color of each row. This is known as zebra striping. This easily done with the following CSS rule.

```
tr:nth-of-type(even)>td {
    background-color: #F4F4F0;
}
```

This returns every even row since the keyword even is used instead of a specific row number. You could also use the odd keyword. However, we don't want to apply the background to the entire row, since the header cell (th) is part of the gradient applied earlier. The > operator is used to indicate only immediate children, and combined with the td element selector, it will return only the table cell elements on the even rows. The result is shown in Figure 13-10.

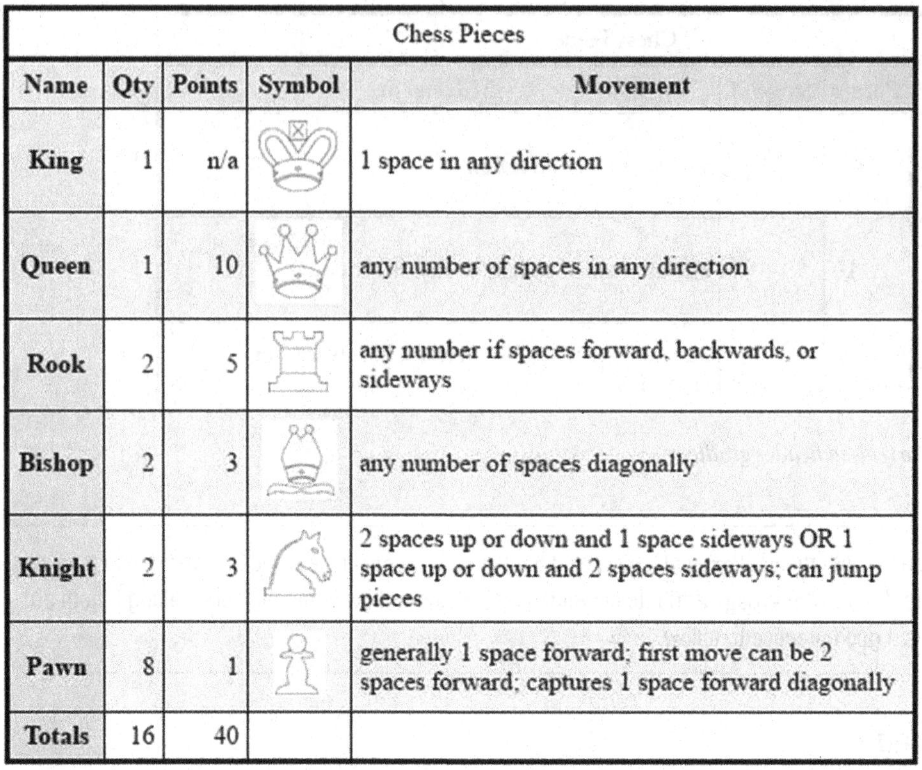

Chess Pieces				
Name	Qty	Points	Symbol	Movement
King	1	n/a		1 space in any direction
Queen	1	10		any number of spaces in any direction
Rook	2	5		any number if spaces forward, backwards, or sideways
Bishop	2	3		any number of spaces diagonally
Knight	2	3		2 spaces up or down and 1 space sideways OR 1 space up or down and 2 spaces sideways; can jump pieces
Pawn	8	1		generally 1 space forward; first move can be 2 spaces forward; captures 1 space forward diagonally
Totals	16	40		

Figure 13-10. Using zebra striping

For one miscellaneous update, I'll increase the font size of the caption using the following rule. As with the rest of the text in this table, you can change all of the font attributes as well. Refer to Chapter 11 for the options available.

```
caption {
    font-size: xx-large;
}
```

Highlighting

You can easily highlight a row by adjusting the background color. This will work much like the zebra striping except you select a single row. Also, in the striping example we didn't update the header cell; in this example, I'll update the header cell as well. However, setting the background on a row has no effect, you need to set the background on the row child elements, the table cells (td) and table header cells (th). The following CSS rule will accomplish this:

```
tr:nth-child(3)>th, tr:nth-child(3)>td {
    background-color: yellow;
}
```

You can also highlight a column using a similar technique. Again, you'll need to combine two selectors: one for the header cells and one for the other cells. The resulting table is shown in Figure 13-11.

```
th:nth-child(3), table td:nth-child(3) {
    background-color: yellow;
}
```

<table>
<tr><td colspan="5" align="center">Chess Pieces</td></tr>
<tr><td>Name</td><td>Qty</td><td>Points</td><td>Symbol</td><td>Movement</td></tr>
<tr><td>King</td><td>1</td><td>n/a</td><td></td><td>1 space in any direction</td></tr>
<tr><td>Queen</td><td>1</td><td>10</td><td></td><td>any number of spaces in any direction</td></tr>
<tr><td>Rook</td><td>2</td><td>5</td><td></td><td>any number if spaces forward, backwards, or sideways</td></tr>
<tr><td>Bishop</td><td>2</td><td>3</td><td></td><td>any number of spaces diagonally</td></tr>
<tr><td>Knight</td><td>2</td><td>3</td><td></td><td>2 spaces up or down and 1 space sideways OR 1 space up or down and 2 spaces sideways; can jump pieces</td></tr>
<tr><td>Pawn</td><td>8</td><td>1</td><td></td><td>generally 1 space forward; first move can be 2 spaces forward; captures 1 space forward diagonally</td></tr>
<tr><td>Totals</td><td>16</td><td>40</td><td></td><td></td></tr>
</table>

Figure 13-11. Highlighting a row and a column

■ **Tip**   Notice that it is actually the fourth row that was highlighted if you count the header. If you look at the markup, the table element has three children: a thead, tbody, and a tfoot element. The head and foot each have a single child, a tr element. The body has six child tr elements. The tr:nth-child(3) selector will return any row that happens to be the third child of its immediate parent. Since the body rows have a different parent, the numbering starts back at 1. Also, I'm using :nth-child instead of :nth-of-type since I know that all the siblings are rows. In this case :nth-child and :nth-of-type produce the same result. I recommend using :nth-of-type in most cases as it will still work if other element types are later added.

■ **Note**   The individual elements within a table are stacked on top of each other, and it's important to know the order of that stack, especially when using multiple backgrounds. The order is fairly intuitive: the table element is on the bottom, on top of that lie the caption, thead, tbody, and tfoot elements. After that, the row (tr) elements are placed and then finally, the cells (th and td). In most cases, only the caption and cells are actually visible. However, if you are playing around with opacity, the other backgrounds can be exposed.

Creating Tables with CSS

If you've searched the Web for articles on HTML tables, you've likely encountered some lively debate regarding the use of HTML table elements. Some people state that you should never use them – that this should be done in CSS. Opponents of this view push back and say that HTML is where this belongs, not CSS. This might give you the notion that HTML tables and CSS tables (as the two views are sometimes referred to) are two different techniques for accomplishing the same thing. But this is not true; these techniques were intended to solve completely different problems.

Tabular data such as team standings, stock positions, or a list of contact details, should be in tables. For example, if you are displaying stock positions and have four pieces of information for each stock: stock symbol, yesterday's closing position, percent gain or loss, and volume traded. Each piece of data such as $35.87, 0.51%, or 1.4 million, has no meaning unless you can associate these to the stock that they belong to. It's only when individual pieces of data (cells) are grouped together (rows) that they can have any meaning. This is what HTML tables should be used for. Another way to look at it is that there is no other logical way to organize these data points. If you tried grouping all the stock symbols together and then all of the closing positions, it wouldn't make any sense. There is inherent structure in the data, which should be captured in the HTML markup.

On the other hand, if you're trying to lay out a web page, perhaps with a set of links on the left side and related articles on the right side, for example, this is not tabular data. This is a job for CSS. The easiest way to distinguish between the two scenarios is to ask is this the only logical way to structure the content. In this case, no, there are lots of ways this could be done. You could put the links across the top of the page, and perhaps the article could be on the left.

Doing this in CSS also makes it a lot easier to adjust the layout when you need to render the page on different devices. Accessibility is another important reason to not use tables for layout. Screen readers, for example, read the HTML, and if you put non-tabular data into tables, the presentation of your site can be very confusing.

Display Attribute

First of all, you need to understand that the table elements work the way they do solely because of the value assigned to the display attribute. In Chapter 10, we looked at a couple of values for the display attribute, primarily block and inline. There are quite a few more values and they are mostly related to tables. Each of the table elements that I explained in Chapter 6 is assigned one of these values as its default display attribute. In fact, it is the specific display value that makes table elements work like they do. Table 13-1 lists each of the elements and the default display value assigned to it.

Table 13-1. *Table Display Attributes*

HTML Element	Default Display Attribute
table	table
tr	table-row
th, td	table-cell
thead	table-header-group
tbody	table-row-group
tfoot	table-footer-group
col	table-column
colgroup	table-column-group
caption	table-caption

CSS Table Demonstration

You can accomplish the same layout with non-tabular elements by simply applying the correct value for the display attribute. To demonstrate this, I'll re-create the same table that was used at the beginning of the chapter using only simple HTML elements such as div and p elements. This uses the class attribute to make it easier to select the appropriate entities later. This is shown in Listing 13-2.

Listing 13-2. Using non-tabular elements

```
<div class="table">
    <div class="head row">
        <h3>Name</h3>
        <h3>Qty</h3>
        <h3>Points</h3>
        <h3>Symbol</h3>
        <h3>Movement</h3>
    </div>
    <div class="body row">
        <h3>King</h3><p>1</p><p>n/a</p>
        <p><img src="king.png" alt="King" /></p>
        <p>1 space in any direction</p>
    </div>
    <div class="body row">
        <h3>Queen</h3><p>1</p><p>10</p>
        <p><img src="queen.png" alt="Queen" />
        <p>any number of spaces in any direction</p>
    </div>
    <div class="body row">
        <h3>Rook</h3><p>2</p><p>5</p>
        <p><img src="rook.png" alt="Rook" /></p>
        <p>any number if spaces forward, backwards, or sideways</p>
    </div>
```

```
    <div class="body row">
        <h3>Bishop</h3><p>2</p><p>3</p>
        <p><img src="bishop.png" alt="Bishop" /></p>
        <p>any number of spaces diagonally</p>
    </div>
    <div class="body row">
        <h3>Knight</h3><p>2</p><p>3</p>
        <p><img src="knight.png" alt="Knight" /></p>
        <p>2 spaces up or down and 1 space sideways OR 1 space up or down and 2 spaces
            sideways; can jump pieces</p>
    </div>
    <div class="body row">
        <h3>Pawn</h3><p>8</p><p>1</p>
        <p><img src="pawn.png" alt="Pawn" /></p>
        <p>generally 1 space forward; first move can be 2 spaces forward;
            captures 1 space forward diagonally</p>
    </div>
    <div class="foot row">
        <h3>Totals</h3><p>16</p><p>40</p><p></p><p></p>
    </div>
</div>
```

To style this using table layout, the entire CSS is provided in Listing 13-3. The `display` attributes are shown in bold. The rest of the CSS declarations are applying the same styles that we did in the previous example. The selectors are different because we're using different elements but conceptually, this is identical to the previous CSS. This will render the table exactly the same as the previous examples.

Listing 13-3. Using tabular layout

```
/* Simulate table layout on non-table elements */
.table {
    display: table;
    border: 3px solid black;
    border-collapse: collapse;
    background-color: #DDB;
    background: linear-gradient(to bottom right, #F4F4F0 0%, #DDB 100%);
}
.row {
    display: table-row;
}
.row>h3, .row>p {
    display: table-cell;
    border: 1px solid black;
    padding: 5px;
    vertical-align: middle;
}
.row img {
    display: table-cell;
    vertical-align: middle;
    margin: 0 auto;
}
```

```
/* Alignment */
.row>h3 {
    text-align: center;
    font-size: medium;
}
.row>p:nth-child(2) { /*Qty*/
    text-align: right;
    }
.row>p:nth-child(3) { /*Points*/
    text-align: right;
    }

/* Background and zebra striping */
.body>p, .foot>p {
    background-color: white;
    background-image: none;
}
.body:nth-child(odd)>p, .body:nth-child(odd)>img {
    background-color: #F4F4F0;
}

/* Highlighting */
.row:nth-child(4)>h3, .row:nth-child(4)>p {
    background-color: yellow;
}
.row>h3:nth-child(3), .row>p:nth-child(3) {
    background-color: yellow;
}
```

■ **Caution**   I created this to demonstrate that there's nothing special about the table elements other than their default styles. You can use table layouts on any HTML elements. However, you should never actually build a table this way. Tabular data should be put into table elements.

Applications

Knowing that you can use table-style layout on any HTML elements, I'll show a couple of scenarios where this can be really useful.

Aligning Elements

Using table layout can help if you have two or more elements that you want to be aligned when rendered on a page. Suppose, for example, that you have a small image and some text and you want them side by side, vertically aligned. This simple HTML markup creates a div with an image and a paragraph element.

```
<div class="centering">
    <div><img src="penny.jpg" alt="penny" /></div>
    <p>Fourscore and seven years ago, our fathers brought forth to this continent
        a new nation...</p>
</div>
```

The first attempt to style this will use display: inline; so the image and text are on the same line. This also fixes the image size. The result is shown in Figure 13-12.

```
.centering div, .centering p {
    display: inline;
}
.centering img {
    width: 50px;
}
```

 Fourscore and seven years ago, our fathers brought forth to this
continent a new nation...

Figure 13-12. *Initial styling attempt*

This is not exactly what I had intended. Let's employ table layout with a simple change to the CSS. I'll change to display: table-cell; that will put the image and the text in their own cell. The cells are automatically aligned; all that's left to do is configure the alignment within the cell. The result is shown in Figure 13-13.

```
.centering div, .centering p {
    /*display: inline;*/
    display: table-cell;
    text-align: left;
    vertical-align: middle;
}
```

Fourscore and seven years ago, our fathers brought forth to this
continent a new nation...

Figure 13-13. *Alignment corrected with tables*

Using table layouts can greatly simply the alignment of elements because the table cells provide structure. Each element is placed in a cell and aligned within the cell. Another great application of this is when styling input forms. A form will have a collection of input fields such as text boxes, radio buttons, and checkboxes as well as labels, buttons, and other content. It is generally a good idea to align these in some way and using table layout is a common and effective approach.

Page Layout

For a final example, I'll use tables to organize the overall page layout. A typical web page will have a header and footer, often a set of navigation links, and sometimes a sidebar. I'll add those around the existing table that I have been using throughout this chapter. The additional elements are shown in Listing 13-4.

Listing 13-4. Adding the remaining page elements

```
<body>
    <header>
        <h1>Chapter 13 - Styling Tables</h1>
    </header>
    <section>
        <nav role="navigation">
            <ul>
                <li>One</li>
                <li>Two</li>
                <li>Three</li>
                <li>Four</li>
            </ul>
        </nav>
        <main>
            <table>
```

... insert the existing table here ...

```
            </table>
        </main>
        <aside>
            <h1>Check out these titles</h1>
            <ul>
                <li>Beginning Workflow 4.0</li>
                <li>Office Workflow 2010</li>
                <li>Project Management with SharePoint 2010</li>
                <li>Pro Access 2010</li>
                <li>Office 365 Development</li>
                <li>HTML5 with Visual Studio 2015</li>
            </ul>
        </aside>
    </section>
    <footer>
        Professional HTML5 - Apress
    </footer>
</body>
```

I will organize these in a fairly common three-column layout that is illustrated in Figure 13-14. I have indicated in each section how the display attribute will be set to achieve the desired layout.

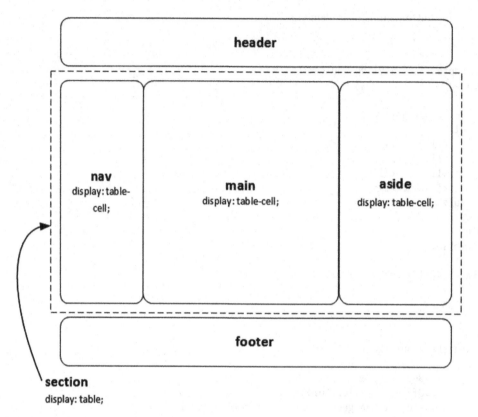

Figure 13-14. *The overall page structure*

The section element is sandwiched between the header and footer elements and will be set up as a table. Its child elements, the nav, main, and aside elements are set up as cells within that table. The following CSS rules apply this table layout along with some basic formatting.

```
section {
    display: table;
    table-layout: fixed;
}
nav, main, aside {
    display: table-cell;
}
nav {
    min-width: 150px;
}
aside {
    width: 25%;
    text-align: center;
}
```

This also sets the table-layout attribute to fixed. Its default value is auto, which means that the table cells are sized to fit the content. In this mode, the browser has to do a lot of work because it has to first determine which row is the longest, and then format the remaining rows using this size. By setting this to fixed, this auto-size logic is disabled and you can set the sizes manually. The nav element is set to 150 pixels and the aside element is 25% of the window width. The remaining area in the middle is assigned to the main element and will grow and shrink based on the width of the window.

In the markup, I'm using an unordered list (ul) element to represent the items in the nav and aside elements. I'm using the following CSS rules to format these as tables.

```
ul {
    display: table;
}
li {
    display: table-row;
    height: 50px;
    text-align: left;
    vertical-align: middle;
}
```

In this example, the unordered list element is set up as a table, and the list item as a row object. With these changes in place, the content is now structured as expected, albeit a little plain looking – like the initial table at the beginning of this chapter. To make this more visually appealing I'll add the following CSS rules. The resulting page layout is shown in Figure 13-15.

```
header, footer {
    border: 1px solid black;
    border-radius: 6px;
    background-color: #F4F4F0;
    text-align: center;
    padding: 5px;
}
nav, aside {
    border: 1px solid black;
    border-radius: 6px;
    background-color: #F0F0F0;
}
aside article:nth-child(even) {
    background-color:  #fafbbf;
}
aside {
    padding: 5px;
    font-family: Verdana;
    font-size: small;
}
```

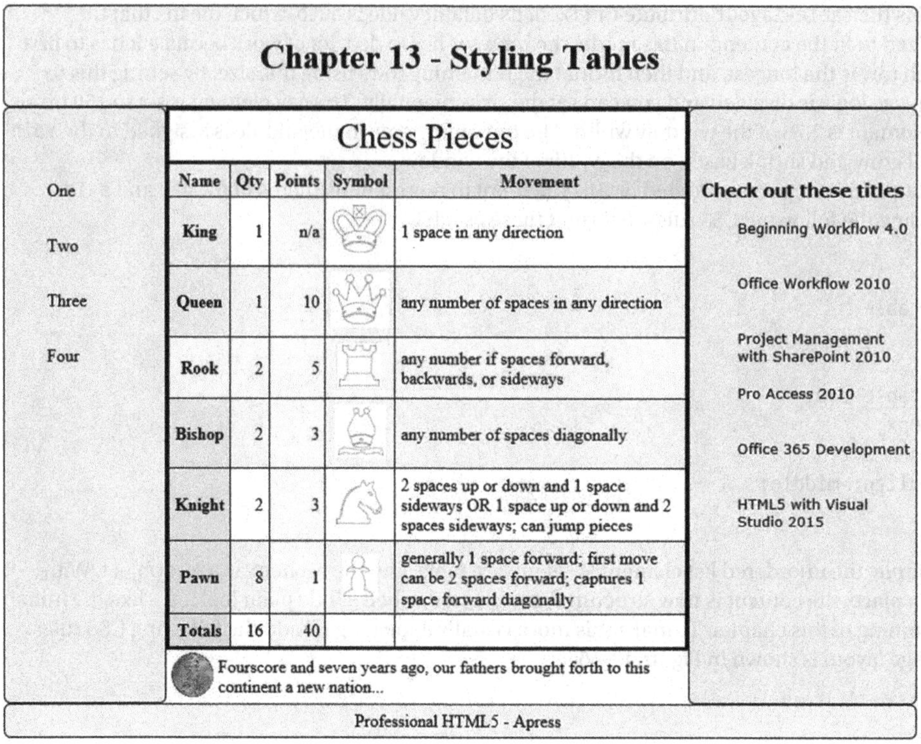

Figure 13-15. *The final page layout*

Responsive Layout

The page elements used the standard, semantic header, nav, main, aside, and footer elements. They are only rendered as a table because that's how we chose to configure them in CSS. We could have just as easily decided to arrange them differently. I'll now show you how to use media queries, which I explained in Chapter 2, to dynamically alter the layout of your page based on its size.

For this page I'll set the threshold at 700px. For a simple example, I'll put the CSS rules that set up the table layout into a media query. The media query and the conditional rules within it are shown in Listing 13-5.

Listing 13-5. Using a media query

```
@media (min-width: 700px) {
    section {
        display: table;
        table-layout: fixed;
    }

    nav, main, aside {
        display: table-cell;
    }

    nav {
        min-width: 150px;
    }
    aside {
        width: 25%;
        text-align: center;
    }
    ul {
        display: table;
    }
    li {
        display: table-row;
        height: 50px;
        text-align: left;
        vertical-align: middle;
    }
}
```

Now if you shrink the window to smaller than 700pixels, the table layout is gone as shown in Figure 13-16.

Chapter 13 - Styling Tables

- One
- Two
- Three
- Four

Chess Pieces

Name	Qty	Points	Symbol	Movement
King	1	n/a		1 space in any direction
Queen	1	10		any number of spaces in any direction
Rook	2	5		any number if spaces forward, backwards, or sideways
Bishop	2	3		any number of spaces diagonally
Knight	2	3		2 spaces up or down and 1 space sideways OR 1 space up or down and 2 spaces sideways; can jump pieces
Pawn	8	1		generally 1 space forward; first move can be 2 spaces forward; captures 1 space forward diagonally
Totals	16	40		

 Fourscore and seven years ago, our fathers brought forth to this continent a new nation...

Check out these titles

Figure 13-16. *Removing table layout*

Styling Lists

As a final side topic, there are styling options available for list items. A list item typical has a marker next to it such as a dot or a number. Through CSS attributes you can control the style and position of the marker.

■ **Note**   List item elements (li) also have a default display attribute, which is set to list-item. The attribute is what causes the browser to add the marker beside the element. In the previous example, this was changed to table-row in the wide screen mode. Notice that the markers are gone. In the narrow mode, however, the default attribute is used and the markers are displayed.

Type

The list-style-type attribute defines the marker that is used. Here are the standard values that are supported:

- none - no marker

- disc - a solid circle (default value for unordered lists)

- circle - a hollow circle

- square - a solid filled square

- decimal - sequential integers (1, 2, 3..., default for ordered lists)

- decimal-leading-zero - same as decimal but leading zeros are added

- lower-alpha - sequential letters (a, b, c...)

- upper-alpha - sequential uppercase letters (A, B, C...)

- lower-roman - roman numerals (i, ii, iii...)

- upper-roman - uppercase roman numerals (I, II, III...)

The first four options (none, disc, circle, and square) are used for unordered lists (ul). The remainder are used only for ordered lists (ol). To be clear, if you use any of the first four options, such as disc, on an ordered list, each list item will have that same marker. The purpose of an ordered list is so the browser can sequentially number them; thus you would have effectively turned it into an unordered list. Conversely, if you use a value like decimal on an unordered list, the items will be sequentially numbered and you now have an ordered list. The only real difference between the ul and ol elements is the default value given to the list-style-type attribute, disc, and decimal, respectively.

For ordered lists, you can also control the marker used by assigning the type attribute in the HTML markup, which I explained in Chapter 4. It supports the values 1, a, A, I, and I, which correspond to the decimal, lower-alpha, upper-alpha, lower-roman, and upper-roman values of the list-style-type attribute in CSS. Note, however, that the style applied in CSS will override markup setting.

▪ **Note** There are several others that are generally supported such as lower-latin and lower-greek. In addition, there are lots of other languages defined with minimal browser support.

Image

If none of these styles are suitable, you can define your own by setting the list-style-image attribute. There are no options for defining the size of the rendered image, so make sure to use an image that has intrinsic dimensions that will work with your content. The following CSS rule will use the pawn.png image as the marker. This is rendered as shown in Figure 13-17.

```
ul {
    list-style-image: url("pawn.png");
}
```

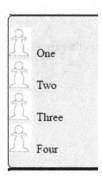

Figure 13-17. *Using a custom image for the list item*

■ **Tip**   When using custom images, you should also specify the list-style-type attribute as well. This should come before the list-style-image declaration. This will be used as a fallback if the image cannot be loaded for some reason.

Position

With the list-style-position attribute you can decide if the marker should be inside the containing block. If the value inside is specified, the marker is aligned with the block and the item is indented to make room for the marker. If you specify outside, the list item is aligned with the block and the marker will be outside of the block.

Shorthand

As with many other CSS attributes, there is a shorthand that enables you to specify all of the list item attributes in a single declaration. The three values – type, image, and position can be provided in any order and separated by a space. For example:

```
list-style: url("pawn.png") outside square;
```

Summary

In this chapter I demonstrated how a table can be styled using CSS. You can easily turn a rather unattractive table into a visually appealing presentation, with a few simple rules. Beyond that, you can apply table layout techniques to other, non-tabular data by changing the display attribute.

A common use of this is to lay out a web page as table elements, while retaining the original semantic elements. Because this layout is performed in CSS, you can use media queries to apply alternate formats depending on the device characteristics.

I also demonstrated how list items can be styled using the supported CSS attributes. Also, using tables to lay out list items is a popular approach.

CHAPTER 14

Flexbox

In this chapter I'll explain yet another value for the display attribute: flex. This is a very flexible (pun intended) way of laying out elements. Conceptually, this is pretty straightforward although the terminology can be confusing, primarily because of its flexibility. When using flex, you need a container element that has child items inside it. There are separate attributes that are configured on the container and the items.

It is supported by IE11 and above as well as all major browsers, although there are some issues with Safari. If you must support these browsers, you will need to provide a fallback solution. However, I believe this will become the preferred approach, especially when supporting responsive web pages.

The terminology is direction agnostic; you won't see any values such as height, width, horizontal, or vertical. Even the flex-direction attribute uses the values row and column. One of the challenges of using flex is that you need to translate the terms. For example, if I refer to an element's height and width, you immediately know what I'm referring to. If I talk about its main size, you'll need to translate based on the flex-direction.

Container Configuration

I'll start by explaining the attributes that can be specified on the container. The first, of course, is the display attribute, which should be set to flex.

```
.container {
    display: -webkit-flex;
    display: flex;
}
```

■ **Caution** To support Safari, you'll need to use the -webkit prefix.

Flex Direction

The most important attribute is the flex-direction, which establishes the framework for the remaining attributes. It is applied to the container element and supports the following values:

- row - (default) the items are laid out horizontally. The actual direction is determined by the direction attribute, either ltr or rtl. If ltr mode is being used, the items will flow from left to right.

- row-reverse - the items are laid out horizontally in the opposite direction of the direction attribute.

© Mark J. Collins 2017

M. J. Collins, *Pro HTML5 with CSS, JavaScript, and Multimedia*, DOI 10.1007/978-1-4842-2463-2_14

- `column` - the items are arranged vertically, from top to bottom.

- `column-reverse` - the items are arranged vertically from bottom to top.

Figure 14-1 illustrates the meaning of the terminology when `flex-direction: row;` is used, assuming `ltr` mode.

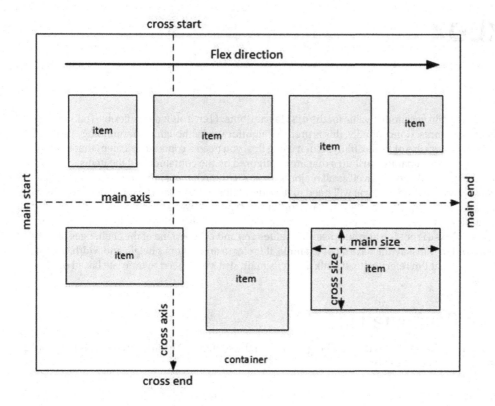

Figure 14-1. *Illustrating flexbox terminology*

Many of the subsequent term are configured based on values that are derived from the `flex-direction`. The *main axis*, for example, is the axis of the `flex-direction`, horizontal in this case and the *cross axis* is vertical. The *main start* and *main end* define the beginning and ending edges of the container element. This is the left and right edges in this example. Similarly, the *cross start* and *cross end* define the container edges along the other dimension – top and bottom in this case. The size of an item within the container is not identified by the width and height, rather they are specified by the *main size* and *cross size* values.

For a specific `flex-direction`, all of these values translate into familiar values such as vertical, left, bottom, and width. When you're first learning to use flex, it may be easier to think of these in more familiar terms. However, be aware that with a different `flex-direction` the meaning of these terms change. This is illustrated in Figure 14-2, which demonstrates these values when `flex-direction: column;` is used.

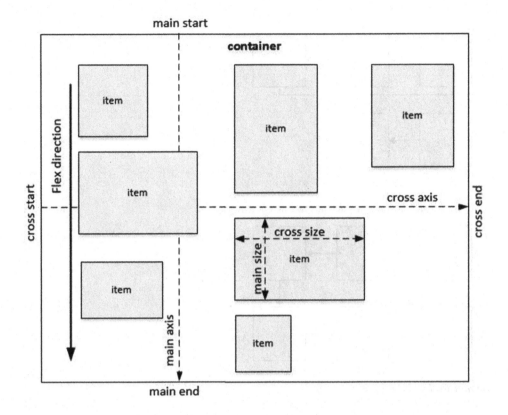

Figure 14-2. *Terms used when flex direction is column*

Flex Wrap

When the flex-direction is row (or row-reverse) the items in the container flow horizontally much like using display:inline; and when the width of the container is filled, the subsequent items wrap to the next row. The flex-wrap attribute controls if and how this is done. There are three possible values:

- nowrap - (default) The items do not wrap but are displayed in a single row (or column).

- wrap - The items will wrap to the next row or column using the same direction as the initial.

- wrap-reverse - The items wrap to the next row or column but do so in reverse order.

The wrap and wrap-reverse options are illustrated in Figure 14-3.

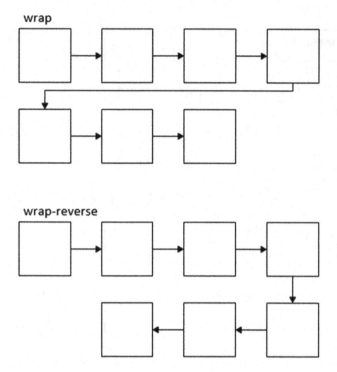

Figure 14-3. *Demonstrating the wrapping options*

When using flex-direction: row-reverse; the wrapping works the same way except the directions are reversed. When using flex-direction: column; the items will flow from top to bottom. If wrap-reverse is specified, they will then flow from bottom to top after wrapping to the next column. The third row or column will use the initial direction.

You can specify both the flex-direction and the flex-wrap attribute with the flex-flow attribute. This expects two values: one for each attribute, which are separated with a space. The default value is row nowrap.

Justification

The justify-content attribute determines how items are arranged within a single row (or column) along the main axis (I'll also explain justification along the cross axis later). There are five available options that are illustrated in Figure 14-4.

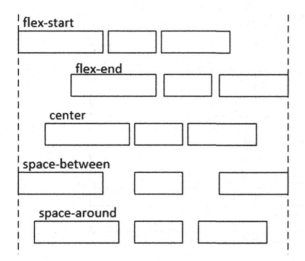

Figure 14-4. *Justification along the main axis*

The flex-start value indicates that the items are justified to the main start edge. Similarly, flex-end aligns the item against the main end edge. When using flex-direction: row; these are translated to left aligned and right aligned as shown in Figure 14-4. However, with row-reverse, the main start and main end edges are reversed. Likewise, if column is used for the flex-direction, these become the top and bottom edges.

The space-between option aligns the first item to the main start edge and the last item to the main end edge. The spacing between the items is then adjusted so they are evenly spaced apart. The space-around option is similar, except that an equal space is inserted before the first item and after the last item.

The resulting rows (or columns) of content can also be justified along the cross axis using the align-content attribute. The available options are similar to justify-content, except there is a sixth option: stretch. These are illustrated in Figure 14-5.

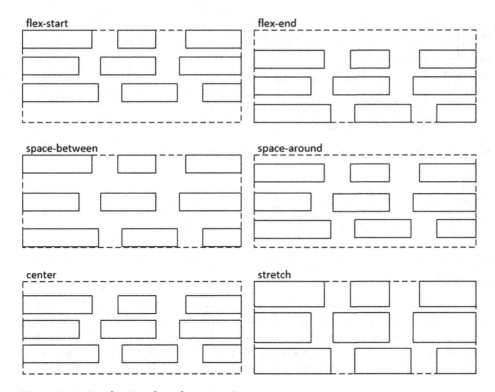

Figure 14-5. *Justification along the cross axis*

The flex-start and flex-end options justify the content against the cross start or cross end edges. If the flex-direction is row or row-reverse, these are the top and bottom edges, respectively, as illustrated in Figure 14-5. For column or column-reverse, these become the left and right edges. The stretch option works like the space-between option, except that the items are then stretched along the cross axis to fill the gaps between the rows (or columns).

■ **Tip** You'll need to remember that the justify-content attribute justifies the items along the main axis, while the align-content attribute justifies the rows (or columns) along the cross axis. The names themselves do not help much here, so make a mental note: justify-content: main axis, align-content: cross axis.

Aligning Items

In all of my illustrations thus far, all of the items had the same cross size. When using flex-direction: row; this translates to the height of the item. If they were different sizes, then you'll need to decide how they should be aligned. The align-items attribute provides five options, which are shown in Figure 14-6. I just explained the align-content attribute, which aligns rows (or columns) within the container. In contrast, the align-items attribute defines how items are arranged within a single row (or column). Both adjust the alignment along the cross axis.

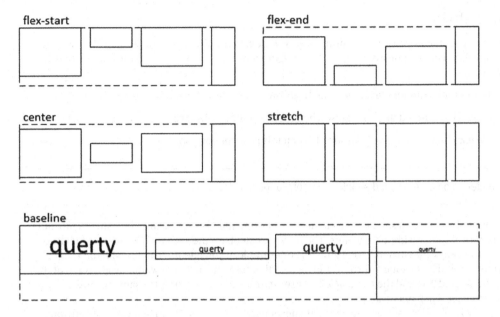

Figure 14-6. *Aligning items in a row*

Again, the flex-start and flex-end options align the items against the cross start and cross end edges, respectively. The center option will center the items along the cross axis. The baseline option aligns the items so their baselines are at the same position within the row.

■ **Tip**   The term *baseline* came from the print world where characters were aligned along a baseline. This is not necessarily the bottom of the text, but is the invisible line that most characters sit on. The baseline provides a visual guide to placing characters so the line appears straight. In CSS, this concept is even more complicated because we're not just dealing with text. If you want to delve into this subject, here is a good article: http://www.smashingmagazine.com/2012/12/17/css-baseline-the-good-the-bad-and-the-ugly.

Item Configuration

So far, I have explained how to configure the container, or parent, which provides the overall structure of how the items are arranged. You can also configure the items to provide fine-tuned control of their alignment.

Grow and Shrink

The items in a flex container can grow or shrink to accommodate the size of the container. This is very important, especially with responsive designs. To configure how this works, there are three facets that you need to work with:

- *Basis* - the optimum size of the item; by default, this is its intrinsic size.

- *Grow* - how should this item grow when there is additional space.

- *Shrink* - how should this item shrink when this is not enough space.

■ **Note**   The terms basis, grow, and shrink only apply to the main axis.

The amount of growth and shrink of an element is set using the flex-grow and flex-shrink attributes. These are numerical values without any units. The browser calculates the amount of space to add based on the ratio of the item's growth to the total growth. For example, if you had three items with the flex-grow attribute set to 1, 2, and 3, the total growth would be 6. In this case, the first item would be given 1/6 of the extra space, the second 2/6, and the third, 3/6. The flex-shrink attribute works the same way except it is used to remove space when necessary.

The flex-grow and flex-shrink attributes are never used simultaneously. The flex-grow attribute is only used when there is extra space and flex-shrink only applies when there is not enough space. Obviously, both cannot be true at the same time. Also, negative values are not allowed for either attribute. A value of zero indicates that the item should not grow (or shrink).

The flex-basis attribute defines the base size of the item. This is a distance unit and can be specified as an absolute value or one of the relative units. The auto value, which is the default value, uses the item's intrinsic size for the basis.

For convenience, you can set all three values – grow, shrink, and basis with the flex shorthand. Make sure to set the three values in that order: grow, shrink, and basis. There are also some special values that you can use to set all three attributes:

- flex: auto; - sets the grow and shrink to 1 and the basis to auto.

- flex: none; - sets the grow and shrink values to 0 and basis to auto. The item will use its intrinsic size and will not grow or shrink.

Demonstration

The concept of basis is often misunderstood. Consider the previous example with three items having flex-grow set to 1, 2, and 3. Some would assume that the second item is always twice as large as the first, and the third is three times the size. However, this is not true, in most cases; only the extra space, beyond its base size, follows this ratio. An example here will help clarify this.

The following markup creates a section element with four child elements: two paragraph elements, a div element and an image. Each of the child elements has a class attribute so we can more easily configure them with CSS.

```
<div class="std1"></div>
<section>
    <p class="i1">Fourscore and seven years ago, our fathers brought forth to this continent,
        a new nation</p>
    <img class="i2" src="king.jpg" alt="King" />
```

```
    <div class="i3">
        <div class="std2"></div>
    </div>
    <p class="i4">This is some text</p>
</section>
```

This also creates a couple of extra div elements that I will set as a fixed size to provide a frame of reference to help visualize the growth (and shrink) behavior. The entire CSS is shown in Listing 14-1.

Listing 14-1. CSS for Flex Demo

```
/* include the border in the sizing values */
* {
    box-sizing: border-box;
}
.std1 {
    height: 30px;
    width: 350px;
    border: 1px solid black;
    background-color: lightblue;
}
.std2 {
    height: 30px;
    width: 50px;
    border: none;
    background-color: lightblue;
}
section {
    display: flex;
    flex-wrap: nowrap;
    justify-content: flex-start;
    align-content: flex-start;
    align-items: stretch;
}

/* Put a border around the children*/
section>* {
    border:  1px solid black;
    margin:  0;
}

.i1 {
    flex: 1 3 350px;
}

/* Not needed, this is the default for images */
.i2 {
    flex: none;
}
```

```
.i3 {
    height: 75px;
    background-color: lightyellow;
    flex: 2 0 50px;
}
.i4 {
    flex: 3 1 auto;
}
```

Most of the CSS rules are there to help set up the demo; I highlighted the declarations that are specific to flex. The container sets the display: flex; attribute and the rest of the attributes are set to the default values and can be omitted. The first item has a base size of 350px. I also set the empty div element with the std1 class to have the same size. Similarly, in the third item, I embedded an empty div element with the std2 class. This has a fixed size of 50px, which is the same as the base size of the third item. The last paragraph element does not have an explicit basis so it will use the intrinsic size, which is essentially an element just wide enough to fit all of this text without wrapping.

For the image, I set the flex attribute to none, which is the default values for images. Images, by default, do not grow or shrink. For the div element, I set the grow to 2 and the shrink to 0; this element will grow but not shrink. For the two paragraph elements, I set different values for grow and shrink to demonstrate how these work.

If you render this in a browser and size the width of the window to be just large enough to fit the base sizes of each child element, it will look like Figure 14-7.

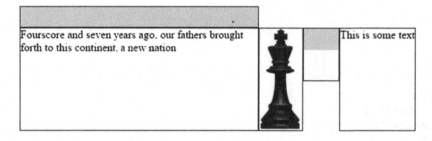

Figure 14-7. *The flex elements with the exact base size*

The two fixed div elements that provide a reference size are shown in blue. As you can see, the child elements have the exact size of their basis. Also, the text of the last child just barely fits without wrapping. If you then expand the window, the image is unchanged, as expected, but the other three child elements grow proportionally to the flex-grow attribute. This is illustrated in Figure 14-8.

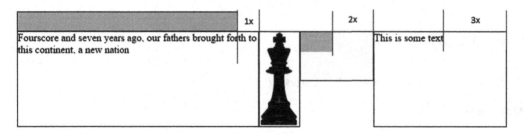

Figure 14-8. *Demonstrating the growth behavior*

When the container is larger than the sum of the item base size, the grow calculation is used. In this case, the actual size allocated to each item can be expressed with the following formula:

```
Base size + Extra space * (Grow / sum of Grow values)
```

Calculating Shrink

If you make the window smaller than the base size, the image and the empty div element do not shrink, but the two paragraph elements do. With a smaller window, the page looks like Figure 14-9.

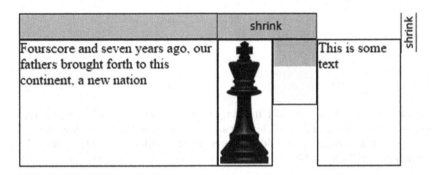

Figure 14-9. *Demonstrating the shrink behavior*

I set the flex-shrink attribute to 3 on the first paragraph and 1 on the last paragraph; however, as you can see in Figure 14-9, the amount of shrink in the first paragraph is more than three times the shrink of the last paragraph. For some reason, the shrink calculation works differently than the grow calculation. It takes into account the base value of the item. When the container is smaller than the total base size, the shrink calculation is used on each item, which can be expressed in the following formula:

```
Base size - Overflow size * (Shrink * Base Size / sum of (Shrink * Base size) )
```

So let's work this out, starting with the final sum. There are two items with a non-zero shrink value. The intrinsic size for the last paragraph is approximately 110 pixels. The sum of both is 3 * 350 + 1 * 110 = 1160. Now the ratios: the first item will be 3 * 350 / 1160 = ~90% and the last paragraph is 1 * 110 / 1160 = ~10%. So only 10% of the amount of the overflow size is removed from the last paragraph. Knowing this, you can adjust the shrink value to account for this. For example, if you want them to shrink at the same rate, in this case, set the shrink value on the first paragraph to roughly .35 to accomplish this.

Uniform Growth

I started out with the more complex case to see how the basis affects both the growth and shrink of the items. However, for a simpler application you can set the basis to zero for all of the items. If the basis is zero, the shrink value doesn't apply either; the item can only grow. To support this, the flex attribute allows a single numeric value, which is applied as the flex-grow attribute. This shorthand also sets the flex-shrink and flex-basis attributes to zero.

To demonstrate this, I'll modify the previous CSS to use this shortcut:

```
.i1 {
    /*flex: 1 3 350px;
    flex: 1 .35 350px;*/
    flex: 3;
}
.i3 {
    height: 75px;
    background-color: lightyellow;
    /*flex: 2 0 50px;*/
    flex: 1;
}
.i4 {
    /*flex: 3 1 auto;*/
    flex: 2;
}
```

In this example the div element has a grow value of 1 and the paragraphs are set to 3 and 2, respectively. The first paragraph will be three times the size of the div element and the last paragraph twice. However, there is one exception, because the div element has a child element with a fixed width, it won't shrink smaller than that. This is demonstrated in Figure 14-10.

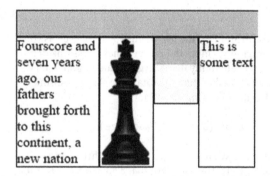

Figure 14-10. *Shrinking beyond the intrinsic size*

The base size of the div element is still zero for the growth calculation. Notice that the last paragraph is 2/3 as wide as the first paragraph because the grow values were set to 2 and 3, respectively. Regardless of the size of the container, these two elements will always maintain this ratio.

Order

By default, items are rendered in the order they exist in the document. With flex items, you can set their order property to explicitly define their order. If not specified, the order value is zero and all items with the same order are displayed based on their order in the document. Negative values are allowed.

This is a really useful feature, especially with responsive web pages. Allowing the order to be controlled by CSS means that they can be adjusted based on media queries. For example, you can set the order to move some particular content to the bottom of the page when a small device is being used.

■ **Tip** You don't have to set the `order` attribute on all of the items. For example, if you want a particular item to be displayed first, set its `order` to -1 and leave the remaining with their initial value. All the other items will have a value of 0, so this item will come first.

Overriding Alignment

I previously explained how the `align-items` attribute on the container controls the cross axis alignment of items with a row (or column). This attribute applies to all of the flex items in the container. However, you can override this on individual items by setting is `align-self` attribute. This supports the same six values as the `align-items` attribute. For a simple example, the following CSS sets this attribute on the first paragraph and the `div` element. The result is shown in Figure 14-11.

```
.i1 {
    /*flex: 1 3 350px;
    flex: 1 .35 350px;*/
    flex: 3;
    align-self: flex-end;
}
.i3 {
    height: 75px;
    background-color: lightyellow;
    /*flex: 2 0 50px;*/
    flex: 1;
    align-self: center;
}
```

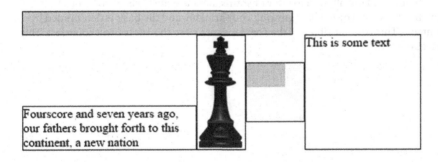

Figure 14-11. *Using the align-self attribute*

Vertical Example

For a simple example using a vertical main axis, I'll set up a typical page layout with a fixed size header and footer. The body will be allowed to grow to fit the existing content. The markup is as follows:

```
<section class="vertical">
    <header>Header</header>
    <footer>Footer</footer>
    <main>
        <p>Lorem ipsum dolor...</p>
    </main>
</section>
```

This section element contains a header, footer, and main element. I put the footer element before the main element to demonstrate the order attribute. To format this, the following CSS is used:

```
.vertical {
    display: flex;
    flex-direction: column;
}
header, footer {
    text-align: center;
    background-color: lightgreen;
    flex: 0 0 35px;
}
main {
    flex: auto;
}
footer {
    order: 3;
}
```

This sets the flex-direction to column so the main axis is now vertical. The item will grow and shrink vertically. The header and footer and not allowed to grow or shrink and have the basis set to 35 pixels. In contrast, the main element has flex: auto; to allow growing and shrinking and the basis is determined by the intrinsic size of its contents. The order attribute of the footer is set to 3 so the footer will come last. This is rendered as shown in Figure 14-12.

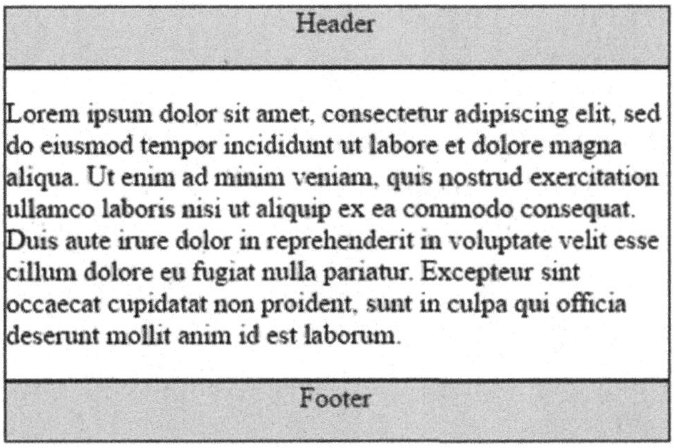

Header

Lorem ipsum dolor sit amet, consectetur adipiscing elit, sed do eiusmod tempor incididunt ut labore et dolore magna aliqua. Ut enim ad minim veniam, quis nostrud exercitation ullamco laboris nisi ut aliquip ex ea commodo consequat. Duis aute irure dolor in reprehenderit in voluptate velit esse cillum dolore eu fugiat nulla pariatur. Excepteur sint occaecat cupidatat non proident, sunt in culpa qui officia deserunt mollit anim id est laborum.

Footer

Figure 14-12. *A vertical example*

Summary

In this chapter I have explained how to use a flexbox to arrange items in a flexible layout. The basic idea is to define predictive rules for arranging HTML elements and then let the browser apply these rules based on the current window size. You configure attributes on the container as well as the items within it.

On the container, you define the direction that the items flow as they are rendered within it. The attributes and terms are direction agnostic, such as start and end instead of top or bottom, so you may have to perform some translation when thinking through a solution. The container properties also enable you to specify how the rows or columns of items are aligned.

On the items, you specify how the items should grow or shrink along the main axis depending on the available space. You can override the alignment along the cross axis. You can also set the order that an item should be displayed, giving you the ability to adjust the order in CSS. This allows you to relocate elements using media queries depending on the device characteristics.

In the next chapter, I will demonstrate how to use animation and transforms to add some interest and pizzazz to your web page.

CHAPTER 15

■ ■ ■

Animation and Transforms

Animation

Animation looks really impressive but is actually quite trivial to implement. An animation is simply modifying one or more attributes over time. This used to require writing JavaScript to set up a timer and then manipulate the attributes with each timer event. Now you can accomplish that with only CSS.

Keyframes

In CSS, the first step in creating animation is to define the *keyframes*. Each keyframe specifies a set of CSS attributes at a specific point in time. This is roughly analogous to an animated movie that is a set pictures, called frames, which are displayed in rapid succession, giving the impression that the pictures are moving. Fortunately, we don't have to supply 30 or 60 frames per second like most videos.

Using keyframes is similar to defining a gradient, which I explained in Chapter 12. You need to define at least the beginning and ending frames, and the browser will provide a gradual transition between them. However, you can define additional frames to control the progress of the animation. An animation has a specified duration and each keyframe is assigned to a specific point along that duration, which is expressed as a percentage. The initial frame is at 0% and the final frame is at 100%.

Keyframes are sometimes referred to as at-rules. They resemble normal CSS rules except a percentage is used as the selector. Inside each frame, you can specify any number of CSS attributes. A simple keyframe might look like this:

```
@keyframes colors {
    0% {
        background-color: yellow;
    }
    100% {
        background-color: blue;
    }
}
```

At the beginning of the animation, the background color is yellow, and by the end of it, the color is gradually changed to blue. You can add more frames as well. Suppose you wanted the color to change from red, to yellow, to blue, and then back to red. The keyframe would be specified like this:

```
@keyframes colors {
    0%, 100% {
        background-color: red;
```

© Mark J. Collins 2017
M. J. Collins, *Pro HTML5 with CSS, JavaScript, and Multimedia*, DOI 10.1007/978-1-4842-2463-2_15

```
    }
    33% {
        background-color: yellow;
    }
    66% {
        background-color: blue;
    }
}
```

Notice that both the initial and final frames have the same value, so they can be specified with the same frame, separating the percentages by a comma, which, in CSS selector syntax, is the logical OR operator. Also, 0% and 100% can be represented with the from and to aliases, respectively. So, the first set of keyframes could also be specified as:

```
@keyframes colors {
    from {
        background-color: yellow;
    }
    to {
        background-color: blue;
    }
}
```

Configuring Animations

An animation is applied to one or more elements. For example, the previous keyframes modifies the background-color attribute. This needs to be applied to an element, and then its background color will be changed by the animation. To provide a simple demo, I'll use an empty div element:

```
<div class="circle"></div>
```

To provide a little more interest, I'll turn this into a red circle with the following CSS rule:

```
.circle {
    width: 300px;
    height: 300px;
    margin: 10px 0 0 0;
    border-radius:  50%;
    background-color: red;
}
```

This creates a div element whose height is equal to its width. Setting the radius to 50% will turn this square into a circle. Finally, to animate the background color, the following rule is used:

```
.circle {
    animation: colors 5s;
}
```

This uses the animation shorthand to specify the two required attributes. This first indicates the name of the keyframe to use, which was created earlier. The second specifies the duration of the animation, 5 seconds in this case. When the page loads, the circle will start out red but gradually change to yellow, then blue, and back to red.

Animation Attributes

There are eight attributes that can be used to configure the animation. I alluded to the first two; here is the complete set with their available options:

- -name - the name of the keyframe that defines the attributes to be set and their relative timing.

- -duration - (default 0s) the total time that a single execution will take to complete.

- -timing-function - (default ease) indicates how the transition occurs between frames. There are a lot of options here, and Mozilla has a good article that describes each of these options in detail at https://developer.mozilla.org/en-US/docs/Web/CSS/timing-function. The following common values are supported:

  - linear - the transition is uniform between frames

  - ease-in - the transition starts slow at the beginning

  - ease-out - the transition slows down at the end

  - ease-in-out - the transition is slower both at the beginning and the end

  - ease - similar to ease-in-out but the slowdown at the beginning is less than at the end

- -delay - (default 0s) the duration of pause between when the page is loaded and when the animation should start.

- -iteration-count - (default 1) how many times the animation should be performed; set to infinite if the animation runs continually.

- -direction - (default normal) indicates if the animation runs forward or backwards through the keyframes. The following values are supported:

  - normal - the animation goes through the keyframes in order from 0% to 100%; if the execution is repeated, it will start back at the beginning.

  - alternate - the animation goes from 0% to 100% on the initial execution but the subsequent execution will go backwards. The odd executions are forward and the even executions are in reverse.

  - reverse - the animation executes backwards from 100% to 0%; subsequent executions are also backwards.

  - alternate-reverse - the initial execution is in reverse, from 100% to 0% but the next execution goes forward. All odd executions are in reverse and the even executions are forward.

- -fill-mode - (default none) specifies how the keyframe attribute should be applied before and after the animation. Note that actual initial frame is controlled by the animation-direction attribute; the final frame is also dependent on how many iterations are executed when the alternate direction is used. The following values are supported:

  - none - the before and after values are not affected by the animation.

  - forwards - the target elements will retain the value of the last keyframe after the animation is completed.

- backwards - if there is a delay in starting the animation, the target element will use the initial keyframe values.

- both - the behavior of both forwards and backwards values are applied.

- -play-state - (default running) indicates if the animation is currently running or paused.

■ **Tip** Time units can be specified in either seconds or milliseconds. The s or ms suffix is required, otherwise the value will be treated as a numeric value. Spaces between the value and unit are not allowed.

Animation Shorthand

As I said, all eight attributes can be set using the animation shorthand. They are technically all optional and have a default value if omitted. However, without specifying the animation-name and animation-duration, you cannot animate anything.

The attributes in the shorthand are separated by a space and can be specified in any order, except for a few details that you'll need to be aware of. There are two time values, animation-duration and animation-delay. The first time value will be assigned to the animation-duration, and the second, if supplied, will be used for the animation-delay.

There are four attributes that have a preset list of supported values, which do not overlap: animation-timing-function, animation-direction, animation-fill-mode, and animation-play-state. These can be supplied in any order as the browser can determined by the value that attributes to assign it to. Any unrecognized value will be assigned to the animation-name attribute.

Some care must be taken if you wanted to give your keyframe a name that is one of the attribute values, such as reverse. You must specify the corresponding attribute, in this example, the animation-direction, first before the animation-name. If you wanted the direction to be reverse, you will need to include the value reverse twice; the first one will be used for animation-direction and the second for the animation-name attribute. You cannot let the browser set a default value. If you wanted the default, normal, you would need to explicitly include normal before reverse.

Multiple Animations

You can define more than one animation on the same target element. For instance, one animation can move an element and another one can change its color. These are applied independently. If you're using the animation shorthand, specify all of the desired attributes for the first animation and then the second animation and so on. A comma is used to separate the attributes of each animation. For example, this will apply two animations to all elements with the circle class:

```
.circle {
    animation: colors 5s 3, otherKey 2s 4s alternate;
}
```

If you're setting the individual attributes, you include an attribute value for each animation, which are separated by a comma. Specify the values in the same order for each attribute. The first value for `attribute-name` will go with the first value for `attribute-direction`, and so on. To demonstrate, the previous animation can be specified as follows:

```
.circle {
    animation-name: colors, otherKey;
    animation-duration: 5s, 2s;
    animation-iteration-count: 3;
    animation-delay: 0s, 4s;
    animation-direction: normal, alternate;
}
```

Notice for `animation-iteration-count`, only one value was specified, which will apply to the first animation. For `attribute-delay` and `attribute-direction`, the default value was needed so the second value can be applied to the second animation.

■ **Caution**   Not all CSS attributes can be animated. Here is article that lists all of the attributes that can be animated: `https://developer.mozilla.org/en-US/docs/Web/CSS/CSS_animated_properties`. The non-animatable attributes are mostly those than cannot be gradually changed over time, such as `font-family`.

Cubic Bézier

As I said, animation is simply adjusting one or more attributes over time. In the simplest case, you define the beginning and ending values and the browser will interpolate the values in between. The `animation-timing-function` attribute determines the function that is used to perform the interpolation. There are several common values that I already mentioned such as `ease-in` and `linear`.

The most straightforward of these is a `linear` function. Suppose you had an animation with a duration of 5 seconds, which modifies the `margin-left` attribute. The beginning value is 0 and the ending value is 250px. With a `linear` function, every second will change the margin by 50px. So after 1 second it is 50px, after 2 seconds it is 100px, and so on. With the `ease-in` function, the animation starts slower and speeds up. After 1 second, the left margin may only be at 30px, for example.

These values such as `ease-in` are merely predefined Bézier curves. A Bézier curve uses a mathematical formula to compute the value of one axis as a function of the other axis. In particular, the timing function uses a cubic Bézier, which uses four points to define the formula. The specific attribute value, `margin-left`, in this case, is computed at every point along a 5-second duration. Figure 15-1 shows a cubic Bézier that illustrates this.

Point P0 is the beginning point that represents the initial (0%) attribute value and the beginning of the duration. Point P3 is the endpoint at the 100% attribute value. The graph is always scaled so that these points are at 0,0 and 1,1, respectively. Points P1 and P2 define the curve of the line connecting P0 and P3.

The cubic Bézier in Figure 15-1 is defined by the values of P1 and P2, which are .8, .25 and .75 and 1.3. This is specified in CSS as:

```
animation-timing-function: cubic-bezier(0.80, 0.25, 0.75, 1.30);
```

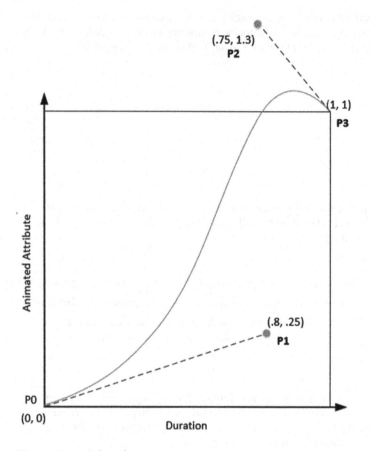

Figure 15-1. *Cubic Bézier*

In this case, the animation starts out slow, like ease-in, but at the end, actually overshoots the desired end value and has to come back before completing the animation.

■ **Tip**   If you want to play with cubic Béziers, check out the website at http://cubic-bezier.com. This allows you to graphically adjust the curve showing the values of P1 and P2 for you to enter into your CSS. Another useful site is at http://easings.net.

To demonstrate this, I'll create another empty div element:

```
<div class="bounce"></div>
```

For some simple styling, I used the following CSS rule:

```
.bounce {
    width: 100px;
    height: 35px;
    margin-left: 300px;
    border-radius: 10px;
    background-color: lightblue;
}
```

This creates a small rectangle with rounded corners. The animation is then configured with the following rule:

```
@keyframes bounce {
    from {
        margin-left: 0;
    }
    to {
        margin-left: 300px;
    }
}

.bounce {
    animation: 3s cubic-bezier(0.80, 0.25, 0.75, 1.30) bounce;
}
```

This will cause the div element to move across the page, slowly at first, and then after passing its final position, have to reverse and come back a little.

Transitions

When a CSS property is changed during runtime, that is after the page is loaded, you can use a transition to make a smoother change rather than an abrupt one. For example, you can change the background color of an element when the mouse is over it by using the :hover pseudo-class. Normally, that change happens immediately as soon as the mouse is over the element. However, you can define a transition so that change is more gradual.

Transitions are very similar to animations and use some of the same techniques. The primary difference is that you do not define keyframes in a transition; a transition only deals with the beginning and ending state of the target element. This is like having a keyframe that only defines the 0% and 100% values.

The other big difference is that a transition, unlike an animation, does not define the beginning and ending states; these are defined outside of the transition. The beginning and ending states are typically defined in CSS. For example, the background-color is a CSS attribute that is applied to the element through a CSS rule. A second rule, using the :hover pseudo-class, applies a different background-color. These two rules define the beginning and ending states. The transition can then be added to manipulate the change from one rule to another, to make it a smooth transition rather than an immediate one.

An example will help demonstrate this. The following markup creates an empty div element. Then a CSS rules defines its height and width along with the border and background color. The next rule modifies the height and width when the mouse is over the element.

```
<div class="tran"></div>

.tran {
    width: 200px;
    height: 100px;
    background-color: lightyellow;
    border: 1px solid black;
}
.tran:hover {
    width: 420px;
    height: 150px;
}
```

If you try this, you'll see that the size jumps to the larger size when you move the mouse over it. Now you can define how that transition occurs. There are four CSS attributes that can be applied:

- transition-property - (default all) specifies the property that the transition should be applied to.

- transition-duration - (default 0s) the length of time to complete the transition.

- transition-delay - (default 0s) the amount of time before the transition starts.

- transition-timing-function - (default ease) - the function that specifies how the transition is made over time. This works just like the animation-timing-function attribute and supports the same values.

Now, I'll use these attributes to make this a smooth transition by adding the following CSS rule. I'm using the same cubic Bézier function that I used with the previous animation.

```
.tran {
    transition-property: width;
    transition-duration: 3s;
    transition-delay: 0s;
    transition-timing-function: cubic-bezier(0.80, 0.25, 0.75, 1.30);
}
```

Now when you hover over the element, the width will change gradually. Notice the slight bounce effect as the width extends beyond the end state and has to come back slightly. The height, however, changed immediately because the transition only applied to the width attribute. You can use the all keyword for the transition-property attribute so the transition will apply to all changing attributes.

You can also define different transition attributes for each target attribute. If you wanted the height transition, for example, to be a quicker transition, you can define its transition separately. To accomplish this, supply multiple values to each attribute separated by commas:

```
transition-property: width, height;
transition-duration: 3s, 1s;
```

This will make the width transition take 3 seconds but the height transition will only take 1 second. The transition-property attribute defines the number of transitions. In this case, since two values were supplied, there will be two transitions. The remaining properties can have the same number of values, which are applied in order, so the 3s duration applies to the width attribute and the 1s duration applies to the height attribute. If fewer values are supplied, the values that are provided will be repeated as necessary so there will be a value for each value provided to the transition-property attribute. Since the transition-delay attribute only has a single value, it will be repeated so a 0s delay will be used for both the width and height attribute. If there are more values supplied than there are for the transition-property attribute, the extra values are ignored.

I applied the transition to the .tran class selector so it will affect both the transition to the hover state as well as the transition back to the initial state. Notice that if you move the mouse away from the element, it uses a gradual transition back to the initial state. If I had applied the change to the .tran:hover selector, the transition to the hover state would be gradual but when you remove the mouse, the transition back is immediate. You can take advantage of this behavior to provide different transitions. For example, you could have a faster transition back to the initial state.

To accomplish this, I'll define a slower transition in the .tran selector and override the duration in the .tran:hover selector to make it longer.

```
.tran {
    width:  200px;
    height:  100px;
    background-color:  lightyellow;
    border:  1px solid black;
    transition-property: width, height;
    transition-duration: 1s;
    transition-delay: 0s;
    transition-timing-function: cubic-bezier(0.80, 0.25, 0.75, 1.30);
}
.tran:hover {
    width: 420px;
    height: 150px;
    transition-duration: 3s, 1s;
}
```

■ **Tip** To demonstrate a transition, I am using the :hover pseudo-class to force an attribute change. However, transitions apply to any attribute change regardless of how it was invoked. In the next section I will explain how you can manipulate both HTML and CSS through JavaScript. If you modify an attribute through client-side scripting, any transition applied to it in CSS will be invoked.

You can also use the transition shorthand to supply all four values in a single declaration. You can supply these in any order; however, like the animation attribute, the first time value will be used as the duration and the second as the delay. If any values are omitted, the default values, which I indicated previously, will be used. For example, this transition will apply to all properties with a 3-second duration using the ease-in timing function. The delay, since it is not specified, will be 0s.

```
transition: all 3s ease-in;
```

If you want to define different transitions, you can use the transition shorthand and separate each with a comma.

```
transition: width 3s 0s ease-in, height 1s;
```

As with other shorthand attributes, any values that are not supplied will use the default values. In this example, for the height attribute, the default ease timing function will be used since it was not specified. When defining multiple transitions, using the individual attributes may be a little easier since a single value will apply to all as I explained previously.

Transforms

You can use the transform attribute to modify how an element is rendered by adjusting its coordinate system. When using the transform attribute, you must specify one of the transformation functions, which can be grouped into the following categories:

- Translation - the element is shifted either horizontally, vertically, or both. The element retains its original size and shape but is moved to a different position.

- Rotation - the element is rotated about one or more axis. As with translation, it maintains its original size and shape.

- Scale - the element is stretched or shrunk along one or more axis. This will change the size and possibly the aspect ratio of the element.

- Skew - the element is twisted or distorted. For example, a rectangle can become a parallelogram.

Applying a transform to an element changes how and where it is rendered on the page. However, this does not affect the placement of its neighboring elements. This can result in overflow conditions where elements are on top of each other.

Translation

Translation is probably the simplest of the transforms. There are three functions that are supported:

- translateX() - moves the element horizontally by the specified distance

- translateY() - move the element vertically

- translate() - accepts two values, one for X and one for Y, and moves the element both horizontally and vertically.

If only one value is specified when calling the translate() function, it will be used to translate the element horizontally. A positive value moves the element to the right (or down); a negative value to the left (or up). The following declaration will move the element up and to the right:

```
transform: translate(30px, -10px);
```

Rotation

When rotating an element, you need to first decide on which axis it should pivot. The X-axis is a horizontal line. Rotating an element on the X-axis means that the top of the element would either get closer to you or further from you, while the bottom would do the opposite. Think of flipping a page by pulling the bottom of the paper up, revealing the next sheet, like you would a calendar. This is sometime called a military flip. The Y-axis is a vertical line and rotating along the Y-axis is similar to turning the page of a book. The Z-axis comes out of the page.

There are four functions available relating to rotation:

- `rotateX()`

- `rotateY()`

- `rotateZ()`

- `rotate()`

The first three are pretty self-explanatory, and they rotate the element along the corresponding axis by the specified angle, which is passed in as a parameter. The `rotate()` function does the same thing as `rotateZ()`. It is provided since the vast majority of the time you will use the Z-axis and this is a sort of shortcut notation.

■ **Caution** Unless you're using 3D transformations, which I'll explain later, rotating along the X- or Y-axis is not very useful. On a two-dimensional system, rotating along the X-axis simply makes the shape shorter and rotating along the Y-axis makes the element narrower. However, rotating 180 degrees (or 1/2 turn) will flip the element. Most of the time, you will rotate along the Z-axis.

When rotating an element, you also need to decide the point on which it is rotated. By default, this will be the center of an element. However, you can use the `transform-origin` attribute to change this. This accepts three values, which specify the X, Y, and Z offsets. The default value is 50% 50% 0, which is the horizontal and vertical center of the element. You can supply absolute or relative values for each and they are expected in that order (X, Y, Z). If only two values are supplied, these will be used as the X and Y values.

There are also some keywords that can be used, including `left`, `right`, `top`, `bottom`, and `center`. For example, specifying `top right`, will rotate the element around the point defined by its top-right corner. The keywords can be entered in any order as the browser can determine which value it applies to. The `center` keyword specifies both X and Y values and is equivalent to the default value (50% 50% 0).

Scale

The scaling functions are fairly straightforward. There is a `scaleX()` and a `scale(Y)` function that will grow or shrink the item along the X- or Y-axis, respectively. If you want to scale in both directions the `scale()` functions accept two values to define the horizontal and vertical scaling. A value of 1 indicates no scaling; values greater than 1 will make the element larger. A value less than one will make the element smaller. Specifying 0.5, for example, will make the element half of its original size for the specified dimension.

The `transform-origin` attribute affects how the scaling is done, or more accurately how the resulting shape is positioned, relative to the original element. If you leave the default value of `center`, the element will expand in both directions, leaving the center of the new shape exactly where the center of the original element was. If you set this to `top left`, for example, the top-left corner will remain fixed and the element will expand down and to the right.

A negative value will invert the element along the opposite axis. For example, using scaleY(-1) will flip the element vertically (along the horizontal axis). So the following functions will accomplish the same thing:

```
transform: rotateX(.5turn);
transform: scaleY(-1);
```

A value of -1 will simply invert it; a value of -2 will invert it and double its size.

Skew

Skewing an element, especially in two dimensions can be a bit tricky to understand. Let's start with a single dimension. Picture a rectangle that is fixed on one side and the opposite side is pulled down, causing the whole element to twist. This would be considered *skewed* and can be accomplished with the skewY() function as illustrated in Figure 15-2. The skewY() function will shift, or skew, the non-fixed size in the vertical dimension. The amount of skew is specified as an angle. The skewX() function will move the non-fixed edge horizontally.

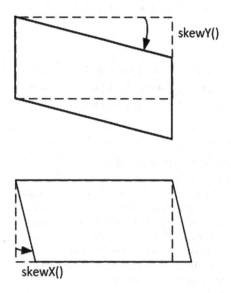

Figure 15-2. *Illustrating skewing*

■ **Note**   In these examples, I'm assuming the left or top edge is fixed. However, this is controlled by the transform-origin attribute, just like with the rotate and scale functions. Changing this does not affect the resulting shape but will change how the element is positioned.

The skew() function allows you to specify both an X and Y value. Skewing in both directions is illustrated in Figure 15-3. This combines the effect of both types of skewing.

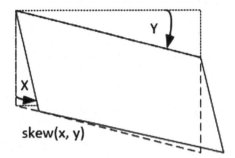

Figure 15-3. *Skewing in two dimensions*

Demonstration

The following will demonstrate all of these transformations. The markup creates four empty div element with class attributes so they can be easily selected.

```
<div class="transform translate">translate</div>
<div class="transform rotate">rotate</div>
<div class="transform scale">scale</div>
<div class="transform skew">skew</div>
```

The CSS first applies some basic styling for all of these div element and then applies the different transforms for each. The result is shown in Figure 15-4.

```
.transform {
    margin: 25px;
    height: 50px;
    width: 100px;
    border: 1px solid black;
    background-color: lightblue;
}
.translate {
    transform: translate(30px, -10px);
}
.rotate {
    transform: rotate(15deg);
    transform-origin: bottom left;
}
.scale {
    transform: scale(1.5, .9);
    transform-origin: bottom left;
}
.skew {
    transform: skew(20deg, 15deg);
    transform-origin: top left;
}
```

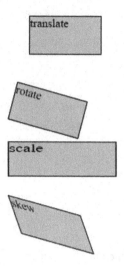

Figure 15-4. *The effects of each transform*

Notice that all of these effects apply not only to the shape of the element but also its contents. The text, for example, is also scaled or skewed.

3D Transforms

Three-dimensional transforms attempt to simulate a 3-dimensional object on a 2-dimensional page. To do that you have to configure some additional information so that the browser knows how to perform the transformation. The additional attributes are the perspective and perspective-origin. To understand how these are used, let me explain some basic drawing techniques.

If you have a 3-dimensional object such as a box and want to draw it on a 2-dimensional piece of paper, the simplest approach is to use a vanishing point. This is done by drawing one side of the box and then define a vanishing point somewhere away from the rectangle. Then draw an imaginary line from each of the corners to that point. A portion of these lines will form the edges of the box. Finally, the back of the box is found by creating a parallel rectangle that intersects these vanishing lines. This is illustrated in Figure 15-5.

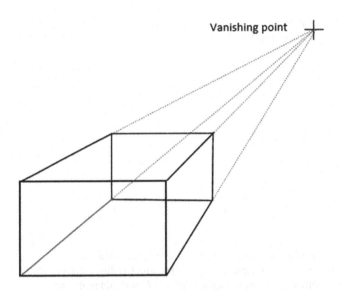

Figure 15-5. *Demonstrating a vanishing point*

You can probably envision how that moving the vanishing point, and dragging the lines with it, will create a different perspective of the same box. This is what these additional attributes allow you to do. The perspective attribute defines the distance from the original image to the vanishing point. The greater the distance, the subtler the 3D effect.

The perspective-origin attribute defines on which side of the image the vanishing point is. In Figure 15-5, the vanishing point is to the top right. This creates the effect of looking down on the box from above and from the right of it. The perspective-origin takes both X and Y values that are expressed as percentages, from 0% to 100%. There are some predefined values as well. For example, 0% 0% can also be entered as left bottom, and 100% 100% is right top. The single value of center is the same as 50% 50% and indicates that vanishing point is directly behind the image.

These perspective details need to be defined on a container element, and not the element that is being transformed. Also, if you want the browser to perform a 3D transform, you need to set the transform-style attribute. The default value for this attribute is flat, which will perform a simple 2D transform. You need to set this to perserve-3d instead.

To demonstrate this, I'll create a div element as the container and put an image inside of it. The div element uses the rotate3D class to make it easier to select.

```
<div class="rotate3D">
    <img src="phonebooth.jpg" alt="Phone booth" />
</div>
```

To aid in the demonstration, I will use a transition so the rotation happens slowly and you can more easily see the 3D effect. The following CSS rules will accomplish this.

```
.rotate3D {
    margin: 100px;
    transform-style: preserve-3d;
    perspective: 360px;
    perspective-origin: left;
}
img {
    transition: all 5s linear;
}
img:hover {
    transform: rotateY(180deg);
}
```

On the container, I set the three transform attributes, transform-style, perspective, and perspective-origin. These attributes are always defined on the container element. On the image element, I defined a 5 second transition on all modified attributes using the linear timing function. Finally, on the :hover pseudo-class I used the same transform attribute that I described earlier with the rotateY() function.

When you hover the mouse over the image, it should slowly rotate with a 3D effect as demonstrated in Figure 15-6.

Figure 15-6. *Demonstrating a 3D transform*

When rotating elements, you might not want to see their backsides, no pun intended. In this example, seeing the back of the phone booth is not a problem. Actually, we're not seeing the back, but rather of the front turned around. You can make the element invisible when turned around by using the backface-visibility attribute to hidden. It's default value is visible. If the back of the box has a different picture, for example, you wouldn't want to show the front image when the box is turned around.

Summary

In this chapter I demonstrated techniques for creating animations. An animation is simply modifying one or more CSS attributes over the duration of the animation. The browser will perform the interpolation so you don't have to define every frame. For a simple animation you can just define the beginning and ending frames.

The gradual change over time is controlled by the timing function, which is defined by a cubic Bézier curve. This is defined by the X and Y coordinates of two points. This provides a lot of flexibility for controlling the actual transition. However, there are also some predefined curves such as linear and ease-in.

A transition is similar to an animation but is invoked when a CSS attribute is changed. The transition does not change the attribute but rather defines the gradual transition when the value is changed. CSS transitions are also invoked when the property is changed through client-side scripting.

Transforms are functions that will adjust the size, shape, or position of an element. These functions fall into one of four categories (translation, rotation, scaling, and skewing). These transforms can apply to either the X, Y, or Z axes. A 3D transform can also be done but requires a few more attributes to be set such as perspective and transform-style.

The next chapter will start a new section regarding JavaScript. This will start with looking at the browser environment and the facilities that are available to your page scripts.

PART IV

■ ■ ■

JavaScript

Using JavaScript in your web application opens up seemingly endless possibilities, making web pages much more dynamic and interactive. I gave a pretty thorough overview of the JavaScript language in Chapter 3. In this section, I'll demonstrate how JavaScript can be used in a web environment. The topics I'll cover are the following:

- 16) Browser environment – this chapter explores the resources available from the Browser Object Model, including the `Screen`, `Location`, `History`, `Navigator`, `Console`, and other resources, using timers, and various caching options such as session storage and cookies.

- 17) Window object – this chapter demonstrates how to create and manipulate a window, including various dialogs and frames.

- 18) DOM manipulation – this chapter explains how to find, create, modify, and move the HTML elements that you learned about in Part 2, through JavaScript.

- 19) Dynamic styling – In this chapter, you'll use JavaScript to dynamically alter the style rules of the web page using several different techniques.

- 20) Events – these are the lifeblood of an interactive application. In this chapter, you'll learn how to register for an event and then use the event object to respond appropriately.

CHAPTER 16

Browser Environment

In Chapter 3 I explained the mechanics of the JavaScript language. In the remaining chapters of this book, I'll demonstrate how to embed JavaScript in your HTML document. You will be using JavaScript extensively so you might want to review Chapter 3 if this is fairly new to you. In the next two chapters, I'll explain the operating environment that the web page will be hosted in. The browser provides quite a lot of functionality that can be manipulated through JavaScript.

Browser Object Model

The facilities provided by the browser, starting with the window object, are informally referred to as the *Browser Object Model* (BOM). There is no official standard defining this, however. Fortunately, the major browser vendors all provide essentially the same properties and methods.

Caution I will describe the features that are generally available in most modern browsers and reasonably safe for you to use. However, you should not assume that everything I mention is available in every browser. Test your code on a lot of browsers, and be sure to provide fallback options for critical functionality.

The window object, which can be found in the global namespace, is the starting point for accessing the browser facilities. It represents a single window or tab. If you have multiple tabs open, there will be a separate instance of the window object for each tab, as well as one for the overall window. Also, if you open a dialog box, a separate window instance will be used for that as well. I will explain how to work with multiple windows and frames in Chapter 17. For now, I'll start with a simple case, with a single window/tab.

In addition to the many properties and functions available on the window object, there are several child objects that provide specific functionality. The main ones are shown in Figure 16-1, and I will describe each of these individually. The document object represents the HTML document that is being rendered in the window. Chapters 18 and 19 will deal exclusively with manipulating this through JavaScript so I won't say much about it here.

© Mark J. Collins 2017
M. J. Collins, *Pro HTML5 with CSS, JavaScript, and Multimedia*, DOI 10.1007/978-1-4842-2463-2_16

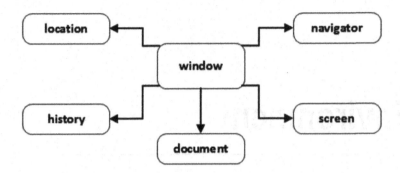

Figure 16-1. *Primary browser objects*

■ **Tip** While these objects are all child objects of the window, they are also available in the global namespace. If you access the screen or document property, for example, from the global namespace, it will return the object associated with the current window or tab.

Before describing the window object itself, I'll start with demonstrating these primary child objects.

Screen

The screen object provides details about the device that the browser is running on. The simplest way to see what it contains is to try it out. If you go to your browser's console and type **window.screen**, you'll see something similar to Figure 16-2.

```
> window.screen
<· ▼ Screen 🔳
      availHeight: 1160
      availLeft: 0
      availTop: 0
      availWidth: 1920
      colorDepth: 24
      height: 1200
    ▼ orientation: ScreenOrientation
        angle: 0
        onchange: null
        type: "landscape-primary"
      ▶ __proto__: ScreenOrientation
      pixelDepth: 24
      width: 1920
```

Figure 16-2. *Displaying the screen object*

As you can see, I'm using a monitor with a resolution of 1920 x 1200 and a color depth of 24. These properties are all read-only as you can't change the device characteristics. This information can be used by your web page. For example, if you were to launch a new window or pop-up dialog, the device characteristics may influence the size and location of the new window.

If you look at the `screen` object in multiple browsers, however, you'll notice that they provide a slightly different set of properties. Here's the basic set the you can pretty much count on:

- `height` - Total height of the device (in pixels)

- `width` - Total width of the device (in pixels)

- `availHeight` - Amount of vertical space not used by the OS (such as for a taskbar)

- `availWidth` - Amount of horizontal space available

- `colorDepth` - the number of bits used to specify the color

- `pixelDepth` - this is the same as `colorDepth`

The device orientation has not standardized; For Firefox and Edge, the prefixed properties, `mozOrientation` and `msOrientation`, respectively, can be used. For Chrome, orientation is provided as an object and you can access it's `type` property (`screen.orientation.type`). However, since you can get the `height` and `width`, you can easily determine the orientation.

Location

The `location` object provides the web address of the document that is loaded in the window. It is also linked to the `document` object so it can be accessed through either `window.location` or `document.location`, or simply `location` as I explained previously. It contains individual properties for each part of the URL:

- `protocol`

- `hostname`

- `port`

- `pathname`

- `search - one or more query string parameters preceded with a question mark (?)`

- `hash - a hashtag (#) followed by a fragment identifier`

There are a few additional properties that are provided for convenience:

- `href` - provides the full URL

- `host` - includes the `hostname` and `port`

- `origin` - includes the `protocol`, `hostname`, and `port`

The `ToString()` method will return the `href` property so you can get the full URL by simply referencing the `location` object. For example, the following code will generate the pop-up shown in Figure 16-3:

```
alert(location);
```

Figure 16-3. *Displaying the URL*

Like the screen object, the location object is generally read-only. The one big exception, is that you can use the location object to navigate to another page, using the assign() method. You could also just assign a URL value to the location object, so either of the following will accomplish the same thing:

```
location.assign("http://www.google.com");
location = "http://www.google.com";
```

You can also modify one of the URL components instead of the entire URL. A useful example is to modify the query string parameters in the search property. If the user changes their search criteria, you can simply update the search property and a new request will be sent to the server.

Instead of using the assign() method, you can use the replace() method, which works the same way except that the current page will not be saved in the history, which I will explain next. The location object also supports the reload() method, which will refresh the current window. The reload() method accepts a Boolean parameter, and if true is passed, the page is refreshed from the server. If this is false, or no parameter is supplied, the browser may refresh the page using its local cache.

History

The history object tracks the pages that were loaded in a single window. This is not the complete browsing history with the sites that were visited yesterday or last week, nor is it aware of pages loaded in other windows or tabs. It is used to support the back button, allowing you to go back to the previous page.

The history object has a length property the indicates how many entries are in the history. This will include the current page so there will always be at least one. You can navigate to the previous page by calling the back() method. Similarly, you can move to the next page using the forward() method. This works the same way as if the user had clicked the back or forward buttons on the browser. The history object also supports a generic go() function, where the direction and number of pages is specified by an integer value. Using go(-1) is equivalent to back() and go(1) is equivalent to forward(). However, you can use the go() method to skip multiple pages, such as go(-2), which will go back two pages in the history.

■ **Note**   If an out-of-range scenario happens, such as calling forward() when on the most recent page, the call is ignored and has no effect.

The history object also supports the pushState() and replaceState() methods that you can use to manipulate the history stack. Calling pushState() will add another history element as if you had actually navigated to a new page (such as using the location.assign() method). The replaceState() method updates the existing history element with the data provided. However, neither method actually navigates to a new page.

Both methods support three parameters:

- state - a JSON string containing any serializable data that you want to store here.

- title - this is currently ignored; you can enter an empty string or a short title describing the page.

- url - the address that will be stored in the history and used for navigating back or forward.

Using the pushState() and replaceState() members, as their name implies, allows you to associate state information with the history. If someone navigated away from your page and then used the back button to go back, your page could take advantage of the state data. Suppose for example, that your page performed a customer lookup and retrieved details about the user. This data can be stored in the history state so when they navigate back to your page, the data can be obtained without performing another lookup.

There are two ways to obtain the state data. First, you can listen for the popstate event, which is fired when navigating through the history. The popstate event is only fired when the current and new URLs are for the same document. So if the user navigates to a completely different site and then navigates back to your page, no event is fired. Also, Chrome only fires the event when navigating back; it is not fired when navigating forward.

Fortunately, you can also obtain the current state data by simply getting it from the history object using the state property. The code in Listing 16-1 demonstrates these state methods and properties.

Listing 16-1. Demonstrating the history state

```
window.onpopstate = function (e) {
    console.log("popstate - url: " + location + ", state: " + JSON.stringify(e.state));
}

console.log("0-length: " + history.length + ", state: " + JSON.stringify(history.state));
history.replaceState({id: 1}, "", location);
history.pushState({id: 2}, "", location);
history.pushState({id: 3}, "", location);
console.log("1-length: " + history.length + ", state: " + JSON.stringify(history.state));
history.go(-1);
history.go(-1);
history.go(1);
history.go(1);
console.log("2-length: " + history.length + ", state: " + JSON.stringify(history.state));
```

This code first implements the popstate event by simply writing the details to the console. The code then uses the replaceState() method to set the state on the current history element. The pushState() method is then used to add two more history entries. Notice that the location object is passed in as the third parameter. This will specify the current value for the URL so no change is being made; only the state is being updated. This code also logs the history length and the current state before any changes are made, after the new history entries are added, and after the navigation is done. The results from the console window are shown in Figure 16-4.

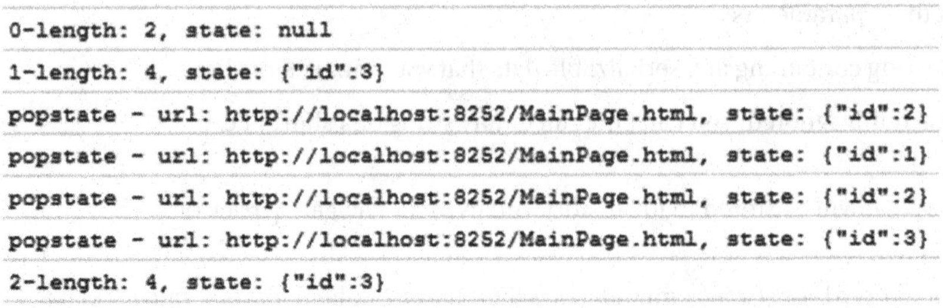

```
0-length: 2, state: null
1-length: 4, state: {"id":3}
popstate - url: http://localhost:8252/MainPage.html, state: {"id":2}
popstate - url: http://localhost:8252/MainPage.html, state: {"id":1}
popstate - url: http://localhost:8252/MainPage.html, state: {"id":2}
popstate - url: http://localhost:8252/MainPage.html, state: {"id":3}
2-length: 4, state: {"id":3}
```

Figure 16-4. *Console in Firefox*

The history length is initially 2, because when I started the browser it loaded the default home page and I then entered the URL for my test site. As expected, the initial state is null. After calling pushState() twice, the length was 4. Each time the go() method was called, the popstate event fired and the state was updated to reflect the new current entry.

Navigator

Like the screen object, the navigator object provides information about the device that the browser is running on. The screen object is limited to details of the device display such as size and color depth. In contrast, the navigator object supports a pretty long list of properties and methods. I'm not going to explain all of them here; however they are listed with a short description in the reference materials in Appendix C.

One increasing useful property of the navigator object is geolocation. This uses the device hardware to determine the current position of the device using either Global Positioning System (GPS), cellular triangularization, Wi-Fi information, or IP lookup depending on the capabilities of the device. I will cover this in detail in Chapter 26.

User Agent

The navigator object includes several properties that indicate the operating system and browser details, including:

- appCodeName
- appName
- appVersion
- platform
- product
- userAgent

Most of this information is inaccurate and difficult to make any good use out of it. For example, I'm running Chrome, Firefox, and Edge on Windows 10, and all three have the same values for appCodeName, appName, and product (Mozilla, Netscape, and Gecko, respectively). The userAgent property is a string that contains most of the information from the other properties. However, this is a bit cryptic. For example, here are the userAgent strings for the three browsers I just mentioned:

- Mozilla/5.0 (Windows NT 10.0; WOW64) AppleWebKit/537.36 (KHTML, like Gecko) Chrome/54.0.2840.71 Safari/537.36

- Mozilla/5.0 (Windows NT 10.0; WOW64; rv:49.0) Gecko/20100101 Firefox/49.0

- Mozilla/5.0 (Windows NT 10.0; Win64; x64) AppleWebKit/537.36 (KHTML, like Gecko) Chrome/51.0.2704.79 Safari/537.36 Edge/14.14393

One of the reasons for this debacle, is that web developers have made the mistake (and continue to do so) of writing logic in their code based on the browser instead of using feature detection; if Chrome do this or else if Firefox do that. So, new browsers set the userAgent property to look like other browsers so the application will take advantage of the browser features.

▪ **Tip** If you want to glean some useful information from the userAgent, I recommend using a parser that someone else has written. There are several to choose from. Just google "parse user agent."

Battery

The battery property returns a BatteryManager object, which provides the following properties:

- charging (true if the device is pulled in and charging).

- chargingTime (the number of seconds remaining until fully charged).

- dischargingTime (the number of seconds until the battery is completely discharged).

- level (a valued from 0 to 1 indicating the current charge level).

You can also listen for events that fire when these values change. These events are called chargingchange, chargingtimechange, on dischargingtimechange, and levelchange.

Window Object

Now let's look at the window object and explore the functionality that it exposes. There is a long list of both properties and methods that are available, and I have listed the standard ones in the reference materials in Appendix C. There are also a large number of events that you can subscribe to and these are listed as well. However, I will explain events in Chapter 20.

Console

The browser console is usually found as part of the developer tools and is a handy resource that allows you to inspect the value of properties and to run ad-hoc JavaScript commands. The console also includes a log where you can write debugging information from your application, which I have already demonstrated. The window object also provides a console object that you use to interact with the console programmatically. As with many of the other objects provided by the window object, the console is also in the global namespace so you can access it with window.console or simply console.

The methods supported by the console object are listed and described in the reference materials in Appendix C. I won't describe all of them here, but I will explain a few of the more useful features.

String Substitution

Many of the console methods including log(), error(), info(), and warn() support string substitution. You can embed one or more percent signs (%) into the text as a placeholder and then provide an additional parameter for each placeholder. Next to the % symbol, you need to also specify one of the following format characters:

- s - string
- d or i - numeric
- f - floating point
- o - object

▪ **Caution** Firefox also supports qualifying the numeric and floating-point formats to specify the number of digits. As of this writing, this is not supported by most other browsers and can causing incorrect formatting in some browsers, including Edge.

For a quick demonstration, the following will output four values with the specified format:

```
console.info("Formatting: %i, %f, %s, %o", 22.651, Math.PI, "text", screen);
```

This will be displayed in the Edge browser as shown in Figure 16-5 and in Chrome as shown in Figure 16-6. Notice the blue circle with an "i" in it to indicate this is an informational entry.

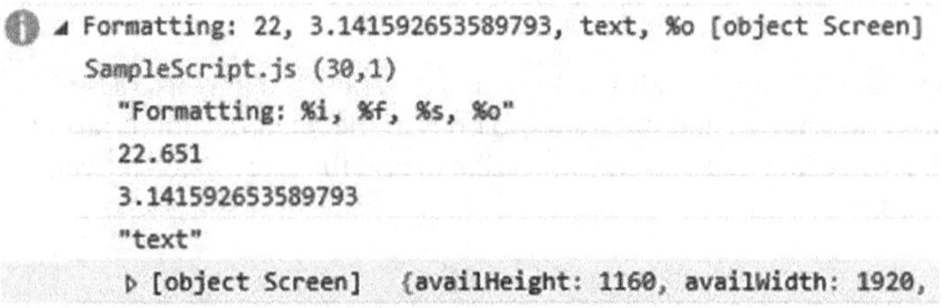

```
ⓘ ⊿ Formatting: 22, 3.141592653589793, text, %o [object Screen]
      SampleScript.js (30,1)
        "Formatting: %i, %f, %s, %o"
      22.651
      3.141592653589793
      "text"
      ▷ [object Screen]    {availHeight: 1160, availWidth: 1920,
```

Figure 16-5. *An informational log entry in Edge*

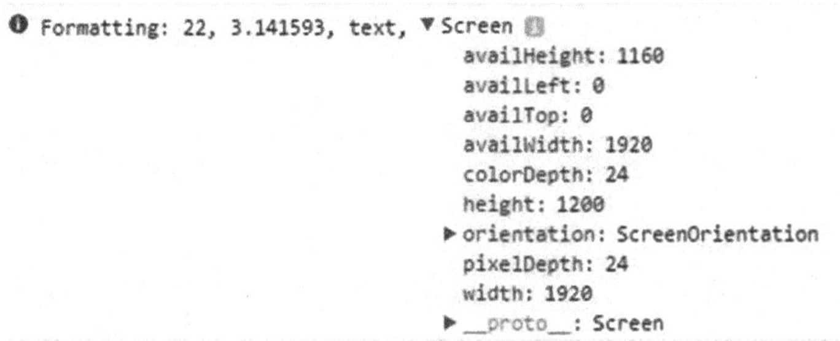

```
❶ Formatting: 22, 3.141593, text, ▼ Screen 🔳
                              availHeight: 1160
                              availLeft: 0
                              availTop: 0
                              availWidth: 1920
                              colorDepth: 24
                              height: 1200
                            ▶ orientation: ScreenOrientation
                              pixelDepth: 24
                              width: 1920
                            ▶ __proto__: Screen
```

Figure 16-6. An informational log entry in Chrome

Profiling

Most browsers provide developer tools that include utilities for evaluating performance. These can be quite powerful and help you see where your application can be tuned to improve responsiveness. This is beyond the scope of this book but I want to give you a couple of links to help you get started. Here's a good explanation of Chrome's Timeline tool: https://developers.google.com/web/tools/chrome-devtools/evaluate-performance/timeline-tool. In addition, Firefox has a Performance tool that is demonstrated in a series of articles starting with this one: https://developer.mozilla.org/en-US/docs/Tools/Performance.

The console object provides facilities for integrating with these performance tools. For example, the profile() method will start a new profile. You can place this call just before code that you want to evaluate. Then call the profileEnd() method to stop the profile and output the results. Google provides a good article that describes these various console functions with tips on how to use them: https://developers.google.com/web/tools/chrome-devtools/console/console-reference.

The time() and timeEnd() method can be used to gather some simple metrics. These methods act like a stopwatch. If you want to know how long a function takes to complete, just wrap these around the function. For example, the following code iterates through a loop 1,000 times and records the total time taken to complete.

```
console.time("Stopwatch");
var j = 1;
for (var i = 0; i < 1000; i++) {
    j += j + i;
}
console.info("j = %i", j);
console.timeEnd("Stopwatch");
```

Performance

On a somewhat related topic, the window object includes a performance property that provides access to the Web Performance API. This API has two properties, navigation and timing that provide details of how the page was loaded and various timing metrics. If you enter **window.performance.timing** in the browser console, you can see a collection of timing details as shown in Figure 16-7. These values are the computed as the number of milliseconds from a specific point in time.

```
window.performance.timing
▲ [object PerformanceTiming]              {connectEnd: 1477780420170, connectStart:
   ▷ [functions]
   ▷ __proto__                            [object PerformanceTimingPrototype] {...}
     connectEnd                           1477780420170
     connectStart                         1477780420170
     domainLookupEnd                      1477780420170
     domainLookupStart                    1477780420170
     domComplete                          1477780420716
     domContentLoadedEventEnd             1477780420713
     domContentLoadedEventStart           1477780420711
     domInteractive                       1477780420711
     domLoading                           1477780420316
     fetchStart                           1477780420170
     loadEventEnd                         1477780420718
     loadEventStart                       1477780420717
     msFirstPaint                         1477780420426
     navigationStart                      1477780420119
     redirectEnd                          0
     redirectStart                        0
     requestStart                         1477780420212
     responseEnd                          1477780420358
     responseStart                        1477780420316
     unloadEventEnd                       8223774009272
     unloadEventStart                     8223774009271
```

Figure 16-7. *Performance timing details*

This API also provides a now() method that will return the number of milliseconds using the same reference point. The API also provides a mark() method that you can use to add a custom performance entry.

Grouping Log Entries

You can also group log entries by using the group() method. After the log entries are added, call the groupEnd() method to close the group. For a simple demonstration, the following code logs three entries inside a group. This is seen in the Firefox console as shown in Figure 16-8.

```
console.group("Logging a group of records...");
console.log("Log entry #1");
console.log("Log entry #2");
console.log("Log entry #3");
console.groupEnd();
```

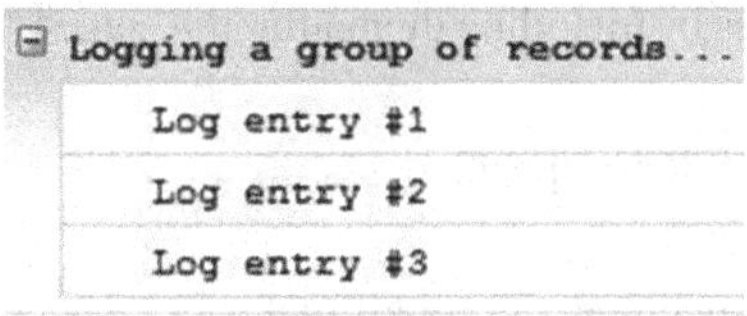

```
⊟ Logging a group of records...
      Log entry #1
      Log entry #2
      Log entry #3
```

Figure 16-8. *Display a log group in Firefox*

Instead of using the group() method, you could use the groupCollapsed() method. This works exactly the same way as the group() method except that the group is collapsed in the console and the user must expand it to see the three log entries.

Cache

Being able to store data on the client has several important applications, including performance and improved user experience. For a long time, this was done exclusively through cookies but HTML introduces localStorage and sessionStorage to address some of the drawback of cookies.

Cookies

Cookies allow you to store small amounts of data on the client. They are actually part of the document object, but I will explain them here along with the other storage mechanisms. All of the cookies for a document are provided as a single string, which is available through the document.cookie property. The cookies are separated by a semicolon and each cookie has the form <name>=<value>. For example, if there were three cookies names Test1, Test2, and Test3, the cookie string might look like this:

```
Test1=Test cookie #1; Test2=Test cookie #2; Test3=Test cookie #3
```

■ **Tip**   One important aspect of cookies is that they are included with every server request. This makes this client-side data available to the server. The server can also set the value of the cookies.

To add a cookie you assign its value using the same document.cookie property. However, you can only set a single cookie value at a time. For example:

```
document.cookie = "Test1=Test value";
```

This will either create a new cookie with the name "Test1" or update an existing cookie if one by the same name already exists. This will not affect any other cookies that were already defined. However, getting the document.cookie property will return all cookies as I previously explained. To get a specific cookie, you'll need to parse the cookies value looking for the desired cookie. To remove a cookie, you need to update its value to an empty string.

When creating a cookie, you can also include some other properties by including them after the cookie value. These are the supported attributes:

- domain= - specifies the domain that has access to this cookie; if not specified this defaults to the domain of the document.

- expires= - indicates when the cookie should expire; if not specified, the cookie will expire when the session is closed. This must be formatted as a UTC string; use the toUTCString() method to assist with formatting.

- max-age= - another way of specifying when the cookie expires; specify the number of seconds before the cookie expires.

- path= - specifies the location where the cookie should be stored.

- secure - indicates that the cookie should only be sent when https is used.

For example, to set the expiration date, create a new cookie like this:

```
document.cookie = "Test=Test cookie; expires=Sun, 30 Oct 2016 12:00:00 UTC";
```

Working with cookies is somewhat tedious, and I suggest that you create (or borrow) some helper functions to simplify accessing them. The code in Listing 16-2 creates three functions that create, remove, and get a cookie. The remaining code then uses these functions, writing the results to the console.

Listing 16-2. Using Cookies

```
function storeCookie(key, value, duration) {
    var expDate = new Date();
    expDate.setTime(expDate.getTime() + duration * 86400000);
    document.cookie = key + "=" + value + ";expires=" + expDate.toUTCString();
}

function removeCookie(key) {
    storeCookie(key, "", 0);
}

function getCookie(key) {
    var cookies = document.cookie.split(';');
    for(var i=0; i<cookies.length; i++) {
        if (cookies[i].trim().indexOf(key + "=") == 0) {
            return cookies[i].trim().substring(key.length + 1);
        }
    }
    return null;
}

storeCookie("Test1", "Test cookie #1", 5);
storeCookie("Test2", "Test cookie #2", 5);
storeCookie("Test3", "Test cookie #3", 5);

console.log(document.cookie);
console.log("Test2:", getCookie("Test2"));
removeCookie("Test2");
console.log("Test2:", getCookie("Test2"));
console.log(document.cookie);
```

The results in the console log is shown in Figure 16-9. After adding three cookies, they are all returned in the cookies property. The getCookie() function returned the specified cookie but then after the cookie was removed, the function returned null. Also, the cookie property only returns two cookies after one was removed.

```
Test1=Test cookie #1; Test2=Test cookie #2; Test3=Test cookie #3
Test2: Test cookie #2
Test2: null
Test1=Test cookie #1; Test3=Test cookie #3
```

Figure 16-9. *Displaying the cookie results*

Storage

HTML5 defines two new storage mechanisms for client-side caching, localStorage and sessionStorage. Both are properties of the window object and they return a Storage object. The only difference between the two is the duration that the data is available. The sessionStorage is cleared when the browser is closed whereas the localStorage is kept indefinitely.

The Storage object holds a set of key/value pairs both of which must be strings. You can store any data in the Storage object that can be serialized. You add an item by calling the setItem() methods passing in both a key and a string value. If the specified key exists, its value will be updated; otherwise a new item is added to storage. You can retrieve an item by calling getItem() passing in the key of the desired item. If the specified key is not found, getItem() will return null.

■ **Caution**   Always check for exceptions when calling setItem() as exceptions can occur. The setItem() will throw an exception if the cache is full. Also, in some browsers it will throw an exception when in private mode.

If you want to remove an item from storage, call the removeItem() method passing in the key of the item. You can also remove all items by calling the clear() method. The Storage methods are demonstrated in the following code:

```
var cache = window.sessionStorage;
cache.clear();
cache.setItem("key1", "This is my saved data");
console.log("Saved data: " + cache.getItem("key1"));
cache.removeItem("key1");
console.log("Saved data: " + cache.getItem("key1"));
```

There are size limits for both local and session storage that vary by browser and operating system. Here is a page that will test your specific browser and verify the storage limits: http://dev-test.nemikor.com/web-storage/support-test/. But generally, you should have around 5MB.

Browser Interface Elements

The browser provides several UI components, such as a menu, toolbar, and status bar, that the user can use to interact with and control the browser's behavior. Each of these components support the BarProp interface that exposes a single property, visible. JavaScript can access these components to determine if a particular element is available to the users. The following window properties are supported:

- locationbar - displays the URL of the current document.

- menubar - any type of menu provided by the browser.

- personalbar - provides user preferences, bookmarks, favorites, etc.

- scrollbar - either a vertical or horizontal scrollbar.

- statusbar - provide status of the current page of the currently selected element on the page. This may include download status of a resource or the URL a link is pointing to.

- toolbar - component containing UI-based commands such as the back button or refresh button.

You cannot hide or show these UI components, but you can determine if they are currently visible. To see if the menu is visible, for example, call the following:

```
if (window.menubar.visible) {
    console.log("Menu is visible");
}
```

Timers

The window object provides two types of timers:

- setTimeout() - calls the specified function after a specified amount of time.

- setInterval() - calls the specified function after a specified amount of time and continues to call that function using the same interval.

Both methods return a handle that you can use to cancel the timer. This is particularly important for setInterval() as it will keep calling the function until it is canceled. To cancel the timer, use the corresponding method, clearTimeout() or clearInterval() passing the return value of the set method.

To see this in action, here is a simple demonstration:

```
function logMessage() {
    console.log("The timer went off!");
}

var timer = setTimeout(logMessage, 2000);

// Don't call this or the timer will never fire
//clearTimeout(timer);
```

I purposely commented out the call to clearTimeout() so the timer would eventually expire. About 2 seconds after the page loads, you should see a new entry in the console log.

Summary

In this chapter I covered a wide range of topics related to the browser environment and the features that are available. There is a lot of information available that you can use to influence the behavior of your application. The `window` object is the starting point and provides access to these capabilities. The primary child objects are:

- `screen` - Provide details of the display device.

- `location` - Provide details of the current web address and can be used to navigate to other pages.

- `history` - Used to support the back button and can be manipulated to change the behavior of the back button. You can also include state information that is available when navigating back to a previous page.

- `navigator` - provides details about the device including hardware, operating system, and browser information. It also provides the `geolocation` object.

The `window` object provides some useful features such as the console log as well as profiling and performance metrics. You can also store client-side data through cookies as well as local and session storage. Timers are also available through the `window` object. There is a lot of functionality that I did not cover in detail but is provided in the reference material.

In the next chapter I will explain more about the window itself, including dialog boxes, frames and multi-tab applications.

Window Object

In this chapter I will explain how you can create and manipulate windows with JavaScript. I will start by opening a pop-up window and demonstrate how to control its size and position as well as other attributes. I'll show how you can use methods on the `window` object to move and resize a window. I also provide an example that simulates a modal dialog using HTML, CSS, and JavaScript. Finally, I will briefly explain how to use an inline frame to embed content from another source.

Create a Window

I'll start by opening a new window using JavaScript on an existing window. Then I'll demonstrate the ways the new window can be manipulated through JavaScript. A new window is easily created by calling the `window.open()` method. This has two required parameters: a name for the window and the web address for its document.

Note The `window` object provides methods for modifying properties such as its size and location. However, as a security measure, you can only adjust windows that were created through JavaScript. So, you cannot change the initial window that was created by the browser. However, you can create a new window using the `open()` method and then manipulate it though JavaScript, which is what I'll be doing here.

In my web project, I have a very simple HTML document named `MainPage.html` with the following markup:

```
<!DOCTYPE html>

<html lang="en">
    <head>
        <meta charset="utf-8" />
        <title>Chapter 17 - Windows</title>
        <script src="SampleScript.js"></script>
    </head>
    <body>
        <p>Hello World!</p>
    </body>
</html>
```

For the new window I also have `PopUp.html` and `PopUp2.html` files that are essentially the same as the initial document with a slight variation on the title and paragraph elements so you can tell them apart. The pop-up document also references a different script file, `PopUp.js`, which is initially empty. The `SampleScript.js` file initially has the following JavaScript code:

```
"use strict";

window.name = "Chapter17";
var popup = window.open("PopUp.html", "popup");
```

A window created through the open( ) method will have its name property set by the second parameter. However, windows created through the browser do not, so this script sets the name property. It then creates a new window using the `PopUp.html` document.

Pop-Up Blocker

When you try this out, unless you have your Pop-Up Blocker disabled, you probably received some sort of warning like the one shown in Figure 17-1, which is from the Chrome browser. Pop-ups are generally pretty annoying and can pose a security threat so all modern browsers can block pop-ups. In most cases, this is the default setting.

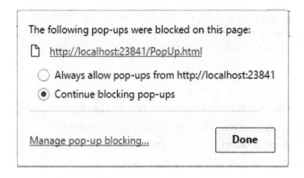

Figure 17-1. *Pop-up warning in Chrome*

I recommend that you click the *Manage pop-up blocking* or equivalent link and selectively allow some pop-ups. If you disable blocking completely, you leave you browser susceptible. However, most of the demos in this chapter won't work if pop-ups are not enabled. In the pop-up exception dialog, you can enter **localhost** as shown in Figure 17-2.

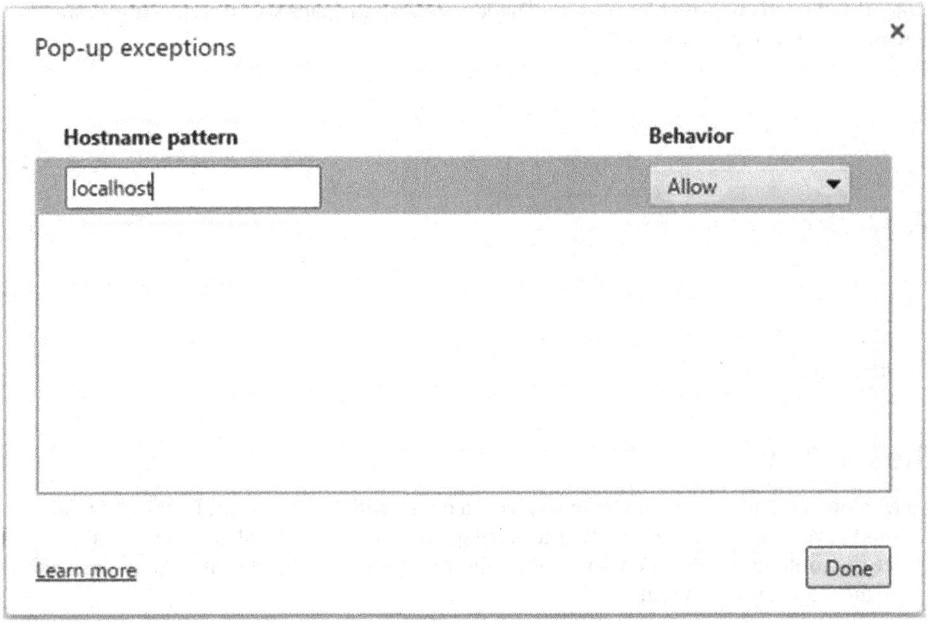

Figure 17-2. *Configuring pop-up exceptions in Chrome*

Each browser has a different interface for reporting blocked pop-ups and for managing which pop-ups are allowed. For example, the warning in Firefox is shown in Figure 17-3 and the warning in Opera is shown in Figure 17-4.

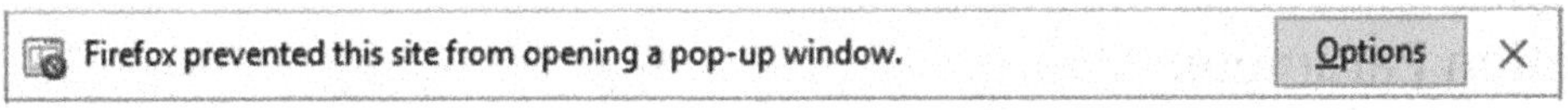

Figure 17-3. *The pop-up blocker in Firefox*

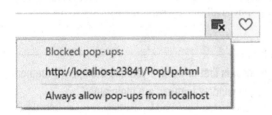

Figure 17-4. *The pop-up blocker in Opera*

Once you have disabled the pop-up blocker, you'll need to refresh the page so the script runs again. You should see another tab as shown in Figure 17-5.

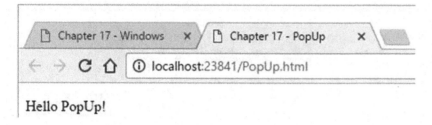

Figure 17-5. *Opening a second tab*

Reusing the Window

When creating a window through JavaScript you must give it a name, which is the second parameter passed to the open() method. If you try to open another window using the same name, it will use the existing window but replace the contents with the new URL. To try this out, go to the initial tab and open the console window. Then type the following command:

```
window.open("PopUp2.html", "popup");
```

Because the name is the same, "popup," the same window will be used, but it will load the specified document, PopUp2.html.

The open() method will also return a window object and, in my example, is stored in the popup variable. You can use that to manipulate the window and I will demonstrate that later in this chapter.

Configuration Parameter

The open() method also accepts a third parameter that contains a configuration string, which is sometimes referred to as the window features string. If you don't provide this parameter or the parameter is an empty string, the new window will be created as a new tab in the existing browser window, as I previously demonstrated. However, supplying any value, even a single space will cause a separate window to be created.

▪ **Tip** The window feature string is only used when the window is first created. If you use the open() method to replace its contents, this parameter is ignored and the existing window features are maintained.

This window features string contains a collection of name/value pairs that are separated by commas, and each defines a feature of the new window. There is a long list of features that can be specified in this string. I have organized them into logical groups.

▪ **Note** The specification states that there should be no whitespace between each name/value pair, only a comma. However, my experience is that spaces between each value are ignored.

Position and Size

The following values related to the new window's position or size are supported, which are fairly self-explanatory:

- `left`
- `top`
- `height`
- `width`
- `outerHeight`
- `outerWidth`

The `left` and `top` values indicate the position of the new window and specify the number of pixels from the left and top edges of the display. The `height` and `width` values specify the area available for the actual content of the document. The `outerHeight` and `outerWidth` values include the space for content as well as the title area, menu, toolbar, etc. If both are specified, the outer values will take precedence.

To demonstrate this, close the second tab and go to the console window of the initial page. Then enter the following command:

```
window.open("PopUp.html", "popup", "height=300,width=400,top=400,left=150");
```

■ **Caution**   Browser support for these features is not consistent. Chrome, IE, and Edge do not support the `outerHeight` and `outerWidth` features. Opera does, but if you use them, the `top` and `left` features are ignored and the window is aligned with the top-left corner of the initial window. Chrome requires the `height` and `width` features; if not supplied, the whole string is ignored, Edge does not support the `top` and `left` features; the new window is always about 20 pixels down and to the right of the initial window.

Chrome Features

The next set of features is related to the UI components of the browser, which is often referred to as the chrome, not to be confused with the Chrome browser. If none of these features are set, the default behavior in most browsers is to include the title bar and location area only; however IE does not include the location by default.

The specification defines the following values. As of this writing, only Firefox and Edge support these, however.

- `location`
- `menubar`
- `personalbar`
- `status`
- `titlebar`
- `toolbar`

These are Boolean values and do not require a specified value; their existence indicates the feature is requested and their absence indicates the opposite. Setting their value to no, such as menubar=no will also disable the feature. To test this, from either Firefox or IE, close the pop-up and enter the following command in the console of the initial window.

```
window.open("PopUp.html", "popup",
    "height=300,width=400,top=400,left=150,location,menubar,status,toolbar");
```

■ **Caution**   The behavior of these flags varies by browser. For example, in IE as I mentioned, the location area is not displayed by default but you can include it by adding location to the window feature string. However, adding the location will suppress the titlebar. In Firefox, if you add the menubar, the new window uses tabs and the page title is in the tab, not the title area.

Window Features

There are additional features that define the window behavior. There is very little support for these so I'll simply list them here as they might be supported later.

- alwaysLowered - puts the new window under the existing one in the z order.
- alwaysRaised - puts the new window above the existing window in the z order.
- close - set to no to disable the close icon.
- dependent - a dependent window is automatically closed when its parent window is closed.
- minimizable - disables the minimize icon.
- fullscreen - puts the new window in fullscreen mode.
- resizable - enables the window to be resized; this is on by default.
- scrollbars - set this to no to disable scrollbars. By default, scrollbars are included when the content doesn't fit into the allocated space.

Manipulating Windows

After creating a new window, you can use the window properties and methods to view and adjust its size, position, and scroll properties.

Properties

The current position and size of a window can be obtained from the window object. The open() method returns the window object that represents the new window. The initial window can use this to find out where the window is. You can also determine the current scroll position of the window. The following properties are available.

- innerHeight - height of the space available for content.
- innerWidth - width of the space available for content.
- outerHeight - total height of the window including the browser UI elements.

- outerWidth - total width of the window including the browser UI elements.

- screenX - the distance between the left edge of the device and the left edge of the window.

- screenY - the distance between the top edge of the device and the top edge of the window.

- scrollX - the number of pixels that the document has been scrolled horizontally.

- scrollY - the number of pixels that the document has been scrolled vertically.

Methods

These properties are all read-only; however, they can be manipulated through a set of methods that are provided on the window object. The following methods are available:

- moveBy() - Move the window by the specified number of pixels; both the horizontal and vertical shifts are specified. Set one to zero if no movement in that direction is desired. A negative value will move the window up or to the left.

- moveTo() - Move the window so the top-left corner is at the specified position.

- resizeBy() - Increase the window size by the amount specified; both a horizontal and vertical increase is specified. Set to negative if the dimension should shrink. The top and left edges remain in the same place.

- resizeTo() - Specify the new window size. The top and left edges remain in the same place.

- scrollBy() - Scroll by the specified number of pixels; both the horizontal and vertical values can be specified.

- scrollByLines() - Scroll the document vertically by the specified number of lines.

- scrollByPages() - Scroll the document vertically the number of specified pages.

- scrollTo() - Scroll to the specified horizontal and vertical positions.

- sizeToContent() - Change the window size to fit the existing content.

Demonstration

To demonstrate these capabilities, I first added a large image to the PopUp2.html file by adding the line in bold. This enables you to see the scrolling behavior as well as the sizeToContent() method.

```
<body>
    <p>Hello PopUp 2!</p>
    <img src="G_Wash_Wide.jpg" alt="George Washington" />
</body>
```

I then replaced the SampleScript.js with the code shown in Listing 17-1.

Listing 17-1. Rewriting the SampleScript.js to test window manipulation

```
"use strict";

window.name = "Chapter17";
var popup = window.open("PopUp2.html", "popup", "height=300,width=400,left=400,top=150,locat
ion,toolbar,menubar,scrollbars");


var i = 1;
var timer = window.setInterval(adjustWindow, 2000);

function adjustWindow() {

    if (i > 9) {
        clearInterval(timer);
    }
    else {
        console.log("outerH: %i, outerW: %i, innerH: %i, innerW: %i, screenX: %i, screenY: %i,
                    scrollX: %i, scrollY: %i",
            popup.outerHeight, popup.outerWidth, popup.innerHeight, popup.innerWidth,
            popup.screenX, popup.screenY, popup.scrollX, popup.scrollY);
    }

    switch (i) {
        case 1:
            popup.scrollBy(50, 30);
            break;
        case 2:
            popup.moveBy(50, 50);
            break;
        case 3:
            popup.moveTo(200, 100);
            break;
        case 4:
            popup.resizeBy(50, 50);
            break;
        case 5:
            popup.resizeTo(700, 500);
            break;
        case 6:
            popup.scrollByLines(5);
            break;
        case 7:
            popup.scrollByPages(1);
            break;
```

```
        case 8:
            popup.sizeToContent();
            break;
        case 9:
            popup.close();
            break;
    }
    i++;
}
```

The adjustWindow() function is called repeatedly, every 2 seconds, by using the setInterval() method that I explained in the previous chapter. Each time it is called it uses a different method to adjust either the size, position, or scroll of the pop-up window. On each iteration, the current window attributes are written to the console log. The last time it is called the pop-up window is closed by calling the close() method. When completed, the console log will look similar to Figure 17-6.

```
outerH: 500, outerW: 600, innerH: 390, innerW: 588, screenX: 400, screenY: 150, scrollX: 0, scrollY: 0
outerH: 500, outerW: 600, innerH: 390, innerW: 588, screenX: 400, screenY: 150, scrollX: 50, scrollY: 30
outerH: 500, outerW: 600, innerH: 390, innerW: 588, screenX: 450, screenY: 200, scrollX: 50, scrollY: 30
outerH: 500, outerW: 600, innerH: 390, innerW: 588, screenX: 200, screenY: 100, scrollX: 50, scrollY: 30
outerH: 550, outerW: 650, innerH: 440, innerW: 638, screenX: 200, screenY: 100, scrollX: 50, scrollY: 30
outerH: 500, outerW: 700, innerH: 390, innerW: 688, screenX: 200, screenY: 100, scrollX: 50, scrollY: 30
outerH: 500, outerW: 700, innerH: 390, innerW: 688, screenX: 200, screenY: 100, scrollX: 50, scrollY: 125
outerH: 500, outerW: 700, innerH: 390, innerW: 688, screenX: 200, screenY: 100, scrollX: 50, scrollY: 213
outerH: 696, outerW: 913, innerH: 586, innerW: 901, screenX: 200, screenY: 100, scrollX: 0, scrollY: 0
```

Figure 17-6. *Results in the console log*

Focus

You can programmatically change which window has the focus. When a new window is opened, it will normally have the focus. If you want to open a new window to display some information but the user is still interacting with the initial window, you should call the focus() method on the initial window after the new window is opened. This will keep the main window in focus.

The window also supports the blur() method. The name may seem odd at first, but the opposite of being focused is to be blurred. Calling the blur() method will remove the focus from the window and the focus will be on which ever window is next in the z order.

Modal Dialog Windows

So far, the windows I have created have been *modeless*, meaning that the user can interact with other windows as well. In contrast a *modal* window gets the focus and disables the rest of the application until the window is closed. Now, I'll show you how to create modal dialog boxes.

Standard Pop-Up Dialogs

Before I explain the more generic modal dialog boxes, I want to first point out that there are three standard modal dialog boxes available through JavaScript. They are quick and easy to use, but they are not very attractive and impossible to style. The first one is the alert box, which I showed you back in Chapter 3. This simply displays a text message with an OK button that will close the dialog box. The second is the confirmation box, which displays a text message but has both an OK and a Cancel button. This also returns true if OK is clicked or false if Cancel was clicked. The last is the prompt box, which displays a text message and a text field for entering a value. The entered value is returned. The following code demonstrates all three dialog boxes

```
window.alert("This is an alert box.\nThis is a second line");

if (window.confirm("Is it OK to proceed?")) {
    var answer = window.prompt("How many pets do you have?", 0);
    console.log("%i pets were entered.", answer);
}
else {
    console.log("Confirmation failed");
}
```

The alert() method demonstrates how you can include a line brake using the \n escape sequence. This is also supported on the other two pop-up dialogs. The confirm() method is nested inside an if statement. If the user clicks the Cancel button, the following code is skipped and a message is written to the console log. The prompt() method takes two parameters. The first is the text that is displayed in the dialog and the second is the default value, which is optional. The dialog boxes that are displayed in Firefox are shown in Figures 17-7, 17-8, and 17-9. Each browser formats these dialog boxes differently.

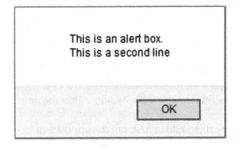

Figure 17-7. *The alert box in Firefox*

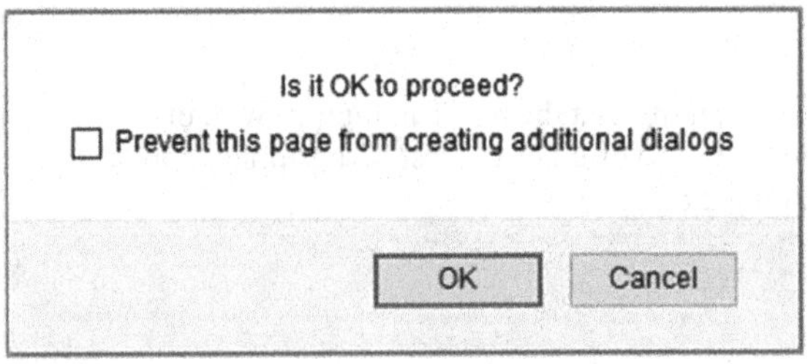

Figure 17-8. *The confirmation box in Firefox*

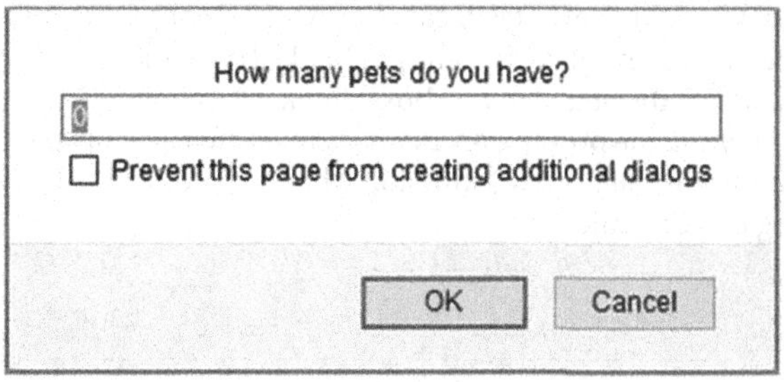

Figure 17-9. *The prompt box in Firefox*

Custom Modal Dialogs

Creating a true modal dialog box in HTML/JavaScript is challenging. There have been a couple of methods kicking around for some time now, openDialog() and showModalDialog(). However due to security vulnerabilities and various implementation issues, these have been deprecated. In fact, this capability has been completely removed from several browsers. You should definitely not use either of these methods for any new applications.

The HTML5 specification has defined a new dialog element that has the promise of simplifying modal dialogs. However, as of this writing there is almost no support for it. There are some jQuery solutions as well as other polyfills that can be employed that are outside of the scope of this book.

I will demonstrate a fairly simple way to approximate a modal dialog box using only native HTML, CSS, and JavaScript that is sometimes referred to as a *glass pane* approach. The basic idea is to overlay the entire window with a transparent, or semitransparent element, referred to as a glass. This is like putting a sheet of glass over a painting; while you can see the painting underneath the glass, you can't actually touch the painting. The actual dialog box and its elements are then placed on top of the glass. You can interact with the dialog box but not the rest of the page. From the user's perspective, this behaves just like a modal dialog box.

■ **Tip** To accomplish this I will need to give you a sneak peek into the next two chapters. You will need to manipulate the DOM elements and their styles through JavaScript.

The HTML for the glass overlay and the dialog elements are included in the main HTML document but they remain hidden until you want to open the dialog. Here is the markup that you'll need.

```
<body>
    <p>Hello World!</p>
    <button onclick="showDialog()">Show Dialog</button>
    <div id="glass" class="glass">
        <div class="dialog">
            <h3>Prompt</h3>
            <p>How many pets do you have?</p>
            <input type="number" value="0" id="numPets" />
            <button id="dialogOK" type="Submit" onclick="OK()">OK</button>
        </div>
    </div>
</body>
```

I have added a button that will show the dialog box; its click event will call the showDialog() function that needs to be implemented. The rest of the markup creates the glass, which is a simple div element. Inside the div element is another div element that contains the actual dialog box content. This includes a header element for the title, a paragraph element containing the prompt, an input element that accepts the user input, and a button to submit the entry. The button will call the OK() function when clicked.

The glass and dialog are styled with the following two CSS rules:

```css
.glass {
    position: fixed;
    left: 0;
    top: 0;
    background-color: rgba(225,225,225,.7);
    height: 100vh;
    width: 100vw;
    z-index: 100;
}

.dialog {
    height: 125px;
    width: 220px;
    margin: 0 auto;
    padding: 15px;
    border: 1px solid black;
    background-color: white;
}
```

The glass uses position: fixed, which as I explained in Chapter 10, will keep the element fixed relative to the window. By setting left and top to 0 and height and width to 100vh and 100vw, respectively, this element will take up the entire area of the window. The z-index is set to 100 to ensure that this element is on top of everything else.

You can adjust the background based on your preference; I set it to a gray background with 30% transparency. This will make it clear that the other controls around the dialog box are not available. You can use a completely transparent background as well. This will make the other elements appear normally, but the user still can't interact with them. You could also use a completely opaque background to hide the other elements. These choices are purely visual and have no effect on how the page functions.

The formatting of the dialog is pretty straightforward, using a fixed size and centering it horizontally using the margin: 0 auto; declaration. I did not add any other formatting to pretty it up, but you can add more declarations as desired.

The JavaScript needed to pull all of this together is shown in Listing 17-2.

Listing 17-2. The dialog implementation

```javascript
// Holds the result from the dialog box
var result = 0;

function showDialog() {
    var dialog = document.getElementById("glass");
    dialog.style.visibility = "visible";
}
```

```
function closeDialog() {
    var dialog = document.getElementById("glass");
    dialog.style.visibility = "hidden";

}
function OK() {
    var input = document.getElementById("numPets");
    result = input.value;
    closeDialog();

    console.log("#Pets: " + result);
}

// Make sure the dialog starts closed
closeDialog();
```

The first two functions, showDialog() and closeDialog(), get the glass element and the set is visibility attributed to either visible or hidden. The OK() function, which is called by the submit button, gets the value from the input element and stores it in the result variable. It also calls the closeDialog() function. After defining these functions, the closeDialog() function is called to ensure the glass is hidden when the page is first loaded. When the Show Dialog button is clicked, the page will look like Figure 17-10.

Figure 17-10. *The modal dialog box*

Frames

You can include an inline frame (iframe) element to embed content from another HTML document. For example, if you want to include a video on your page that is hosted on another site, such as YouTube, an iframe is just what you need. I explained inline frames briefly in Chapter 4.

■ **Caution**   Prior to HTML5 the frame element was used to organize parts of a page such as header or sidebar. Each was a window in its own right with a separate document and could be sized and moved independently of the other frames. This was a difficult pattern to work with. With HTML5 the frame element has been deprecated in favor of the sectioning elements that I explained in Chapter 4. Inline frames were kept, however. They provide the ability to embed another document while still anchored within the parent document. If you're familiar with frames, don't try to implement the frame approach using inline frames; use the sectioning elements and style with CSS.

Simple Example

An inline frame is embedded by using an iframe element, setting its src attribute to the location of the document that should be included in it. For example:

```
<iframe src="http://www.apress.com"></iframe>
```

Like other elements, you can style it with CSS. The following rule sets the width to 95%, allowing some room for the border. It also sets the height and applies a blue border. The result is shown in Figure 17-11.

```
iframe {
    width: 95vw;
    height: 300px;
    border: 3px solid blue;
    margin-top: 5px;
}
```

Hello World!

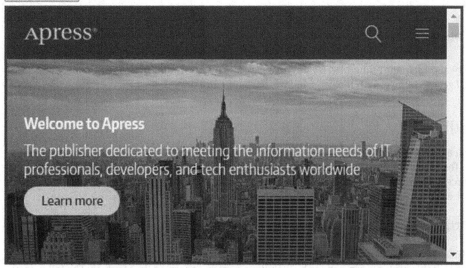

Figure 17-11. *Using a simple iframe*

The inline frame element supports several attributes that you can set in the markup.

- `allowfullscreen` - include this if you want the embedded window to be able to switch to fullscreen mode.

- `height` - the height of the element in pixels.

- `name` - the name of the frame; this can be used to create a link to this element.

- `sandbox` - this is used to specify restrictions on the window, which I'll describe later.

- `src` - the URL of the document to be loaded in the frame.

- `srcdoc` - used in conjunction with the `sandbox` attribute.

- `width` - the width of the element in pixels.

Accessing Frames

As I mentioned, the frame is actually another window and operates independently from the parent window. This includes styles, which do not cascade down to content inside a frame. These child windows are available in JavaScript through the `window` object, which has a `frames` property. For example, you can see how many frames there are by calling `window.frames.length`, or access the first frame by calling `window.frames[0]`. The later returns a `window` object that represents the frame. However, if you try to access any of its properties you'll get a cross-origin error as demonstrated in Figure 17-12.

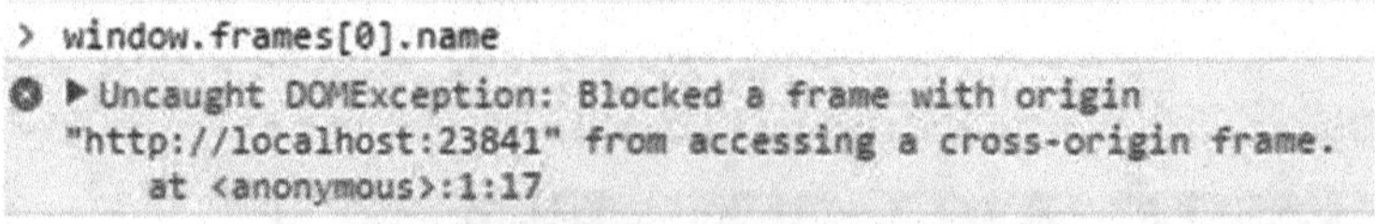

```
> window.frames[0].name
⊗ ▶ Uncaught DOMException: Blocked a frame with origin
    "http://localhost:23841" from accessing a cross-origin frame.
       at <anonymous>:1:17
```

Figure 17-12. *Displaying a cross-origin exception*

Similarly, JavaScript in the embedded frame can access the outer window by calling `window.parent`. Of course, you'll get the same error if the two windows have different origins.

Using Sandbox

As I'm sure you can imagine, embedding someone else's web page inside your own can open up some vulnerabilities. To minimize this risk, you can create the inline frame and specify the sandbox attribute, which will enforce a number of restrictions on the embedded window. To use sandbox mode, add `sandbox=""` to the `iframe` element:

```
<iframe src=http://www.apress.com sandbox=""></iframe>
```

You can also selectively allow some of these features by listing them inside the value of the `sandbox` attribute. You can disable multiple restrictions by including a space-separated list of values. The following values have been defined, although not all browsers support all of them.

- `allow-forms`
- `allow-modals`
- `allow-orientation-lock`
- `allow-pointer-lock`
- `allow-popups`
- `allow-popups-to-escape-sandbox`
- `allow-presentation`
- `allow-same-origin`
- `allow-scripts`
- `allow-top-navigation`

Summary

In this Chapter I explained the properties and methods on the `window` object that allow you to create and manipulate windows. Creating a pop-up window is easy but this needs to be allowed by the pop-up blocker. Only windows that are created through JavaScript can be manipulated through JavaScript. I demonstrated the standard modal dialog boxes and how to create a custom model dialog through HTML, CSS, and JavaScript. I also explained how to use an inline frame and briefly covered the options that are available for minimizing risk.

In the next chapter, I'll show you how to manipulate the DOM using JavaScript. This will provide a lot of flexibility and give you tools to improve the functionality of your web page.

DOM Elements

An HTML document is a specialized XML document and, like all XML documents, is comprised of a hierarchy of node elements. Each node can have a parent node and zero or more child nodes. In previous chapters, you created these nodes through some type of HTML editor or possibly a simple text editor. In this chapter, I will show you how you can read and manipulate these nodes through JavaScript.

Document Object Model

For a quick review, here is a very simple HTML document. It contains a head element that contains four child elements: a meta, title, link, and script element. It also contains a body element that has a single paragraph element. The word "Hello" is inside a strong element.

```
<!DOCTYPE html>

<html lang="en">
    <head>
        <meta charset="utf-8" />
        <title>Chapter 18 - DOM Elements</title>
        <link rel="stylesheet" href="Sample.css" />
        <script src="SampleScript.js" defer></script>
    </head>
    <body>
        <p><strong>Hello</strong> World!</p>
    </body>
</html>
```

Each of these elements is a node in the document. This is illustrated in Figure 18-1.

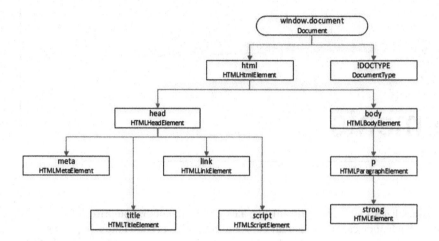

Figure 18-1. A simple HTML document

As I mentioned in Chapter 16, the window object contains a document property that gives you access to the HTML document. To demonstrate this, if you go to the browser console and type **window.document. childNodes**, an array of nodes will be listed, with two elements: !DOCTYPE and html.

Element Inheritance

In Figure 18-1, for each node, I indicated the HTML element name as well as the object type that represents that element in JavaScript. Because each element has a different behavior, the object type that represents it must be different as well. There is quite a long list of these object types as you might imagine. While not every HTML element has a specialized class in JavaScript, many do.

Fortunately, these object types use inheritance so a common set of base objects are implemented by most elements. The link element, for example, is represented by the HTMLLinkElement object. The object inherits properties and methods from the HTMLElement object, as do all of the other HTML element objects such as script, p, and strong. The HTMLLinkElement object provides additional capability that is unique to link elements. Figure 18-2 illustrates the inheritance hierarchy of some of the more common objects.

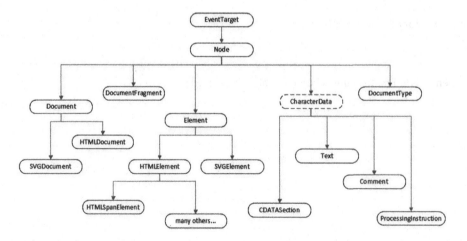

Figure 18-2. The inheritance hierarchy

■ **Tip**   All of the JavaScript objects that represent HTML elements are derived from the HTMLElement object. I did not show them in the diagram because there are dozens of them. However, the reference material in Appendix C includes a table that lists all of the HTML elements and the JavaScript object that represents it.

The EventTarget object provides the properties and methods needed to receive and handle events. The Node object provides the ability to have a parent and zero or more child nodes as well as methods for traversing and modifying them. The Element object adds more capability for manipulating elements within the overall document. One of the more important capabilities of the Element object is to view and update the attributes on an element. The HTMLElement object extends this further, providing capability such as defining the language and assigning styles.

Simple Demonstration

Before getting into the details, for a quick demonstration, I'll remove the contents of the body element from the HTML file and create this using JavaScript. The HTML markup will have an empty body element. The SampleScript.js file that is referenced in the head element and includes the populateBody() function. I'll explain each of these method calls in more detail later.

```
function populateBody() {
    var body = document.getElementsByTagName("body")[0];
    var paragraph = document.createElement("p");
    paragraph.innerHTML = "<strong>Hello</strong> World!";
    body.appendChild(paragraph);
}

populateBody();
```

The first call gets the body element using the getElementsByTagName() method. This returns an array of all the elements in the document of that type. Since there should only be one body element, it simply takes the first instance. The next call creates a paragraph element by calling the createElement() method, specifying the element type. This returns an HTMLParagraphElement object. The contents of the paragraph element are set by updating the innerHTML property. Finally, the paragraph is inserted into the body element by calling the appendChild() method. Now, to invoke this function, simply call it inside the SampleScript.js file.

Basic DOM Manipulation

This simple example demonstrates the four basic operations that you'll use to manipulate the DOM:

- finding one or more elements
- creating a new element
- positioning an element
- modifying an element

Finding Elements

Generally, the first step in manipulating the DOM is to find the element that you need to access. In the previous example, I had to get the body element so I could modify its content. There are several methods available for this depending on what data you're using to search on.

The simplest method is to retrieve the element based on its id attribute. Since the id attribute must be unique within a document, this will return zero or one elements. If no matching element is found, a null is returned.

```
var element = document.getElementById(id);
```

The next two methods return an array of elements that match either the element type or the class attribute. The first of these was used in the initial demonstration:

```
var elementArray = document.getElementsByTagName(name);
var elementArray = document.getElementsByClassName(names);
```

The latter of these allows you to provide a space-separated list of class names. If multiple names are supplied, only elements that have all of the specified class names will be returned. If there are no matching elements found, both of these methods will return an empty array.

In Chapter 9, I explained the capabilities of CSS selectors. You can leverage this functionality in JavaScript using the querySelector() and querySelectorAll() method. With both of these methods, you pass in a selector that is just like the selectors used in CSS. The querySelectorAll() method returns all matching elements, while the querySelector() method only returns the first one. You can use complex selectors, for example:

```
var elementArray = document.querySelectorAll("header+p, .book, p:first-child");
```

■ **Tip**   In these examples, I'm calling the search methods on the document object. This will perform the search across the entire document. These methods are also supported by all of the elements, so you could call them from one of the child nodes. This will perform the search starting from the element on which it is called. This will ignore its parent and siblings.

Creating Elements

As I already demonstrated, you create a new element by using the createElement() method, passing in the element type, such as div, p, or span. The new element is provided in the return value. The actual object type that is returned will vary depending on the element type that was specified.

In addition to element nodes, a document also has *text nodes*. Text nodes contain the content between the opening and closing tags of an element. For example, to create a paragraph element and set its content:

```
var p = document.createElement("p");
var text = document.createTextNode("This is a test");
p.appendChild(text);
```

If you inspect the document after the JavaScript has been executed, you will see the element defined like this:

```
<p>This is a test</p>
```

You can accomplish the same thing by setting the textContent property. For example:

```
p.textContent = "This is a test";
```

You can also set the innerHTML property like I did in the initial example. When using the innerHTML property the contents of the element can include child elements. In the first example, part of the text was inside a strong element. When setting the innerHTML property, its contents are replaced with the specified document fragment. In contrast, the createTextNode() method only updates the content of the element with text. If you try to embed elements in the string passed to it, they will be treated as literal text.

■ **Caution**   There are security implications when setting the innerHTML property. To avoid cross-site scripting attacks, script elements are ignored if included in the innerHTML property. You should still be careful when setting the innerHTML property. Don't insert user input into the DOM using the innerHTML property. Use the textContent property instead.

Moving Elements

Creating an element, or a text node, merely creates the node; it doesn't put it anywhere. For it to be included in the document, you need to add it, either as the document's root node or a child element of an existing node. A document can only have one root node and, unless you are completely building the document in JavaScript, you will likely be adding the new element to an existing node.

To do that, the appendChild() method was used in the initial example. You need to first find the element that you want to add the new element to. The appendChild() method will then make the new element a child node of that element. The method is called on the parent element and the child element is passed as a parameter. The child node, the node being added, is also returned by the appendChild() method.

```
var child = parentNode.appendChild(childNode);
```

If the parent node already has child elements, the new one will come after the existing children. If that's not where you want it, you can call the insertBefore() method instead. This works like appendChild() except there is an extra parameter to specify the sibling that the new element should come before.

```
var child = parentNode.insertBefore(childNode, sibling);
```

You call the insertBefore() method on the parent node and the first parameter is the element being added. If you pass a null for the sibling, the element will be added as the last child; this is equivalent to calling the appendChild() method.

■ **Tip**   Since there is an `insertBefore()` method, you might be expecting an `insertAfter()` method as well. But no, this is not provided. However, this can be accomplished easily enough by using the `nextSibling` property: `parentNode.insertBefore(childNode, sibling.nextSibling)`. The `Node` object, from which all HTML elements inherit, provides a `nextSibling` property. Inserting after an element is the same thing as inserting before the element's next sibling. If the element happens to be the last child, its `nextSibling` property will be null and the `insertBefore()` method will add the new element as the last child.

You can also remove an element using the `removeChild()` method. Like the `appendChild()` and the `insertBefore()` methods, the `removeChild()` method is called on the parent node, and the element to be removed is passed in as a parameter. The element still exists, but it is no longer part of the document. Like the other methods, the removed element is returned by the method call.

```
var removedElement = parentNode.removeChild(childNode);
```

If you want to move an element, you can use the `removeChild()` method to delete it from its original location and then use `appendChild()` or `insertBefore()` to move it to a new location.

■ **Note**   It may seem odd to need the parent element to remove a node but that's how it works. You can easily get the parent by using the element's `parentNode` property. So, if you have the element that you want removed, call `element.parentNode.removeChild(element)`.

Lastly, you can replace an existing element with another element using the `replaceChild()` method. It works much like the other methods; it is called on the parent element. It takes two parameters: the first is the element that should be added and the second is the element that should be removed. The new element is added in the same location as the removed element. The element that was removed is returned by the method call.

```
var removedElement = parentNode.replaceChild(newElement, existingElement);
```

Modifying Elements

Most HTML elements consist of its contents (the text between the opening and closing tags) as well as the attributes that are specified in the opening tag. Some elements such as images don't have any content and are defined solely by their attributes. As I've already explained, the element's content can be set using either:

- Creating a text node and appending it to the element
- Setting the `textContent` property
- Setting the `innerHTML` property

To manipulate the attributes, each element has an `attributes` property that contains all the attributes that have been defined on that element. This is a collection of name/value pairs. You can see if a particular attribute has been specified by calling the `hasAttribute()` method, passing in the name of the attribute. You can also add attributes to this collection or modify existing ones. The following code demonstrates how to access the `attributes` property. It will write the attributes of the first `link` element to the console. The output is shown in Figure 18-3.

```
var link = document.getElementsByTagName("link")[0];
var attr = link.attributes;
for (var i=0; i < attr.length; i++) {
    console.log(attr[i].name + "='" + attr[i].value + "'");
}
```

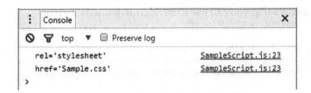

Figure 18-3. *Displaying the element attributes*

However, the attributes are also available as individual properties. You can simply get or assign a value to these properties directly. The `HTMLElement` object supports all of the global attributes such as `id` and `class`. To illustrate this, I'll modify the previous sample to set the `id`, `class`, and `lang` attributes. These will then be included in the `attributes` property as shown in Figure 18-4.

```
var link = document.getElementsByTagName("link")[0];
link.id = "myID";
link.className = "myClass";
link.lang = "en";
var attr = link.attributes;
for (var i=0; i < attr.length; i++) {
    console.log(attr[i].name + "='" + attr[i].value + "'");
}
```

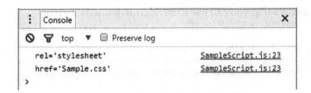

Figure 18-4. *Displaying the additional attributes*

■ **Caution**   The property name may be different from the attribute name. In this case, class is a reserved word in JavaScript, so the property is called className.

Other specialized objects such as HTMLImageElement inherit the global attributes from HTMLElement and provide additional properties specific to that element. For example, HTMLImageElement exposes the alt, src, and srcset attributes.

Related Elements

As I mentioned, each element is a node in the document and can have a parent node (all nodes have a parent except the root node). A node can also have zero or more child nodes. After you have obtained an element from the document, there are several properties that you can use to navigate to related elements. The following properties are available:

- parentNode - the node's immediate parent; null for the root node only

- children - an HTMLCollection object that contains all of the node's immediate children

- firstChild - the first element in the children collection

- lastChild - the last element in the children collection

- previousSibling - an element that has the same immediate parent as the current node and comes just before the current node in the parent's children collection. This is null if the current element is the parent's first child node.

- nextSibling - the element that has the same parent as the current node and comes just after the current node. This will be null if the current element is its parent's last child.

■ **Tip**   There are literally hundreds of properties, methods, and events available on the objects that represent the HTML elements. I have explained the more commonly used features but this is not an exhaustive set. Mozilla has a really good API reference that I recommend if you're looking for more details. I would start here: https://developer.mozilla.org/en-US/docs/Web/API/HTMLElement. This article describes the members of the HTMLElement object and has links to other objects

Using jQuery

■ **Note**   In this book, I have focused on native HTML, CSS, and JavaScript capabilities. However, there are a lot of libraries and frameworks that extend this functionality. Of course, they come with their own set of advantages and shortcomings. If you are doing any serious web development you will want to consider one or more of these, but I have carefully avoided them in this book. However, when it comes to DOM manipulation, jQuery has become a de facto standard.

In Chapter 3, I explained how to define a namespace to keep variables out of the global namespace. If you define a function such as log() in your namespace called MyNamespace, you then execute it by specifying the namespace along with the function name. This avoids any possible conflicts with other scripts that may also define a log() function.

```
MyNamespace.log("Hello World");
```

In jQuery, all of the members are defined in a namespace, which happens to be named "$." Whenever you see a $. or $(). you'll know that a jQuery member is being used.

Fundamentals

Using jQuery is pretty easy to use, but there are some basics that you'll need to understand.

Selecting Elements

The basic pattern to all jQuery operations is to select something and then do something with it. The syntax looks like this:

```
$(selector).action();
```

The selector will return zero or more elements. The specified action is then performed on each of the elements in this set. The selector can be any valid CSS selector, which were described in Chapter 9. jQuery also supports additional capabilities. Here's an article that lists all of the selectors with samples and documentation: http://codylindley.com/jqueryselectors/.

You can split the selection and action into two separate calls. For example:

```
var $elements = $(selector);
$elements.action();
```

This is especially useful if you have multiple actions to perform on the set of elements as it avoids having to perform the selection again. Keep in mind, however, that the results from the selector are static; they are not updated if there are changes to the document. To reflect the most recent state, you'll need to re-execute the selector.

You can also pass in an object to the selector, instead of a selector string. The most common example is using the document object. For example, this will assign the anonymous function to be executed when the document is ready:

```
$(document).ready(function(){... add code here ...});
```

jQuery provides a number of index-related selectors that select elements based on the relative order with their parent object. The index is zero-based so :eq(0) is equivalent to using the first() method. You can also use :lt(), :gt(), :even(), and :odd(). If you specify a negative value for :eq(), :lt(), or :gt(), the index is counted from the end rather than the beginning. So :eq(-1) is equivalent to last().

jQuery Object

It's important to keep in mind that the objects returned from a jQuery selector are jQuery objects, not the native DOM objects such as HTMLElement. The native object is wrapped by a jQuery object and supports the methods that I will demonstrate later. If you need the native object, call the get() method on the jQuery object.

The methods provided by the jQuery object will have similar functionality as the native objects but they will have different names. You'll need to keep track of what type of object you're working with because they have a different set of properties and methods. A common practice is to prefix all jQuery variables with a "$" character. This should not be confused with the $ namespace, however.

Also, the object returned from a jQuery selector is an object, not an array of objects. It is similar to an array in that it has a length property and a first() method, for example. But it has a lot more capabilities as well. For a complete list, see the article at http://api.jquery.com/.

All of the jQuery methods return a jQuery object that supports a collection of elements. Even the first() method returns a jQuery object that has a collection of one element. The get() method will return the native DOM object from a jQuery object; however, you must supply the index. For example, to get an HTMLElement object that represents the body element, use this:

```
var body = $("body").get(0);
```

Manipulating DOM Elements

jQuery doesn't have a createElement() equivalent function, although you can create elements inline when calling some of the other jQuery methods, which I'll demonstrate shortly. You can create a native object using createElement() and then use jQuery to add it to the document.

To add an element to the document, use the append() method. The selector will determine which element(s) the new element is added to. This is roughly equivalent to the appendChild() function. If the selector returns multiple elements, however, a clone of the new element will be added to each one. Like the appendChild() method, append() adds the new element as a child element of the selected element, as the last child element, after any existing elements. If you wanted to insert the element before the existing child elements, use prepend(), instead.

Both append() and prepend() accept a variety of input types. You can pass in a native DOM object, such as HTMLElement or a jQuery object containing one or more elements. You can also provide multiple comma-separated parameters, or an array parameter if you want to add multiple elements. You could also specify an HTML string. For example, passing in "<p></p>" will create a new paragraph element. The HTML string can include more complex HTML with embedded child elements. This is similar to setting the innerHTML property. However, the elements defined by the HTML string are appended (or prepended) to the existing child element, instead of replacing them.

With both the append() and prepend() methods, the selector determines the target element(s), where the elements will be inserted, and the parameter specifies the element(s) to be added. jQuery also provides appendTo() and prependTo() that accomplishes the same result with a different syntax. With these methods, the selector determines the elements to be added and the parameter specifies the target element.

The html() method replaces the innerHTML property with the HTML script that is passed in. If the selector matches multiple elements, they will all be updated. If no parameter is passed it, it will not update the element but rather return the existing HTML string, including any child elements. If the selector matches multiple elements, only the innerHTML of the first element will be returned.

All of these methods add the new content as child elements to the specified parent. jQuery also provides the before() and after() methods that add the content as siblings to the specified target. The before() method is similar to the insertBefore() method, except that you don't need to specify the parent. The new element is inserted just before the target as its sibling. Similarly, the after() method inserts the element just after the target.

With the before() and after() methods, the selector determines the target where the new elements should be added, and the parameter specifies the element to be added. The parameter can be any of the values described with the append() method. jQuery also provides the insertBefore() and insertAfter() methods, These accomplish the same result as before() and after() but have their syntax reversed like the appendTo() method. The selector determines the elements to be added and the parameter specifies the target.

The wrap() method is used to insert an element as the parent object of the targets specified by the selector. If you had some image elements in your document, you could nest each of them inside a new div element, for example. The selector would find the image elements and the parameter would specify the new elements that are placed inside:

```
$("img").wrap("<div class='image'></div>");
```

In contrast, the unwrap() method removes the immediate parent from the element returned by the selector. This will undo the effect of calling the wrap() method.

With the wrap() method, each selected element is wrapped with a new parent element. The wrapAll() method will wrap all selected elements in a single parent element. If there are unmatched elements in between the matching elements, they will not be included in the new parent but will follow immediately after.

The wrapInner() methods works like the wrap() method except only the content is wrapped instead of the entire element. For example, you could add a strong element around the contents of a paragraph tag. If the original HTML was:

```
<p class="myClass">Hello World</p>
```

You could call the wrapInner() method like this:

```
$("p").wrapInner("<strong></strong>");
```

The resulting HTML would be:

```
<p class="myClass"><strong>Hello World</strong></p>
```

Elements can be removed from the document through either the remove() or detach() methods. With both methods, the elements returned by the selector are removed. However, the detach() method will return the set of removed elements so they can added be added back later. Use detach() when you want to move the elements to a different location. The empty() method will remove all of the child elements from the elements that are returned by the selector.

You can also replace elements using the replaceWith() method. The selector specifies the elements that should be removed. For each one, the elements passed to the method are inserted in its place. Like the detach() methods, the set of removed elements is returned. The replaceAll() has the syntax reversed; the selector specifies the elements that are to be added, and the parameter identifies the elements that are to be replaced.

Summary

In this chapter, I explained the methods available to manipulate the DOM elements using JavaScript. There are several methods that you can use to find one or more elements, depending on how you need to perform the search. The most flexible method is the querySelectorAll() method that enables you to use any of the supported CSS selectors. After creating an element, you then need to call one of several methods to insert it into the document. You need to specify the parent element when adding an element to the document. You can also remove elements. There are methods available for extracting and setting the attributes of an element. However, in most cases you can simply access the attribute as a property of the element.

I briefly described how to use jQuery to manipulate the document. The jQuery library provides an easier and more feature-rich approach to DOM manipulation. You should consider using jQuery if you need to access and modify the document elements.

In the next chapter, I'll show you how to use similar techniques to manipulate the styling of the document elements.

CHAPTER 19

■ ■ ■

Dynamic Styling

In the previous chapter, I explained how you can dynamically change the HTML content using JavaScript. There are methods available to create new DOM elements as well as to rearrange or modify the existing elements. Similar capability exists for modifying the styling of those elements. In this chapter, I will describe four techniques that you can use to dynamically change the style rules using JavaScript:

- replacing style sheets

- changing the style rules

- modifying the CSS classes

- adjusting inline styles

These scenarios provide increasingly finer control of the styles applied to the document, starting with replacing an entire style sheet and finishing with updating the style of a single element.

Changing Style Sheets

The first approach I'll explain is to replace the entire style sheet. This technique is useful if you want to support several themes, for example. Each style sheet would contain a set of rules that present a particular look to the web page. A specific style sheet is then applied based on user preferences, user input, or some other rule. You should put the common rules into a separate style sheet that is always used. The thematic elements are put into separate style sheets that can be applied dynamically.

■ **Tip**   You can add new external style sheets to the document by creating a `link` element as I explained in the previous chapter. You can also create a new `style` element to create an internal style sheet.

Enabling Style Sheets

The style sheets that are available can be accessed through the `document.styleSheets` property. This returns a collection of the style sheets that have been loaded. After adding a style sheet to the HTML document with the `link` element, it can be viewed in the console as shown in Figure 19-1:

```
<link rel="stylesheet" href="Sample.css" title="Shared" />
```

M. J. Collins, *Pro HTML5 with CSS, JavaScript, and Multimedia*, DOI 10.1007/978-1-4842-2463-2_19

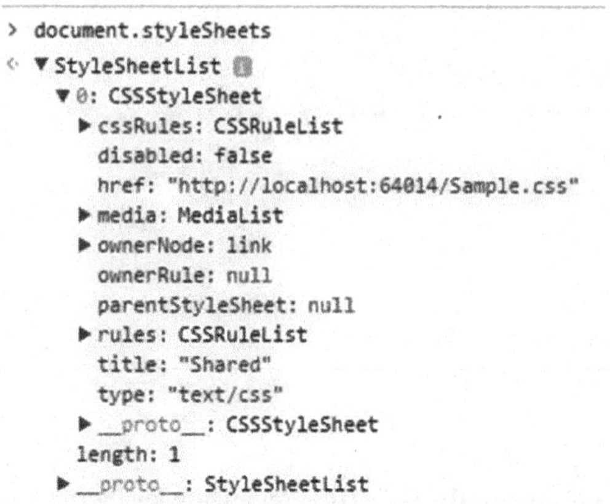

```
>  document.styleSheets
◁  ▼ StyleSheetList 🚼
     ▼ 0: CSSStyleSheet
       ▶ cssRules: CSSRuleList
         disabled: false
         href: "http://localhost:64014/Sample.css"
       ▶ media: MediaList
       ▶ ownerNode: link
         ownerRule: null
         parentStyleSheet: null
       ▶ rules: CSSRuleList
         title: "Shared"
         type: "text/css"
       ▶ __proto__: CSSStyleSheet
       length: 1
     ▶ __proto__: StyleSheetList
```

Figure 19-1. *Viewing the style sheet properties*

The stylesheets collection has a `length` of 1 since there is only one style sheet loaded. The `link` element includes the `title` attribute and this is available on the `CSSStyleSheet` object.

Most of the properties on this object are read-only; however, you can change the `disabled` property. To demonstrate that, I'll add a button on the page to toggle the `disabled` property. Here is the complete HTML document.

```
<!DOCTYPE html>

<html lang="en">
    <head>
        <meta charset="utf-8" />
        <title>Chapter 19 - Dynamic Styling</title>
        <link rel="stylesheet" href="Sample.css" title="Shared" />
        <script src="SampleScript.js" defer></script>
    </head>
    <body>
        <p><strong>Hello</strong> World!</p>
        <button onclick="toggleSS()">Toggle</button>
    </body>
</html>
```

The `Sample.css` file has a single style rule that uses a larger font:

```
p {
    font-size: xx-large;
}
```

The toggleSS() function is implemented in the SampleScript.js file:

```
"use strict";

function toggleSS() {
    for (var i = 0; i < document.styleSheets.length; i++ ) {
        if (document.styleSheets[i].title == "Shared") {
            document.styleSheets[i].disabled = !document.styleSheets[i].disabled;
            break;
        }
    }
}
```

This function iterates through all of the style sheets and if the title is "Shared," it toggles the disabled property.

Choosing a Style Sheet

We can apply this approach to dynamically choose a style sheet. The document will load several style sheets and then will enable one and disable the others based on user input. For this example, I'll use three more style sheets, each setting a different color. The page will have buttons to select a color, which calls a JavaScript function to enable/disable the appropriate style sheets.

The new style sheets each have a single rule to set the color attribute, like this:

```
p {
    color: red;
}
```

I'll add the new style sheets with the following link elements inside the head element. I'm not using the title attribute and I'll explain why later in the chapter.

```
<link rel="stylesheet" href="Red.css" />
<link rel="stylesheet" href="Green.css" />
<link rel="stylesheet" href="Blue.css" />
```

I'll also add four buttons that can be used to select the corresponding style sheets.

```
<button onclick="disableAll()">Black</button>
<button onclick="enable('Red')" style="color: red">Red</button>
<button onclick="enable('Green')" style="color: green">Green</button>
<button onclick="enable('Blue')" style="color: blue">Blue</button>
```

The first button calls the disableAll() function, which will disable all three style sheets. In this case, the content will use the default black font. The other buttons call the enable() function that will enable the specified style sheet and disable the others. We'll need to add these two methods to the SampleScript.js file:

```
function disableAll() {
    for (var i = 0; i < document.styleSheets.length; i++ ) {
        if (document.styleSheets[i].title != "Shared") {
            document.styleSheets[i].disabled = true;
        }
    }
}
```

```
function enable(color) {
    for (var i = 0; i < document.styleSheets.length; i++ ) {
        if (document.styleSheets[i].href.includes(color)) {
            document.styleSheets[i].disabled = false;
        }
        else if (document.styleSheets[i].title != "Shared") {
            document.styleSheets[i].disabled = true;
        }
    }
}
```

To find the corresponding style sheet, the enable() function uses the href property and checks to see if the specified color is part of the URL. Both functions will ignore the shared style sheet. The style sheets are all enabled by default, so Blue.css, being loaded last will be applied. If you want the black font to be used, initially, you can call the disableAll() function when the page is loaded.

■ **Tip**   IE doesn't support the includes() method. There are a few easy polyfills that you can use instead. See this article for details: http://stackoverflow.com/questions/31221341/ie-does-not-support-includes-method.

Alternate Style Sheets

As I've demonstrated, you can enable or disable style sheets using JavaScript. However, some browsers provide native support for this approach using *alternate stylesheets*. This is controlled through the rel and title attributes of the link element. Elements that don't have a title attribute are always applied to the document. These are referred to as *persistent* style sheets. As I've shown, however, they can be disabled through JavaScript.

Style sheet links that have a title attribute are dynamic and can be enabled or disabled through user actions. If the rel attribute does not include the alternate keyword, the style is known as the *preferred* style; it is enabled by default. You can only have one preferred style; if there are more than that, only one will be applied. Preferred styles are enabled by default but are disabled if an alternate style is selected. If the rel attribute includes the alternate keyword, the style is called an *alternate* style. Alternate styles are disabled by default. These rules are summarized in Table 19-1.

Table 19-1. *Style sheet types*

Type	Has Title	Alternate	Comments
Persistent	no	no	These style sheets are always applied.
Preferred	yes	no	Applied by default; disabled if alternate selected.
Alternate	yes	yes	Disabled by default.

Based on these rules, the correct way to add the style sheets for the previous example would be as follows. The Sample.css is always applied and has no title attribute. The Red.css, Green.css, and Blue.css are alternate stylesheets; they have a title and the alternate keyword.

```
<link rel="stylesheet" href="Sample.css" />
<link rel="alternate stylesheet" href="Red.css" title="Red"/>
<link rel="alternate stylesheet" href="Green.css" title="Green"/>
<link rel="alternate stylesheet" href="Blue.css" title="Blue"/>
```

With no JavaScript, these styles can be selectively enabled through the browser. For example, in Firefox, an alternate style can be selected from the View menu as shown in Figure 19-2.

Figure 19-2. Selecting an alternate style sheet in Firefox

If you wanted the green style to be enabled by default, for example, remove the alternate keyword, rel="stylesheet". It will be enabled when the page is loaded, but will be disabled when the red or blue style is selected.

■ **Caution**   Chrome and Opera do not support alternate style sheets. There is no UI to select one of the alternate styles. Also, if more than one link element has the title attribute, only the first will be enabled. The others cannot be enabled, even with JavaScript. In the JavaScript example, the style sheets were added without the title attribute so it would work in Chrome.

Using Style Elements

In the previous examples, I used external style sheets that were included through the link element. You can also use internal style sheets that are embedded in a style element; these are also available through the document.styleSheets property. Of course, these will not have the href property so you'll need identify them through the title attribute.

You can replace the link elements that include the Red.css, Green.css, and Blue.css with the following style elements.

```
<style title="Red">
    p { color: red;}
</style>
<style title="Green">
    p { color: green;}
</style>
<style title="Blue">
    p { color: blue;}
</style>
```

In Firefox, the same UI to select alternate styles works equally well with internal style sheets. The View menu shows the same Red, Green, and Blue options based on the title attribute in the style elements.

The JavaScript functions, however, will need to look at the title property instead of the href property. Listing 19-1 shows an implementation of these functions that will support either, depending which properties are present.

Listing 19-1. Final JavaScript for alternate styles

```
"use strict";

function toggleSS() {
    for (var i = 0; i < document.styleSheets.length; i++ ) {
        if ((document.styleSheets[i].href &&
             document.styleSheets[i].href.includes("Sample")) ||
            document.styleSheets[i].title == "Shared") {
            document.styleSheets[i].disabled = !document.styleSheets[i].disabled;
            break;
        }
    }
}

function disableAll() {
    for (var i = 0; i < document.styleSheets.length; i++ ) {
        if (!(document.styleSheets[i].href &&
              document.styleSheets[i].href.includes("Sample")) &&
             document.styleSheets[i].title != "Shared") {
            document.styleSheets[i].disabled = true;
        }
    }
}

function enable(color) {
    for (var i = 0; i < document.styleSheets.length; i++ ) {
        if ((document.styleSheets[i].href &&
             document.styleSheets[i].href.includes(color)) ||
            document.styleSheets[i].title == color) {
            document.styleSheets[i].disabled = false;
        }
```

```
        else if (!(document.styleSheets[i].href &&
                document.styleSheets[i].href.includes("Sample")) &&
                document.styleSheets[i].title != "Shared") {
            document.styleSheets[i].disabled = true;
        }
    }
}

disableAll();
```

■ **Caution**   The Chrome limitation that I mentioned previously applies to the style elements as well. And since there is no href property to use instead of the title, this will not work in Chrome or Opera. To work around this, you would need to use the id attribute on the style element and select them using the getElementById() method, which I described in the previous chapter.

Modifying Rules

In the previous section, I demonstrated how to dynamically apply an entire style sheet, which is a set of preconfigured style rules. You can also modify the rules on an existing style sheet. Use this option if you need to make minor adjustments.

To view the existing rules, go back to the document.styleSheets property. Each style sheet has a cssRules property that enumerates the rules included in the style sheet. This is a collection of CSSStyleRule objects as illustrated by Figure 19-3.

```
>  document.styleSheets
<· ▼ StyleSheetList 🔢
      ▼ 0: CSSStyleSheet
        ▼ cssRules: CSSRuleList
          ▼ 0: CSSStyleRule
              cssText: "p { font-size: xx-large; }"
              parentRule: null
            ▶ parentStyleSheet: CSSStyleSheet
              selectorText: "p"
            ▶ style: CSSStyleDeclaration
              type: 1
            ▶ __proto__: CSSStyleRule
            length: 1
          ▶ __proto__: CSSRuleList
```

Figure 19-3. *Viewing the style rules*

Each CSSStyleRule object is assigned a sequential index. As I explained in Chapter 2, the order that rules are included can affect how conflicts are resolved. The index is also important because you'll need this to remove a rule.

For a simple demonstration, I'll add the following JavaScript code. The newRuleIndex variable will store the index of the newly added rule, which adds a thin, black border. The toggleRule() function will either add a new rule if this is not set, or use the variable to remove the rule.

```
var newRuleIndex = -1;

function toggleRule() {
    if (newRuleIndex == -1) {
        newRuleIndex = document.styleSheets[0].insertRule("p {border: 1px solid black;}", 1)
    }
    else {
        document.styleSheets[0].deleteRule(newRuleIndex);
        newRuleIndex = -1;
    }
}
```

I'm taking some shortcuts here, simply adding the rule to the first style sheet. You may need to first select the style sheet that you want to modify. Finally, we'll need a button on the page to call this function. When the button is clicked, the border is added as shown in Figure 19-4.

```
<button onclick="toggleRule()">Border</button>
```

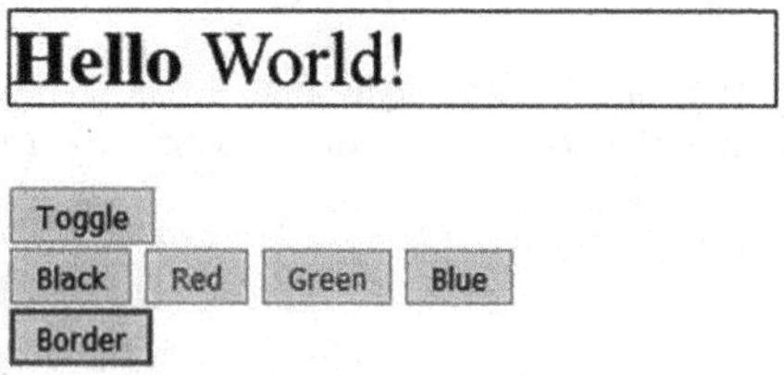

Figure 19-4. *Adding a border*

■ **Note**   This adds a new rule to the first style sheet, which is Sample.css. This also has the larger font rule. If you click the Toggle button, the entire style sheet is disabled, which will remove both the larger font and the border. Even though the style sheet is disabled, clicking the Border button will modify the style sheet; it just won't affect the page until it is enabled.

Modifying a style sheet through the insertRule() or deleteRule() methods does not affect the original source document. For internal styles, the HTML document is not affected by these changes, nor are the CSS files for external style sheets. If the page is refreshed, the styles will revert to their original state until the JavaScript is rerun to modify them.

Modifying Classes

The last scenario modified the rules in a stylesheet, which depending on the change, can affect multiple elements in the document. However, in many cases you simply need to make an existing rule apply to a specific element in certain situations. The pseudo-classes are a good example of this. Pseudo-classes such as :enabled, :selected, or :hover allow you to apply a style rule under certain dynamic conditions. These conditions, however, are limited.

If a suitable pseudo-class is not available, you can create a style rule that uses a class selector. Then you can dynamically apply the appropriate class as needed using JavaScript. To try this out, I'll first add a rule with a class selector to the Sample.css file. This will set the opacity to 50%.

```
.special {
    opacity: .5;
}
```

Every element has a classList property that contains the list of classes that have been assigned to the element. It supports four methods that you can use to manipulate this list:

- contains() - returns a Boolean value indicating if the class exists.

- add() - adds a new class.

- remove() - removes the specified class.

- toggle() - adds the class if it doesn't exist or removes it if it does.

The following JavaScript function demonstrates all of these methods. It will check to see if the class exists and either adds or removes it.

```
function toggleClass() {
    var paragraph = document.querySelector("p");
    if (paragraph) {
        if (paragraph.classList.contains("special")) {
            paragraph.classList.remove("special");
        }
        else {
            paragraph.classList.add("special");
        }

        // This could also be done with the following
        //paragraph.classList.toggle("special");
    }
}
```

■ **Tip**   This can all be done by simply calling the toggle() method, but I'm implementing it this way to demonstrate the other methods.

Finally, I'll add a button to call this function:

```
<button onclick="toggleClass()">Opacity</button>
```

Each element also supports the className property. This is a string that contains a space-separated list of classes, just like you would see in the class attribute in the markup. You can manipulate this string directly, if you prefer, but the classList property is easier to work with.

The one exception, however, is if you want to remove all of the classes. Rather than enumerating the classList property, simply set the className property to an empty string:

```
paragraph.className = "";
```

Modifying Inline Styles

The previous scenario only affects a single element. However, adding or removing a class can apply or remove multiple style rules, as well as multiple declarations on each of those rules. In this final scenario, I'll show you how to apply inline styles to a single element. Generally, applying inline styles is a bad idea because you lose the ability to adjust the style with a CSS change. But there can be times when you need to and don't want to make CSS changes that can break other elements.

Using CSSStyleDeclaration

The style attribute is available on all HTML elements and can be accessed from JavaScript through the style property. It is represented in JavaScript by the CSSStyleDeclaration object, which is a collection of name/value pairs. Style declarations can be modified on this object through the following methods.

- setProperty() - adds a declaration; takes two required parameters, property and value, and an optional priority parameter that can be either blank or the "important" keyword.

- getPropertyValue() - the property name is passed as a parameter and the corresponding value is returned.

- getPropertyPriority() - returns "important" if the specified property has the important keyword.

- cssText - returns all of the declarations on this style, formatted as it would be in a CSS document.

- removeProperty() - removes the specified property.

For a quick demonstration, the following solution will update the background color. First, I'll add a button that will call the toggleBackground() function when the button is clicked:

```
<button onclick="toggleBackground()">Background</button>
```

The toggleBackground() function gets the first paragraph element using the querySelector() method. It checks the length property of the style property, which indicates how many declarations have already been set of this object. If there are none, the background-color attribute is added; otherwise it is removed.

```
function toggleBackground() {
    var p = document.querySelector("p");
    console.log("Initial style = " + p.style.cssText);

    if (p.style.length == 0) {
        p.style.setProperty("background-color", "yellow", "important");
```

```
        console.log("Value: " + p.style.getPropertyValue("background-color"));
        console.log("Priority: " + p.style.getPropertyPriority("background-color"));
    }
    else {
        p.style.removeProperty("background-color");
    }
    console.log("Updated style = " + p.style.cssText);
}
```

This code also writes some entries to the console log. After clicking the Background button, the console log should look like Figure 19-5.

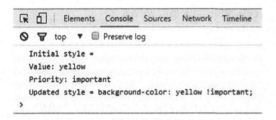

Figure 19-5. *The console output*

Setting Style Properties

The CSSStyleDeclaration object has a property for every CSS property and you can simply get or set these properties. For example:

```
var p = document.querySelector("p");
p.style.fontStyle = "italic";
p.style.fontSize = "xx-small";

console.log("Current color is " + p.style.color);
```

The name of the property in JavaScript is the same as the CSS property except that all hyphens are removed and the first character of the next word is made uppercase. So, font-size becomes fontSize in JavaScript.

You also need to be careful regarding reserved words in JavaScript such as float. The property names for these will be prefixed with "css." To set the float value, for example, use cssFloat.

■ **Tip**   The CSSStyleRule object, as I explained earlier, represents a style rule. I demonstrated how a new rule can be added by specifying the CSS entry for it. The CSSStyleRule object also has a style property that can be manipulated through these methods, just like other style properties.

Using setAttribute

A third way to set the style properties is through the setAttribute() method. You can set the value of any HTML attribute through this method. It takes two parameters: the name of an attribute and the value you want it set to. For example, the style attribute can be set like this:

```
var p = document.querySelector("p");
p.setAttribute("style", "font-style:italic; font-size:xx-small;");
```

■ **Caution**   When setting a specific style property such as style.color, only that property is affected. However, using the setAttribute() method will replace the entire existing inline style rules with whatever you provide in the second parameter. Any existing value for the style attribute is overwritten.

Computed Style

As I've explained before, the styles that are applied to an element come from various sources such as external and internal style sheets and inline style properties. Each style rule affects elements based on the selector and there can be multiple rules that apply to a particular element. Some of these rules are applied dynamically such as with pseudo-classes.

However, at any given point in time, there is a fixed set of style property values that have been computed for an element. You can get this information in JavaScript by calling the window.getComputedStyle() method and passing in the element in question. For example, if you run this in the console, you will see the properties and their values as illustrated in Figure 19-6:

```
var p = document.querySelector("p");
window.getComputedStyle();
```

```
animationName: "none"
animationPlayState: "running"
animationTimingFunction: "ease"
backfaceVisibility: "visible"
background: "rgba(0, 0, 0, 0) none repeat scroll 0% 0% / auto padding-box border-box"
backgroundAttachment: "scroll"
backgroundBlendMode: "normal"
backgroundClip: "border-box"
backgroundColor: "rgba(0, 0, 0, 0)"
backgroundImage: "none"
backgroundOrigin: "padding-box"
backgroundPosition: "0% 0%"
backgroundPositionX: "0%"
backgroundPositionY: "0%"
```

Figure 19-6. *Displaying the computed styles*

■ **Tip**   The style property of an element will only return the inline styles. If you want to see the net effect of all of the style sheets and inline styles, use the getComputedStyle() method.

Summary

In this chapter, I explained four basic approaches for adjusting the styles in JavaScript. These techniques range from replacing the entire style sheet to modifying a single property on an element. I also gave some examples of scenarios where these approaches are useful. You have a lot of capability for dynamically configuring the style rules. The first step however, is to decide what you want to accomplish and then which approach is the best fit.

In the next chapter, I will demonstrate how to use events in JavaScript to implement functional logic to respond to user- and system-initiated events.

Events

Events are an integral part of most web pages: they allow you to take an action when something happens. The "something happens" is called an event, and there are dozens of them that have been defined in the web standard (see `http://www.w3.org/TR/DOM-Level-3-Events/#events-module`). The "an action" is called an event handler, which is just a simple JavaScript function.

Initial Example

I'll start with a simple example and then describe the pieces. A basic HTML document is shown in Listing 20-1.

Listing 20-1. The initial HTML document

```
<!DOCTYPE html>

<html lang="en">
    <head>
        <meta charset="utf-8" />
        <title>Chapter 20 - Events</title>
        <link rel="stylesheet" href="Sample.css" />
        <script src="SampleScript.js" defer></script>
    </head>
    <body>
        <section>
            <div id="div1">
                <div id="div2">
                    <p>Some text</p>
                    <p>Some more text</p>
                </div>
            </div>
        </section>
    </body>
</html>
```

This document has two paragraph elements inside a pair of nested div elements. To help visualize the area used by these elements, I'll put a border around the div elements and use a background color on the paragraph elements. I'll also use padding and margin to put some space between them.

```
div {
    border: 1px solid black;
    padding: 10px;
}

p {
    margin: 5px;
    background-color: yellow;
}
```

To set up the event logic, the event handler is a function called someAction() that simply raises an alert. To configure this handler, the script gets the inner div element and then calls the addEventListener() method, assigning the handler to the click event. The addEventListener() method is available on all HTML elements and has two required parameters: the name of the event and a reference to the function that will be called when the event occurs. The EventTarget object implements the addEventListener() methods and as I explained in Chapter 18, is the base object that all elements are derived from.

```
"use strict";

function someAction() {
    alert("Taking some action...");
}

var div = document.getElementById("div2");
div.addEventListener("click", someAction);
```

If you click inside the inner div element, you'll see the alert box as shown in Figure 20-1.

Figure 20-1. *Responding to an event*

Event Registration

Event registration is the process of linking three things together: an event to an event handler for a specific DOM element. It is saying that 1) this **element** responds to 2) this **event** by executing 3) this **handler**. The addEventListener() method is the preferred way to accomplish this. There are other ways to do this, however.

One approach, known as *inline* registration, is to include the registration in the markup. For example:

```
<div id="div2" onclick="someAction()">
```

While this technique has been around for decades and is still used fairly frequently, this should be avoided. This includes JavaScript code inside your HTML document, an obvious violation of separation of concerns.

Another approach is to assign the event handler to an event property of the DOM element. Each DOM element has a property for each event that it supports. These event properties hold a reference to the event handler for the corresponding event. For example, the `onclick` property can store a reference to an event handler that will be called when the `click` event occurs. We can rewrite the initial demonstration like this:

```
//div.addEventListener("click", someAction);
div.onclick = someAction;
```

This approach, sometimes referred to as the *traditional* method, is the safest and most universally supported event registration method. It has been around since the Netscape days and is supported by IE4 and later, as well as all modern browsers.

■ **Caution**   The event properties, such as `onclick`, expect a function reference. Don't add the parenthesis after the function name as this will cause the function to be executed, and the return value will be registered as the event handler.

One issue with the both the inline and traditional approaches is that you can only have a single event handler per event for each element. If you try to register a second event handler, if will replace the first one. For example, if you have two JavaScript libraries that use a different event handler for their own purposes, they cannot coexist if the traditional approach is used.

A third approach, which is supported only by Internet Explorer uses the an `attachEvent()` method that is similar to `addEventListener()`. IE did not support the `addEventListener()` method until version 9, so if you need to support IE8 and earlier, you'll need to use `attachEvent()` (or the traditional method) as a polyfill.

■ **Tip**   The `addEventListener()` method (as well as `attachEvent()` in IE) will allow you to assign multiple event handlers for the same event.

Event Propagation

When registering an event listener, a handler function is assigned on a specific element for particular event. The previous example listened for the `click` event on the inner `div` element. However, you can click anywhere in the `div` element, including on either of the two paragraph elements, and the alert will be displayed. This works because of the way events are propagated.

The paragraph elements are part of the content of the inner `div`, so it makes sense that clicking on them is treated as if the `div` was clicked. In the same way, the inner `div` is part of the outer `div`, the outer `div` is part of the `section`, and so on. What would happen if the event was registered on the `document` or `window` object? As you might expect, a click on any of its descendants would execute the event handler.

When an event occurs, such as a mouse click, it is first sent to the `window` object. It is then propagated downward through the document hierarchy until it reaches the element that was actually clicked, which is called the *target*. Lastly, it is propagated back through the same objects in reverse, until it reaches the `window` object. This is illustrated in Figure 20-2.

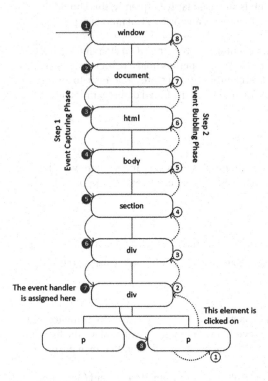

Figure 20-2. *Event propagation*

In our initial example, a total of 16 events were raised: 8 on the way down and 8 on the way back up. However, we only registered a single event handler so 15 of these were ignored.

Propagating the events downward is called the capturing phase and going back up the chain is referred to as the bubbling phase. This terminology may not be very helpful although, since bubbles tend to rise to the top; you can remember that the bubbling phase goes up.

The `addEventListener()` method supports a third parameter that you can use to specify if you want to listen for the capture event or the bubble event. Pass a true value to listen for the capture event. Omit the third parameter or pass in false to listen for the bubble event.

To demonstrate this behavior, I'll replace the previous JavaScript with the code shown in Listing 20-2. This defines a pair of variables to record the number of times a capture or bubble event was handled. It then defines two event handlers that simply increment these counters. The event is first raised on the `window` object and it also ends on the `window` object. I'll use two special event handlers for the `window` object. The `clearCount()` function will be called on the capture event and will clear the counters. The `reportCounts()` function will be called on the bubble event and will raise an alert with the value of the counters.

Listing 20-2. Record event counts

```
var captureCount = 0;
var bubbleCount = 0;

function incrementCapture() {
    captureCount++;
}
function incrementBubble() {
    bubbleCount++;
}
function clearCounts() { // called on window capture
    captureCount = 1; // include this event in the count
    bubbleCount = 0;
}
function reportCounts() { // called on window bubble
    bubbleCount++;   // include this event in the count
    alert("Capture: " + captureCount + ", Bubble: " + bubbleCount);
}

var elements = document.querySelectorAll("*");
for (var i = 0; i < elements.length; i++ ) {
    elements[i].addEventListener("click", incrementCapture, true);
    elements[i].addEventListener("click", incrementBubble, false);
}

document.addEventListener("click", incrementCapture, true);
document.addEventListener("click", incrementBubble, false);

window.addEventListener("click", clearCounts, true);
window.addEventListener("click", reportCounts, false);
```

To set up the event handlers, I used the querySelectorAll() method that I described in Chapter 18. This uses the all selector (*) and will return all of the HTML elements. This includes the html element and all of its descendants. It does not return the window or document objects, so I added these event handlers separately.

With these event handlers wired up, if you click on one of the paragraph elements, you'll see an alert like the one shown in Figure 20-3. As I described in Figure 20-2, there will be eight capture events and eight bubble events handled, as the event is propagated down and up the element hierarchy.

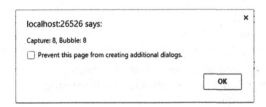

Figure 20-3. *Reporting the event counts*

If you click on the inner div (but not on the paragraph element) there will be only seven events handled. Likewise, if you click the outer div, there will be only six events handled. The section and body elements do not take up any space of their own so you can't click on them. If you click anywhere on the page, but not in the outer div element, there will be three events handled. The event handlers assigned to the window, document, and html objects will be called.

■ **Note** The addEventListener() method is the only way to register for the capture events. The other techniques that I mentioned previously can only register the bubble events.

If you just need to know when a button is clicked, for instance, it doesn't really matter whether you listen for the capture event or the bubble event. However, if you have multiple handlers assigned to different elements, having these two options can be useful. For example, if you have different handlers on both a parent and a child element, when using a capture event, the parent's handler will be executed first. This order is reversed when listening for the bubble event.

Event handlers are executed serially; the current event handler must complete before the next one is called. If you have multiple event handlers on the same element, they are also executed serially, in the order that they were registered.

Unregistering Events

You can remove an event handler, although the process will be different, depending on how the event handler was originally registered. If you used addEventListener() (or attachEvent()), multiple event handlers can be assigned to a single element. In order to remove the correct one, you need to specify all of the same information that was used to register the event handler.

For example, the following code will remove the handler that was set up in the previous example. Notice the parameters are exactly the same as was used when registering the event handler

```
function removeHandlers() {
    var div = document.getElementById("div2");
    div.removeEventListener("click", someAction, false);
}
```

In order for this to work, all four pieces of information must match the original registration details:

- The element the event was registered on.
- The event type.
- The handler function that was registered.
- The flag indicating if this was registered on the capture or bubbling phase.

If you used the attachEvent() method to register the event handler, use the detachEvent() method to remove it. This works just like removeEventListener() except there is no capture/bubbling flag.

The other registration methods don't allow multiple event handlers, so removing them is a simpler process. Just set the appropriate event property to null. For example:

```
div.onclick = null;
```

Event Interface

When an event occurs and a corresponding listener has been registered, the assigned event handler will be called. I've explained that in some detail. Another very important aspect about event handling is the event itself. When an event happens, an event object is created that contains details of the event and this is passed to the event handler(s). If a mouse button was clicked, for example, you might want to know what element was clicked on or which button was used.

Common Event Properties

Your event handler can access this event object by declaring a function parameter. You can name the parameter anything you want, although the accepted convention is to use e. For example:

```
function someAction(e) {
...
}
```

There is a base Event object that provides some common properties and methods. However there are dozens of derived objects that provide specialized information depending on the type of event. The primary shared properties are:

- type - the type of event; this is helpful if you have a single event handler for multiple events. For example, you might have a handler to respond to both mouseup and mousedown events.

- target - the element that triggered the event.

- currentTarget - the element that event handler was registered on.

I'll go back to the initial example with just a single event handler. Instead of creating an alert, I'll change it to log some details about the event. The console will look like Figure 20-4.

```
function someAction(e) {
    console.log(e.type);
    console.log(e.target);
    console.log(e.currentTarget);
    //alert("Taking some action...");
}
```

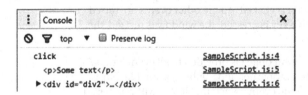

Figure 20-4. *Displaying event details in the console*

The event type is click, as expected. I clicked the first paragraph element and the event target confirms this. The currentTarget property is the inner div element where the event handler was registered.

Canceling Events

There are several methods that are common to all events. These are used to modify how events are handled. These methods are called on the event object.

- stopPropagation()

- stopImmediatePropagation()

- preventDefault()

I described earlier how an event is propagated from the window object down to the target and back up to the window object. However, if you call the stopPropagation() method on the event object, no further propagation will occur. If you handle an event during the capture phase and stop propagation, the remaining capture and all of the bubble events will be suppressed.

The stopImmediatePropagation() method also stops the propagation as I just described but also performs an additional step; it prevents any other handlers on the current element from being executed. To illustrate this behavior, assume you had registered three event handlers on the inner div element (from the previous example) for the click event in the bubbling phase. When the event finally propagated to the div element, all three event handlers would be executed, one at a time, in the order they were registered. If the first event handle called the stopImmediatePropagation() method, the other two handlers would not be called. However, if the stopPropagation() method was called instead, the other two event handlers would be executed. In both cases, no further propagation to other elements would occur, however.

The browser performs a default action in response to some events. For example, if you click on a link, the browser will navigate to that URL or if you right-click on certain elements, a context menu will appear. However, your custom events will be executed before the default browser action is taken. If you want to disable the default action, the event handler can call the preventDefault() method on the event object. If you wanted to block a link under certain situations, for instance, you can set up a custom handler to respond to the click event. The custom handler can then call preventDefault() if the link should not be used.

Exploring Events

Now that you understand the fundamentals of event processing, you can use any of the events that are supported. They all work the same way. The difference between each event boils down to just two things:

- **When is the event raised?** I've used the click event in all the examples in this chapter. It is raised when a mouse button is clicked. All the other events are raised under certain conditions such as when a key is pressed, the window is resized, the network access has been lost, etc.

- **What event details are provided?** An event object is provided to all event handlers and I've explained some of the common properties and methods available. Most events will provide additional details in the event object; the details will vary based on the event. The event object for a keypress event, for instance, should indicate which key was pressed.

I'm not going to list all of the available events here; there are hundreds of them. However, this article by Mozilla provides a pretty good overview, organizing events into categories and including links for more details: https://developer.mozilla.org/en-US/docs/Web/Events

Each event will provide a specific event object although related events will often use the same interface. For example, the MouseEvent interface is provided on most of the mouse events, such as click, dblclick, and mousedown. There is a hierarchy of event interfaces. The MouseEvent is derived from UIEvent, which is, in turn, derived from Event.

■ **Tip** You can also create your own custom events. This is outside the scope of this book, but if you're interested, check out this article: https://developer.mozilla.org/en-US/docs/Web/Guide/Events/ Creating_and_triggering_events

---

Summary

In this chapter I demonstrated how you can use event handlers to respond to user input or system-initiated events. You need to register an event handler, which ties three things together:

- the event
- the event handler
- the DOM element

When the specified event is raised for the specified element, the registered handler is executed.

The preferred method of registering an event handler is to use the addEventListener() method. There are other legacy methods supported as well but these do not include all the functionality of addEventListener().

When an event occurs on an element, referred to as the target, the event is raised on all of the objects in the DOM hierarchy. The event starts at the window object and trickles down to the target in the capturing phase. It then bubbles up back through the chain until it reaches the window object again.

In the next section of this book, I will provide example solutions that demonstrate some of the advanced capabilities of HTML5. We'll start with custom embedding of audio and video elements.

PART V

■ ■ ■

Advanced Applications

This section is different from the rest of the book, being a little more hands-on. Each chapter uses a series of exercises that takes you step by step to complete a solution. For some of these exercises you will need some files from the source code download that is available at www.apress.com. There are some image and media files that I can't include in the text. There are also some large blocks of code that are tedious and time consuming to type, and I've provided these to save you some time.

For each project, you can either work through the code on your own as you read the text, or just open the final solution from the download and follow along in the book. If you choose the latter, spend a few minutes to make sure you understand what the code is doing.

The solutions that you will create are these:

- 21) Creating custom audio and video controls.

- 22) Using Scalar Vector Graphics (SVG) to build an interactive map of the United States.

- 23) Simulating a game of Chess using canvas. You'll also use canvas to create a simple model of the solar system and demonstrate compositing.

- 24) Use the Drag and Drop (DnD) API to implement the game of Checkers.

- 25) Rewrite the Chess simulation using IndexedDB, storing the moves and the status of each piece in a client-side database.

- 26) Use Geolocation to find the current position and map this using the Bing Mapping API along with pushpins to identify related locations.

CHAPTER 21

■ ■ ■

Audio and Video

In Chapter 7, I introduced the audio and video elements and demonstrated how they could be embedded into your HTML document using the native controls provided by the browser. In this chapter, you'll use your own controls that are wired up to the audio and video elements through JavaScript. All of the DOM elements and events are available in JavaScript, so it's a fairly straightforward process to create your own controls to work with the audio or video element. However, there are several facets that you'll need to control, so it's not a trivial exercise.

Overview

There are three areas that you'll need to address:

- Play/Pause

- Displaying progress and fast-forwarding/rewinding

- Adjust volume/mute

I'll start by creating custom controls for audio, but as you'll see, the process for video is essentially the same. You will need to respond to events from both the UI controls as well as the audio element. You'll start by adding all the necessary controls to the page. Then I'll show you how to implement the event handlers that are needed for each area. The input elements that you'll use to control the audio element are as follows:

- Play/Pause button: The label will toggle between "Play" and "Pause" depending on the state of the audio element.

- Seek: This is a range control (introduced in Chapter 8) that will serve both to show the progress and allow the user to seek a specific location.

- Duration: This is a span element that displays both the current location and the total duration of the audio file.

- Mute button: The label will toggle between "Mute" and "Unmute."

- Volume: This is another range control that is used to specify the volume level.

The audio events that you'll provide handlers for include the following:

- play: Raised when the audio is started

- pause: Raised when the audio is paused

- ended: Raised when the audio has completed

© Mark J. Collins 2017
M. J. Collins, *Pro HTML5 with CSS, JavaScript, and Multimedia*, DOI 10.1007/978-1-4842-2463-2_21

- timeupdate: Raised periodically as the audio clip is played

- durationchange: Raised when the duration changes, which occurs when the file is loaded

- volumechange: Raised when the volume level changes or the mute property has changed

Custom Audio Controls

You'll start by creating an HTML document that has an audio element. Then you'll add input elements that will be used to control the audio.

EXERCISE 21-1. CREATING THE MARKUP

1. Create an HTML document with a single audio element. You'll need to provide your own audio file so the src attribute will be different from what is shown here. This also has the controls attribute so the native controls will be used but you'll remove that later. The page, in Chrome, will look like Figure 21-1.

```
<!DOCTYPE html>

<html lang="en">
    <head>
        <meta charset="utf-8" />
        <title>Chapter 21 - Audio and Video</title>
        <link rel="stylesheet" href="Sample.css" />
        <script src="SampleScript.js" defer></script>
    </head>
    <body>
        <audio id="audio" src="Media/Linus and Lucy.mp3" controls >
            <p>HTML5 audio is not supported on your browser</p>
        </audio>
    </body>
</html>
```

Figure 21-1. The initial audio element

2. Now you'll remove the `controls` attribute from the `audio` element and add your own controls as follows. The new controls are standard input elements and are in a separate `div` element.

```
<div id="audioControls">
    <input type="button" value="Play" id="play" />
    <input type="range" id="audioSeek" />
    <span id="duration"></span>
    <input type="button" id="mute" value="Mute" />
    <input type="range" id="volume" min="0" max="1" step="any" />
</div>
```

There are two range controls; the first one will show the progress as the audio clip is played. The user can also use this to rewind or fast-forward to a new place in the file. The `min` and `max` attributes will be set in JavaScript based on the length of the audio file. The second range control is used to adjust the volume. The `min` and `max` attributes are set to 0 and 1, respectively. A volume of 1 indicates 100% and the actual value should be between 0 and 1.

There are also two buttons; the first serves as both the Play and Pause buttons. The label will change depending on the current state of the audio element. The second button toggles the mute flag. Again, its label will change depending on if the audio is currently muted. There is a span element in the middle of these controls that has no content, initially. This will display the length of the file and the current position.

Supporting Play and Pause

With all the elements on the page, it's time to start writing some JavaScript. This first exercise will wire up the Play button and perform the initial configuration of the range control.

EXERCISE 21-2. SUPPORTING PLAY AND PAUSE

1. Create a new JavaScript file named **SampleScript.js**. Since the `audio` element will be referenced in numerous places, you'll declare a variable to store it. This will avoid the need to search through the DOM every time it is used.

    ```
    "use strict";

    var audio = document.getElementById("audio");
    ```

2. You'll need an event handler to set up the initial duration value. The `setupSeek()` method is called in response to the `durationchange` event on the `audio` element. When the page is first loaded, it doesn't know how long the audio clip is until the file is opened and the metadata is loaded. As soon as the metadata has been loaded, the duration can be determined, and the event is raised. The `duration` property is expressed in seconds. The `setupSeek()` function uses the `duration` property to set the `max` attribute of the `audioSeek` range control. It is also used to set the initial value of the `span` element. Notice that the `Math.round()` function is called to round this value to the nearest integer (second).

```
function setupSeek() {
    var seek = document.getElementById("audioSeek");
    seek.min = 0;
    seek.max = Math.round(audio.duration);
    seek.value = 0;
    var duration = document.getElementById("duration");
    duration.innerHTML = "0/" + Math.round(audio.duration);
}
```

3. The `togglePlay()` method is called when the user clicks the Play button. If the current state of the `audio` element is paused or ended, it calls the `play()` function. Otherwise, it calls the `pause()` method.

```
function togglePlay() {
    if (audio.paused || audio.ended) {
        audio.play();
    }
    else {
        audio.pause();
    }
}
```

4. The `updatePlayPause()` method is registered on the `audio` element for both the `play` and `pause` events. It sets the label of the Play button to reflect the state of the `audio` element. If the audio is currently playing, the text is changed to "Pause" since that will be the result if the button is clicked. Otherwise, the text is set to "Play."

```
function updatePlayPause() {
    var play = document.getElementById("play");
    if (audio.paused || audio.ended) {
        play.value = "Play";
    }
    else {
        play.value = "Pause";
    }
}
```

■ **Tip** The `togglePlay()` function responds to the Play button being clicked, and the `updatePlayPause()` function responds to the `audio` element being started or paused. When the button is clicked, the `togglePlay()` method will change the state of the `audio` element. This state change will raise either a `play` or `pause` event, which are both handled by the `updatePlayPause()` function. This is done this way because it is possible that the audio can be played or paused through means other than clicking the Play button. For example, if you left the `controls` attribute, you would have both the native controls as well as the custom controls. Responding to the `play` and `pause` events ensures the button label is always correct regardless of how the `audio` element is manipulated.

---

5. Finally, the endAudio() function is registered with the audio element in response to the ended event, which is raised when the audio has finished playing. This performs some synchronization including setting the button label and initializing the range and span controls.

```
function endAudio() {
    document.getElementById("play").value = "Play";
    document.getElementById("audioSeek").value = 0;
    document.getElementById("duration").innerHTML = "0/" + Math.round
    (audio.duration);
}
```

6. Now you'll need to register the event handlers using the following code:

```
// Wire-up the event handlers
audio.addEventListener("durationchange", setupSeek, false);
document.getElementById("play").addEventListener("click", togglePlay, false);
audio.addEventListener("play", updatePlayPause, false);
audio.addEventListener("pause", updatePlayPause, false);
audio.addEventListener("ended", endAudio, false);
```

Supporting Progress and Seek

We'll want to be able to use the slider to move to a different position in the audio file. The next exercise will configure this to both report the current position as well as to change the position.

EXERCISE 21-3. PROGRESS AND SEEK

1. Just like with the Play button, there is one event handler, seekAudio(), which responds to the input element and a separate event handler, updateSeek(), which responds to the audio element. The seekAudio() function is called when the user moves the slider on the range control. It simply sets the currentTime property using the value selected by the range control.

```
function seekAudio() {
    var seek = document.getElementById("audioSeek");
    audio.currentTime = seek.value;
}
```

2. The updateSeek() function is called when the ontimeupdate event is raised by the audio element. This updates the range control to reflect the current position within the file. It also updates the span control to show the actual position (in seconds). Again, the currentTime property is rounded to the nearest integer.

```
function updateSeek() {
    var seek = document.getElementById("audioSeek");
    seek.value = Math.round(audio.currentTime);
    var duration = document.getElementById("duration");
```

```
        duration.innerHTML = Math.round(audio.currentTime) + "/" +
            Math.round(audio.duration);
    }
```

3. Now you'll need to register the event handlers using the following code:

```
document.getElementById("audioSeek").addEventListener
("change", seekAudio, false);
audio.addEventListener("timeupdate", updateSeek, false);
```

Controlling the Volume

This exercise will set up the controls to adjust the volume, including the Mute button.

EXERCISE 21-4. CONTROLLING THE VOLUME

1. As its name suggests, the toggleMute() function toggles the muted property of
    the audio element. When this is changed, the volumechange event is raised by the
    audio element.

    ```
    function toggleMute() {
        audio.muted = !audio.muted;
    }
    ```

2. The updateMute() function responds to the volumechange event and sets the
    button label according to the current value of the muted property. Again, doing it
    this way ensures the button label is correct.

    ```
    function updateMute() {
        var mute = document.getElementById("mute");
        if (audio.muted) {
            mute.value = "Unmute";
        }
        else {
            mute.value = "Mute";
        }
    }
    ```

3. Finally, the setVolume() function is called when the user moves the slider on the
    second range control. It sets the volume property of the audio element to whatever
    was selected on the range control.

    ```
    function setVolume() {
        var volume = document.getElementById("volume");
        audio.volume = volume.value;
    }
    ```

4. Register the event handlers as follows:

```
document.getElementById("mute").addEventListener("click",
toggleMute, false);
audio.addEventListener("volumechange", updateMute, false);
document.getElementById("volume").addEventListener("change",
setVolume, false);
```

■ **Note**   The `volume` property has a value between 0 and 1. You could think of this as 0 percent and 100 percent. When you defined the `range` control, the `min` attribute was set to 0 and `max` was set to 1, so the scale is correct. You can simply set the `volume` property using the range value. If you want to display the actual value of the `volume` property, just convert it to a percentage.

Adjusting the Style

Now you're ready to try your custom controls. Save your changes and browse to your page. The page should look similar to Figure 21-2.

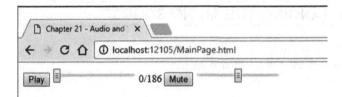

Figure 21-2. *The custom audio controls*

The styling here is pretty boring; a little CSS will help. Add the following CSS rules to change the size of the buttons and the range controls. The result is shown in Figure 21-3.

```
input[type="button"] {
    width: 75px;
    background-color: lightblue;
    border-radius: 5px;
}
#audioSeek {
    width: 300px;
}
#volume {
    width: 50px;
}
```

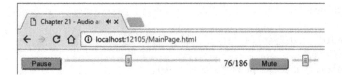

Figure 21-3. *The style controls*

■ **Tip** Changing the style of a range control is possible but requires using vendor prefixes and is different for every browser. If you're interested, here's an article with some details: `http://brennaobrien.com/blog/2014/05/style-input-type-range-in-every-browser.html`.

Changing the Audio Source

In this example, the audio source was defined in the markup. However, you can easily control this using JavaScript. If you're using a single `src` attribute as you did initially, you just need to change this attribute to reference a different file. However, if you're using multiple `source` elements, you'll need to update all of these and then call the `load()` method.

EXERCISE 21-5. CHANGING THE AUDIO SOURCE

1. To try this, add a button that will change the source to a second audio clip and play that one instead. Here's the markup to add a new button to the page:

    ```
    <div>
        <input type="button" value="Track2" id="track2" />
    </div>
    ```

2. Add the following event handler that will be executed when the button is clicked.

    ```
    function nextFile() {
        audio.src = "Media/Sample.mp3";
        //audio.load(); needed if there are multiple sources
        audio.play();
    }
    ```

3. Register the event handler with the Next button

    ```
    document.getElementById("track2").addEventListener("click",
    nextFile, false);
    ```

Note I explained how to set up multiple sources in Chapter 7. This was important back in the day when you needed two or more audio files to support multiple browsers. A single MP3 file is now supported by all major browsers. If there are multiple sources, you'll need to update all of them and then call the `load()` method. If you're using a single source, you don't need to call `load()`.

Custom Video Controls

Creating custom video controls is identical to audio controls. You need to provide the ability to play and pause the video, adjust the volume, and move to a particular point in the file. I'll add the same video element from Chapter 7.

```
<video src="Media/BigBuckBunny.mp4" id="video"
        poster="Media/BBB_Poster.png" width="852" height="480">
    <p> HTML5 video is not supported on your browser</p>
</video>
```

Since the implementation is nearly identical as the audio controls, the JavaScript is shown in its entirety in Listing 21-1. The functions are equivalent to their audio counterparts.

Listing 21-1. Implementing custom video controls

```
var video = document.getElementById("video");

function setupSeekVideo() {
    var seek = document.getElementById("videoSeek");
    seek.min = 0;
    seek.max = Math.round(video.duration);
    seek.value = 0;
    var duration = document.getElementById("durationVideo");
    duration.innerHTML = "0/" + Math.round(video.duration);
}

function togglePlayVideo() {
    if (video.paused || video.ended) {
        video.play();
    }
    else {
        video.pause();
    }
}
```

```
function updatePlayPauseVideo() {
    var play = document.getElementById("playVideo");
    if (video.paused || video.ended) {
        play.value = "Play";
    }
    else {
        play.value = "Pause";
    }
}

function endVideo() {
    document.getElementById("playVideo").value = "Play";
    document.getElementById("videoSeek").value = 0;
    document.getElementById("durationVideo").innerHTML = "0/"
        + Math.round(video.duration);
}

// Wire-up the event handlers
video.addEventListener("durationchange", setupSeekVideo, false);
document.getElementById("playVideo").addEventListener("click", togglePlayVideo, false);
video.addEventListener("play", updatePlayPauseVideo, false);
video.addEventListener("pause", updatePlayPauseVideo, false);
video.addEventListener("ended", endVideo, false);

// Support progress and seek
function seekVideo() {
    var seek = document.getElementById("videoSeek");
    video.currentTime = seek.value;
}

function updateSeekVideo() {
    var seek = document.getElementById("videoSeek");
    seek.value = Math.round(video.currentTime);
    var duration = document.getElementById("durationVideo");
    duration.innerHTML = Math.round(video.currentTime) + "/"
        + Math.round(video.duration);
}

document.getElementById("videoSeek").addEventListener("change", seekVideo, false);
video.addEventListener("timeupdate", updateSeekVideo, false);

// Support volume and mute
function toggleMuteVideo() {
    video.muted = !video.muted;
}

function updateMuteVideo() {
    var mute = document.getElementById("muteVideo");
    if (video.muted) {
        mute.value = "Unmute";
    }
```

```
    else {
        mute.value = "Mute";
    }
}

function setVolumeVideo() {
    var volume = document.getElementById("volumeVideo");
    video.volume = volume.value;
}

document.getElementById("muteVideo").addEventListener("click", toggleMuteVideo, false);
video.addEventListener("volumechange", updateMuteVideo, false);
document.getElementById("volumeVideo").addEventListener("change", setVolumeVideo, false);
```

■ **Note** The audio and video elements are represented in JavaScript by the HTMLAudioElement and HTMLVideoElement objects, respectively. Both of these are derived from HTMLMediaElement.

Summary

In the previous chapter I explained how to use events in JavaScript. You can see, from the examples in this chapter, just how important events are. Whether responding to user actions or system notifications, all of the logic was implemented in event handlers. In this chapter, the event handlers were used to primarily sync the UI elements with the audio or video elements they were controlling.

The current state of the audio or video is available through properties such as duration, currentTime, and volume. Some of these properties, including currentTime and volume can be set as well, allowing you to adjust them based on user input. To create your own custom controls, you just need to wire up the necessary event handlers so changes in the state of the audio or video are reflected in the UI elements, and vice versa.

In the next chapter, you'll use Scalable Vector Graphics (SVG) to create some impressing graphic applications. SVG is a technique for drawing graphics that scales without any loss of image quality. One of the really useful features of SVG is that the drawing elements can be styled using CSS.

CHAPTER 22

■ ■ ■

Scalable Vector Graphics

In this chapter, I'll show you how to use Scalable Vector Graphics (SVG) in an HTML5 web application. There are a lot of really cool things that you can do with SVG. I've picked out a fun demonstration that can be easily applied to many business applications. But first, let me give you an introduction to what SVG is.

Most people think of a graphic element as some form of bitmap, with an array of rows and columns of pixels, and each pixel is assigned a specific color. In contrast, however, vector graphics express an image as a collection of formulas. For example, draw a circle with a center at point x,y and a radius r. More complex images are defined as a collection of graphic elements including circles, lines, and paths. While the rendering engine will ultimately determine the specific pixels that need to be set, the image definition is based on a formula. This fundamental difference provides two significant advantages to using vector graphics.

First, as its name suggests, vector graphics are scalable. If you want to expand the size of the image, the rendering engine simply recalculates the formula based on the new size and there is no loss of clarity. If you zoom in on a bitmap image, you'll quickly start to see graininess and the image becomes blurry.

Second, each element in the image can be manipulated independently. If there are several circles in the image, for example, you can highlight one by simply changing the color of that image. Since vector graphics are formula based, you can easily adjust the formula to modify the image. What makes this particularly useful is that these elements can be styled using CSS, employing the powerful selectors and formatting capabilities that I showed you in previous chapters.

Introducing SVG

You'll begin by creating a page that uses simple geometric shapes to draw a picture. Then you'll apply styles to these shapes using CSS. I'll show you how to save these markup elements in an .svg image file. This image file can be used just like other image files such as .jpg and .png files.

Adding Some Simple Shapes

To demonstrate how an svg element works, you'll add some simple shapes such as circles, rectangles, and lines. Most images can be expressed as a collection of geometrical shapes, as I will demonstrate here.

© Mark J. Collins 2017
M. J. Collins, *Pro HTML5 with CSS, JavaScript, and Multimedia*, DOI 10.1007/978-1-4842-2463-2_22

389

EXERCISE 22-1. BUILDING A SNOWMAN

1. Insert the following svg element in the body of your HTML document:

    ```
    <svg xmlns:svg="http://www.w3.org/2000/svg" version="1.1"
        width="100px" height="230px"
        xmlns="http://www.w3.org/2000/svg"
        xmlns:xlink="http://www.w3.org/1999/xlink">
    </svg>
    ```

■ **Note** The width and height attributes define the element's intrinsic dimensions. With most browsers, if the width and height are not specified, the image will be clipped to some default size.

---

2. Inside the svg element, add the following elements. These are just simple shapes, mostly circle elements with a rectangle (rect), line, and polygon.

    ```
    <circle class="body" cx="50" cy="171" r="40" />
    <circle class="body" cx="50" cy="103" r="30" />
    <circle class="body" cx="50" cy="50" r="25" />
    <line class="hat" x1="30" y1="25" x2="70" y2="25" />
    <rect class="hat" x="40" y="10" width="20" height="15" />
    <circle class="button" cx="50" cy="82" r="4" />
    <circle class="button" cx="50" cy="100" r="4" />
    <circle class="button" cx="50" cy="118" r="4" />
    <circle class="eye" cx="42" cy="42" r="4" />
    <circle class="eye" cx="58" cy="42" r="4" />
    <polygon class="nose" points="45,60 45,50 60,55" />
    ```

A circle is expressed as a center point, cx and cy and a radius, r. A line is specified as a beginning point, x1 and y1; and an endpoint, x2 and y2. A rectangle (rect) element is described by the top-left corner location, x and y; a width; and a height. A polygon is defined by a set of points in the form of x1,y1 x2,y2 x3,y3. You can specify any number of points. It is rendered by drawing a line segment between each of these points and a line segment from the last point, back to the first point.

3. Save your changes and view your web page in a browser. The page should look like Figure 22-1.

Figure 22-1. *The initial SVG image without styling*

Adding Styles

The default style for these elements is a solid black fill, and because some of these shapes are on top of each other, several are not currently visible. Notice that you assigned a `class` attribute to each element. Now you'll apply styles for these elements using a `class` selector.

1. Add the following rules to the CSS file. Save these changes and refresh the browser to view the updated web page, which should look like Figure 22-2.

```
.body {
    fill: white;
    stroke: gray;
    stroke-width: 1px;
}

.hat {
    fill: black;
    stroke: black;
    stroke-width: 3px;
}

.button {
    fill: black;
}

.eye {
    fill: black;
}

.nose {
    fill: orange;
}
```

Figure 22-2. *The SVG image with styling applied*

Using SVG Image Files

In addition to embedding an svg element, you can save this as a stand-alone image file with an .svg extension. This file can then be used just like other graphic images. I'll show you how to create a stand-alone SVG image and then use it on a page.

Creating an SVG Image

I'll first show you how to create a stand-alone .svg file; you'll use it later as a background image. This will also demonstrate the scalability of SVG images.

EXERCISE 22-2. CREATING AN SVG IMAGE

1. Create a new file in your web application called **snowman.svg**.

2. Enter the following markup instructions:

   ```
   <?xml version="1.0" standalone="no"?>
   <!DOCTYPE svg PUBLIC "-//W3C//DTD SVG 1.1//EN"
   "http://www.w3.org/Graphics/SVG/1.1/DTD/svg11.dtd">
   ```

3. Copy and paste the entire svg element from the previous HTML document.

4. You'll need the style rules in the same file as the svg element. To do that, add a style element inside the svg element. Copy the style rules from the CSS file to the style element.

The snowman.svg file should have the DOCTYPE entry indicating this is an SVG file and an svg element. The CSS rules will be inside the style element, which is inside the svg element.

5. To test your image, open the snowman.svg file from your desktop. This should launch a browser and display the snowman image.

Using an SVG Background

Now you have an image file that you can use just like other images. To demonstrate this, you'll use the snowman.svg file as the background image for the initial web page.

1. In the initial CSS file, add the following style rule:

```
body {
    background-image: url(snowman.svg);
    background-size: cover;
}
```

2. This uses the new snowman.svg image and configures it to expand to fit the window. After refreshing your browser, in addition to the small image, you should also see a larger version of your image, as shown in Figure 22-3. Notice that there is no loss of image quality when expanding the size of the image.

Figure 22-3. *The page with the snowman background*

Creating an Interactive Map

Drawing pictures of snowmen may be fun, but let's move on to some more practical uses of SVG. You will create a map of the United States with each state represented by a separate SVG path element, which I'll explain later. The path definitions will be stored in a separate JavaScript file. Once you have the map displayed, I'll show you some CSS tricks to style the map using both static and dynamic styles. Finally, you'll add some animation to add a little flair to your web page.

Using Path Elements

The path element is the most versatile of all SVG elements. It is a collection of "move to," "line to," and various "curve to" commands. The shape is drawn by following the path commands. Each command starts from the current position and either moves to a new position or draws a line to the next position. Here's an example:

- Move to 25, 50.

- Draw a line to 50, 50.

- Draw a line to 50, 25.

- Draw an arc to 25, 50.

This is expressed as follows:

```
<path d="M25,50 L50,50 L50,25 A25,25 0 0,0 25,50 z" />
```

The "move to" and "line to" commands are pretty straightforward. The "arc to" command, as well as all the other curve commands, is more complicated because you need to provide additional control points that describe how the curve should be drawn. Each command uses a single letter, as shown in Table 22-1.

Table 22-1. *The Available Path Commands*

Command	Abbr.	Description
Move to	M	Moves to the specified position
Line to	L	Draws a line to the specified position
Horizontal line to	H	Draws a horizontal line to the specified x coordinate
Vertical line to	V	Draws a vertical line to the specified y coordinate
Arc to	A	Draws an arc to the specified position
Curve to	C	Draws a cubic Bézier curve
Shorthand curve to	S	Draws a simplified cubic Bézier curve
Quadratic curve to	Q	Draws a quadratic Bézier curve
Shorthand quadratic curve to	T	Draws a simplified quadratic Bézier curve
Close path	Z	Closes the figure by drawing a line to the starting position

For each of these commands, an uppercase letter is used when absolute coordinates are used. You can also specify relative coordinates and use a lowercase letter to indicate the values that are relative to the current position. For more information about constructing a path element, see the article at http://www.w3.org/TR/SVG/paths.html#PathData.

As you can probably envision, drawing a complex shape like the state of Alaska will take a lot of commands. You won't want to edit this by hand. Fortunately, there are tools available to help build a path definition. For example, a free web-based tool is available at http://code.google.com/p/svg-edit. Just for grins, Listing 22-1 shows the path element for Alaska.

Listing 22-1. The Path Element Definition for Alaska

```
<path d="M 158.07671,453.67502 L 157.75339,539.03215 L 159.36999,540.00211 L
162.44156,540.16377 L 163.8965,539.03215 L 166.48308,539.03215 L 166.64475,541.94205 L
173.59618,548.73182 L 174.08117,551.3184 L 177.47605,549.37846 L 178.1227,549.2168 L
178.44602,546.14524 L 179.90096,544.52863 L 181.0326,544.36697 L 182.97253,542.91201 L
186.04409,545.01361 L 186.69074,547.92352 L 188.63067,549.05514 L 189.7623,551.48006 L
193.64218,553.25833 L 197.03706,559.2398 L 199.78529,563.11966 L 202.04855,565.86791 L
203.50351,569.58611 L 208.515,571.36439 L 213.68817,573.46598 L 214.65813,577.83084 L
215.14311,580.9024 L 214.17315,584.29729 L 212.39487,586.56054 L 210.77826,585.75224 L
209.32331,582.68067 L 206.57507,581.22573 L 204.7968,580.09409 L 203.98849,580.9024 L
205.44344,583.65065 L 205.6051,587.36885 L 204.47347,587.85383 L 202.53354,585.9139 L
200.43195,584.62061 L 200.91693,586.23722 L 202.21021,588.0155 L 201.40191,588.8238 C
201.40191,588.8238 200.59361,588.50048 200.10863,587.85383 C 199.62363,587.20719
198.00703,584.45895 198.00703,584.45895 L 197.03706,582.19569 C 197.03706,582.19569
196.71374,583.48898 196.06709,583.16565 C 195.42044,582.84233 194.7738,581.71071
194.7738,581.71071 L 196.55207,579.77077 L 195.09712,578.31582 L 195.09712,573.30432 L
194.28882,573.30432 L 193.48052,576.6992 L 192.34888,577.1842 L 191.37892,573.46598 L
190.73227,569.74777 L 189.92396,569.26279 L 190.24729,574.92094 L 190.24729,576.05256 L
188.79233,574.75928 L 185.23579,568.77781 L 183.13419,568.29283 L 182.48755,564.57462 L
180.87094,561.66472 L 179.25432,560.53308 L 179.25432,558.26983 L 181.35592,556.97654 L
180.87094,556.65322 L 178.28436,557.29986 L 174.88947,554.87495 L 172.30289,551.96504 L
167.45306,549.37846 L 163.41152,546.79188 L 164.70482,543.55866 L 164.70482,541.94205 L
162.92654,543.55866 L 160.01664,544.69029 L 156.29843,543.55866 L 150.64028,541.13375 L
145.14381,541.13375 L 144.49717,541.61873 L 138.03072,537.73885 L 135.92912,537.41553 L
133.18088,531.59573 L 129.62433,531.91905 L 126.06778,533.374 L 126.55277,537.90052 L
127.68439,534.99062 L 128.65437,535.31394 L 127.19941,539.67879 L 130.43263,536.93055 L
131.07928,538.54716 L 127.19941,542.91201 L 125.90612,542.58869 L 125.42114,540.64875 L
124.12785,539.84045 L 122.83456,540.97208 L 120.08632,539.19381 L 117.01475,541.29541 L
115.23649,543.397 L 111.8416,545.4986 L 107.15342,545.33693 L 106.66844,543.23534 L
110.38664,542.58869 L 110.38664,541.29541 L 108.12338,540.64875 L 109.09336,538.22384 L
111.35661,534.34397 L 111.35661,532.5657 L 111.51827,531.75739 L 115.88313,529.49413 L
116.85309,530.78742 L 119.60134,530.78742 L 118.30805,528.20085 L 114.58983,527.87752 L
109.57834,530.62576 L 107.15342,534.02064 L 105.37515,536.60723 L 104.24352,538.87049 L
100.04033,540.32543 L 96.96876,542.91201 L 96.645439,544.52863 L 98.908696,545.4986 L
99.717009,547.60018 L 96.96876,550.83341 L 90.502321,555.03661 L 82.742574,559.2398 L
80.640977,560.37142 L 75.306159,561.50306 L 69.971333,563.76631 L 71.749608,565.0596 L
70.294654,566.51455 L 69.809672,567.64618 L 67.061434,566.67621 L 63.828214,566.83787 L
63.019902,569.10113 L 62.049939,569.10113 L 62.37326,566.67621 L 58.816709,567.96951 L
55.90681,568.93947 L 52.511924,567.64618 L 49.602023,569.58611 L 46.368799,569.58611 L
44.267202,570.87941 L 42.65059,571.68771 L 40.548995,571.36439 L 37.962415,570.23276 L
35.699158,570.87941 L 34.729191,571.84937 L 33.112578,570.71775 L 33.112578,568.77781 L
36.184142,567.48452 L 42.488929,568.13117 L 46.853782,566.51455 L 48.955378,564.41296 L
51.86528,563.76631 L 53.643553,562.958 L 56.391794,563.11966 L 58.008406,564.41296 L
58.978369,564.08964 L 61.241626,561.3414 L 64.313196,560.37142 L 67.708076,559.72478 L
69.00137,559.40146 L 69.648012,559.88644 L 70.456324,559.88644 L 71.749608,556.16823 L
75.791141,554.71329 L 77.731077,550.99508 L 79.994336,546.46856 L 81.610951,545.01361 L
81.934272,542.42703 L 80.317657,543.72032 L 76.922764,544.36697 L 76.276122,541.94205 L
74.982838,541.61873 L 74.012865,542.58869 L 73.851205,545.4986 L 72.39625,545.33693 L
```

70.941306,539.51713 L 69.648012,540.81041 L 68.516388,540.32543 L 68.193068,538.3855 L
64.151535,538.54716 L 62.049939,539.67879 L 59.463361,539.35547 L 60.918305,537.90052 L
61.403286,535.31394 L 60.756645,533.374 L 62.211599,532.40404 L 63.504883,532.24238 L
62.858241,530.4641 L 62.858241,526.09925 L 61.888278,525.12928 L 61.079966,526.58423 L
54.936843,526.58423 L 53.481892,525.29094 L 52.835247,521.41108 L 50.733651,517.85452 L
50.733651,516.88456 L 52.835247,516.07625 L 52.996908,513.97465 L 54.128536,512.84303 L
53.320231,512.35805 L 52.026941,512.84303 L 50.895313,510.09479 L 51.86528,505.08328 L
56.391794,501.85007 L 58.978369,500.23345 L 60.918305,496.51525 L 63.666554,495.22195 L
66.253132,496.35359 L 66.576453,498.77851 L 69.00137,498.45517 L 72.23459,496.03026 L
73.851205,496.67691 L 74.821167,497.32355 L 76.437782,497.32355 L 78.701041,496.03026 L
79.509354,491.6654 C 79.509354,491.6654 79.832675,488.75551 80.479317,488.27052 C
81.125959,487.78554 81.44928,487.30056 81.44928,487.30056 L 80.317657,485.36062 L
77.731077,486.16893 L 74.497847,486.97723 L 72.557911,486.49225 L 69.00137,484.71397 L
63.989875,484.55231 L 60.433324,480.83411 L 60.918305,476.95424 L 61.564957,474.52932 L
59.463361,472.75105 L 57.523423,469.03283 L 58.008406,468.22453 L 64.798177,467.73955 L
66.899773,467.73955 L 67.869736,468.70951 L 68.516388,468.70951 L 68.354728,467.0929 L
72.23459,466.44626 L 74.821167,466.76958 L 76.276122,467.90121 L 74.821167,470.00281 L
74.336186,471.45775 L 77.084435,473.07437 L 82.095932,474.85264 L 83.874208,473.88268 L
81.610951,469.51783 L 80.640977,466.2846 L 81.610951,465.47629 L 78.21606,463.53636 L
77.731077,462.40472 L 78.21606,460.78812 L 77.407756,456.90825 L 74.497847,452.22007 L
72.072929,448.01688 L 74.982838,446.07694 L 78.21606,446.07694 L 79.994336,446.72359 L
84.197528,446.56193 L 87.915733,443.00539 L 89.047366,439.93382 L 92.765578,437.5089 L
94.382182,438.47887 L 97.130421,437.83222 L 100.84863,435.73062 L 101.98027,435.56896 L
102.95023,436.37728 L 107.47674,436.21561 L 110.22498,433.14405 L 111.35661,433.14405 L
114.91316,435.56896 L 116.85309,437.67056 L 116.36811,438.80219 L 117.01475,439.93382 L
118.63137,438.31721 L 122.51124,438.64053 L 122.83456,442.35873 L 124.7745,443.81369 L
131.88759,444.46033 L 138.19238,448.66352 L 139.64732,447.69356 L 144.82049,450.28014 L
146.92208,449.6335 L 148.86202,448.82518 L 153.71185,450.76512 L 158.07671,453.67502 z M
42.973913,482.61238 L 45.075509,487.9472 L 44.913847,488.91717 L 42.003945,488.59384 L
40.225672,484.55231 L 38.447399,483.09737 L 36.02248,483.09737 L 35.86082,480.51078 L
37.639093,478.08586 L 38.770722,480.51078 L 40.225672,481.96573 L 42.973913,482.61238 z M
40.387333,516.07625 L 44.105542,516.88456 L 47.823749,517.85452 L 48.632056,518.8245 L
47.015444,522.5427 L 43.94388,522.38104 L 40.548995,518.8245 L 40.387333,516.07625 z M
19.694697,502.01173 L 20.826327,504.5983 L 21.957955,506.21492 L 20.826327,507.02322 L
18.72473,503.95166 L 18.72473,502.01173 L 19.694697,502.01173 z M 5.9534943,575.0826 L
9.3483796,572.81934 L 12.743265,571.84937 L 15.329845,572.17269 L 15.814828,573.7893 L
17.754763,574.27429 L 19.694697,572.33436 L 19.371375,570.71775 L 22.119616,570.0711 L
25.029518,572.65768 L 23.897889,574.43595 L 19.533037,575.56758 L 16.784795,575.0826 L
13.066588,573.95097 L 8.7017347,575.40592 L 7.0851227,575.72924 L 5.9534943,575.0826 z M
54.936843,570.55609 L 56.553455,572.49602 L 58.655048,570.87941 L 57.2001,569.58611 L
54.936843,570.55609 z M 57.846745,573.62764 L 58.978369,571.36439 L 61.079966,571.68771 L
60.271663,573.62764 L 57.846745,573.62764 z M 81.44928,571.68771 L 82.904234,573.46598 L
83.874208,572.33436 L 83.065895,570.39442 L 81.44928,571.68771 z M 90.17899,559.2398 L
91.310623,565.0596 L 94.220522,565.86791 L 99.232017,562.958 L 103.59687,560.37142 L
101.98027,557.94651 L 102.46525,555.52159 L 100.36365,556.81488 L 97.453752,556.00657 L
99.070357,554.87495 L 101.01029,555.68325 L 104.89016,553.90497 L 105.37515,552.45003 L
102.95023,551.64172 L 103.75853,549.70178 L 101.01029,551.64172 L 96.322118,555.19827 L
91.472284,558.10817 L 90.17899,559.2398 z M 132.53423,539.35547 L 134.95915,537.90052 L
133.98918,536.12224 L 132.21091,537.09221 L 132.53423,539.35547 z" />

■ **Tip** This data, as well as the data for all the other states, was downloaded from `http://en.wikipedia.` `org/wiki/File:Blank_US_Map.svg`. You can find a lot of similar material by going to `http://commons.` `wikimedia.org` and entering **svg map** in the search criteria.

Implementing the Initial Map

You'll start by creating the initial map with only basic styles applied. The paths are defined in a `States.js` file that you can download from `www.apress.com`. You'll create a new HTML document that will display the map and the actual path DOM elements will be created with JavaScript.

EXERCISE 22-3. CREATING THE INITIAL MAP

1. Create a new HTML document with the following markup. This is similar to the previous page; notice, however, that the height and width are different because this will have a different intrinsic size.

```
<!DOCTYPE html>

<html lang="en">
    <head>
        <meta charset="utf-8" />
        <title>Chapter 22 - US Map</title>
        <link rel="stylesheet" href="Map.css" />
        <script src="States.js" defer></script>
        <script src="Map.js" defer></script>
    </head>
    <body>
        <svg xmlns:svg="http://www.w3.org/2000/svg" version="1.1"
            width="959px" height="593px"
            xmlns="http://www.w3.org/2000/svg"
            xmlns:xlink="http://www.w3.org/1999/xlink"
            id="map">
        </svg>
    </body>
</html>
```

2. Download the `States.js` file from `www.apress.com`. This defines a variable named `States`, which is an array of objects. Each object has a `StateCode`, `StateName`, and `Path` property.

3. Create a `Map.js` file and use the following code for its implementation. This gets the `svg` element and adds the `path` elements as children. The `StateCode` is used for the `id` and the `StateName` is used for the `class` attribute.

```
var map = document.getElementById("map");

for (var i=0; i<States.length; i++) {
    var path = document.createElementNS("http://www.w3.org/2000/svg", "path");
    path.id = States[i].StateCode;
    path.setAttribute("class", States[i].StateName)
    path.setAttribute("d", States[i].Path);
    map.appendChild(path);
}
```

■ **Note** Because the path element is not part of the standard HTML namespace, you must use the `createElementNS()` method and specify the svg namespace.

---

4. Create the `Map.css` file and enter the following rule. This will change the fill color so the state outlines will be visible.

```
path {
    stroke: black;
    fill: khaki;
}
```

5. Save your change and display the `Map.html` file in a browser. The map should look like Figure 22-4.

Figure 22-4. *The initial map*

Styling the State Elements

Now that all the mechanical work is done, you can have some fun styling the path elements. As I demonstrated earlier with the snowman image, each element can be styled using CSS. You can also style them dynamically using JavaScript. I will show you how to use solid-color fills, gradients, and background images to format each element.

Using Basic Fill Colors

■ **Note** Throughout this chapter you will be using colors to style each state differently. In the print version of this book, some of these colors might not display well when converted to grayscale. You will want to work through the exercise or download the project to see the results of the styles being applied.

You'll start by adding some simple fill rules. Using a simple element selector, you already set the stroke color to black and the fill color to khaki. Now, to add some variety and to demonstrate using attribute selectors, you'll change the fill color based on the state code.

| **EXERCISE 22-4. ADDING BASIC FILL COLORS** |

The id attribute contains the two-letter state code, and the class attribute contains the state name. Using the first letter of the id attribute, you'll set the fill color as follows:

- A: Red
- N: Yellow
- M: Green
- C: Blue
- O: Purple
- I: Orange

1. Enter the following style rules to the Map.css file.

```
path[id^="A"] {
    fill: red;
}
path[id^="N"] {
    fill: yellow;
}
path[id^="M"] {
    fill: green;
}
path[id^="C"] {
fill: blue;
}
```

```
path[id^="O"] {
    fill: purple;
}
path[id^="I"] {
    fill: orange;
}
```

2. Refresh your browser, and the map should now look like Figure 22-5.

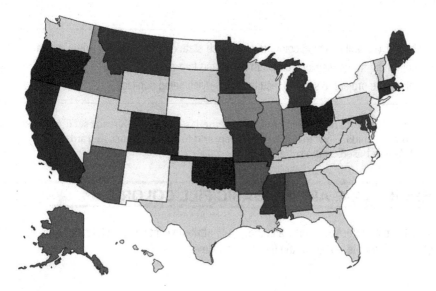

Figure 22-5. *The map with some basic styling*

3. As you're moving the mouse around the map, it would be nice to highlight the state that the mouse is currently pointing to. Add the following rule to the Map.css file:

```
path:hover {
    opacity: .5;
}
```

Using Gradient Fills

You can use gradient fills with SVG elements, but they are implemented differently than typical HTML elements. You first have to define the gradient in the HTML markup and then reference it using a URL.

EXERCISE 22-5. ADDING A GRADIENT FILL

1. Add the following defs element to the HTML document, inside the svg element:

```
<defs>
    <linearGradient id="blueGradient"
                    x1="0%" y1="0%"
                    x2="100%" y2="100%"
                    spreadMethod="pad">
        <stop offset="0%"   stop-color="#ffffff" stop-opacity="1"/>
        <stop offset="50%" stop-color="#6699cc" stop-opacity="1"/>
        <stop offset="100%" stop-color="#4466aa" stop-opacity="1"/>
    </linearGradient>
</defs>
```

The defs element is used to define something that can be referred to later in the document. It doesn't do anything until it is actually referenced. Here you are defining a linearGradient element and giving it the id blueGradient. You will reference it using the id attribute.

The attributes are different from the gradients you used in Chapter 12 but accomplish basically the same thing. The x1, y1, x2, and y2 attributes define a vector that specifies the direction of the gradient. In this case, it will start from the top-left corner and go to the bottom-right corner. This specifies three color values that define the gradient color at the beginning, midpoint, and end.

2. Now add the following rule at the end to the Map.css file. This will use the new gradient for the state of Wyoming.

```
path[id="WY"] {
    fill: url(#blueGradient);
}
```

3. Refresh the browser, and you should see a gradient fill for Wyoming, as shown in Figure 22-6.

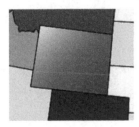

Figure 22-6. *Using a gradient fill*

Using a Background Image

You can also use an image file for the shape background. You will need to first define this as a pattern in the defs element and then reference it just like you did with the gradient. For this exercise, you'll use an image of the state flag of Texas and make this the background for that state.

EXERCISE 22-6. USING A BACKGROUND IMAGE

1. In the source code download for Chapter 22 there is a TX_Flag.jpg file; download this file.

2. Add the following code to the defs element in the HTML document that you created earlier. This will define the background image and specifies that the pattern should use the TX_Flag.jpg image file and stretch it to 377 x 226 pixels. This will make it large enough to cover the path element without needing to repeat.

```
<pattern id="TXflag" patternUnits="objectBoundingBox" width="1"
height="1">
    <image xlink:href="TX_Flag.jpg" x="0" y="0"
        width="377" height="226" />
</pattern>
```

3. Add the following rule to the Map.css file, which will use the new pattern for the state of Texas.

```
path[id="TX"] {
    fill: url(#TXflag);
}
```

4. Save your changes and refresh the browser. You should see the background image, as shown in Figure 22-7.

Figure 22-7. Using a background image

Since this is a chapter on SVG, I felt a little funny about using a bitmap image. You can see the degraded image quality when the image is stretched. The state flag of Texas is one of the easiest to draw with SVG, but I wanted to demonstrate that bitmapped images can be used within an SVG definition. But just for the record, Listing 22-2 shows the flag expressed in SVG (this was downloaded from the same Wikimedia Commons site I mentioned earlier and reformatted slightly).

Listing 22-2. The Texas State Flag in SVG

```
<rect width="1080" height="720" fill="#fff"/>
<rect y="360" width="1080" height="360" fill="#bf0a30"/>
<rect width="360" height="720" fill="#002868"/>
<g transform="translate(180,360)" fill="#fff">
    <g id="c">
        <path id="t" d="M 0,-135 v 135 h 67.5"
              transform="rotate(18 0,-135)"/>
        <use xlink:href="#t" transform="scale(-1,1)"/>
    </g>
    <use xlink:href="#c" transform="rotate(72)"/>
    <use xlink:href="#c" transform="rotate(144)"/>
    <use xlink:href="#c" transform="rotate(216)"/>
    <use xlink:href="#c" transform="rotate(288)"/>
</g>
```

Notice that the group element, g, is used to define a single path. This is rotated with five different angles to create a five-pointed star.

Altering Styles with JavaScript

One of the primary uses of this kind of application is to dynamically style each element based on some external data. For example, you might want to highlight states where you have sales locations. Or perhaps you want to set the colors based on some type of demographic such as population. So far, you have used only static styles, but you can just as easily set the styles using JavaScript.

In this example, you will first set the fill attribute on all path elements to khaki using JavaScript. This will replace the CSS property that sets the default color. This code will then set the fill color of the path element for Virginia. In a real application, you would normally define the style based on external data.

This exercise will also show you how to use JavaScript to respond to the mouseover and mouseout events. You will replace the path:hover rule and accomplish this using these event handlers.

EXERCISE 22-7. ADJUSTING STYLES USING JAVASCRIPT

1. Add the following function to the Map.js script:

```
function adjustStates() {
    var paths = document.getElementsByTagName("path");
    for (var i = 0; i < paths.length; i++) {
        paths[i].setAttribute("fill", "khaki");
    }

    var path = document.getElementById("VA");
    path.setAttribute("fill", "teal");
}
```

2. Call the adjustStates() method from the Map.js script.

   ```
   adjustStates();
   ```

3. In the Map.css file, remove the default khaki fill like this:

   ```
   path {
   stroke: black;
   /*fill: khaki; */
   }
   ```

4. Refresh the browser, and Virginia should no longer use the default color, as shown in Figure 22-8.

Figure 22-8. *Virginia styled with JavaScript*

5. Now you'll also use JavaScript to implement the hover style. You can use the event.target property to get the path element that triggered the event. You can then determine the state code by accessing its id attribute. Add the following methods to the Map.js script:

   ```
   function hoverState(e) {
       var event = e || window.event;
       var state = event.target.getAttribute("id");
       var path = document.getElementById(state);
       path.setAttribute("fill-opacity", "0.5");
   }

   function unhoverState(e) {
       var event = e || window.event;
       var state = event.target.getAttribute("id");
       var path = document.getElementById(state);
       path.setAttribute("fill-opacity", "1.0");
   }
   ```

6. Then bind the mouseover and mouseout event handlers by adding the code shown in bold to the adjustStates() function. This uses the addEventListener() method to bind hoverState() and unhoverState() event handlers to each path element.

```
function adjustStates() {
    var paths = document.getElementsByTagName("path");
    for (var i = 0; i < paths.length; i++) {
        paths[i].setAttributeNS(null, "fill", "khaki");

        paths[i].addEventListener("mouseover", hoverState, true);
        paths[i].addEventListener("mouseout", unhoverState, true);
    }

    var path = document.getElementById("VA");
    path.setAttributeNS(null, "fill", "teal");
}
```

■ **Caution**   In Internet Explorer, the `event` object is not passed to the event handler. Instead, it is made available through the global `window.event` property. The event handlers can be coded to work with either model by setting the event variable like this: `var event = e || window.event`. This will use the object passed in, if available, and if not, it will use the global `window.event` object. For this to work, however, you must register the event handlers by using the `addEventListener()` method. You cannot simply set the `mouseover` attribute.

---

7. Remove the `path:hover` style rule like this:

```
/*path:hover {
    opacity: .5;
}*/
```

8. Save your changes and refresh the browser. As you move the mouse around, the states should highlight just like they did with the `path:hover` style.

Adding Animation

A typical application of a map like this will allow the user to select a region and have something happen as a result of that selection. The page will display some information based on the item that was selected. To demonstrate that, you'll add some animation when the user clicks a state.

The CSS animation that I showed you in Chapter 15 does not work on SVG elements. Instead, you'll implement the animation using JavaScript. When a state is selected, you'll first make a copy of the selected element. Then you'll use a timer to gradually change its rotation angle. You need to make a copy so that as the image rotates, it doesn't leave a hole in the map. Also, the new element will be on top of all the others, so you don't have to worry about it being hidden by the other elements.

Once the copy of the element has completed its animation, you'll remove it from the document. Then you'll display an alert showing the state code and state name of the `path` that was selected.

EXERCISE 22-8. ADDING ANIMATION

1. Because this uses a 3D transform, you'll need to set some of the transform properties on the path elements. Add the following rule to the Map.css file:

```
path {
    transform-style: preserve-3d;
    perspective: 200px;
}
```

2. Then add the code shown in Listing 22-3 to the Map.js script.

Listing 22-3. Adding Functions to Support Animation

```
// Setup some global variables
var timer;
var stateCode;
var stateName;
var animate;
var angle;

function selectState(e) {
    var event = e || window.event;

    // Get the state code and state name
    stateCode = event.target.getAttribute("id");
    stateName = event.target.getAttribute("class");

    // Get the selected path element and then make a copy of it
    var path = document.getElementById(stateCode);
    animate = path.cloneNode(false);

    // Set some display properties and add the copy to the document
    animate.setAttribute("fill-opacity", "1.0");
    animate.setAttribute("stroke-width", "3");
    document.getElementById("map").appendChild(animate);

    angle = 0;

    // Setup a timer to run every 10 msec
    timer = setInterval(function () { animateState(); }, 10);
}
```

```
function animateState() {
    angle += 1;

    // If we've rotated 360 degress, stop the timer, destroy the copy
    // of the element, and show an alert
    if (angle > 360) {
        clearInterval(timer);
        animate.setAttribute("visibility", "hidden");
        var old = document.getElementById("map").removeChild(animate);

        alert(stateCode + " - " + stateName);

        return;
    }

    // Change the image rotation
    animate.style.transform = "rotateY(" + Math.round(angle) + "deg)";
}
```

The selectState() function gets the state code and state name from the selected path element. It then gets the path element and uses its cloneNode() method to make a copy of it. Because the mouse is currently over the selected path, it will have the opacity set to 50%. So, this code changes the opacity of the copy to 100%. It also sets the stroke width to give this element a wider border. The copy is then added to the document, and a timer is started to cause the animation.

Every 10 milliseconds, the animateState() function is called, which increments the angle and redraws the image. If the rotation has reached 360 degrees, this method cancels the timer and removes the copy of the path element. It also raises an alert to display the state code and state name.

3. Add another event handler by adding the code shown in bold to the adjustStates() function. This will call the selectState() method when the user clicks a path element.

```
function adjustStates() {
    var paths = document.getElementsByTagName("path");
    for (var i = 0; i < paths.length; i++) {
        paths[i].setAttribute("fill", "khaki");

        paths[i].addEventListener("mouseover", hoverState, true);
        paths[i].addEventListener("mouseout", unhoverState, true);
        paths[i].addEventListener("click", selectState, true);
    }

    var path = document.getElementById("VA");
    path.setAttribute("fill", "teal");
}
```

4. Refresh the browser and click a state, and you should see it fly off the page, as shown in Figure 22-9.

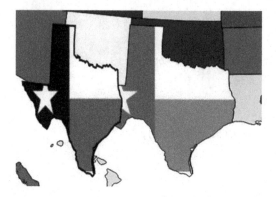

Figure 22-9. *Animating the selected state*

5. The image will then fly back into place, and an alert will appear, as shown in Figure 22-10.

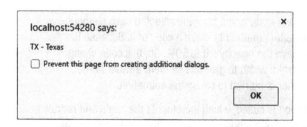

Figure 22-10. *The alert showing the name of the selected state*

Summary

In this chapter, I introduced SVG with a couple of fairly simple applications. An SVG image consists of multiple elements, which can be simple elements such as lines, circles, and rectangles or more complex options such as polygons and paths. The key feature of SVG is that each individual element can be styled independently both statically and dynamically. This enables much greater control and interaction. Also, because the image is based on an expression, the images can be scaled without affecting the image quality.

In the exercises in this chapter, you did the following:

*   Designed an image using simple geometric shapes

*   Created a stand-alone .svg image file

*   Displayed a map as a collection of path elements

*   Styled the path elements using a variety of selectors

*   Implemented animation on an SVG element

In the next chapter, I'll show you how to use the canvas element, which is a very different approach to graphical content in HTML5.

CHAPTER 23

Canvas

In this chapter, I'll show you how to use the canvas element in HTML5 to create some fun graphics. As you'll see, it is very different from SVG, which you explored in the previous chapter. I will discuss the differences in more detail later, but the main thing you'll notice is that canvas is completely implemented in JavaScript. The only part that is in the markup is a simple element definition like this:

```
<canvas id="myCanvas" width="400" height="400">
    Canvas is not supported on this browser
</canvas>
```

Instead, you'll define the content by calling the various drawing methods using JavaScript. Just like with the audio and video elements, the markup within the canvas element is used when the browser does not support canvas. You can use this to provide the appropriate fallback content.

Through the exercises in the chapter, you will create three different canvas implementations that, collectively, will demonstrate the capability of canvas. You will create the following:

- A chess board with moving chess pieces

- A simple model of the solar system

- A page that demonstrates the various ways shapes can be composited

Of course, you can use your imagination to apply these principles in any number of fun and compelling graphical applications.

Creating a Chess Board

In the first application, you'll draw a chess board, which is just a series of squares with alternating colors. I'll show you how to use a gradient to make the board a little more interesting. You'll use image files to draw the chess pieces in the appropriate squares. Finally, you'll apply a little bit of animation to move the pieces around the board. This will give you a good sense of how basic drawing techniques are used before getting into more advanced topics.

The canvas element is appropriately named because it provides an area that you can use to draw on. When you create a canvas element, you define its size using the height and width attributes. You can specify other attributes through markup or CSS to specify the margin, padding, and border. These attributes affect where the element is positioned within the page. However, you cannot modify any of the content within the element. The canvas element itself simply defines a blank area on which you can create your masterpiece.

When you create a canvas element in HTML, you will generally assign an id attribute so you can access it in JavaScript using the getElementById() method. You don't have to; you can access it using the getElementsByTagName() method or use the new query selectors I described in Chapter 18.

© Mark J. Collins 2017

M. J. Collins, *Pro HTML5 with CSS, JavaScript, and Multimedia*, DOI 10.1007/978-1-4842-2463-2_23

Once you have the canvas element, you'll then get its drawing context by calling getContext(). You must specify which context to use. The context specifies a set of API functions and drawing capabilities. The only one that is generally available is 2d, and we will be using that exclusively in this chapter.

■ **Note** The other possible context is not 3d as you might expect; it's WebGL or, in some browsers, experimental-webgl. This is not quite ready for prime time and it is very different from the 2d context.

Drawing Rectangles

Unlike SVG, the only shape that you can draw directly is a rectangle. You can draw more complex shapes using paths, which I'll explain later. There are three methods that you can use to draw rectangles.

- clearRect(): Clears the specified rectangle
- strokeRect(): Draws a border around the specified rectangle with no fill
- fillRect(): Draws a filled-in rectangle

Each of these methods takes four parameters. The first two define the x and y coordinates of the top-left corner of the rectangle. The last two parameters specify the width and height, respectively. The drawing context has the strokeStyle and fillStyle properties that control how the border or fill will be drawn. You set these before drawing the rectangle. Once set, all subsequent shapes are drawn with these properties until you change the properties.

■ **Tip** Just like SVG, in canvas, the top-left corner of the canvas element has the x and y coordinates of 0, 0.

To demonstrate drawing rectangles, you'll start by drawing the chess board, which contains eight rows of eight squares each.

EXERCISE 23-1. DRAWING A SIMPLE CHESS BOARD

1. Create a new web page called **Chess.html**, using the basic markup:

```
<!DOCTYPE html>

<html lang="en">
    <head>
        <meta charset="utf-8" />
        <title>Chapter 23 - Chess</title>
        <script src="Chess.js" defer></script>
    </head>
    <body>
    </body>
</html>
```

2. Add a `canvas` element by inserting the following markup in the `body` element:

```
<canvas id="board" width ="600" height ="600">
    Not supported
</canvas>
```

3. Then create a `Chess.js` script file using the following code.

```
"use strict";

// Get the canvas context
var chessCanvas = document.getElementById("board");
var chessContext = chessCanvas.getContext("2d");
```

4. Add a function to draw the chessboard to the `Chess.js` file and then call this function using the following code.

```
// Draw the chess board
function drawBoard() {

    chessContext.clearRect(0, 0, 600, 600);

    chessContext.fillStyle = "red";
    chessContext.strokeStyle = "red";

    // Draw the alternating squares
    for (var x = 0; x < 8; x++) {
        for (var y = 0; y < 8; y++) {
            if ((x + y) % 2) {
                chessContext.fillRect(75 * x, 75 * y, 75, 75);
            }
        }
    }

    // Add a border around the entire board
    chessContext.strokeRect(0, 0, 600, 600);
}

drawBoard();
```

The `drawBoard()` function first clears the area on which it will be drawing. It then uses nested `for` loops to draw the squares. The `fillStyle` and `strokeStyle` attributes are both set to red; by default these are both black. Notice that it draws only the red squares. Since the entire area was cleared first, any area not drawn on will be white. This code uses nested `for` loops to iterate through the eight rows and eight columns. The red squares are the ones where the sum of the row and the column is odd. For even-numbered rows (0, 2, 4, and 6), the odd columns (1, 3, 5, and 7) will be red. For odd-numbered rows, the even-numbered columns will be red. To clean up the edge squares, a red border is drawn around the entire board.

5. Save your changes and display the Chess.html page in a browser. The page should look like Figure 23-1.

Figure 23-1. *The initial chessboard*

Using Gradients

You can also use a gradient to fill a shape instead of a solid color. To do that, you must first create a gradient object using the drawing context's createLinearGradient() method. This method takes four parameters, which are the x and y coordinates of the beginning and ending points of the gradient. This allows you to specify whether the gradient should go from top to bottom, left to right, or corner to corner. The gradient is computed across the entire canvas. You cannot define gradients for individual elements.

You must then define the color stops. Each color stop defines a position along the gradient and a color. At a minimum, you'll need color stops at 0 and 1, which define the beginning and ending colors. You can also add color stops in between these if you want to control the transition. For example, if you want to define the color at the halfway point, use 0.5.

Finally, you'll use this gradient to specify the fillStyle property. To try it, add the following code shown in bold:

```
function drawBoard() {

    chessContext.clearRect(0, 0, 600, 600);

    var gradient = chessContext.createLinearGradient(0, 600, 600, 0);
    gradient.addColorStop(0.0, "#D50005");
    gradient.addColorStop(0.5, "#E27883");
    gradient.addColorStop(1.0, "#FFDDDD");

    chessContext.fillStyle = gradient;
    chessContext.strokeStyle = "red";
```

Save your changes and refresh the browser. The page should now look like Figure 23-2. Notice that the color transitions across the canvas, not across each square.

Figure 23-2. *The board using a gradient fill*

Using Images

Now you're ready to add the chess pieces, which will be drawn using image files. It is really easy to add an image to a canvas. You create an Image object, set its src property as the location of the image file, and then call the drawing context's drawImage() method like this:

```
var myImage = new Image();
myImage.src = "images/sample.jpg";
context.drawImage(myImage, 0,0, 50, 100);
```

The first parameter of the drawImage() method specifies the image that will be drawn. This can be an Image object, as I've shown here. Alternatively, you can also specify an img, video, or canvas element that is already on the page. The next two parameters specify the x and y locations of the top-left corner of the image. The fourth and fifth parameters are optional and specify the width and height, respectively, that the image will be scaled to fit into. If you don't specify these parameters, the image will be drawn using its intrinsic size.

The drawImage() method also allows you to supply four additional parameters. These are used to specify only the portion of the image that should be displayed on the canvas. These additional parameters include an x coordinate and a y coordinate that specify the top-left corner, as well as a width and height to define the specified portion. Use the last four parameters if you want only a portion of the image to be drawn. If these are omitted, the entire image will be displayed.

In this application you will be drawing 32 pieces using 12 different images. Also, later in this chapter you will be adding code to move the pieces around. To facilitate this, you'll add some structure to your application. You will define a class that will store attributes about a chess piece such as the image to use and its location on the board. Then you'll implement a generic drawing function that uses the details from these attributes.

EXERCISE 23-2. DRAWING CHESS PIECES

1. Create a new folder in your web application, called **Images**, to store the image files.

2. The images for the chess pieces are included in the source code download file. You'll find these in the Chapter23\Images folder. Drag all 12 files to your Images folder.

3. Add the following variable declarations to the beginning of Chess.js file (just after the chessCanvas and chessContext variables). This will define a variable to reference an Image object for each of the 12 image files. It will also define an array that you will be using to store the 32 chess pieces.

```
// Define the chess piece images
var imgPawn = new Image();
var imgRook = new Image();
var imgKnight = new Image();
var imgBishop = new Image();
var imgQueen = new Image();
var imgKing = new Image();
var imgPawnW = new Image();
var imgRookW = new Image();
var imgKnightW = new Image();
var imgBishopW = new Image();
var imgQueenW = new Image();
var imgKingW = new Image();

// Define an array to store 32 pieces
var pieces = new Array(32);
```

4. Add the loadImages() function to the Chess.js file.

```
function loadImages() {
    imgPawn.src = "Images/pawn.png";
    imgRook.src = "Images/rook.png";
    imgKnight.src = "Images/knight.png";
    imgBishop.src = "Images/bishop.png";
    imgQueen.src = "Images/queen.png";
    imgKing.src = "Images/king.png";
    imgPawnW.src = "Images/wpawn.png";
    imgRookW.src = "Images/wrook.png";
    imgKnightW.src = "Images/wknight.png";
    imgBishopW.src = "Images/wbishop.png";
    imgQueenW.src = "Images/wqueen.png";
    imgKingW.src = "Images/wking.png";
}
```

5. Now you're ready to define the chess pieces. You'll use an object definition that will store the properties needed to draw the chess piece. The `image` property contains a reference to the appropriate `Image` object. The x and y properties specify the square that the piece is in, from 0 to 7, left to right and top to bottom. The `height` and `width` properties indicate the size of the image, which will vary depending on the type of piece. The `killed` property is used to indicate whether the piece has been captured. Captured images are not displayed. Add the following code to the `Chess.js`:

```
// Define a class to store the piece properties
function ChessPiece() {
    this.image = null;
    this.x = 0;
    this.y = 0;
    this.height = 0;
    this.width = 0;
    this.killed = false;
}
```

6. Add the following functions to the `Chess.js` file. This implements the `drawPiece()` function that draws a single chess piece based on the class properties. It also implements a `drawAllPieces()` function that will draw each of the pieces defined in the `pieces` array.

```
// Draw a chess piece
function drawPiece(p) {
    if (!p.killed)
        chessContext.drawImage(p.image,
                        (75 - p.width) / 2 + (75 * p.x),
                        73 - p.height + (75 * p.y),
                        p.width,
                        p.height);
}

// Draw all of the chess pieces
function drawAllPieces() {
    for (var i = 0; i < 32; i++) {
        if (pieces[i] != null) {
            drawPiece(pieces[i]);
        }
    }
}
```

7. Now you need to create 32 instances of the `ChessPiece` class and specify all of the appropriate properties. Add the `createPieces()` function shown in Listing 23-1. This function creates the instances of the `ChessPiece` class, storing them in the `pieces` array, and sets the properties of each one.

■ **Tip** Since this is rather long and tedious, I made this function available in the source code download as a separate file. If you prefer, instead of typing the function from Listing 23-1, you can find the `createPieces.js` file in the `Chapter23` folder and drag this to your web project. Then add this reference in the `head` element:

`<script src="createPieces.js" defer></script>`

Listing 23-1. Implementing the createPieces() Function

```
function createPieces() {
    var piece;

    // Black pawns
    for (var i = 0; i < 8; i++) {
        piece = new ChessPiece();
        piece.image = imgPawn,
        piece.x = i;
        piece.y = 1;
        piece.height = 50;
        piece.width = 28;

        pieces[i] = piece;
    }

    // Black rooks
    piece = new ChessPiece();
    piece.image = imgRook;
    piece.x = 0;
    piece.y = 0;
    piece.height = 60;
    piece.width = 36;
    pieces[8] = piece;

    piece = new ChessPiece();
    piece.image = imgRook;
    piece.x = 7;
    piece.y = 0;
    piece.height = 60;
    piece.width = 36;
    pieces[9] = piece;

    // Black knights
    piece = new ChessPiece();
    piece.image = imgKnight;
    piece.x = 1;
    piece.y = 0;
    piece.height = 60;
    piece.width = 36;
    pieces[10] = piece;
```

```
piece = new ChessPiece();
piece.image = imgKnight;
piece.x = 6;
piece.y = 0;
piece.height = 60;
piece.width = 36;
pieces[11] = piece;

// Black bishops
piece = new ChessPiece();
piece.image = imgBishop;
piece.x = 2;
piece.y = 0;
piece.height = 65;
piece.width = 30;
pieces[12] = piece;

piece = new ChessPiece();
piece.image = imgBishop;
piece.x = 5;
piece.y = 0;
piece.height = 65;
piece.width = 30;
pieces[13] = piece;

// Black queen
piece = new ChessPiece();
piece.image = imgQueen;
piece.x = 3;
piece.y = 0;
piece.height = 70;
piece.width = 32;
pieces[14] = piece;

// Black king
piece = new ChessPiece();
piece.image = imgKing;
piece.x = 4;
piece.y = 0;
piece.height = 70;
piece.width = 28;
pieces[15] = piece;

// White pawns
for (var i = 0; i < 8; i++) {
    piece = new ChessPiece();
    piece.image = imgPawnW,
    piece.x = i;
    piece.y = 6;
    piece.height = 50;
    piece.width = 28;

    pieces[16 + i] = piece;
}
```

```
// White rooks
piece = new ChessPiece();
piece.image = imgRookW;
piece.x = 0;
piece.y = 7;
piece.height = 60;
piece.width = 36;
pieces[24] = piece;

piece = new ChessPiece();
piece.image = imgRookW;
piece.x = 7;
piece.y = 7;
piece.height = 60;
piece.width = 36;
pieces[25] = piece;

// White knights
piece = new ChessPiece();
piece.image = imgKnightW;
piece.x = 1;
piece.y = 7;
piece.height = 60;
piece.width = 36;
pieces[26] = piece;

piece = new ChessPiece();
piece.image = imgKnightW;
piece.x = 6;
piece.y = 7;
piece.height = 60;
piece.width = 36;
pieces[27] = piece;

// White bishops
piece = new ChessPiece();
piece.image = imgBishopW;
piece.x = 2;
piece.y = 7;
piece.height = 65;
piece.width = 30;
pieces[28] = piece;

piece = new ChessPiece();
piece.image = imgBishopW;
piece.x = 5;
piece.y = 7;
piece.height = 65;
piece.width = 30;
pieces[29] = piece;
```

```
// White queen
piece = new ChessPiece();
piece.image = imgQueenW;
piece.x = 3;
piece.y = 7;
piece.height = 70;
piece.width = 32;
pieces[30] = piece;

// White king
piece = new ChessPiece();
piece.image = imgKingW;
piece.x = 4;
piece.y = 7;
piece.height = 70;
piece.width = 28;
pieces[31] = piece;
}
```

8. Modify the `drawBoard()` function to also call `drawAllPieces()` after the board has been drawn.

```
// Add a border around the entire board
chessContext.strokeRect(0, 0, 600, 600);

    drawAllPieces();
}
```

9. Finally, replace the call to `drawBoard()` function in the `Chess.js` file with the following code. This will call the `loadImages()` and `createPieces()` functions and wait 1 second before calling `drawBoard()`.

```
loadImages();
createPieces();

setTimeout(drawBoard, 1000);
```

10. Save your changes and refresh the browser. You should now see the chess pieces, as shown in Figure 23-3.

Figure 23-3. *The chess board with the pieces displayed*

■ **Note**   When you create an Image object and set its src property, the specified image file is downloaded asynchronously. It's possible that the file has not been loaded before the drawImage() function is called. If this happens, the image is not displayed. The 1-second delay is a simple solution to this problem. You could implement the onload event handler for each Image object, which is called when the image has been loaded. This is a bit complicated since you'll need to wait for all 12 images to be loaded.

Adding Simple Animation

To demonstrate simple animation using canvas, you'll move the pieces around. The function that draws each piece computes the location based on the square that the piece is in. To move a piece, you just need to update the x or y property and then redraw it.

When you redraw a piece in its new location, it is still visible in the old location as well. Also, if you were to capture a piece by moving a piece in the same square as another, you would end up with two pieces in the same square. You could implement some complex logic to clear the square and redraw a red or white square before moving the piece. However, for this demonstration, you will simply clear the entire canvas and redraw the board and all of the pieces.

To implement the automation, you'll create a makeNextMove() function. This will adjust the x and y positions of a chess piece and then redraw the board and all of the pieces. You'll use the setInterval() function to call this repeatedly so the pieces will move in succession.

EXERCISE 23-3. ANIMATING THE CHESS PIECES

1. Add the following variables shown in bold near the beginning of the
    Chess.js file:

```
// Define an array to store 32 pieces
var pieces = new Array(32);
var moveNumber = -1;
var timer;
```

2. Implement the makeNextMove() function in the Chess.js file using the following
    code. This code "moves" a piece by adjusting its x and y properties. It keeps track
    of the move number and uses this to adjust the appropriate piece. The seventh
    move captures a piece and sets its killed property. Since this ends the animation,
    the seventh move also uses the clearTimer() function so no more timer events
    will occur. After each move, the board and all the pieces are redrawn. After the
    seventh move, this function also uses the fillText() method, which is used to
    write text to the canvas.

```
function makeNextMove() {
    function inner() {
        if (moveNumber === 1) {
            pieces[20].y--;
        }
        if (moveNumber === 2) {
            pieces[4].y += 2;
        }
        if (moveNumber === 3) {
            pieces[29].y = 4;
            pieces[29].x = 2;
        }
        if (moveNumber === 4) {
            pieces[6].y++;
        }
        if (moveNumber === 5) {
            pieces[30].x = 5;
            pieces[30].y = 5;
        }
        if (moveNumber === 6) {
            pieces[7].y++;
        }
        if (moveNumber === 7) {
            pieces[30].x = 5;
            pieces[30].y = 1;
            pieces[5].killed = true;
            clearInterval(timer);
        }
```

```
            moveNumber++;

            drawBoard();
            drawAllPieces();

            if (moveNumber > 7) {
                chessContext.font = "30pt Arial";
                chessContext.fillStyle = "black";
                chessContext.fillText("Checkmate!", 200, 220);
            }
        }

        return inner;
    }
```

3. Add the following code to the Chess.js file. This will call the makeNextMove() function every 2 seconds.

   ```
   timer = setInterval(makeNextMove(), 2000);
   ```

4. Save your changes and refresh the browser. After a series of moves, the page should look like Figure 23-4.

Figure 23-4. *The completed chess board*

▪ **Note** The makeNextMove() function uses an often misunderstood feature of JavaScript called closure, which was covered in Chapter 3. This function defines another function called inner(), which does the actual work. The inner() function is then returned. The makeNextMove() function will be called by the window object when the timer expires. However, all of the variables that it uses, such as the array of chess pieces, will be out of scope. The inner() function will be able to access these variables, so this works around the scope issue.

Modeling the Solar System

For the next canvas, you'll draw a moving model of the solar system. For the sake of time, you'll show only the earth, sun, and moon. This implementation will take advantage of these two important features of canvas:

- Paths
- Transformations

Using Paths

As I mentioned earlier, the only simple shape that canvas supports is the rectangle, which you used in the previous example. For all other shapes you must define a path. The basic approach to defining paths in canvas is similar to SVG. You use a move command to set the starting point and then some combination of line and curve commands to draw a shape.

In canvas, you always start with a beginPath() command. After calling the desired drawing commands, the path is completed by calling either stroke() to draw an outline of the shape or fill() to fill in the shape. The shape is not actually drawn to the canvas until either stroke() or fill() is called. If you call beginPath() again, before completing the current shape (with a call to stroke() or fill()), the canvas will ignore the previous uncompleted commands. The same strokeStyle and fillStyle properties that you used with rectangles also define the color of the path.

The actual drawing commands are as follows:

- moveTo()
- lineTo()
- arcTo()
- bezierCurveTo()
- quadraticCurveTo()

In addition, these functions can be used for drawing:

- closePath(): This performs a lineTo() command from the current position to the starting position to close in the shape. If you use the fill() command, the closePath() function is automatically called if you're not currently at the starting position.

- arc(): This draws an arc at the specified location; you don't have to move there first. However, this is still treated as a path; you need to first call beginPath(), and the arc is not actually drawn until you call either stroke() or fill().

Drawing Arcs

The arc() command is one that you'll likely use a lot and will be important in this example. The arc() command takes the following parameters:

```
arc(x, y, radius, start, end, counterclockwise)
```

The first two parameters specify the x and y coordinates of the center point. The third parameter specifies the radius. The fourth and fifth parameters determine the starting and ending points of the arc. These are specified as an angle from the x-axis. The 0° angle is the right side of the circle; a 90° angle would be the bottom edge of the circle. The angles are specified in radians, however, not degrees.

Unless you're drawing a full circle, the direction of the arc is important. For example, if you drew an arc from 0° to 90°, the arc would be 1/4 of a circle, from the right side to the bottom. However, using the same endpoints but drawing in a counterclockwise direction, that arc would be 3/4 of the circle. The final parameter, if true, indicates that the arc should be drawn in a counterclockwise direction. This parameter is optional. If you don't specify it, it will draw the arc in a clockwise direction.

Using Transformations

At first, transformations in canvas may seem a bit confusing, but they can be quite helpful once you understand how they work. First, transformations have no effect on what has already been drawn on the canvas. Instead, transformations modify the grid system that will be used to draw subsequent shapes. I will demonstrate three types of transformations in this chapter.

- Translating
- Rotating
- Scaling

As I mentioned earlier, a canvas element uses a grid system where the origin is at the top-left corner of the canvas. So, a point at 100, 50 will be 100 pixels to the right and 50 pixels down from that corner. Transformations simply adjust the grid system. For example, the following command will shift the origin 100 pixels to the right and 50 pixels down:

```
context.translate (100, 50);
```

This is illustrated in Figure 23-5.

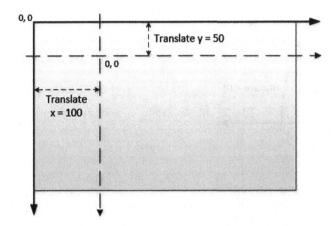

Figure 23-5. *Translating the context origin*

Now when you move to 10, 20, since this is relative to the new origin, the actual position (relative to the canvas), will be 110, 70. You might be wondering why you would want to do this. Well, suppose you were drawing a picture of the U.S. flag, which has 50 stars on it. A five-pointed star is a fairly complex shape to draw, which will require a number of drawing commands. Once you have drawn the first star, you'll need to repeat the process 49 more times, each time using different values.

By simply translating the context to the right a little, you can repeat the same commands using the same values. But now the star will be in a different location. Granted, you could accomplish the same thing by creating a drawStar() function that accepted x, y parameters. Then call this 50 times, passing in different values. However, once you get used to using transformation, you will find this easier, especially with the other types such as rotation.

The rotate transformation doesn't move the origin; instead, it rotates the x- and y-axes by the specified amount. A positive amount is used for a clockwise rotation, and a negative value is used to rotate counterclockwise. Figure 23-6 demonstrates how a rotate transformation works.

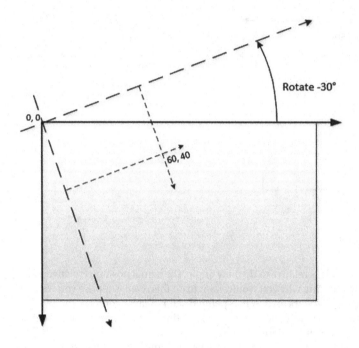

Figure 23-6. *Rotating the drawing context's grid*

■ **Note** I indicated the rotation angle as 30° since that is what most people are familiar with. However, the `rotate()` command expects the value in radians. If your geometry is a little rusty, a full circle is 360° or 2π radians. In JavaScript, you can use the `Math.PI` property to get the value of π (Pi). For example, 30° is 1/12 of a full circle, so you can write this as (`Math.PI*2/12`). In general, radians are calculated as `degrees` * (`Math.PI/180`).

You can use multiple transformations. For example, you can translate the origin and then rotate the x- or y-axis. You can also rotate the grid some more and translate again. Each transformation is always relative to the current position and orientation.

Saving the Context State

The state of a drawing context includes the various properties such as `fillStyle` and `strokeStyle` that you have already used. It also includes the accumulation of all transformations that have been applied. If you start using multiple transformations, getting back to the original state may be difficult. Fortunately, the drawing context provides the ability to save and then restore the state of the context.

The current state is saved by calling the `save()` function. Saving the state pushes the current state onto a stack. Calling the `restore()` function pops the most recently saved state off the stack and makes that the current state. This is illustrated in Figure 23-7.

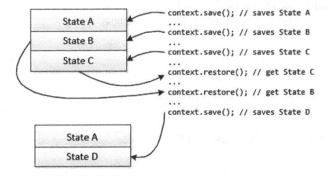

Figure 23-7. *Saving and restoring the drawing context state*

You should generally save the state before doing any transformations, especially complex ones. When you have finished drawing whatever elements needed the transformation, you can restore the state to the way it was. Remember, changing the state by setting the fillStyle or performing a transformation does not affect what has already been drawn.

Drawing the Solar System

With these features at your disposal, let's draw a simple model of the solar system.

EXERCISE 23-4. MODELING THE SOLAR SYSTEM

1. Create a new web page, **Solar.html**, using the basic markup:

```
<!DOCTYPE html>

<html lang="en">
    <head>
        <meta charset="utf-8" />
        <title>Chapter 23 - Solar System</title>
        <script src="Solar.js" defer></script>
    </head>
    <body>
    </body>
</html>
```

2. Add the canvas element inside the body element.

```
<canvas id="solarSystem" width="450" height="400">
    Not supported
</canvas>
```

3. Add a new `Solar.js` script using the following code. This code gets the `canvas` element and then obtains the `2d` drawing context, just like the previous example.

```
"use strict";

// Get the canvas context
var solarCanvas = document.getElementById("solarSystem");
var solarContext = solarCanvas.getContext("2d");
```

4. Add the `animateSS()` function to the `Solar.js` file using the following code.

```
function animateSS() {
    var ss = document.getElementById('solarSystem')
    var ssContext = ss.getContext('2d');

    // Clear the canvas and draw the background
    ssContext.clearRect(0, 0, 450, 400);
    ssContext.fillStyle = "#2F1D92";
    ssContext.fillRect(0, 0, 450, 400);

    ssContext.save();

    // Draw the sun
    ssContext.translate(220, 200);
    ssContext.fillStyle = "yellow";
    ssContext.beginPath();
    ssContext.arc(0, 0, 15, 0, Math.PI * 2, true);
    ssContext.fill();

    // Draw the earth orbit
    ssContext.strokeStyle = "black";
    ssContext.beginPath();
    ssContext.arc(0, 0, 150, 0, Math.PI * 2);
    ssContext.stroke();

    ssContext.restore()
}
```

The `animateSS()` function is what does the real work. It clears the entire area and then fills it with dark blue. The rest of the code relies on transformations, so it first saves the drawing context and then restores it when finished.

This `animateSS()` function uses the `translate()` function to move the origin to the approximate midpoint of the canvas. The sun and the earth orbits are drawn using the `arc()` function. Notice the center point for both is 0, 0 since the context's origin is now in the middle of the canvas. Also, notice the start angle is 0 and the end angle is specified as `Math.PI * 2`. In radians, this is a full circle or 360°. The arc for the sun is filled in, and the orbit is not.

5. Call the `setInterval()` function to call the `animateSS()` function every 100 milliseconds.

```
setInterval(animateSS, 100);
```

6. Display the page in the browser. So far, the drawing is not very interesting; it's a sun with an orbit drawn around it, as shown in Figure 23-8.

Figure 23-8. *The initial solar system drawing*

Now you'll draw the earth and animate it around the orbit. Normally the earth will revolve around the sun once every 365.24 days, but we'll speed this up a bit and complete the trip in 60 seconds. To determine where to put the earth each time the canvas is redrawn, you must calculate the number of seconds. The amount of rotation per second is calculated as `Math.PI *2 / 60`. Multiply this value by the number of seconds to determine the angle where the earth should be.

7. Add the following code that is shown in bold. This code uses the `rotate()` function to rotate the drawing context the appropriate angle. Since the arc for the earth orbit is 150px, this code then uses the `translate()` function to move the context 150 pixels to the right so the earth can be drawn at the adjusted 0,0 coordinate. Notice that this is combining two separate transforms, one to rotate based the earth position in its orbit and one to translate the appropriate distance from the sun. The earth is then drawn using a filled arc with a center point of 0,0, the new origin of the context.

```
// Draw the earth orbit
ssContext.strokeStyle = "black";
ssContext.beginPath();
ssContext.arc(0, 0, 150, 0, Math.PI * 2);
ssContext.stroke();

// Compute the current time in seconds (use the milliseconds
// to allow for fractional parts).
var now = new Date();
var seconds = ((now.getSeconds() * 1000) + now.getMilliseconds()) / 1000;
```

```
//------------------------------------------------
// Earth
//------------------------------------------------
// Rotate the context once every 60 seconds
var anglePerSecond = ((Math.PI * 2) / 60);
ssContext.rotate(anglePerSecond * seconds);
ssContext.translate(150, 0);

// Draw the earth
ssContext.fillStyle = "green";
ssContext.beginPath();
ssContext.arc(0, 0, 10, 0, Math.PI * 2, true);
ssContext.fill();

ssContext.restore()
```

8. Save your changes and refresh the browser. Now you should see the earth make its way around the sun, as shown in Figure 23-9.

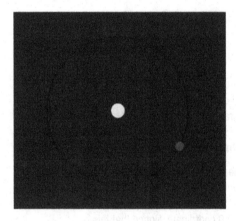

Figure 23-9. *Adding the earth to the drawing*

Now you'll show the moon revolving around the earth, which will demonstrate the real power of using transformations. The specific position of the moon is based on two moving objects. While it's certainly possible to compute this using some complex formulas (scientists have been doing this for centuries) with transformations, you don't have to. The drawing context was rotated the appropriate angle based on current time (number of seconds). It was then translated by the radius of the orbit, so the earth is now at the origin of the context. It doesn't really matter where the earth is; you can simply draw the moon relative to the current origin.

9. You will now draw the moon just like you drew the earth. Instead of the origin being at the sun and rotating the earth around the sun, the origin is on the earth, and you'll rotate the moon around the earth. The moon will rotate around the earth approximately once each month; in other words, it will complete about 12 revolutions for each earth orbit. So, you'll need to rotate 12 times faster. The `anglePerSecond` is now computed as `12 * ((Math.PI * 2) / 60)`. Add the following code shown in bold.

```
// Draw the earth
ssContext.fillStyle = "green";
ssContext.beginPath();
ssContext.arc(0, -0, 10, 0, Math.PI * 2, true);
ssContext.fill();

//---------------------------------------------
// Moon
//---------------------------------------------
// Rotate the context 12 times for every earth revolution
anglePerSecond = 12 * ((Math.PI * 2) / 60);
ssContext.rotate(anglePerSecond * seconds);
ssContext.translate(0, 35);

// draw the moon
ssContext.fillStyle = "white";
ssContext.beginPath();
ssContext.arc(0, 0, 5, 0, Math.PI * 2, true);
ssContext.fill();

ssContext.restore()
```

■ **Note** There are about 12.368 lunar months per solar year. You can make your model more accurate by using this figure instead of 12 in the preceding code.

10. Save your changes and refresh the browser. You should now see the moon rotating around the earth, as shown in Figure 23-10.

Figure 23-10. Including the moon

Applying Scaling

Before you finish this model, there's one minor correction that you'll make. The earth's orbit is not actually a perfect circle. This attribute is known as eccentricity. (If you're curious about orbital eccentricity, check out the article at http://en.wikipedia.org/wiki/Orbital_eccentricity). To model this in your drawing, you'll stretch the orbit, making it a little bit wider than it is tall. To do this, you'll use scaling.

The scale() function performs the third type of transformation. This function takes two parameters that specify the scaling along the x- and y-axes. A scale factor of 1 is the normal scale. A factor less than 1 will compress the drawing, and a factor greater than 1 will stretch it. While the imperfection in the earth's orbit is extremely slight, you'll exaggerate it here and use a scale factor of 1.1 for the x-axis.

Add the following code shown in bold just before the earth orbit is drawn:

```
// Draw the earth orbit
ssContext.scale(1.1, 1);
ssContext.strokeStyle = "black";
```

Refresh the browser; the page should look like Figure 23-11.

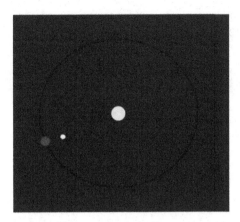

Figure 23-11. *Adding scaling*

You now have a slightly out-of-shape orbit. By simply changing the scale factor, all the various drawing elements were adjusted proportionally. Also, after restoring the context, the scaling is restored to normal so subsequent elements are drawn correctly.

■ **Note**   The alignment in Figure 23-11 demonstrates a solar eclipse, where the moon passes between the earth and the sun, casting a shadow over the earth.

Clipping a Canvas

I want to cover one more feature related to paths. Earlier I said that after you call beginPath() and then the desired drawing functions, you can call either stroke() or fill(). There is one more function you can call as well: clip(). The clip() function will use the path that you just defined and will not allow anything to be drawn outside of that path. This doesn't affect what has already been drawn, but any future shapes will be restricted to the clipping area defined by this path.

To demonstrate this, you'll go back to the chess board example and define a clipping path using an arc. Go to the chess.js script and add the code shown in bold to the drawBoard() function.

```
var gradient = chessContext.createLinearGradient(0, 600, 600, 0);
gradient.addColorStop(0, "#D50005");
gradient.addColorStop(0.5, "#E27883");
gradient.addColorStop(1, "#FFDDDD");

// Clip the path
chessContext.beginPath();
chessContext.arc(300, 300, 300, 0, (Math.PI * 2), true);
chessContext.clip();

chessContext.fillStyle = gradient;
chessContext.strokeStyle = "red";

// Draw the alternating squares
```

This defines a circle on the board, and anything outside of that circle will not be visible. Display the Chess.html file in a browser, which should look like Figure 23-12.

Figure 23-12. *The chess board with a clipping path*

■ **Note**   If you define the clipping path after the board is drawn, the entire board will be drawn, but the pieces will be cropped, so any part that is outside the clipping area will be hidden.

Understanding Compositing

With all the shapes you have drawn so far, the one drawn last overlaid, or hid, whatever preceded it. This behavior is referred to as compositing. The default behavior, called source-over, is to draw the current shape on top of whatever may already be on the canvas, as you've seen. The compositing terminology uses *source* to refer to the shape being drawn and *destination* as the result of what was previously drawn. In addition to source-over, there are 10 other behaviors that you can configure using the globalCompositeOperation property. These are best explained by seeing a sample of each.

In this exercise, you will overlap a red square with a blue circle. You will do this 11 times, each time using a different value for the globalCompositeOperation property. To make this work correctly, you'll create 11 canvas elements, drawing the same elements on each.

EXERCISE 23-5. EXPLORING COMPOSITING

1. Create a new web page, **Compositing.html**, using the basic markup:

```
<!DOCTYPE html>

<html lang="en">
    <head>
        <meta charset="utf-8" />
        <title>Chapter 23 - Compositing</title>
        <script src="Compositing.js" defer></script>
        <link rel="stylesheet" href="Compositing.css" />
    </head>
    <body>
    </body>
</html>
```

2. In the body element, create 11 new canvas elements using the following markup.

```
<div>
    <canvas id="composting1" width="120" height="120"></canvas>
    <br />source-over
</div>
<div>
    <canvas id="composting2" width="120" height="120"></canvas>
    <br />destination-over
</div>
<div>
    <canvas id="composting3" width="120" height="120"></canvas>
    <br />source-in
</div>
<div>
    <canvas id="composting4" width="120" height="120"></canvas>
    <br />destination-in
</div>
<div>
    <canvas id="composting5" width="120" height="120"></canvas>
    <br />source-out
</div>
<div>
    <canvas id="composting6" width="120" height="120"></canvas>
    <br />destination-out
</div>
<div>
    <canvas id="composting7" width="120" height="120"></canvas>
    <br />source-atop
</div>
<div>
    <canvas id="composting8" width="120" height="120"></canvas>
    <br />destination-atop
</div>
```

435

```
<div>
    <canvas id="composting9" width="120" height="120"></canvas>
    <br />xor
</div>
<div>
    <canvas id="composting10" width="120" height="120"></canvas>
    <br />copy
</div>
<div>
    <canvas id="composting11" width="120" height="120"></canvas>
    <br />lighter
</div>
```

3. Create a `Compositing.css` file with the following style rule. This will format the canvas elements into three columns so you can see all 11 examples on one screen.

```css
body div {
    -webkit-column-count: 3;
    -moz-column-count: 3;
    column-count: 3;
}
```

4. Add the **Compositing.js** file with the following code.

```javascript
"use strict";

for (var i = 1; i <= 11; i++) {
    var c = document.getElementById("composting" + i);
    var cContext = c.getContext("2d");

    cContext.fillStyle = "red";
    cContext.fillRect(10, 20, 80, 80);

    switch (i) {
        case 1: cContext.globalCompositeOperation = "source-over"; break;
        case 2: cContext.globalCompositeOperation = "destination-over"; break;
        case 3: cContext.globalCompositeOperation = "source-in"; break;
        case 4: cContext.globalCompositeOperation = "destination-in"; break;
        case 5: cContext.globalCompositeOperation = "source-out"; break;
        case 6: cContext.globalCompositeOperation = "destination-out"; break;
        case 7: cContext.globalCompositeOperation = "source-atop"; break;
        case 8: cContext.globalCompositeOperation = "destination-atop"; break;
        case 9: cContext.globalCompositeOperation = "xor"; break;
        case 10: cContext.globalCompositeOperation = "copy"; break;
        case 11: cContext.globalCompositeOperation = "lighter"; break;
    }

    cContext.fillStyle = "blue";
    cContext.beginPath();
    cContext.arc(65, 75, 40, 0, (Math.PI * 2), true);
    cContext.fill();
}
```

This code uses a for loop to process all 11 canvas elements. It gets the corresponding element and then obtains its drawing context. It adds a red square and then sets the globalCompositeOperation property. Finally, it adds a blue circle, which is offset slightly from the position of the square.

5. Save your changes and open the Compositing.html file in a browser. The web page should look like Figure 23-13.

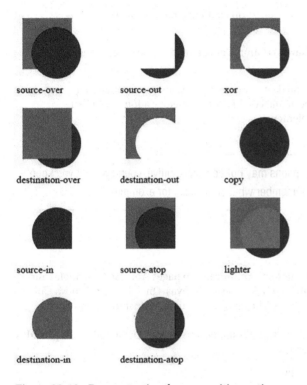

Figure 23-13. *Demonstrating the compositing options*

The compositing options are as follows:

- source-over: This is the default operation. The source element (the element being added) is drawn on top of the destination (whatever is already in this location).

- destination-over: This is the opposite of source-over, where the source element is added underneath the existing elements.

- source-in: Only the portion of the source object that is also in a destination element is displayed. Note that none of the destination element is displayed; it is being used like a clipping shape.

- destination-in: Only the portion of the destination object that is also in the source element is displayed.

- source-out: Only the portion of the source element that does not overlap the destination element is displayed.

- destination-out: Only the portion of the destination element that does not overlap the source element is displayed.

- source-atop: The source is displayed on top of the destination element, but the entire shape is clipped by the destination element.

- destination-atop: The source is displayed beneath the destination element, but the entire shape is clipped by the source element.

- xor: Only the portions of the source and destination elements that do not overlap are displayed.

- copy: The name is misleading. This draws the source element and clears everything else.

- lighter: This draws both the source and destination elements, and the overlapping area is displayed in a lighter color. The actual color is determined by adding the color values of the source and destination elements.

■ **Tip** Some of the names of these compositing options may not be very intuitive. I suggest that you keep this figure handy to refer to later in case you don't remember what copy does, for example.

Summary

In this chapter, you used the canvas element to create some graphical web pages. You used rectangles and paths to draw shapes on the canvas. You also included images on your canvas. One of the really powerful features of canvas is the ability to apply transformations. The appropriate use of transformations can really simplify some complex drawing applications.

Canvas is fundamentally different from SVG. In SVG, each shape is a separate DOM node. This provides two important features that you cannot do with canvas:

- Attach event handlers to individual shapes.

- Individual shapes can be manipulated. A good example of this is defining the :hover pseudo-rule, which allows the shape's attributes to be changed when the mouse is hovered over it.

In contrast to SVG, canvas is pixel based, which means it is resolution dependent. Notice that all of the drawing commands used pixel locations or sizes. When you draw a shape on a canvas element, the pixels of that canvas are adjusted as appropriate and all that is remembered is the resulting pixel content.

Canvas will tend to be more efficient because of its raw pixel manipulation. SVG, on the other hand, must perform a lot of rendering (and re-rendering). However, larger images with less dense content, such as maps, will generally perform better in SVG.

In the next chapter, you will use the drag-and-drop capability to implement a game of Checkers.

Drag and Drop

The ability to select an element and drag it to another location is an excellent example of a natural user experience. I can still remember the early Apple computers where you could delete a file by dragging it onto a trash can icon. This action, and hundreds more like it, is a key component of user experiences found on desktop applications. Web applications, however, have lagged far behind in this arena. With the drag-and-drop (DnD) API in HTML5, you'll find web applications rapidly catching up.

In this chapter, you'll build a web application that implements a checkers game, using the DnD API to move the pieces around the board. I will first explain the concepts and how a DnD application is structured. Then I'll dive into the code, demonstrating the various aspects. I'll finish up with some advanced features including dragging between browser windows.

Understanding Drag and Drop

Before I get into building an application, I want to explain the basic concepts of the DnD API. This will help you put this in context as you start to write code. I will first explain the events that are raised; it is important to know when each is raised and on which object. Then you'll look at the dataTransfer object, which you'll use to pass information from the object being dragged to each of the events and eventually to the drop action. You can also use this to configure various aspects of the dragging operation. Finally, I'll show you how to make objects draggable.

Handling Events

As with its desktop counterpart, DnD is an event-based API. As the user selects an item, moves it, and drops it, events are raised, allowing the application to control and respond to these actions. To effectively use this API, you'll need to know when these events are raised and on which element they are raised. At first, this may seem confusing, but it's pretty straightforward once you see this in perspective.

Tip I explained the fundamentals of using events in Chapter 20.

In a DnD operation, two elements are involved:

- The element that is being dragged, sometimes referred to as the source

- The element being dropped on, usually called the target

You can think of this as the source being an arrow that is being dropped onto a target, as illustrated in Figure 24-1.

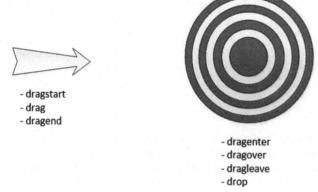

- dragstart
- drag
- dragend

- dragenter
- dragover
- dragleave
- drop

Figure 24-1. *The source and target elements*

During a DnD operation, events are fired on both elements, and I've indicated which events are raised on each. On the source element, the dragstart, drag, and dragend events are comparable to the mousedown, mousemove, and mouseup events in a Windows application. When you click an element and start to move the mouse, the dragstart event is raised. This is immediately followed by the drag event, and the drag event is also repeatedly raised with each move of the mouse. Finally, the dragend event is raised when the mouse button is released.

The events on the target element are a little more interesting. As the mouse is moved around the page, when it enters the area defined by an element, the dragenter event is raised on that element. As the mouse continues to move, the dragover event is raised on the target element. If the mouse moves outside of that element, the dragleave event is fired on the target element. Presumably, the mouse is now on a different element, and a dragenter event is raised on that element. However, if the mouse button is released while over the target element, instead of a dragleave event, the drop event will be raised.

Now let's walk through a typical scenario and see the order of these events. This is illustrated in Table 24-1.

Table 24-1. *Sequence of Events*

Element	Event	Notes
Source	dragstart	Raised when the mouse is clicked and starts to move
Source	drag	Raised with each mouse move
Target	dragenter	Raised when the mouse enters the target element's space
Target	dragover	Raised with each mouse move when the pointer is over the target
Source	drag	Continues to be raised as the mouse moves
Target	dragleave	Raised when the mouse is moved past the current target
Target	dragenter	Raised when mouse moves to a new target element
Target	drop	Raised when the mouse button is released
Source	dragend	Ends the drag-and-drop operation

Now that you understand the events that are used, you can implement a DnD operation by providing appropriate handlers for each of these events.

Using the Data Transfer Object

There is one more DnD concept that you should understand. Simply dragging an element around a page is not all that useful; what you're really after is the data associated with the element. In the example I gave earlier with dragging a file to the trash can, seeing the icon swallowed up by the trash may be fun to watch, but the ultimate goal is to delete the file. In this case, you're passing a file specification to the recycle bin so it can perform the requested action in the file system.

Storing Data

In the DnD API, the dataTransfer object is used to store the data associated with the operation. The dataTransfer object is usually initialized in the dragstart event handler. Recall that this event is raised on the source element. The event handler can access the data from the source element and store it in the dataTransfer object. This is then provided to all of the other event handlers so they can use it in their specific processing. Ultimately, this is used by the drop event handler to take the appropriate action on this data.

The dataTransfer object is provided as a property of the event object that is passed to each of the event handlers. You use the setData() method to store data in the dataTransfer object. To indicate the type of data, an appropriate MIME type needs to be supplied as well. For example, to add some simple text, call the method like this:

```
e.dataTransfer.setData("text", "Hello, World!");
```

To access this data in a subsequent event, such as the drop event, use the getData() method like this:

```
var msg = e.dataTransfer.getData("text");
```

You'll need to use the same MIME type when retrieving the data as was used when the data was stored.

■ **Caution** Not all browsers recognize all MIME types. In this example, you might expect text/plain to be used. This works fine in Firefox and Opera but is not supported in Chrome or IE. However, if you use just text, this will work on all of these browsers.

Using Drop Effects

Another purpose for the dataTransfer object is to provide feedback to the user as to the action that will occur when the item is dropped. This is called the drop effect, and there are four possible values.

- copy: The selected element will be copied in the target location.

- move: The selected element will be moved to the target location.

- link: A link to the selected item will be created in the target location.

- none: The drop operation is not allowed.

When you start dragging an item, the cursor will change to indicate the drop effect that will occur when the item is dropped on the current target. This is standard UI, and you can try this on most applications. For example, using any text editor, select some text and then start dragging it. You should see the cursor change to either a move cursor or a "not allowed" cursor depending on where you are trying to move it. If you hold down the Ctrl key before moving it, you should see the copy cursor instead of the move cursor.

In the dragstart event handler, you can specify the drop effects that are allowed based on the source element that is selected. You can specify more than one allowed effect by simply concatenating them (for example, copyMove) or specify all effects like this:

```
e.dataTransfer.effectAllowed = "all"; // "copy", "link", "move", "copyLink", "linkMove",
"copyMove"
```

Then, in the dragover event, you'll specify the drop effect that will occur if the source element is dropped there. If that drop effect is one of the allowed effects, the cursor will change to indicate that drop effect. If that effect is not allowed, however, the cursor will use the "not allowed" icon. If this is not a valid location to accept the drop, set the drop effect to none like this:

```
if (validLocation) {
    e.dataTransfer.dropEffect = "move";
}
else {
    e.dataTransfer.dropEffect = "none";
}
```

Enabling Draggable Elements

So now you know you can disable the drop event on an element by setting the drop effect to none in the dragover event. But how do you control which elements can be dragged to start with? The answer is simple: just set the draggable attribute in the markup for the element. For example, to create a div that can be dragged, enter the markup like this:

```
<div id="myDiv" draggable="true">
    <p>This div is draggable</p>
</div>
```

By default, images and links are draggable. Go to google.com and try dragging the Google logo. You should see a somewhat muted copy of this image being dragged as you move the cursor.

If you drag this image onto a Firefox browser window, Firefox will navigate to this image. You've just seen drag and drop in action. Because using drag and drop is such a natural way of working, browsers try to accommodate this out of the box as best they can. For example, if you drag some text from a text editor that appears to be a URL onto a browser, it will try to navigate to that address. If you drag an image file onto a browser, it will either navigate to it or download it.

Sometimes the default action can cause issues with your custom code. I will show you in Exercise 24-3 how to disable this.

■ **Note**   For more information on the DnD API, check out the W3C specification at http://dev.w3.org/html5/spec/single-page.html#dnd.

Creating the Checkers Application

To demonstrate the DnD API, you'll create a web application that displays a typical checkers board of alternating red-and-white squares. You'll use image files to represent the checkers and display them in their initial starting position. Then you'll create event handlers that will allow you to move a piece to a different square. Finally, you'll add logic to disable illegal moves.

▧ **Tip** Throughout this chapter, you will be adding and modifying code in this project as you add features to the application. If there is any question about where each change should be made, the final code is listed in Appendix B, and it is also available with the source download.

Creating the Project

For this chapter, you'll create a single web page called Checkers.

EXERCISE 24-1. CREATING THE WEB PROJECT

1. Create an HTML file called **Checkers.html** and start with the typical markup.

```
<!DOCTYPE html>

<html lang="en">
    <head>
        <meta charset="utf-8" />
        <title>Chapter 24 - Checkers</title>
        <link rel="stylesheet" href="Checkers.css" />
        <script src="Checkers.js" defer></script>
    </head>
    <body>
    </body>
</html>
```

2. Create a new **Checkers.js** script file; you'll add code to this as you work through the exercises.

3. Create a new **Checkers.css** file to hold the style rules.

4. The source code download for this chapter includes an Images folder with five images. Create an **Images** folder in your web project and copy all five images there.

Drawing the Checkers Board

To draw the board, you'll use a separate div element for each square. You'll need 8 rows with 8 div elements each. You could manually create 64 div elements in the HTML document. However, for efficiency, you'll create them using JavaScript.

■ **Note**   In the previous chapter, you drew a chess board using a canvas element. However, that won't work for this application because you need separate DOM elements for each square. You might be tempted to use SVG to create the board since each rect element is a separate DOM element; however, the SVG elements do not support the DnD API.

EXERCISE 24-2. DRAWING THE BOARD

1. Insert a div element in the body element; this will contain the checker board.

    ```
    <body>
        <div id="board">
        </div>
    </body>
    ```

2. Add the following implementation to the Checkers.js file.

    ```
    "use strict";

    function createBoard() {
        var board = document.getElementById("board");

        for (var y=0; y < 8; y++) {
            var row = document.createElement("div");
            row.className = "row";
            board.appendChild(row);

            for (var x=0; x < 8; x++) {
                var square = document.createElement("div");
                square.id = x.toFixed() + y.toString();
                if ((x + y) % 2) {
                    square.className = "bblack";
                }
                else {
                    square.className = "bwhite";
                }
    ```

```
            square.setAttribute("draggable", "false");
            row.appendChild(square);
        }
    }
}

createBoard();
```

This code uses two nested `for` loops to create the `div` elements. The first loop will create a div for the row. Inside the second for loop, the `id` variable is computed by concatenating the `x` and `y` variables. The `class` alternates between `bwhite` and `bblack`. For even-numbered rows, the even columns are black, and the odd columns are white. This reverses for odd-numbered rows. The `draggable` attribute is set to false because we don't want squares being dragged, only pieces.

3. Now you'll need to add some style rules to set the size and color of each square. The rows use `display: table-row` and the squares use `display: table-cell` (see Chapter 13 for details). Add the following style rules to the `Checkers.css` file.

```css
.row {
    display: table-row;
    margin: 0;
    padding: 0;
}
.bblack, .bwhite {
    display: table-cell;
    border-color: #b93030;
    border-width: 1px;
    border-style: solid;
    width: 48px;
    height: 48px;
    margin: 0;
    padding: 0;
}
.bblack {
    background-color: #b93030;
}
.bwhite {
    background-color: #f7f7f7;
}
```

4. Save your changes and display the `Checkers.html` file in a browser. The page should look like Figure 24-2.

Figure 24-2. *The initial board*

5. Now you'll add the checkers by including an img element inside the appropriate
    div elements. Add the code shown in bold to the createBoard() function.

```
else {
    square.className = "bwhite";
}

// If the square should have a piece in it...
if ((x + y) % 2 != 0 && y != 3 && y != 4) {
    var img = document.createElement("img");
    if (y < 3) {
        img.id = "w" +square.id;
        img.src = "Images/WhitePiece.png";
    }
    else {
        img.id = "b" + square.id;
        img.src = "Images/BlackPiece.png";
    }

    img.className = "piece";
    img.setAttribute("draggable", "true");
    square.appendChild(img);
}

square.setAttribute("draggable", "false");
row.appendChild(square);
```

To determine the appropriate squares, the first rule is that checkers are only on the black (or red in this
case) squares. So, the code uses the same (x + y) % 2 != 0 logic that was used to compute the
class attribute. Then, checkers are placed only on the top three and bottom three rows, so the code
excludes rows 3 and 4. If the row is less than 3, this will add a white checker and use a black checker
for the other rows. The code computes the id for the img element by prefixing the id of the square with
either w or b. Notice that the draggable attribute is set to true.

6. The `class` attribute for the `img` elements was set to `piece`. Now add the following rule to the existing `Checkers.css` file, which will add padding so the checker will be centered in the square.

```
.piece {
    margin-left: 4px;
    margin-top: 4px;
}
```

7. Refresh the browser, and you should now see the checkers, as demonstrated in Figure 24-3.

Figure 24-3. *The initial checker board with checkers*

Adding Drag-and-Drop Support

The `img` elements were added with the `draggable` attribute so you should be able to select one and drag it. However, you'll notice that none of the squares will accept the drop, and the cursor shows the "not allowed" icon. If you want to try some default browser functionality, try dragging an image to the address bar; the browser will navigate to the image's URL. You will now add code that will enable a drop so you can start moving the pieces. Then you'll refine this code to ensure that only legal moves are allowed.

Allowing a Drop

You have draggable elements, and all you need to complete a drag-and-drop operation is an element that will accept a drop. To do that, you'll need an event handler for the `dragover` event that sets the drop effect. By default the `effectAllowed` property is set to all so setting the drop effect to move, copy, or link will all be valid settings.

EXERCISE 24-3. IMPLEMENTING THE DROP

1. Add the `allowDrop()` function to the `Checkers.js` script using the following code. This code uses the `querySelectorAll()` function that I described in Chapter 16 to get all of the black squares. It then iterates through the collection that is returned and registers an event handler for the `dragover` event.

```
function allowDrop() {
    // Wire up the target events on all the black squares
    var squares = document.querySelectorAll('.bblack');
    var i = 0;
    while (i < squares.length) {
        var s = squares[i++];
        // Add the event listeners
        s.addEventListener('dragover', dragOver, false);
    }
}
```

2. Implement the `dragover` event handler using the following code. The `dragover()` function calls the `preventDefault()` function to cancel the browser's default action. It then gets the `dataTransfer` object and sets the `dropEffect` property to move.

```
// Handle the dragover event
function dragOver(e) {
    e.preventDefault();
    e.dataTransfer.dropEffect = "move";
}
```

3. Add the call to the `allowDrop()` function to the `Checkers.js` file.

```
allowDrop();
```

4. Refresh the browser and try dragging a checker. You should now get a move cursor on all the black squares but a "not allowed" cursor on the white squares. Try dropping the checker on an empty black square. Since you have not yet implemented a `drop` event handler, the browser will execute its default drop action. Depending on the browser, this may navigate to the image file.

Performing the Custom Drop Action

The default action is not what you're looking for here, so you'll need to implement the drop event handler and provide your own logic. The drop event handler is where all the real work happens. This is where the file is deleted if it's a trash can. For this application, the drop action will create a new img element at the target location and remove the previous image.

To implement the drop, you'll also need to provide the dragstart event handler. In the dragstart event handler, you will store the id of the img element that is being dragged in the dataTransfer object. This will be used by the drop event handler so it will know which element to remove.

1. Add the following function to the Checkers.js script, which will be used as the dragstart event handler. This code gets the id of the source element (remember the dragstart event is raised on the source element), which is the selected checker image. This id is stored in the dataTransfer object. This function also specifies that the allowed effects should be move since you'll be moving this image.

```
// Handle the dragstart event
function dragStart(e) {
    e.dataTransfer.effectAllowed = "move";
    e.dataTransfer.setData("text", e.target.id);
}
```

2. To provide the drop event handler, add the following code to the Checkers.js script.

```
// Handle the drop event
function drop(e) {
    e.stopPropagation();
    e.preventDefault();

    // Get the img element that is being dragged
    var droppedID = e.dataTransfer.getData("text");
    var droppedPiece = document.getElementById(droppedID);

    // Create a new img on the target location
    var newPiece = document.createElement("img");
    newPiece.src = droppedPiece.src;
    newPiece.id = droppedPiece.id.substr(0, 1) + e.target.id;
    newPiece.draggable = true;
    newPiece.classList.add("piece");
    newPiece.addEventListener("dragstart", dragStart, false);
    e.target.appendChild(newPiece);

    // Remove the previous image
    droppedPiece.parentNode.removeChild(droppedPiece);
}
```

This code first calls the stopPropagation() function to keep this event from bubbling up to the parent element. It also calls preventDefault() to cancel the browser's default action. It then gets the id from the dataTransfer object and uses this to access the img element. This function then creates a new img element and sets all the necessary properties and adds the necessary event handlers. As I explained, the drop event is raised on the target element, which is the element being dropped on. The id for the new img element is computed using the id of the new location, which is obtained from the target property of the event object. The ID prefix (b or w) is copied from the existing img element. Finally, this code removes the existing img element.

3. Now you'll need to wire up the event handlers. To do that, add the following code shown in bold to the allowDrop() function.

```
var squares = document.querySelectorAll('.bblack');
var i = 0;
while (i < squares.length) {
    var s = squares[i++];
    // Add the event listeners
    s.addEventListener('dragover', dragOver, false);
    s.addEventListener('drop', drop, false);
}

// Wire up the source events on all of the images
i = 0;
var pieces = document.querySelectorAll('img');
while (i < pieces.length) {
    var p = pieces[i++];
    p.addEventListener('dragstart', dragStart, false);
}
```

The drop event handler is added to the squares since these are the target elements. The dragstart event must be added to the img elements. This code gets all of the img elements using the querySelectorAll() function.

4. Restart the browser; you should be able to drag a checker to any unoccupied red square.

Providing Visual Feedback

When dragging an element, it's a good idea to provide some visual feedback indicating the object that was selected. By setting the dropEffect property in the dragover event handler, the cursor indicates if a drop is allowed or not. However, you should do more than that. Both the source and target elements should stand out visually so the user can easily see that if they release the mouse button, the piece will be moved from here to there.

To do this, you'll dynamically add a class attribute to the source and target elements. Then you can style them with normal CSS style rules. For the source element, you'll use the dragstart and dragend events to add and then remove the class attribute. Likewise for target element, you'll use the dragenter and dragleave events.

EXERCISE 24-4. ADDING VISUAL FEEDBACK

1. You already have a dragstart event handler; add the following code in bold to the dragStart() function. This will add the selected class to the element.

```
function dragStart(e) {
    e.dataTransfer.effectAllowed = "all";
    e.dataTransfer.setData("text/plain", e.target.id);
    e.target.classList.add("selected");
}
```

2. Add the dragEnd() function using the following code that will simply remove the selected class when the drag operation has completed.

```
// Handle the dragend event
function dragEnd(e) {
    e.target.classList.remove("selected");
}
```

3. Add the dragEnter() and dragLeave() functions using the following code. This adds the drop class to the element and then removes it.

```
// Handle the dragenter event
function dragEnter(e) {
    e.target.classList.add('drop');
}

// Handle the dragleave event
function dragLeave(e) {
    e.target.classList.remove("drop");
}
```

4. Since you've added three new event handlers, you'll need to add code to register the event listeners. Add the code shown in bold to the allowDrop() function.

```
var squares = document.querySelectorAll('.bblack');
var i = 0;
while (i < squares.length){
    var s = squares[i++];
    // Add the event listeners
    s.addEventListener('dragover', dragOver, false);
    s.addEventListener('drop', drop, false);
    s.addEventListener('dragenter', dragEnter, false);
    s.addEventListener('dragleave', dragLeave, false);
}
```

```
i = 0;
var pieces = document.querySelectorAll('img');
while (i < pieces.length){
    var p = pieces[i++];
    p.addEventListener('dragstart', dragStart, false);
    p.addEventListener('dragend', dragEnd, false);
}
```

5. Now you'll need to make a couple of changes to the drop event handler. You added
    the drop class to the target element in the dragenter event and then removed
    it in the dragleave event. However, if they drop the image, the dragleave event
    is not raised. You'll also need to remove the drop class in the drop event as well.
    Also, when creating a new img element, you'll need to wire up the dragend event
    handler.

6. Add the code shown in bold.

```
// Create a new img on the target location
var newPiece = document.createElement("img");
newPiece.src = droppedPiece.src;
newPiece.id = droppedPiece.id.substr(0, 1) + e.target.id;
newPiece.draggable = true;
newPiece.classList.add("piece");
newPiece.addEventListener("dragstart", dragStart, false);
newPiece.addEventListener("dragend", dragEnd, false);
e.target.appendChild(newPiece);

// Remove the previous image
droppedPiece.parentNode.removeChild(droppedPiece);

// Remove the drop effect from the target element
e.target.classList.remove('drop');
```

7. Finally, you'll need to define the CSS rules for the drop and selected values. I've
    chosen to set the opacity attribute, but you could just as easily add a border,
    change the background color, or implement any number of effects to achieve the
    desired purpose. Add the following rules to the Checkers.css file:

```
.bblack.drop {
    opacity: 0.5;
}
.piece.selected {
    opacity: 0.5;
}
```

8. Refresh the browser and try dragging an image to a red square; you should see the
    expected visual feedback, as shown in Figure 24-4.

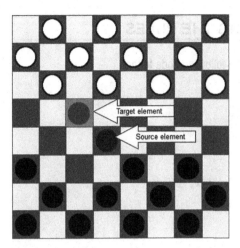

Figure 24-4. Displaying the drag-and-drop visual feedback

Enforcing the Game Rules

You've probably noticed that you can move a piece to any red square. The current implementation doesn't enforce any rules to ensure a legal move is being made. You'll now add that logic. This will be needed by the following events:

- dragover: To set the dropEffect to none for illegal moves
- dragenter: To change the style only for valid drop locations
- drop: To perform the move only if it's a legal move

You'll implement an isValidMove() function that will evaluate the attempted move and return false if this is an illegal move. Then you'll call this function in each of these three event handlers.

Verifying a Move

Fortunately, the rules in checkers are fairly simple. Because the dragover event handler is not added to the white squares, dropping a piece there is already disabled, which further simplifies the work needed. The following are the rules that you'll enforce:

- You cannot move to a square already occupied.
- Pieces can move only forward.
- Pieces can move only one space diagonally or two spaces (diagonally) if jumping an occupied square.
- You can jump only a piece of a different color.
- A jumped piece must be removed from the board.

■ **Note** You'll later add logic to handle promoting a piece to a king.

EXERCISE 24-5. ENFORCING THE RULES

1. Implement the isValidMove() function by adding the following code to the Checkers.js script.

```
function isValidMove(source, target, drop) {
    // Get the piece prefix and location
    var startPos = source.id.substr(1, 2);
    var prefix = source.id.substr(0, 1);

    // Get the drop location, strip off the prefix, if any
    var endPos = target.id;
    if (endPos.length > 2) {
        endPos = endPos.substr(1, 2);
    }

    // You can't drop on the existing location
    if (startPos === endPos) {
        return false;
    }

    // You can't drop on occupied square
    if (target.childElementCount != 0) {
        return false;
    }

    // Compute the x and y coordinates
    var xStart = parseInt(startPos.substr(0, 1));
    var yStart = parseInt(startPos.substr(1, 1));
    var xEnd = parseInt(endPos.substr(0, 1));
    var yEnd = parseInt(endPos.substr(1, 1));

    switch (prefix) {
        // For white pieces...
        case "w":
            if (yEnd <= yStart)
                return false; // Can't move backwards
            break;

        // For black pieces...
        case "b":
            if (yEnd >= yStart)
                return false; // Can't move backwards
            break;
    }

    // These rule apply to all pieces
    if (yStart === yEnd || xStart === xEnd)
        return false; // Move must be diagonal
```

```
        // Can't move more than two spaces
        if (Math.abs(yEnd - yStart) > 2 || Math.abs(xEnd - xStart) > 2)
            return false;

        // If moving two spaces, find the square that is jumped
        if (Math.abs(xEnd - xStart) === 2) {
            var pos = ((xStart + xEnd) / 2).toString() +
                      ((yStart + yEnd) / 2).toString();
            var div = document.getElementById(pos);
            if (div.childElementCount === 0)
                return false;   // Can't jump an empty square
            var img = div.children[0];
            if (img.id.substr(0, 1).toLowerCase() === prefix.toLowerCase())
                return false; // Can't jump a piece of the same color

            // If this function is called from the drop event
            // Remove the jumped piece
            if (drop) {
                div.removeChild(img);
            }
        }

        return true;
    }
```

The parameters to the isValidMove() function include the source and target elements. Remember, the source is an img element, and its id attribute is a combination of the color (w or b) and the x and y coordinates. The target is a div element, and its id attribute is just the x and y coordinates. I've added lots of comments to this code, so it should be fairly self-explanatory, but I will point out a few of the more interesting points.

- To determine whether a square is occupied, you can simply check the childElementCount property. This will be 0 for empty squares.

- For white pieces, moving forward means the y coordinate is increasing, but for black pieces the opposite is true. To handle this, the function uses a switch statement to apply a different rule for each.

- If the piece is moving two spaces, then the function needs to check the square that is being jumped. Its location is determined by averaging the starting and ending positions.

- If the square is occupied, then the code checks to see whether the piece is the same color. The code first gets the child element, which will be the img on that square. The color is determined by the prefix of the id attribute. The code converts the prefix to lowercase before comparing. I'll explain that later.

- If a piece of a different color is being jumped, then you'll remove it since the code already has the img element. However, you want to do this only if this method is called from the drop event, which is specified by the third parameter to this function. The other two events (dragOver and dragEnter) use this method to validate the move but don't actually make the move, and they will pass false for the third parameter.

2. Now you'll need to change dragover event to validate the move before setting the dropEffect. Replace the existing implementation of the dragOver() function with the following code. The new code gets the id of the img that is being dragged from the dataTransfer object and then uses the id to get the element. This is passed in to the isValidMove() function along with the target element, which is obtained from the event object (e.target). The dropEffect is set to move only if this is a valid move.

```
function dragOver(e) {
    e.preventDefault();

    // Get the img element that is being dragged
    var dragID = e.dataTransfer.getData("text");
    var dragPiece = document.getElementById(dragID);

    // Work around - if we can't get the dataTransfer, don't
    // disable the move yet, the drop event will catch this
    if (dragPiece) {
        if (e.target.tagName === "DIV" &&
            isValidMove(dragPiece, e.target, false)) {
            e.dataTransfer.dropEffect = "move";
        }
        else {
            e.dataTransfer.dropEffect = "none";
        }
    }
}
```

■ **Caution** As of this writing, Chrome, IE, and Opera won't allow you to access the dataTransfer object in the dragEnter and dragOver events. This does work, however, in the drop event. The work around in the dragOver event is to allow the move if the source object is not available. The game will still work because the drop event will ignore any invalid moves, but the user experience is not ideal. The dragEnter event is used to apply the drop class for styling purposes, and this will not work as well. For the rest of this chapter, I will be using Firefox to test the application.

3. Replace the implementation of the dragEnter() function with the following code. This code is essentially the same as the dragOver() function, except it adds the drop class to the element instead of setting the dropEffect.

```
function dragEnter(e) {
    // Get the img element that is being dragged
    var dragID = e.dataTransfer.getData("text");
    var dragPiece = document.getElementById(dragID);
```

```
    if (dragPiece &&
        e.target.tagName === "DIV" &&
        isValidMove(dragPiece, e.target, false)) {
        e.target.classList.add('drop');
    }
}
```

4. For the `drop()` function, wrap the code that performs the drop inside an `if` statement that validates the move by adding the code shown in bold. This time, the code is passing `true` for the third parameter to the `isValidMove()` function.

```
if (droppedPiece &&
    e.target.tagName === "DIV" &&
    isValidMove(droppedPiece, e.target, true)) {
    // Create a new img on the target location
    var newPiece = document.createElement("img");
    newPiece.src = droppedPiece.src;
    newPiece.id = droppedPiece.id.substr(0, 1) + e.target.id;
    newPiece.draggable = true;
    newPiece.classList.add("piece");
    newPiece.addEventListener("dragstart", dragStart, false);
    newPiece.addEventListener("dragend", dragEnd, false);
    e.target.appendChild(newPiece);

    // Remove the previous image
    droppedPiece.parentNode.removeChild(droppedPiece);

    // Remove the drop effect from the target element
    e.target.classList.remove('drop');
}
```

5. With these changes now in place, try running the application. You should be allowed to make only legal moves. If you jump a checker, it should be removed from the board.

Promoting to King

In checkers, when a piece moves all the way to the last row, it is promoted to a king. A king works just like a regular piece except that it can move backward. You'll now add code to check whether a piece needs to be promoted. To promote a piece, you'll change the image that is displayed to indicate it is a king. You'll also change the prefix, making it a capital B or W. Then you can allow different rules for kings.

You'll put all this logic in a single function called kingMe(), and you'll call this every time a drop occurs. If the piece is already a king or if it's not on the last row, the function just returns. Otherwise, it performs the promotion.

EXERCISE 24-6. ADDING PROMOTION

1. Add the kingMe() function to the Checkers.js script.

```
function kingMe(piece) {

    // If we're already a king, just return
    if (piece.id.substr(0, 1) === "W" || piece.id.substr(0, 1) === "B")
        return;

    var newPiece;

    // If this is a white piece on the 7th row
    if (piece.id.substr(0, 1) === "w" && piece.id.substr(2, 1) === "7") {
        newPiece = document.createElement("img");
        newPiece.src = "Images/WhiteKing.png";
        newPiece.id = "W" + piece.id.substr(1, 2);
    }

    // If this is a black piece on the 0th row
    if (piece.id.substr(0, 1) === "b" && piece.id.substr(2, 1) === "0") {
        var newPiece = document.createElement("img");
        newPiece.src = "Images/BlackKing.png";
        newPiece.id = "B" + piece.id.substr(1, 2);
    }

    // If a new piece was created, set its properties and events
    if (newPiece) {
        newPiece.draggable = true;
        newPiece.classList.add("piece");

        newPiece.addEventListener('dragstart', dragStart, false);
        newPiece.addEventListener('dragend', dragEnd, false);

        var parent = piece.parentNode;
        parent.removeChild(piece);
        parent.appendChild(newPiece);
    }
}
```

The kingMe() function simply returns if the id prefix is either B or W, which indicates this is already a king. It then checks to see whether this is a white piece on row 7 or a black piece on row 0. If so, a new img element is created with the appropriate src and id properties. If a new img was created, the function then sets all of the properties and events, removes the existing img element from the div element, and adds the new one.

2. Modify the `drop()` function to call the `kingMe()` function after a drop has been performed by adding the line shown in bold.

```
// Remove the previous image
droppedPiece.parentNode.removeChild(droppedPiece);

// Remove the drop effect from the target element
e.target.classList.remove('drop');

// See if the piece needs to be promoted
kingMe(newPiece);
```

■ **Tip** When you implemented the `isValidMove()` function, the rule that prevents the piece from moving backward applies only to b and w prefixes. Since a king has a capital B or W, this rule doesn't apply so the king can move backward. Also, when jumping a piece, the comparison was done after first converting to lowercase. This will allow a white piece to jump either a black piece or a black king.

3. Try moving the pieces around until you move one to the last row. You should see the image change to indicate this is now a king, as shown in Figure 24-5.

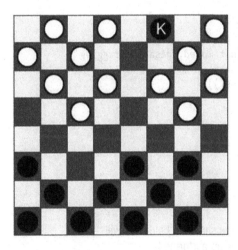

Figure 24-5. The check board with a king

4. Once you have a king, try moving it backward and also try jumping pieces with it.

459

Moving in Turn

You've probably noticed that the application does not enforce each player alternating turns. You'll implement this logic now. After each move is made (drop event processed), you'll set the draggable attribute to false for all the pieces of the color that just moved. That will keep you from moving a piece of the same color. However, there is one exception to this rule that will require a little extra work. If you jump a piece, then that same piece can make another move as long as it is another jump.

You'll start by implementing the general rule first. This will be performed by creating a new function called enableNextPlayer(). This function will use the querySelectorAll() function to get all of the img elements. The draggable attribute will be set to either true or false depending on the id prefix. Then you'll later add special logic that will handle the jump condition.

EXERCISE 24-7. TAKING TURNS

1. Add the enableNextPlayer() function to the Checkers.js script.

```
function enableNextPlayer(piece) {

    // Get all of the pieces
    var pieces = document.querySelectorAll('img');

    var i = 0;
    while (i < pieces.length) {
        var p = pieces[i++];

        // If this is the same color that just moved, disable dragging
        if (p.id.substr(0, 1).toUpperCase() ===
            piece.id.substr(0, 1).toUpperCase()) {
            p.draggable = false;
        }
        // Otherwise, enable dragging
        else {
            p.draggable = true;
        }
    }
}
```

2. At the end of the isValidMove() function, add the code shown in bold. This will call the enableNextPlay() function when a drop is being performed.

```
// Set the draggable attribute so the next player can take a turn
if (drop) {
    enableNextPlayer(source);
}
return true;
}
```

■ **Note** Normally it might make more sense to put this call in the drop() function. However, only the isValidMove() function knows that a jump occurred, and you'll need to add the override logic here. This needs to be after the general rule has been applied.

3. The drop() function creates a new img element and currently sets the draggable attribute to true. Now you'll need to make this conditional based on the draggable attribute of the existing piece. Replace the existing line with the following code shown in bold to the drop() function:

    ```
    // Create a new img on the target location
    var newPiece = document.createElement("img");
    newPiece.src = droppedPiece.src;
    newPiece.id = droppedPiece.id.substr(0, 1) + e.target.id;

    newPiece.draggable = droppedPiece.draggable;

    newPiece.classList.add("piece");
    newPiece.addEventListener("dragstart", dragStart, false);
    newPiece.addEventListener("dragend", dragEnd, false);
    e.target.appendChild(newPiece);
    ```

4. Now you'll need to change the dragStart event handler to ignore this event if the element is not draggable. Add the following code shown in bold to the dragStart() function:

    ```
    function dragStart(e) {
        if (e.target.draggable) {
            e.dataTransfer.effectAllowed = "move";
            e.dataTransfer.setData("text/plain", e.target.id);

            e.target.classList.add("selected");
        }
    }
    ```

Now you'll implement the special jump logic. If the piece just made a jump, you'll set the draggable attribute back to true so it will be allowed to make another move. However, you'll also add the jumpOnly class to the classList so you can enforce that the only move that it is allowed to make is another jump.

5. Add the code shown in bold to the isValidMove() function. This will look for jumpOnly in the classList and set the jumpOnly flag accordingly.

    ```
    var jumpOnly = false;
    if (source.classList.contains("jumpOnly")) {
        jumpOnly = true;
    }

    // Compute the x and y coordinates
    var xStart = parseInt(startPos.substr(0, 1));
    var yStart = parseInt(startPos.substr(1, 1));
    ```

461

6. Now add the code shown in bold to the isValidMove() function. The first part adds the rule to make sure a jump is being made if jumpOnly is true. The second part sets the jumped flag to indicate that this move is making a jump.

```
// These rule apply to all pieces
if (yStart === yEnd || xStart === xEnd)
    return false; // Move must be diagonal

// Can't move more than two spaces
if (Math.abs(yEnd - yStart) > 2 || Math.abs(xEnd - xStart) > 2)
    return false;

// Only jumps are allowed
if (Math.abs(xEnd - xStart) === 1 && jumpOnly)
    return false;

var jumped = false;

// If moving two spaces, find the square that is jumped
if (Math.abs(xEnd - xStart) === 2) {
    var pos = ((xStart + xEnd) / 2).toString() +
                ((yStart + yEnd) / 2).toString();
    var div = document.getElementById(pos);
    if (div.childElementCount === 0)
        return false;  // Can't jump an empty square
    var img = div.children[0];
    if (img.id.substr(0, 1).toLowerCase() === prefix.toLowerCase())
        return false; // Can't jump a piece of the same color

    // If this function is called from the drop event
    // Remove the jumped piece
    if (drop) {
        div.removeChild(img);
        jumped = true;
    }
}
```

7. At the end of the isValidMove() function, add the code shown in bold. This will override the draggable attribute if a jump was made and add jumpOnly to the classList.

```
if (drop) {
    enableNextPlayer(source);

    // If we jumped a piece, we're allowed to go again
    if (jumped) {
        source.draggable = true;
        source.classList.add("jumpOnly"); // But only for another jump
    }
}
```

■ **Note**   The enableNextPlayer() function disabled all of the current player's pieces and enabled the other player's. Then this code enabled the piece that just jumped. So, both are enabled; this piece could jump again or the next player could make a move. Both are valid, so we need to allow them both.

---

8. Modify the drop() function to also add jumpOnly to the classList when creating the new img element by adding the code shown in bold.

```
// Create a new img on the target location
var newPiece = document.createElement("img");
newPiece.src = droppedPiece.src;
newPiece.id = droppedPiece.id.substr(0, 1) + e.target.id;

newPiece.draggable = droppedPiece.draggable;

if (droppedPiece.draggable){
    newPiece.classList.add("jumpOnly");
}

newPiece.classList.add("piece");
```

9. Now you'll need to clear jumpOnly from the classList when the next move is completed. You'll do that in the enableNextPlayer() function by adding the code shown in bold.

```
function enableNextPlayer(piece) {

    // Get all of the pieces
    var pieces = document.querySelectorAll('img');

    var i = 0;
    while (i < pieces.length) {
        var p = pieces[i++];

        // If this is the same color that just moved, disable dragging
        if (p.id.substr(0, 1).toUpperCase() ===
            piece.id.substr(0, 1).toUpperCase()) {
            p.draggable = false;
        }
        // Otherwise, enable dragging
        else {
            p.draggable = true;
        }

        p.classList.remove("jumpOnly");
    }
}
```

10. Now test the application and make sure that each player must alternate turns. Also, verify that you can make successive jumps.

■ **Note**   The draggable attribute is set to true, initially, for both the white and black pieces so either color can make the first move. If you wanted to specify which color went first, you would change the createBoard() function that creates the initial img elements to set the draggable attribute to false for one color. I did some research to see what color was supposed to go first but found mixed results. Some places indicated black goes first and others said that the white goes first. Some, however, said it's just a game, what difference does it make? I decided to implement this logic, so either can go first.

Using Advanced Features

Before I finish this chapter, there are a couple of things I will discuss briefly. First, I'll show you how to use a custom drag image. Then, I'll demonstrate dragging elements across browser windows.

Changing the Drag Image

When you drag an element, a copy of the element follows the cursor as you move it around the page. This is referred to as the drag image. However, you can specify a different image to be used. This is done with the setDragImage() method of the dataTransfer object.

There is a smiley face image in the Images folder. Add the code shown in bold to the dragStart() function to use this as the drag image.

```
function dragStart(e) {
    if (e.target.draggable) {
        e.dataTransfer.effectAllowed = "move";
        e.dataTransfer.setData("text", e.target.id);

        e.target.classList.add("selected");

        // Use a custom drag image
        var dragIcon = document.createElement("img");
        dragIcon.src = "Images/smiley.jpg";
        e.dataTransfer.setDragImage(dragIcon, 0, 0);
    }
}
```

Try the application, and as you move pieces, you should see the smiley face shown in Figure 24-6.

Figure 24-6. *Changing the drag image*

Dragging Between Windows

As I mentioned at the beginning of the chapter, there are separate events raised on the source element and on the target element. It is possible that these elements can be in different browser windows or even different applications. The process, however, works the same way.

To demonstrate this, open a second instance of the browser and navigate to the checkers application. You should see two browser windows each showing the checker board. Select a checker on one window and drag it to a square in the second window. You'll notice that you can drop it only on squares relative to its original location in the first window. When you drop it, the piece is moved to the drop location but is removed from the second window, not the image you initially selected.

The key to cross-window dragging is the dataTransfer object. This is provided in the dragenter, dragover, and dragleave events on the target object. It doesn't really matter where the drag initiated; this information is placed in the dataTransfer object and provided to any window that supports these events. When the drop event received this information, it removed the img element at the location specified in the dataTransfer object. Because the drop event was processed on the second window, the img element was removed from the second window.

The drag and dragend events are raised on the source element. Whatever logic was written on these event handlers is executed in the first window. Notice that the selected img element was muted during the drag but went back to normal when the drop was executed. This is because the dragend event fired on the source element clears the selected class.

When you control both sides of the operation as you do here, you can decide what data needs to be transferred and implement both sets of event handlers. In many cases, you can control only one side of the process. For example, a user could drag a file from Windows Explorer onto your web page. The dragstart, drag, and dragend events (or their equivalents) are raised in the Windows Explorer application, which you can't control. However, the dragenter, dragover, dragleave, and drop events are all fired on your web page. You can decide whether you will accept the drop based on the element it is being dropped on and the contents of the dataTransfer object. You also control the process that occurs when the drop is completed.

Summary

In this chapter, I explained all of the events that are raised as part of the DnD API and which elements they are raised on. The source element receives the following events:

- dragstart: When the element is selected and the mouse is moved

- drag: Called continuously while the mouse is moved

- dragend: When the mouse button is released

The following events are raised on the target element:

- dragenter: When the mouse first enters the target's space

- dragover: Continuously while the mouse is moved and over the target

- dragleave: When the mouse leaves the target's space

- drop: When the mouse button is released

The dataTransfer object is used to pass information about the source element. This is provided in all of the event handlers. It is used especially by the drop event handler to perform the necessary processing. This also enables dragging across applications.

The dragover event handler sets the dropEffect, which controls the cursor that is used. Setting this to None will cause the "not allowed" cursor to be used, signaling that the source cannot be dropped there.

To provide some visual feedback, the dragstart and dragend event handlers should modify the source element to indicate that it is selected and being dragged. Likewise, the dragenter and dragleave event handers should highlight the target element. This will provide an easy way for the user to see where the selected element will be dropped.

The sample application that you created implemented some complex rules for determining which elements could be dragged and where they could be dropped.

In the next chapter, I'll explain how to use the Indexed DB technology, which provides client-side database-like functionality.

CHAPTER 25

■ ■ ■

Indexed DB

As browser capabilities have evolved, providing more and more functionality on the client device, the need to store and manipulate data locally has increased as well. To address this need, the Indexed DB technology has emerged. This is an API for storing and retrieving objects using keys and indices.

This chapter will demonstrate how to use Indexed DB to store and use data on the client. If you are used to working with SQL databases, I will warn you, this is not a SQL database. It is quite powerful and useful once you get the hang of it, but you'll need to adjust your perspective and set aside your SQL experience as you work through this chapter.

To explore the capabilities of Indexed DB, you will rewrite the chess board application that you created using canvas in Chapter 23. As I explain each of the exercises, I will not go into much detail about canvas; however, refer to Chapter 23 if you need more information. Your new version of the application will create object stores to define the positions of each piece and then manipulate this data as the pieces are moved.

Introducing Indexed DB

Before I get started with the detailed demonstration, there are a few key points that I think will help you better understand how Indexed DB works. Like other databases, the data is placed in a persistent data store. In this case, it's on the local hard drive. The data is permanent.

I will explain each of these entities in more detail, but I will first introduce them and their relationships. A database consists of *object stores*. Each object store is a collection of objects, with each object identified by a unique key. An object store can have one or more indices. Each *index* provides an alternate way of identifying the key to an object store. This is illustrated in Figure 25-1.

© Mark J. Collins 2017
M. J. Collins, *Pro HTML5 with CSS, JavaScript, and Multimedia*, DOI 10.1007/978-1-4842-2463-2_25

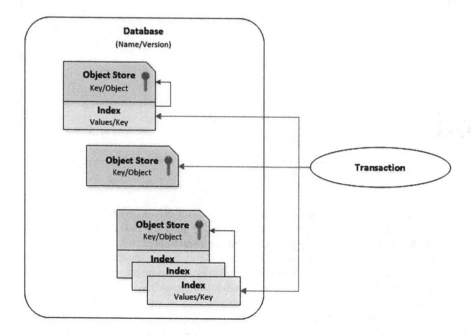

Figure 25-1. *The database entities*

Object stores are accessed through a *transaction* object. When creating the transaction, you must define its scope. This indicates which object stores it will reference and whether it will be reading or writing data to the database.

Using Object Stores

The primary storage unit is called an object store. This is aptly named because they are simply a collection of objects that are referenced by a key. You can think of this as a set of name-value pairs, the value being an object with a set of properties. You can use an inline key, where one of the object properties serves as the key. For example, if the object has an id property with unique values, you can use that as the inline key. If you use out-of-line keys, then you will specify a key when adding an object to the store. Alternatively, you can use a key generator, where the object store will assign incremental key values for you. The following code demonstrates these alternatives:

```
// Using an inline key
var typeStore = db.createObjectStore("pieceType", { keyPath: "id" });
typeStore.add(pieceType);

// Using an out-of-line key
var sampleStore = db.createObjectStore("sample", { });
sampleStore.add(sample, 5);
```

```
// Using a key generator
var pieceStore = db.createObjectStore("piece", { autoIncrement: true });
pieceStore.add(piece);
```

As its name implies, you can also create an index on an object store; in fact, you can create as many indices as you want. An index enables you to find a specific object or collection of objects quickly. An index is a collection of name-value pairs, where the value is a key into the object store. For example, if you have a customer object store and want to search by last name, you can create an index on the lastName property of the object. The database will automatically create an entry in the index for each object in the store. This entry will contain the last name and the corresponding key to that object. The following code demonstrates how to use an index:

```
// Create an index on the lastName property
customerStore.createIndex("lastName", "id", { unique: true });
```

```
// Get the index
var index = customerStore.index("lastName");
index.get(lastName).onsuccess = function();       // get the object
index.getKey(lastName).onsuccess = function();   // get the key
```

The second parameter to the createIndex() function, id in this case, specifies the key path. This tells the database engine how to extract the key from an object. For inline keys, this is the name of the property used to define the unique key.

Indexed DB does not support relationships between object stores. You can't enforce a foreign key relationship, for example. You can certainly use foreign keys, where a property in one object store is a key into another, as I will demonstrate later. However, the database does not enforce this constraint. Also, you can't perform joins between object stores.

Defining the Database

When you open a database, you need to implement three event handlers.

- onsuccess: The database is opened; do something with it.

- onerror: An error occurred, likely an access issue.

- onupgradeneeded: The database needs to be created or upgraded.

When opening a database, if it doesn't exist, it will be created automatically; however, the onupgradeneeded event will be raised. You must implement an event handler for this event, which will create object stores and populate them with any default data. This is the only place where you are allowed to alter the database structure. The important thing to remember is that the onupgradeneeded event is fired before the onsuccess event.

The open() call also specifies a version number. If this is not the current version, the onupgradeneeded event is raised in this scenario also. Your event handler needs to handle altering the structure to match the version requested by the caller. You can query the database's current version like this:

```
var request = dbEng.open("Sample", 2); // get version 2
```

```
request.onupgradeneeded = function (event) {
    alert("Configuring database - current version is " + e.oldVersion +
          ", requested version is " + e.newVersion);
}
```

Based on the current version, the code may need to perform different actions.

Processing Asynchronously

A key aspect of Indexed DB that may take some getting used to is its asynchronous processing; almost all database operations are done asynchronously. The general pattern is to call a method to perform a database operation such as opening a database or retrieving a set of records (objects). This will return a request object. You must then implement the onsuccess and onerror event handlers for that request object. If the request was successful, the onsuccess handler is called, and the result of the method call is passed through the event object.

For complex processing that requires several database calls, you'll need to be careful to nest the event handlers and consider when they are executed. For example, if you needed to make three database requests, your code might look like this:

```
var request = dbCall1()
request.onsuccess = function (e1) {
    f1(e1.target.result);

    dbCall2().onsuccess = function (e2) {
        f3(e2.target.result, e1.target.result);

        dbCall3().onsuccess = function (e3) {
            f5(e3.target.result, e2.target.result, e1.target.result);
        }

        f4(e2.target.result);
    }

    f2(e1.target.result);
}

request.onerror = function(e) {
    alert("The call failed");
}
```

This code calls dbCall1(), dbCall2(), and dbCall3(), in that order, and they will be processed sequentially. In other words, dbCall2() will not start until dbCall1() has completed, and only if it was successful. Each call provides an onsuccess event handler, which makes the next call. If the first call fails, an alert is raised. What may be unexpected is the order that the non-database calls are executed. The database calls return immediately, and the event handler is called later, when the operation has completed. As soon as the call to dbCall2() is made, the function returns, and f2() will be executed. Later, the dbCall2() completes, its event handler is called, and f3() is executed.

■ **Tip** The onerror event is bubbled up the hierarchy. For example, an error that occurs on the request object, if not handled, will be raised on the transaction object. If not handled there, it will be raised on the database object. In many cases, you can use just a single event handler at the database level and handle all the errors there.

Because of the nesting approach, the event handler has access to the event object from previous calls. For this reason, you should use unique names for the event parameter. This will avoid ambiguity. Also, notice the use of closure to access these event objects. As I mentioned, f2() is called before f3(), so the event handler for dbCall1(), which defines the e1 parameter, has completed and is no longer in scope by the time the event handler for dbCall2() is executed. The closure feature of JavaScript allows the subsequent event handlers to access this object. This is important because if you need to access all three object stores to complete an operation, you will need to wait until all three have completed and then access all three results.

■ **Tip**   To avoid closure, you could extract the properties that you need from the first two database calls and store them in local variables (declared prior to the dbCall1() call). Then in the f5() call, you can use these variables instead of the e1 and e2 event objects. This is just a matter of preference because either approach will work fine.

Using Transactions

All data access, both reading and writing, is done within a transaction, so you must first create a transaction object. When the transaction is created, you specify its scope, which is defined by the object stores it will access. You also specify the mode (read-only or read-write). You can then obtain an object store from the transaction and get or put data from/into the store like this:

```
var xact = db.transaction(["piece", "pieceType"], "readwrite");
var pieceStore = xact.objectStore("piece");
```

For read-write transactions, the data changes are not committed until the transaction completes. The interesting question to ask is, "when does a transaction complete?" A transaction is complete when there are no more outstanding requests for it. Remember, everything is request based. You make a request and then implement an event handler to do something when it finishes. If that event handler issues another request on that transaction, then the transaction stays alive. This is another important reason for nesting the event handlers. If you end an event handler without issuing another request, the transaction will complete, and all changes are committed. If you try to use the transaction after that, you will get a TRANSACTION_INACTIVE_ERR error.

Another thing to remember is that read-write transactions cannot have overlapping scopes. If you create a read-write transaction, you can create a second one as long as they don't both include some of the same object stores. If they have overlapping scopes, you must wait for the first transaction to complete before creating the second one. Read-only transactions, however, can have overlapping scopes.

Creating the Application

You'll start by creating a chess board using canvas and configuring images for the chess pieces like you did in Chapter 23.

Creating the Web Project

You'll start by creating an HTML document and a script file. You'll also need the images files for the chess pieces.

EXERCISE 25-1. CREATING THE WEB PROJECT

1. Create a new web page called **Chess.html**, using the basic markup:

```
<!DOCTYPE html>

<html lang="en">
    <head>
        <meta charset="utf-8" />
        <title>Chapter 25 - Chess</title>
        <script src="Data.js" defer></script>
        <script src="Chess.js" defer></script>
    </head>
    <body>
    </body>
</html>
```

2. Then create a **Chess.js** script file using the following code.

```
"use strict";
```

3. Add a div element in the empty body element of the Chess.html file, using the following markup:

```
<div>
    <canvas id="board" width ="600" height ="600">
        Not supported
    </canvas>
</div>
```

4. Add an **Images** folder in the web project.

5. The images for the chess pieces are included in the source code download file. These are the same images used in Chapter 23. You'll find these in the Chapter23\ Images folder. Drag all 12 files to the Images folder to your web project.

Drawing the Canvas

Now you'll design the canvas element using JavaScript. The initial design will just draw an empty board, and you'll add the chess pieces later. Refer to Chapter 23 for more explanation about working with a canvas element. Add the code from Listing 25-1 to the Chess.js script.

Listing 25-1. Designing the Initial Canvas

```
// Get the canvas context
var chessCanvas = document.getElementById("board");
var chessContext = chessCanvas.getContext("2d");
```

```
drawBoard();

function drawBoard() {
    chessContext.clearRect(0, 0, 600, 600);

    var gradient = chessContext.createLinearGradient(0, 600, 600, 0);
    gradient.addColorStop(0, "#D50005");
    gradient.addColorStop(0.5, "#E27883");
    gradient.addColorStop(1, "#FFDDDD");

    chessContext.fillStyle = gradient;
    chessContext.strokeStyle = "red";

    // Draw the alternating squares
    for (var x = 0; x < 8; x++) {
        for (var y = 0; y < 8; y++) {
            if ((x + y) % 2) {
                chessContext.fillRect(75 * x, 75 * y, 75, 75);
            }
        }
    }

    // Add a border around the entire board
    chessContext.strokeRect(0, 0, 600, 600);
}
```

Display the Chess.html file in a browser, which should look like Figure 25-2.

Figure 25-2. *The initial (blank) chess board*

Configuring the Pieces

You will be using image files to represent the chess pieces. Before adding them to the canvas, you'll need to create an Image object for each one and specify its src attribute. You'll also put these into an array to make it easier to programmatically select the desired image.

In addition, you'll need to define the data that will be loaded into the object stores. The pieceTypes[] array defines the properties needed to display each piece such as height and width. It also specifies the corresponding index in the images[] array for both the black and white images. The pieces[] array contains the same details used in the previous chapter such as row and column and defines the starting position for each of the 32 pieces.

Add the code shown in Listing 25-2 to a new Data.js script file. This file is also provided in the source code download so you can simply copy it to your web project instead of rekeying this data.

Listing 25-2. Defining the static data

```
// Define the chess piece images
var imgPawn = new Image();
var imgRook = new Image();
var imgKnight = new Image();
var imgBishop = new Image();
var imgQueen = new Image();
var imgKing = new Image();
var imgPawnW = new Image();
var imgRookW = new Image();
var imgKnightW = new Image();
var imgBishopW = new Image();
var imgQueenW = new Image();
var imgKingW = new Image();

// Specify the source for each image
imgPawn.src = "images/pawn.png";
imgRook.src = "images/rook.png";
imgKnight.src = "images/knight.png";
imgBishop.src = "images/bishop.png";
imgQueen.src = "images/queen.png";
imgKing.src = "images/king.png";
imgPawnW.src = "images/wpawn.png";
imgRookW.src = "images/wrook.png";
imgKnightW.src = "images/wknight.png";
imgBishopW.src = "images/wbishop.png";
imgQueenW.src = "images/wqueen.png";
imgKingW.src = "images/wking.png";

// Define an array of Image objects
var images = [
        imgPawn ,
        imgRook ,
        imgKnight ,
        imgBishop ,
        imgQueen ,
        imgKing ,
        imgPawnW ,
```

```
        imgRookW ,
        imgKnightW ,
        imgBishopW ,
        imgQueenW ,
        imgKingW
];

var pieceTypes = [
    { name: "pawn", height: "50", width: "28", blackImage: 0, whiteImage: 6 },
    { name: "rook", height: "60", width: "36", blackImage: 1, whiteImage: 7 },
    { name: "knight", height: "60", width: "36", blackImage: 2, whiteImage: 8 },
    { name: "bishop", height: "65", width: "30", blackImage: 3, whiteImage: 9 },
    { name: "queen", height: "70", width: "32", blackImage: 4, whiteImage: 10 },
    { name: "king", height: "70", width: "28", blackImage: 5, whiteImage: 11 }
];

var pieces = [
    { type: "pawn", color: "white", row: 6, column: 0, pos: "a2", killed: false },
    { type: "pawn", color: "white", row: 6, column: 1, pos: "b2", killed: false },
    { type: "pawn", color: "white", row: 6, column: 2, pos: "c2", killed: false },
    { type: "pawn", color: "white", row: 6, column: 3, pos: "d2", killed: false },
    { type: "pawn", color: "white", row: 6, column: 4, pos: "e2", killed: false },
    { type: "pawn", color: "white", row: 6, column: 5, pos: "f2", killed: false },
    { type: "pawn", color: "white", row: 6, column: 6, pos: "g2", killed: false },
    { type: "pawn", color: "white", row: 6, column: 7, pos: "h2", killed: false },
    { type: "rook", color: "white", row: 7, column: 0, pos: "a1", killed: false },
    { type: "rook", color: "white", row: 7, column: 7, pos: "h1", killed: false },
    { type: "knight", color: "white", row: 7, column: 1, pos: "b12", killed: false },
    { type: "knight", color: "white", row: 7, column: 6, pos: "g1", killed: false },
    { type: "bishop", color: "white", row: 7, column: 2, pos: "c1", killed: false },
    { type: "bishop", color: "white", row: 7, column: 5, pos: "f1", killed: false },
    { type: "queen", color: "white", row: 7, column: 3, pos: "d1", killed: false },
    { type: "king", color: "white", row: 7, column: 4, pos: "e1", killed: false },
    { type: "pawn", color: "black", row: 1, column: 0, pos: "a7", killed: false },
    { type: "pawn", color: "black", row: 1, column: 1, pos: "b7", killed: false },
    { type: "pawn", color: "black", row: 1, column: 2, pos: "c7", killed: false },
    { type: "pawn", color: "black", row: 1, column: 3, pos: "d7", killed: false },
    { type: "pawn", color: "black", row: 1, column: 4, pos: "e7", killed: false },
    { type: "pawn", color: "black", row: 1, column: 5, pos: "f7", killed: false },
    { type: "pawn", color: "black", row: 1, column: 6, pos: "g7", killed: false },
    { type: "pawn", color: "black", row: 1, column: 7, pos: "h7", killed: false },
    { type: "rook", color: "black", row: 0, column: 0, pos: "a8", killed: false },
    { type: "rook", color: "black", row: 0, column: 7, pos: "h8", killed: false },
    { type: "knight", color: "black", row: 0, column: 1, pos: "b8", killed: false },
    { type: "knight", color: "black", row: 0, column: 6, pos: "g8", killed: false },
    { type: "bishop", color: "black", row: 0, column: 2, pos: "c8", killed: false },
    { type: "bishop", color: "black", row: 0, column: 5, pos: "f8", killed: false },
    { type: "queen", color: "black", row: 0, column: 3, pos: "d8", killed: false },
    { type: "king", color: "black", row: 0, column: 4, pos: "e8", killed: false }
];
```

Creating the Database

Now you're ready to create and use a local Indexed DB database to configure and display the chess pieces. Initially, the data will be loaded from static data, and you will simply display the starting position. Later you will animate the pieces by updating their location in the object store.

You will need to populate the database with some data. For this application, you will just use the data declared in the Data.js script and copy it to the object store. For other applications, this could be downloaded from a server or entered from user input.

Opening the Database

Add the code shown in Listing 25-3 to the Chess.js script, just after the call to drawBoard() (and before the implementation of the drawBoard() function).

Listing 25-3. Opening the Database

```
var dbEng = window.indexedDB ||
            window.webkitIndexedDB || // Chrome
            window.mozIndexedDB ||    // Firefox
            window.msIndexedDB;       // IE

var db;  // This is a handle to the database

if (!dbEng)
    alert("IndexedDB is not supported on this browser");
else {
    var request = dbEng.open("Chess", 1);

    request.onsuccess = function (event) {
        db = event.target.result;
    }

    request.onerror = function (event) {
        alert("Please allow the browser to open the database");
    }

    request.onupgradeneeded = function (event) {
        configureDatabase(event);
    }
}
```

If you can't access the indexedDB object, then the browser does not support it. For this demo you can simply use alert() to notify the user and stop further processing.

This code then uses the indexedDB object to open the Chess database, specifying that version should be used. The open() method returns an IDBOpenDBRequest object, as I described earlier. You will attach three event handlers for this request.

- onsuccess: This event handler simply saves the reference to the database. You will add more logic here later. Notice that the database is obtained from the event.target.result property, which is how all results are returned.

- onerror: The primary reason that the browser fails to open a database is that the browser has the IndexedDB feature blocked. This can be disabled for security reasons. In this case, the user is prompted to allow access. Alternatively, you could choose to display the error message instead.

- onupgradeneeded: This is raised if the database does not exist or if the specified version is not the current version. This calls the configureDatabase() function, which you'll implement now.

Defining the Database Structure

Add the code shown in Listing 25-4 to the Chess.js script to implement the configureDatabase() function.

Listing 25-4. Defining the Database Structure

```
function configureDatabase(e) {
    alert("Configuring database - current version is " + e.oldVersion +
        ", requested version is " + e.newVersion);

    db = e.currentTarget.result;

    // Remove all existing data stores
    var storeList = db.objectStoreNames;
    for (var i = 0; i < storeList.length; i++) {
        db.deleteObjectStore(storeList[i]);
    }

    // Store the piece types
    var typeStore = db.createObjectStore
        ("pieceType", { keyPath: "name" });

    for (var i in pieceTypes){
        typeStore.add(pieceTypes[i]);
    }

    // Create the piece data store (you'll add
    // the data later)
    var pieceStore = db.createObjectStore
        ("piece", { autoIncrement: true });

    pieceStore.createIndex
        ("piecePosition", "pos", { unique: true });
}
```

■ **Caution** The `configureDatabase()` function will be called if the database does not exist or if it is not the current version. For version changes, you can get the current version by using the `db.version` property and then make the necessary adjustments. Also, the `event` object passed to the `onupgradeneeded` event handler will have the `e.oldVersion` and `e.newVersion` properties. To simplify things in this project, you'll simply remove all object stores and rebuild the database from scratch. This will wipe out all existing data. That is fine for this example, but in most cases, you'll need to preserve the data where possible.

The `objectStoreNames` property of the database object contains a list of the names of all the object stores that have been created. To remove all the existing object stores, each of the names in this list is passed to the `deleteObjectStore()` method.

Initially, you'll create two data stores using the `createObjectStore()` method.

- `pieceType`: Contains an object for each type of piece such as pawn, rook, or king

- `piece`: Contains an object for each piece, 16 black and 16 white

Specifying the Object Key

When creating an object store, you must specify a name for the store when calling the `createObjectStore()` method. You can also specify one or more optional parameters. Only two are supported.

- `keypath`: This is specified as a collection of property names. If you're using a single property, you can specify this as a string rather than a collection of strings. This defines the object property (or properties) that will be used as the key. If no `keypath` is specified, the key must be defined out-of-line using a key generator or providing the key as explained later in this section.

- `autoIncrement`: If true, this indicates that the keys are sequentially assigned by the object store.

Every object in a store must have a unique key. There are three ways to specify the key.

- Use the `keypath` parameter to specify one or more properties that define a unique key. As objects are added, the `keypath` is used to generate a key based on the object's properties.

- Use a key generator. If `autoIncrement` is specified, the object store will assign a key based on an internal counter.

- Provide the key value when adding the object. If you don't specify a key path or use a key generator, you must supply a key when adding an object to a store.

For the `pieceType` store you'll use a `keypath`. The `name` property will specify the type such as pawn or knight. This will be a unique value for each object. This is also the value that will be used to retrieve an object, so this is a perfect candidate for a key path. After creating the object store, the data from the `pieceTypes[]` array is then copied to the `pieceType` store.

■ **Note** While in the `onupgradeneeded` event handler, data can be added to an object store without explicitly creating a transaction. There is an implicit transaction created in response to the `onupgradeneeded` event.

Creating an Index

For the piece store there is no natural key available in the pieces data, so you'll use a key generator. It will generate unique keys, but the keys will have no real meaning; they're just a synthetic key used to satisfy the unique constraint. Initially when you're drawing the board, you'll retrieve all of the objects, so you don't need to know what the key is.

Later you'll need to retrieve a piece so you can move it. You will find the desired piece based on its position on the board. To facilitate that, you'll add an index to the store based on the pos property. Since no two pieces can occupy the same space, the pos property can be used as a unique index. By specifying this as a unique index, you will get an error if you try to insert an object with the same position as an existing object.

■ **Caution**   Since the pos property is unique, you might be tempted to use it as the key. However, since you will be moving pieces, their position will change, and it's considered a poor design pattern to use a key that changes often. For Indexed DB, this is especially problematic since you can't actually change a key; you must delete the current object and then add it with the new key.

When creating an index, you must specify a keypath like this:

```
pieceStore.createIndex
    ("piecePosition", "pos", { unique: true });
```

In this case, the pos property is the keypath for this index. The keypath may include more than one property, in which case the index will be based on the combination of the selected properties. When an object store has an index, the index is automatically populated when an object is added to the store.

Resetting the Board

You created the piece object store but have not populated it yet. You'll do that in a separate function. To understand why, let me explain the database life cycle. The first time the web page is displayed, the database is opened, and since it doesn't exist, a new database will be created. This happens because the onupgradeneeded event is raised, and you implemented this event handler to create the object stores. When the page is displayed again (or simply refreshed), this step will be skipped since the database already exists.

Later, when you start moving the pieces around as well as deleting them, you'll want to move them back to their initial position when the page is reloaded. You can use this method to do that. You'll now add a resetBoard() function to the Chess.js script using the following code. This will be called not when the database is created but when the page is loaded.

```
function resetBoard() {
    var xact = db.transaction(["piece"], "readwrite");
    var pieceStore = xact.objectStore("piece");
    var request = pieceStore.clear();
    request.onsuccess = function(event) {
        for (var i in pieces) {
            pieceStore.put(pieces[i]);
        }
    }
}
```

This code creates a transaction using the read-write mode and specifies only the piece object store since that is the only one you'll need to access. Then the piece store is obtained from the transaction. The clear() method is used to delete all the objects from the store. Finally, all the objects in the pieces[] array are copied to the object store.

Now add the following code shown in bold to the onsuccess event handler. This will call the resetBoard() function after the database has been opened.

■ **Note** The onupgradeneeded event is raised, and its event handler must complete before the onsuccess event is raised. This ensures that the database has been properly configured before it is used.

```
var request = dbEng.open("Chess", 1);

request.onsuccess = function (event) {
    db = event.target.result;

    // Add the pieces to the board
    resetBoard();
}
```

■ **Tip** In the resetBoard() function, you called the put() method (repeatedly, 32 times). However, you did not get any response objects or implement any event handlers. This code appears to be working synchronously. Actually, these calls are processed asynchronously, and a response object is returned in both cases, but the return value was ignored. You could implement both onsuccess and onerror event handlers for these requests. In this case, you cheated a little. Since you don't need the result value like you would when retrieving data, you don't have to handle the onsuccess event. Because these calls are within a transaction, subsequent use of these object stores by a different transaction will be blocked until the updates are complete.

Drawing the Pieces

So far you have opened the database, configuring the object stores, if necessary. You have also populated the piece store with the initial positions. Now you're ready to draw the pieces. To do that you'll implement a drawAllPieces() function to iterate through all of the pieces and a drawPiece() function to display a single image. These functions will be similar to the functions you created in Chapter 23 with the same names. However, the data for these functions will be retrieved from the new database.

The drawAllPieces() function will use a cursor to process all the objects in the piece object store. For each piece, this will extract the necessary properties and pass them to the drawPiece() function. The drawPiece() function must then access the pieceType store to obtain the type properties such as height and width and display the image in the appropriate location.

Using a Cursor

When retrieving data from an object store, if you want to retrieve a single record using its key, use the get() method, which I will describe next. You can also select one or more objects using an index, and I will explain that later in this chapter. To get all the pieces, you'll need to access the entire object store, which you'll do using a cursor.

After creating the transaction and obtaining the object store, you'll call its openCursor() method. This returns an IDBRequest object, and you'll need to provide an onsuccess event handler for it. When the event fires, it provides the first object only. You can obtain the next object by calling the continue() method. To demonstrate this, add the function shown in Listing 25-5 to the Chess.js script.

Listing 25-5. Drawing the Pieces

```
function drawAllPieces() {

    var xact = db.transaction(["piece", "pieceType"]);

    var pieceStore = xact.objectStore("piece");
    var cursor = pieceStore.openCursor();
    cursor.onsuccess = function (event) {
        var item = event.target.result;
        if (item) {
            if (!item.value.killed) {
                drawPiece(item.value.type,
                          item.value.color,
                          item.value.row,
                          item.value.column,
                          xact);
            }
            item.continue();
        }
    }
}
```

This code creates a transaction that will use both the piece and pieceType object stores. The mode is not specified, and the default value is readonly. It then gets the piece object store and calls its openCursor() method. The onsuccess event handler gets the first object from the event object (using event.target.result). If the piece has not been captured, the drawPiece() function is called to display it, which you'll implement next. I'll explain the killed property later. You pass in all the properties that it will need such as type, color, row, and column. You'll also pass in the transaction object so the drawPiece() function can use the same transaction to access the pieceType store.

Calling the continue() method will cause the same event to be raised again, this time supplying the next object in the event.target.result property. If there are no more objects, the result property will be null. This is how you'll know all the objects have been processed.

The openCursor() method provides some basic capabilities to filter the objects that are returned. If no parameters are supplied, it will return all the objects in the store. You can specify a key range using one of the following:

- IDBKeyRange.only(): Specifies a single value and only records that match are returned.

- IDBKeyRange.lowerBound(): Returns only key values greater than the value specified. By default this is inclusive, so it will also return objects with keys that have an exact match as well, but you can change this to only return values that are greater.

- IDBKeyRange.upperBound(): Works just like lowerBound() except it returns values less than or equal to the value specified. I will demonstrate this later in the chapter.

- IDBKeyRange.bound(): Allows you to specify both a lower and upper bound. You can also indicate whether either of these values is inclusive. The default value for these is false, meaning not inclusive.

You can also pass a second parameter to the openCursor() function to specify the direction that the records are returned. The supported values for this are defined in the IDBCursorDirection enum. The possible values are as follows:

- next: Returns the next record in increasing key order (this is the default value)

- prev: Returns the previous record

- nextunique: Returns the next record that has a different key; this ignores duplicate keys

- prevunique: Returns the previous record, ignoring duplicate keys

The following example will return objects where the key is greater than 3 and less than or equal to 7 and return them in descending order. The last two parameters when creating the key range indicate that the lower bound is not inclusive but the upper bound is. When opening the cursor, the second parameter specifies the reverse direction should be used.

```
var keyRange = IDBKeyRange.bound(3, 7, false, true);
store.openCursor(keyRange, IDBCursorDirection.prev);
```

Retrieving a Single Object

Now you'll implement the drawPiece() function that will draw a single piece on the board. It must first access the pieceType object store to get the image details. In this case, you'll retrieve a single object using its key. The key to the pieceType object store is the type property. Add the function shown in Listing 25-6 to the Chess.js script.

Listing 25-6. Drawing a Single Piece

```
function drawPiece(type, color, row, column, xact) {
    var typeStore = xact.objectStore("pieceType");
    var request = typeStore.get(type);
    request.onsuccess = function (event) {
        var img;
```

```
    if (color === "black") {
        img = images[event.target.result.blackImage];
    }
    else {
        img = images[event.target.result.whiteImage];
    }

    chessContext.drawImage(img,
                (75 - event.target.result.width) / 2 + (75 * column),
                73 - event.target.result.height + (75 * row),
                event.target.result.width,
                event.target.result.height);
    }
}
```

This code uses the same transaction object, which is passed in. It obtains the pieceType object store and then calls its get() method. The onsuccess event handler gets the necessary properties and calls the canvas drawImage() method. Refer to Chapter 23 for more information about drawing images on a canvas.

Now add the call to drawAllPieces() in the onsuccess event handler for the open() call by adding the code shown in bold.

```
request.onsuccess = function (event) {
    db = event.target.result;

    // Add the pieces to the board
    resetBoard();

    // Draw the pieces in their initial positions
    drawAllPieces();
}
```

Testing the Application

Now you're ready to test the application, which will display the initial starting positions. Refresh the browser and you should see an alert letting you know that the database is being configured, as shown in Figure 25-3.

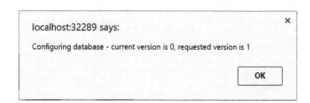

Figure 25-3. The alert showing the database is being configured

When you run this application again, this configuration will not be necessary. The chess board should look like Figure 25-4.

Figure 25-4. *The completed chess board with static positions*

■ **Tip**   If you want to remove the database from your machine, you can find the folder where they are stored and delete the corresponding subfolder. In Firefox, on my machine, the path is C:\Users\Mark\AppData\ Roaming\Mozilla\Firefox\Profiles\p1i1rsab.default\storage\default. In this folder there is a subfolder for each database. The subfolder name includes the protocol (http); domain name; and port, if applicable. For my application, this is http+++localhost+25519. Delete this folder and restart the browser. The page should reconfigure the database since it must create a new one. For Chrome, the file is found at: C:\Users\Mark\AppData\Local\Google\Chrome\User Data\Default\IndexedDB

If you open the Chess.html file in Chrome, you can access this database through the developers' tools. Select the Application link and then expand the IndexedDB item in the Storage section as shown in Figure 25-5.

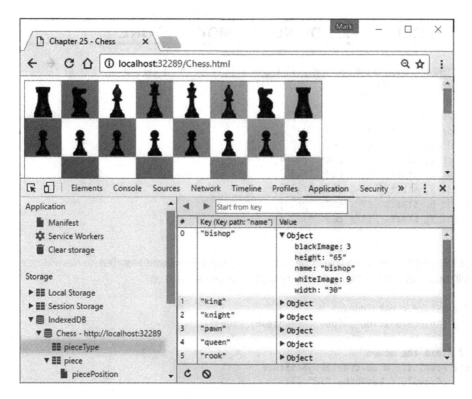

Figure 25-5. *Viewing the database in Chrome*

Moving the Pieces

Now you're ready to animate the board by moving the pieces. You'll use the same canned moves that were used in Chapter 23. A piece can be moved by simply updating its position and then redrawing the board. There is one complication, however; if a move captures a piece, you need to remove it from the board. For now, you'll simply delete the object from the store, but I'll show you a better way at the end of the chapter.

Defining the Moves

Since you're so database savvy now, you'll store the moves in the database as well. A move is defined by the starting and ending positions. For example, "move the piece at e2 to e3." You'll number these moves from 1 to 7 so they will be applied in the correct order. You'll need a new object store to hold the move details. To do that, you'll need to specify a new version, which will raise the onupgradeneeded event. Then you'll add logic the configureDatabase() function to create the new store.

EXERCISE 25-2. ADDING THE MOVES STORE

1. Add the following code to the beginning of the Chess.js script before the call to the drawBoard() function.

```
var moves = [
    { id: 1, start: "e2", end: "e3" },
    { id: 2, start: "e7", end: "e5" },
    { id: 3, start: "f1", end: "c4" },
    { id: 4, start: "h7", end: "h6" },
    { id: 5, start: "d1", end: "f3" },
    { id: 6, start: "g7", end: "g6" },
    { id: 7, start: "f3", end: "f7" }
];
```

2. Add the following code shown in bold to the end of the configureDatabase() function. This will create and populate the move store when the database is configured.

```
pieceStore.createIndex
    ("piecePosition", "pos", { unique: true });

// Store the moves
var moveStore = db.createObjectStore
    ("move", { keyPath: "id" });

for (var i in moves) {
    moveStore.add(moves[i]);
}
}
```

3. On the open() call, change the version to 2 as shown in bold. This will cause the onupgradeneeded event to be raised the next time the page is loaded.

```
if (!dbEng)
    alert("IndexedDB is not supported on this browser");
else {
    var request = dbEng.open("Chess", 2);
```

■ **Caution**   In this example, the configureDatabase() function simply removes all the existing data stores and then re-creates them. You could do this because you didn't need to be concerned about maintaining any of the existing data; it was reloaded using canned values. In many scenarios you will not be able to do that. Instead, you'll need to make specific changes based on the current version. For example, if version 5 is requested and the current version is 2, you'll need to add the version 3 changes and then the version 4 changes and finally the version 5 changes. Keep this in mind when planning your structure changes.

Converting the Position

The objects in the piece store have the row, column, and pos properties. The row and column properties follow the same convention that was used in Chapter 23, where the top-left square is at 0,0. That is consistent with how canvas works and simplifies the drawPiece() implementation. In contrast, the pos property uses the notation widely used in chess where the columns (files) go from a to h as you move left to right. The rows (ranks) go from 1 to 8 as you move from the bottom of the board to the top. Thus, a1 is the bottom-left square.

Before you get into the heavy work of moving the pieces, you'll create a function that will convert the pos property into row and column properties. When a piece is moved to e3, for example, you'll need to convert e3 into the corresponding row and column coordinates, which would be 5 (row) and 4 (column). Add the function shown in Listing 25-7 to the Chess.js script.

Listing 25-7. Implementing the computeRowColumn() Function

```
function computeRowColumn(oStart, end) {
    oStart.pos = end;
    switch (end.substring(0, 1)) {
        case "a": oStart.column = 0; break;
        case "b": oStart.column = 1; break;
        case "c": oStart.column = 2; break;
        case "d": oStart.column = 3; break;
        case "e": oStart.column = 4; break;
        case "f": oStart.column = 5; break;
        case "g": oStart.column = 6; break;
        case "h": oStart.column = 7; break;
    }

    oStart.row = 8 - parseInt(end.substr(1, 1));
}
```

The oStart parameter is the object from the piece store that was found at the starting position (e2 in our example). The end parameter is the ending position, e3, which is copied to the pos property since this will be the piece's new position.

This code then uses a switch statement to convert the a-h file notation into a 0–7 coordinate. This is then stored in the column property. The row property is computed by taking the last digit from the position and subtracting it from 8.

Making a Move

Just like you did in Chapter 23, you'll use a timer to make the next move every two seconds. You'll need a timer variable so you can clear the timer when the animation is done. You'll also need to keep track of the current move. Add the two variables shown in bold to the Chess.js script just before the drawBoard() method is called.

```
var moveNumber = 1;
var timer;

drawBoard();
```

Moving a piece will require making up to five database calls:

1. Get the next object from the move store (this defines the start and end positions).

2. Get the object at the start position.

3. Get the object at the end position (there will be only one if the move is capturing a piece).

4. Remove the object at the end position (this step will be needed only on some moves).

5. Update the object at the start position (to move it to the end position).

These calls will all be made using the same transaction. As I demonstrated at the beginning of the chapter, you'll need to nest the onsuccess event handlers for each of these calls. Add the makeNextMove() function shown in Listing 25-8 to the Chess.js script.

Listing 25-8. Implementing the makeNextMove() Function

```
function makeNextMove() {

    var xact = db.transaction(["move", "piece"], "readwrite");
    var moveStore = xact.objectStore("move");

    moveStore.get(moveNumber).onsuccess = function (e1) {
        var startPos = e1.target.result.start;
        var endPos = e1.target.result.end;
        var startKey = null;
        var oStart = null;

        var pieceStore = xact.objectStore("piece");
        var index = pieceStore.index("piecePosition");

        index.getKey(startPos).onsuccess = function (e2) {
            startKey = e2.target.result;

            index.get(startPos).onsuccess = function (e3) {
                oStart = e3.target.result;

                // If there is a piece at the ending location, we'll
                // need to update it to prevent a duplicate pos index
                removePiece(endPos, oStart, startKey, pieceStore);
            }
        }
    }
}
```

This function creates a transaction that will access both the move and piece stores. The mode is set to readwrite because the objects in the piece store will be modified. It then gets the move store and calls its get() method specifying the current move, which is the key to the table. This will return a single object, and the start and end positions are extracted from the result in the onsuccess event handler.

■ Tip Notice that this code doesn't explicitly define a request variable. Instead, the onsuccess event handler is attached directly to the database call. In the previous examples, I declared a request variable and then attached the event handler to it to help you see what was happening. However, attaching the event handler directly to the method accomplishes the same thing but simplifies the code a little.

Obtaining the Object Key

For the piece store, you used a key generator, so the key is not part of the object. The code in the makeNextMove() function will use the index based on the pos property to retrieve the object at the start position (and also at the end position if there is a piece there). To update or delete an object, you will need its key.

When retrieving the piece object at the start position, this code first gets the piece store from the transaction. It then gets the piecePosition index from the store. To get the key value, you'll need to call index.getKey() method, which returns the key for the requested start position. This is stored in the startKey variable.

To get the desired object, you'll call the index.get() method passing in the position to search for. This returns the object at the requested start position and stores it in the oStart variable.

In both cases, the data is returned in the result property. Again, the event handlers that process the results are nested.

With the necessary data obtained, the removePiece() method is called, passing in the following parameters:

- end: The ending position of the piece being moved

- oStart: An object representing the piece being moved

- startID: The key to the oStart object

- pieceStore : The piece store that will be used to perform the update

Performing the Update

Now you'll implement the removePiece() function. This is perhaps misnamed since it will remove a piece only when necessary. Add the code shown in Listing 25-9 to the Chess.js script to implement the removePiece() function:

Listing 25-9. The removePiece() implementation

```
function removePiece(endPos, oStart, startKey, pieceStore) {
    var index = pieceStore.index("piecePosition");
    index.getKey(endPos).onsuccess = function (e4) {
        var endKey = e4.target.result;
        if (endKey) {
            pieceStore.delete(endKey).onsuccess = function (e5) {
                movePiece(oStart, startKey, endPos, pieceStore)
            }
        }
        else
            movePiece(oStart, startKey, endPos, pieceStore);
    }
}
```

This code gets the key at the ending position. If there is a piece there, it calls the delete() method to remove it and then calls the movePiece() function in the onsuccess handler for the delete() method. Notice that it does not retrieve the object; only the key is needed to perform the delete. If there is no piece there, it just calls the movePiece() function. When calling the movePiece() function, all the data it needs is passed to it including the object, its key, the end position, and the object store that it will use.

Now you'll implement the movePiece() function that will finally perform the actual update. To update an object, you call the put() method. Unlike the add() method that you used earlier to add the pieces, the put() method requires both the object and the key. If there is no object with the specified key, the object will be added. Add the movePiece() method shown in Listing 25-10 to the end of the Chess.js script.

Listing 25-10. Implementing the movePiece() Function

```
function movePiece(oStart, startID, end, pieceStore) {
    computeRowColumn(oStart, end);

    var startUpdateReq = pieceStore.put(oStart, startID);
    startUpdateReq.onsuccess = function (event) {

        moveNumber++;

        drawBoard();
        drawAllPieces();

        if (moveNumber > 7) {
            clearInterval(timer);
            chessContext.font = "30pt Arial";
            chessContext.fillStyle = "black";
            chessContext.fillText("Checkmate!", 200, 220);
        }
    }
}
```

This code first computes the row and column properties using the computeRowColumn() function that you created earlier. It then updates the object. In the onsuccess event handler, it increments the moveNumber variable and draws the board and all of the pieces using the existing functions. Finally, if this is the last move, the timer is cleared and the "Checkmate!" text is drawn on the canvas.

Starting the Animation

The last step is to start the timer that will cause the makeNextMove() function to be called. You'll do this in the onsuccess event handler for the open() call. Add the code shown in bold:

```
var request = dbEng.open("Chess", 2);

request.onsuccess = function (event) {
    db = event.target.result;

    // Add the pieces to the board
    resetBoard();

    // Draw the pieces in their initial positions
    drawAllPieces();
```

```
// Start the animation
timer = setInterval(makeNextMove, 2000);
}
```

Save your changes and refresh the browser. You should see the alert letting you know that the database is being configured since you changed the database version. After a series of moves, you should see the completed chess board shown in Figure 25-6.

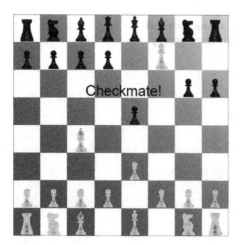

Figure 25-6. *The completed chess board*

Tracking the Captured Pieces

When capturing a piece, you simply deleted the object, and that works since the piece doesn't need to be displayed. However, if your application wants to keep track of the pieces that were captured, you might want to keep the object in the store. Now I'll show you how to change this to update the object instead of deleting it. I also show you how to query this store to list the pieces that have been captured.

The first step is to change the removePiece() function. Instead of deleting the object at the end position, you'll update it and set the killed property. You'll also need to change the pos property since there is a unique index on this. Since the piece is not displayed, the position can be anything. To ensure it is unique, you'll prefix its unique ID with an X. Also, by prefixing these with an X, you'll be able to query for them, as I'll explain later.

Comment out the delete() call and add the code shown in bold:

```
function removePiece(end, oStart, startID, pieceStore) {
    var index = pieceStore.index("piecePosition");
    index.getKey(end).onsuccess = function (e4) {
        var endKey = e4.target.result;
```

```
        if (endKey) {
            //pieceStore.delete (endKey).onsuccess = function (e5) {
            //     movePiece(oStart, startID, pieceStore);
            //}

            index.get(endPos).onsuccess = function (e5) {
                var oEnd = e5.target.result;
                oEnd.pos = 'x' + endKey;
                oEnd.killed = true;
                pieceStore.put(oEnd, endKey).onsuccess = function (e6) {
                    movePiece(oStart, startKey, endPos, pieceStore);
                }
            }
        }
        else
            movePiece(oStart, startID, end, pieceStore);
    }
}
```

Now add the code shown in Listing 25-11 to the Chess.js script to implement the displayCapturedPieces() function:

Listing 25-11. The displayCapturedPieces() implementation

```
function displayCapturedPieces() {
    var xact = db.transaction(["piece"]);
    var textOut = "";

    var pieceStore = xact.objectStore("piece");
    var index = pieceStore.index("piecePosition");

    var keyRange = IDBKeyRange.lowerBound("x");
    var cursor = index.openCursor(keyRange);

    cursor.onsuccess = function (event) {
        var item = event.target.result;
        if (item) {
            textOut += " - " + item.value.color + " " +
                                item.value.type + "\r\n";
            item.continue();
        }
        else if (textOut.length > 0)
            alert("The following pieces were captured:\r\n" + textOut);
    }
}
```

This code creates a read-only transaction using only the piece store. It then gets the store and its piecePosition index. It defines a key range using a lower bound of x. This will only return objects that begin with x or greater. Since the pieces on the board will have a position that starts with a through h, these will be excluded. The code then iterates through the cursor and concatenates the piece details into a text string. The result is displayed using an alert() function.

■ **Caution**   Be aware that the string comparisons in the key range are case sensitive. If you had used an uppercase X, this would not have worked since a lowercase a comes after an uppercase X. The W3C specification provides some details on how comparisons are supposed to work. For details, see the article at www.w3.org/TR/IndexedDB/#key-construct.

Now you'll need to call this function after the animation is completed. Add the following line of code to the movePiece() function after the "Checkmate!" text is displayed:

```
displayCapturedPieces();
```

Save your changes and refresh the browser. After the animation has finished, you should see the alert shown in Figure 25-7.

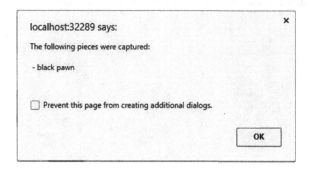

Figure 25-7. *Listing the captured pieces*

Summary

In this chapter, you took a crash course in Indexed DB. There is a lot that you can do with Indexed DB. Because the data is on the client, you avoid round trips to the server. Through a fairly simple application, you utilized most of the capabilities of this new technology. Probably the biggest challenge is to get used to the asynchronous processing. The sample application provides lots of examples of nesting successive calls through the onsuccess event handler. The following are some of the key concepts to remember:

- Create the database and create its structure by responding to the onupgradeneeded event handler when the database is opened. Use the version to force an upgrade, if necessary.

- Objects in a store must have a unique key, which can be defined either by a key path for inline keys or by a key generator for out-of-line keys. You can also supply the key manually when the object is added.

- All data access (read and write) must be done through a transaction object. When creating the transaction, you must specify the scope, which is the list of object stores that it will use as well as the type of access that is required.

- You can add one or more indices to an object store. Each index maps a key path in the object to the object's key.

- Use a cursor to process multiple objects in an object store. The objects that are selected can be filtered by specifying a key range.

- Add an object to the object store and update it later.

- Retrieve an object from an object store.

- Delete an object from an object store by specifying the object's key.

- Obtain the key for an object by using the getKey() method of the index.

- Use the put() method of an object store to add or update an object. The put() method requires both the object and the key. This will add the object if the specified key is not found.

The next chapter will demonstrate how you can use geolocation and mapping in your web page.

CHAPTER 26

■ ■ ■

Geolocation and Mapping

This chapter will demonstrate two technologies that provide powerful features that enable you to easily create some useful web sites. Geolocation provides a standardized API that is used to determine the client's location. Mapping technology adds the ability to display this location on a map along with other points of interest. Together, these form a platform that has many useful applications.

In this chapter, you'll use the geolocation API to find your current position. The accuracy of that position will vary greatly depending on available hardware and the environment. However, HTML5 defines a standard API that is used on all devices so you can provide device-independent solutions.

Just knowing your location in terms of latitude and longitude is not very helpful. To put this data to use, you'll use the Bing Maps API to display that location on a map. Then you can map additional points of interest and see them in relation to your current location.

Understanding Geolocation

While not technically part of the HTML5 specification, the WC3 has defined a standard API for accessing geolocation information, which is supported by all major current browser versions. The technology that determines the location, however, varies greatly depending on the device capabilities and the client's environment.

Surveying Geolocation Technologies

Several technologies can be used to determine the current location, including the following:

- Global positioning system (GPS): GPS communicates with satellites to determine the current location with extremely high accuracy, particularly in rural areas. Tall buildings in an urban area can affect the accuracy, but in most cases GPS provides good results. The biggest limitation is that this doesn't work indoors well. To use GPS, the device must have specific GPS hardware, but this is becoming increasingly common on mobile devices.

- Wi-Fi positioning: Wi-Fi networks have a relatively short range and systems such as Skyhook Wireless maintain a large database of Wi-Fi networks and their locations. Simply being connected to a Wi-Fi network will give a pretty good idea of where you are. Often, however, you may be within range of multiple networks, and the system can use triangulation to determine the location with even greater accuracy. Of course, this requires that you have a device that is Wi-Fi enabled, and it doesn't work in rural areas where there are no Wi-Fi networks.

© Mark J. Collins 2017

M. J. Collins, *Pro HTML5 with CSS, JavaScript, and Multimedia*, DOI 10.1007/978-1-4842-2463-2_26

- Cell tower triangulation: This uses the same principle as Wi-Fi positioning except it uses cellular telephone towers. It is not as accurate, however, because a cell tower has a much larger range. Since all cell phones will have the ability to communicate with cell towers, this technology has a broad application.

- IP block: Every device that connects to the Internet will have an IP address, which is usually provided by the ISP. Each ISP will have a block of IP addresses that it can use, which are typically assigned by geographical location. So, the IP address with which you connect to the Internet can provide a general location, usually a metropolitan area. There are several factors, however, that can yield incorrect results, such as NAT'ed addresses.

Each of these technologies has different hardware requirements and provide varying levels of accuracy. With the geolocation specification, you can easily request the current location from the browser and let it determine the best way to supply that based on the current hardware and access to external sources including satellites, cell towers, and Wi-Fi networks.

Using Geolocation Data

Most people think of geolocation as a device that provides turn-by-turn directions, but that is only one application of this technology. Of course, this requires precise location that can be obtained only through GPS. However, even when the current location is far less accurate, your web site can still make valuable use of this information. Even if the location is determined only by the IP address, this will usually be sufficient to set the default language, for example. You may need to allow the end user to override this, but most of your audience will see the initial page in their native language.

When retrieving the current location, the geolocation service also returns the estimated accuracy. Your application should use this to determine the features that will be provided. Suppose, for example, that you're creating a web page for the U.S. Postal Service that shows where the nearest post offices are. If the current location is known with high accuracy, the web page can show a map and indicate the current location as well as the nearby post offices. In addition, it could provide the estimated driving time to each.

However, if the location is known with lesser accuracy, the page could display a map that shows where the post offices are in that general area. Presumably, the user will know where they are and can use this information to determine the best location to use. However, if the accuracy is poor, the page should prompt for a ZIP code and then display the nearest post offices based on the user input. So, depending on the accuracy, the application can gracefully degrade the functionality.

Using the Geolocation API

To demonstrate how to use the geolocation API, you'll create a simple web page that calls the API to determine your current location. Initially, this data will be displayed on the web page as text. Later you'll display this location on a map.

Creating the Web Project

You'll start by creating a web page that is set up much like the projects in the previous chapters.

EXERCISE 26-1. CREATING THE WEB PROJECT

1. Create a new web page called **Geolocation.html**, using the basic markup:

```
<!DOCTYPE html>

<html lang="en">
    <head>
        <meta charset="utf-8" />
        <title>Chapter 26 - Geolocation</title>
        <script src="Geolocation.js" defer></script>
    </head>
    <body>
    </body>
</html>
```

2. Then create a **Geolocation.js** script file using the following code.

```
"use strict";
```

3. Add a div element in the empty body element of the Geolocation.html file, using the following markup:

```
<div>
    <span id="lbl"> </span>
</div>
```

Using the Geolocation Object

The geolocation API is provided by the geolocation object, which you can access through the navigator object like this:

```
navigator.geolocation
```

If a falsy value is returned such as null or undefined, then geolocation is not supported on the current browser. You can check for support using code like this:

```
if (!navigator.geolocation) {
    alert("Geolocation is not supported");
}
else
    // do something with geolocation
```

To get the current location, use the getCurrentPosition() function, which takes three parameters:

- A callback function that is executed when the call is successful
- An error callback function that is called when an error occurs
- A PositionOptions collection that contains zero or more options

The last two parameters can be omitted. The following options are supported:

- maximumAge: The browser can cache previous positions and return this without actually trying to determine the location. However, the maximumAge attribute specifies how long (in milliseconds) a previous position can be reused without re-querying the current location.

- timeout: The timeout attribute specifies how long the browser should wait for a response from the geolocation object. This is also expressed in milliseconds.

- enableHighAccuracy: This is just a hint to the browser. If you don't need greater accuracy for a particular purpose, setting this to false may yield a faster response or use less power, which is a consideration for mobile devices.

If the call was successful, the position is passed to the callback function that was specified. The Position object includes a coords object that contains the following required properties:

- latitude (specified in degrees)

- longitude (specified in degrees)

- accuracy (specified in meters)

In addition, the following optional properties may be provided depending on the environment and the available hardware. If these are not supported, they will be set to null. (The optional properties are typically available only when GPS is used).

- altitude (specified in meters)

- altitudeAccuracy (specified in meters)

- heading (specified in degrees; north = 0, west = 90, and so on, NaN if stationary)

- speed (specified in meters/second, 0 if stationary)

These properties can be obtained by the callback function like this:

```
function successCallback(pos) {
    var lat = pos.coords.latitude;
    var long = pos.coords.longitude;
    var accuracy =  pos.coords.accuracy + " meters";
}
```

If the call was not successful, the PositionError object is passed to the error callback function. This object includes a code property and a message property. The error code will have one of three possible values.

- 1: PERMISSION_DENIED

- 2: POSITION_UNAVAILABLE

- 3: TIMEOUT

■ **Caution**   Your application will get the location and simply display it (and later map it). However, your script could easily pass this information back to the server, which is a potential privacy issue. Since the browser cannot control what the client does with this information, for privacy reasons the browser may block the access to the geolocation object. In this case, the PERMISSION_DENIED error code is returned. I will demonstrate this later.

If the client is moving and you want to continuously monitor the current location, you could call the getCurrentLocation() function repeatedly using a setInterval() function. To simplify this, the geolocation object includes a watchPosition() function. This takes the same three parameters as the getCurrentLocation() function (success callback, error callback, and options). The callback function is then invoked whenever the position changes. The watchPosition() function returns a timer handle. You can pass this handle to the clearWatch() function when you want to stop monitoring the position like this:

```
var handle = geolocation.watchPosition(callback);
...
geolocation.clearWatch(handle);
```

Displaying the Location

Now you'll add code to your application to get the current location and display it. The web page has a span element with an id of lbl. You'll get the geolocation object and call its getCurrentLocation() function. Both the success and error callback functions will display the appropriate results in the span element.

EXERCISE 26-2. DISPLAYING THE LOCATION

1. Add the following code to the Geolocation.js script.

    ```
    var lbl = document.getElementById("lbl");
    var latitude = 0;
    var longitude = 0;

    if (navigator.geolocation) {
        navigator.geolocation
            .getCurrentPosition(showLocation,
                                errorHandler,
                                {
                                    maximumAge: 100,
                                    timeout: 6000,
                                    enableHighAccuracy: true
                                });
    }
    else {
        alert("Geolocation not suported");
    }

    function showLocation(pos) {
        // Save the coordinates for later
        latitude = pos.coords.latitude;
        longitude = pos.coords.logitude;

        lbl.innerHTML =
            "Your latitude: " + pos.coords.latitude +
            " and longitude: " + pos.coords.longitude +
            " (Accuracy of: " +  pos.coords.accuracy + " meters)";
    }
    ```

```
        function errorHandler(e) {
            if (e.code === 1) { // PERMISSION_DENIED
                lbl.innerHTML = "Permission denied. - " + e.message;
            } else if (e.code === 2) { //POSITION_UNAVAILABLE
                lbl.innerHTML = "Make sure your network connection is active and " +
                    "try this again. - " + e.message;
            } else if (e.code === 3) { //TIMEOUT
                lbl.innerHTML = "A timeout ocurred; try again. - " + e.message;
            }
        }
```

2. Display the Geolocation.html file in a browser. The first time a site tries to access the geolocation object, you will get a prompt like the one shown in Figure 26-1.

Figure 26-1. Prompting for geolocation access

■ **Note**   I'm using the Edge browser for this demonstration. If you're using a different browser, this prompt may work a little differently.

---

3. To test the error handler, choose the "No" option. The page should display an error message like the one shown in Figure 26-2.

Permission denied. - This site doesn't have permission to ask for your location.

Figure 26-2. Displaying the access denied error

4. Open the Geolocation.html file with a different browser. Your current location should be displayed as shown in Figure 26-3.

Your latitude: 37.811079 and longitude: -122.410546 (Accuracy of: 1812 meters)

Figure 26-3. Displaying the current location

I'm using a normal LAN-connected machine without cell or GPS support, so it is using the IP address to determine the location. Consequently, the accuracy estimate is 1.8km (just over a mile).

■ **Note**   Geolocation works on all current browsers. However, if you try this application on an older browser such as IE 8, you'll see the alert that geolocation is not supported.

Using Mapping Platforms

Simply displaying the latitude and longitude is not interesting (or helpful). However, showing your location relative to other points of interest is much more useful. And displaying them on a map with roads and other reference points can really put this information to work. Fortunately, mapping technology has become so sophisticated and accessible that this is really easy to do.

■ **Note**   For the demonstration in this chapter, I will be using Bing Maps. There are other mapping platforms available. If you're interested, check out the article at http://en.wikipedia.org/wiki/Comparison_of_web_map_services for an overview of the different mapping services.

Creating a Bing Maps Account

To use Bing Maps, you'll need to first set up an account, which is free for developers. Once your account is created, you'll receive a key that you'll need to include when accessing the mapping API. I will take you through the process of setting up an account.

EXERCISE 26-3. CREATING A BING MAPS ACCOUNT

1. Go to the Bing Maps site at this address: www.microsoft.com/maps/create-a-bing-maps-key.aspx.

2. You need to get a key that will allow you to access the mapping API. Go to the Basic Key tab. A free, basic key is fine for working through these exercises. Click the Get the Basic Key link near the bottom of the page.

3. In the next page, you'll need to log in with a Windows Live ID. If you don't have one, click the Create button to create an account.

4. Once you have signed in, you should see the "Create account" page shown in Figure 26-4.

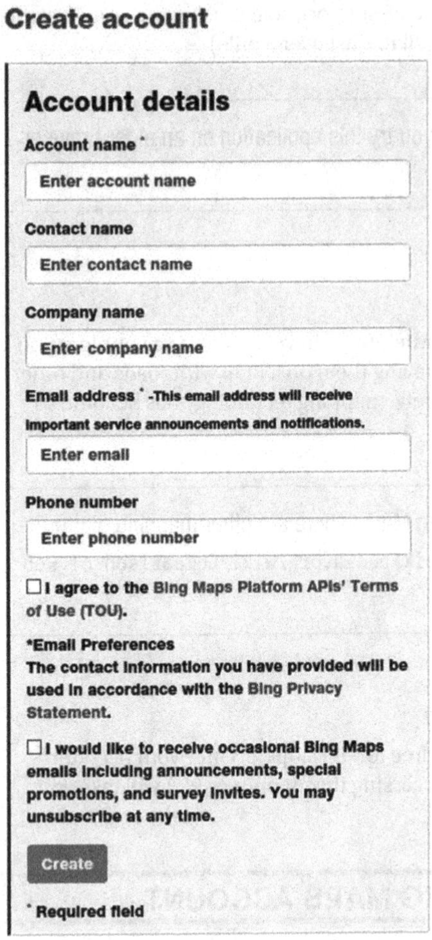

Create account

Account details

Account name *

```
Enter account name
```

Contact name

```
Enter contact name
```

Company name

```
Enter company name
```

Email address * -This email address will receive
important service announcements and notifications.

```
Enter email
```

Phone number

```
Enter phone number
```

☐ I agree to the Bing Maps Platform APIs' Terms
of Use (TOU).

*Email Preferences
The contact information you have provided will be
used in accordance with the Bing Privacy
Statement.

☐ I would like to receive occasional Bing Maps
emails including announcements, special
promotions, and survey invites. You may
unsubscribe at any time.

Create

* Required field

Figure 26-4. *The "Create account" page*

5. Enter an account name. This is just for you to identify it if you have multiple
    accounts; testing is fine. The email address should default in from your Windows
    Live account. Make sure you select the check box agreeing to the terms of use.
    Click the Save button to create the account.

6. From the My account menu, select the "My keys" link. You probably won't have any existing keys shown and you will be presented with the Create key dialog. If not, click the link to create a new key.

7. In the "Create key" page, enter an application name such as HTML5 Test. For the URL, enter **http://localhost** and select Universal Windows App for the application type, as shown in Figure 26-5. Click the Submit button.

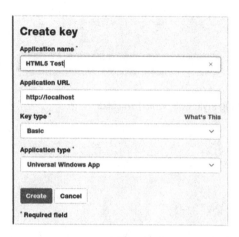

Figure 26-5. *Creating a key*

■ **Note** Bing Maps monitors the use of your key. However, since you're not actually deploying this to a public-facing web site, this is not really applicable. If you are developing a commercial application, you can use a free key for development purposes, but you will need to purchase a key for the live web site.

---

8. After the key has been generated, you should see it displayed on the page. Save this because you will need it later.

Adding a Map

Now you'll add a map to your web page. You'll first add a div element to the page that will contain the map. You'll also need to add a reference to the script that is used to manipulate the map. Then you'll display the map, centering it on your current location.

```
                    EXERCISE 26-4. ADDING A MAP
```

1. Add the code shown in bold to the body element, which will add the div that the map will be displayed in.

   ```
   <body>
       <div>
           <span id="lbl"> </span>
       </div>
       <div id="map">
       </div>
   </body>
   ```

2. Create a **Geolocation.css** style sheet with the following style rule, which will size the div that will contain the map.

   ```
   #map {
       width: 800px;
       height: 1000px;
       border: 1px solid black;
   }
   ```

3. Add the following link element to the head element, which will reference the Geolocation.css stylesheet.

   ```
   <link rel="stylesheet" href="Geolocation.css" />
   ```

4. Add the following script element inside the head element. This will enable your page to call the map API. This needs to come after the Geolocation.js script element.

   ```
   <script
       src=http://www.bing.com/api/maps/mapcontrol?branch=release&callback=
       DisplayMap
       async defer>
   </script>
   ```

This will load the mapping script asynchronously and then call the DisplayMap() function when it has finished loading.

5. Add the DisplayMap() function to the Geolocation.js script using the following code. You'll need to insert your API key that was obtained earlier in Exercise 26-3.

```
function DisplayMap() {
    var map = new Microsoft.Maps.Map(document.getElementById('map'),
        {
        credentials: '<use your key here>',
        center: new Microsoft.Maps.Location(latitude, longitude),
        mapTypeId: Microsoft.Maps.MapTypeId.aerial,
        zoom: 20
        });
```

The call to the Map() function takes two parameters; the first is the HTML element that will display the map. This is the div element you set up earlier and is obtained by using the getElementById() method. The second parameter is a JSON object with a series of options. The credentials field contains your API key, the center field specifies center point of the map, which is the location returned by the geolocation object. In addition, the mapTypeId specifies that the aerial view should be used and zoom is set to 20.

6. Refresh the browser. Depending on your location, your page should look like Figure 26-6. Notice the controls at the top-right corner of the page. You can use this to zoom in or out and pan in any direction. You can also change the view to Road or Streetside.

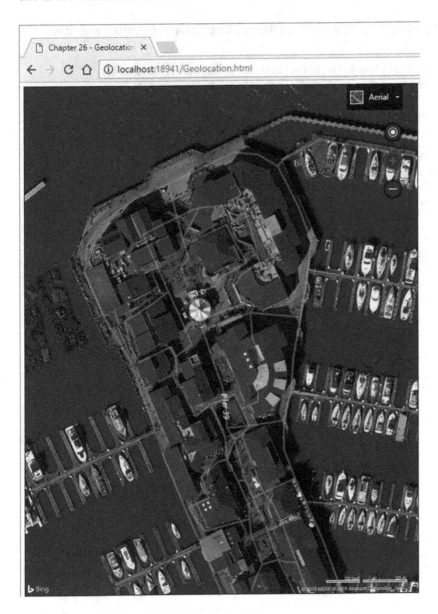

Figure 26-6. *Displaying the initial map*

When calling the Map() function to specify the center location, this code also set the zoom to 20. Depending on your application, you may not want to zoom in that far initially. Try this code using 15 or 16 to see how that looks. Of course, the user can also adjust the zoom once the map is displayed.

Adding Pushpins

Now you'll display some pushpins on the map. To add a pushpin, you first create a Pushpin object, specifying its location. Then add it to the map's entities collection. First, you will add a default pushpin at the current location. Later, you'll add custom pushpins to indicate points of interest.

Add the following code shown in bold to the end of the DisplayMap() function:

```
function DisplayMap() {
    var map = new Microsoft.Maps.Map(document.getElementById('map'),
        {
        ...
        });

    var pushpin = new Microsoft.Maps.Pushpin(map.getCenter(), {
        color: 'orange',
        text: 'X',
        title: 'You are here'
    });
    map.entities.push(pushpin);
}
```

The Pushpin() method takes a location and a JSON object with options. For the location, I'm simply using the getCenter() method to get the center point of the map, which was specified when the map was loaded. I could also have created a location object like this:

```
new Microsoft.Maps.Location(latitude, longitude)
```

For the options, I'm setting the color to orange, putting an "X" on the pushpin and adding a "You are here" label. Refresh the browser and you should see a pushpin indicating the current location, as shown in Figure 26-7.

Figure 26-7. *Adding a pushpin in the current location*

One of the most common uses of maps in a web page is to show where there are nearby locations. For example, you might have multiple store locations, and you'll want to show where each one is. Or perhaps you are in a police department and want to map out where certain crimes have been committed. You could have a public transit system and want to show where all the bus or train stops are.

Each of these scenarios is basically the same; you have a collection of locations that you want to show on a map. You can add as many locations as you want. For each, just create a pushpin object and add it to the entities collection. If you have more than one location, you should make the pushpins look different so the user can easily distinguish between them.

For this demonstration, you will indicate where there are nearby restrooms. Instead of a standard pushpin, you will use an image with a familiar restroom icon. Normally you would query the server to get a list of locations based on the where the client is. However, to simplify this exercise, these will be hard-coded.

■ **Caution** I am hard-coding the location of the restrooms, which are probably nowhere near where your current location is. You can either provide different restroom locations that are near you or simply override your current location to match mine. This will be consistent with the restroom locations.

EXERCISE 12-5. ADDING CUSTOM PUSHPINS

1. The source code download contains a `restroom.gif` image file. Drag this into your web project.

2. Add the following declaration at the top of the existing `Geolocation.js` script. This defines the locations of the restrooms.

```
var restrooms = [
    { lat: 37.810079, long: -122.410806 },
    { lat: 37.809579, long: -122.410206 },
    { lat: 37.811279, long: -122.410446 }
];
```

3. Add the following code to the `DisplayMap()` function just before creating the map object. This will override your current location to be near where the restrooms are.

```
// Override these for testing purposes
latitude = 37.810579;
longitude = -122.410546;
```

4. Add the following functions to the end of the Geolocation.js script. The markRestrooms() function iterates through this array, calling the markRestroom() function for each. The markRestroom() function adds a single pushpin. This first creates an options collection that defines the image file to use as well as the size of the image. This is passed in when creating the Pushpin object.

```
function markRestrooms(map) {
    for (var i in restrooms) {
        markRestroom(map, restrooms[i].lat, restrooms[i].long);
    }
}

function markRestroom(map, lat, long) {
    var pushpinOptions = { icon: '/images/restroom.gif', width: 35, height: 35 };
    var pushpin = new Microsoft.Maps.Pushpin
        (new Microsoft.Maps.Location(lat, long), pushpinOptions);
    map.entities.push(pushpin);
}
```

5. Add this function call at the end of the DisplayMap() function to display the additional pushpins:

```
// Display the restroom locations
markRestrooms(map);
```

6. Refresh the browser and you should now see pushpins where the restrooms are located, as shown in Figure 26-8.

Figure 26-8. Adding the restroom pushpins

■ **Caution** This is purely fictional data. If you happen to be at San Francisco's Pier 39 while reading this book, don't use this map to try to find a restroom.

There is a lot more that you can do with the mapping API. For example, you can display directions for getting to a selected point of interest. You can even display where the traffic is currently heavy. Check out the interactive SDK at http://www.bing.com/api/maps/sdk/mapcontrol/isdk. You can try each feature, and the corresponding JavaScript code is displayed underneath the map.

Summary

In this chapter, you combined the features of geolocation with Bing Maps to create a really useful web site. Geolocation requests are processed asynchronously. After getting the geolocation object, you call its getCurrentPosition() function and specify the success and error callback functions. The Position object is passed to the callback function when the location has been retrieved. It contains the latitude, longitude, and estimated accuracy. If the client has GPS capability, the Position object will also include the altitude, speed, and direction.

Mapping platforms such as Bing Maps are really easy to use and integrate into your web page. In this application, you displayed the map and centered in on the current location. You also added pushpins to show where the nearby restrooms are.

APPENDIX A

AJAX

In traditional web applications (sometimes called the old way of doing things), a page is rendered, which the user interacts with; perhaps they log in, enter some search criteria, or choose an option. This information is then posted back to the server and a new page is returned and rendered on the browser. This, of course, requires a server round trip as well as downloading and rendering a new page. However, there is another way that is much more responsive. You can simply update the current page using the DOM manipulation techniques I showed you in Chapter 18. However, you'll need to get some data from the server to do that, and this is where Ajax comes in. Another common use of Ajax is to download only a partial page initially. While the user is reading the part that has been downloaded, Ajax is used in the background to load the remainder of the page.

Ajax is an acronym that stands for Asynchronous JavaScript And Xml. Ajax is not so much a technology but rather a design pattern that uses a collection of technologies. In a nutshell, Ajax is basically JavaScript code running on the client that makes a server call to retrieve data. While making the call, a callback function is registered to handle the response. When this technology was first developed, XML was the expected format for the response, hence the name. However, the response does not have to be XML; today, in most cases, it will be JSON or HTML.

The concept was first introduced in Internet Explorer 5 with an ActiveX object named XMLHTTP. Other browsers followed suit with an XMLHttpRequest object that provides similar functionality. With IE7, Microsoft also supports the XMLHttpRequest object.

Note   Ajax is used for communicating with RESTful web services. To be able to use Ajax you'll need to understand the basics of RESTful web services such as HTTP verbs and request and response headers. If this is new to you, I suggest reading this article: http://www.drdobbs.com/web-development/restful-web-services-a-tutorial/240169069

Making a Request

To make a request you'll need to create an instance of the XMLHttpRequest object. Then you'll need to do the following:

- Assign a callback function to handle the readystatechange event; I'll cover this a bit later.
- Open the connection; you'll need to specify the HTTP verb such as GET, POST, PUT, or DELETE and the URL of the web service that you are calling.
- Set any request headers that are needed.
- Send the request.

© Mark J. Collins 2017
M. J. Collins, *Pro HTML5 with CSS, JavaScript, and Multimedia*, DOI 10.1007/978-1-4842-2463-2_27

For a simple GET request, the code might look like this:

```
var myRequest = new XMLHttpRequest();
myRequest.onreadystatechange = displayResults;
myRequest.open("GET", url);
myRequest.setRequestHeader("Content-Type", "application/json");
myRequest.send();
```

If using a POST or PUT verb, you would likely have data to pass in the body of the request. In this case, the body is passed this in the send() method. For example:

```
myRequest.send(body);
```

▪ **Caution**   In general, Ajax calls can only be made to services in the same domain as the page they are called from. If your page origin is http://someDomain.com, for example, you can only call services whose URL starts with http://someDomain.com. There are ways around these restrictions that are beyond the scope of this book. For more information, see the following article: https://developer.mozilla.org/en-US/docs/Web/HTTP/Access_control_CORS

Handing the Response

You may have noticed that there is a single callback function that will be called whenever the ready state (or just state) of the request changes. The state will change when the response is received or when an error occurs, so your callback function needs to handle both scenarios. There are five possible state values and the function will be called whenever the state changes to any of them:

- 0 - UNSENT
- 1 - OPENED
- 2 - HEADERS_RECEIVED
- 3 - LOADING
- 4 - DONE

In most cases, you won't care about the interim states and only need to know when the request is complete. You can use the constant XMLHttpRequest.DONE, which has the value 4. The callback function will typically start with code like this to ignore all other state transitions.

```
if (myRequest.readyState === XMLHttpRequest.DONE) {
    ... do something
}
```

You should also wrap this code in a try/catch block because some errors, such as network errors, will generate an exception. The next thing that you'll need to do is to check the status of the request. The ready state just tells you that the request has completed; you still don't know if it was successful. This is done by checking the status property, like this:

```
switch(myRequest.status) {
    case 500: // server error
        ...
        break;
    case 404: // not found
        ...
        break;
    case 200: // success
        ...
        break;
}
```

■ **Tip** The status values that are returned are the standard HTTP status codes defined by the HTTP specification (http://www.w3.org/Protocols/rfc2616/rfc2616-sec10.html). This Mozilla article provides a more condensed version: https://developer.mozilla.org/en-US/docs/Web/HTTP/Status.

Assuming you get a successful status, 200, you then need to extract the data from the response message. The data will be in the responseText property and you'll need to convert this depending on the format you're expecting. For example, if JSON is being returned, you can get the actual object like this:

```
var data = JSON.parse(myRequest.responseText);
```

Summary

You'll generally use a function to send the request, and there will be a different function to handle the response. The XMLHttpRequest object needs to be shared by both functions, so you'll need to declare it outside of the function scope. Putting it all together, a simple solution is shown in Listing A-1.

Listing A-1. A simple Ajax example

```
var myRequest;
var responseData;

function getData() {
    myRequest = new XMLHttpRequest();
    myRequest.onreadystatechange = getResponse;
    myRequest.open("GET", "http://someDomain.com/resource");
    myRequest.setRequestHeader("Content-Type", "application/json");
    myRequest.send();
}
```

```
function getResponse() {
    try {
        if (myRequest.readyState === XMLHttpRequest.DONE) {
            switch(myRequest.status) {
                case 500:
                    break;
                case 404:
                    break;
                case 200:
                    responseData = JSON.parse(myRequest.responseText);
                    break;
            }
        }
    }
    catch(ex) {
        console.log("Ajax error: " + ex.Description);
    }
}
```

When the getData() function is called, assuming the request is successful, the responseData object will hold the data returned from the server. Of course, you'll probably need to do something with this data. To do that, the getResponse() function should call another function that will use the data that was just extracted.

APPENDIX B

■ ■ ■

Drag and Drop Source Code

Listing B-1 contains the final JavaScript implementation for the Drag and Drop application that was demonstrated in Chapter 24.

Listing B-1. Chapter 24 source code

```javascript
"use strict";

function createBoard() {
    var board = document.getElementById("board");

    for (var y=0; y < 8; y++) {
        var row = document.createElement("div");
        row.className = "row";
        board.appendChild(row);

        for (var x=0; x < 8; x++) {
            var square = document.createElement("div");
            square.id = x.toFixed() + y.toString();
            if ((x + y) % 2) {
                square.className = "bblack";
            }
            else {
                square.className = "bwhite";
            }

            // If the square should have a piece in it...
            if ((x + y) % 2 != 0 && y != 3 && y != 4) {
                var img = document.createElement("img");
                if (y < 3) {
                    img.id = "w" +square.id;
                    img.src = "Images/WhitePiece.png";
                }
                else {
                    img.id = "b" + square.id;
                    img.src = "Images/BlackPiece.png";
                }
            }
```

© Mark J. Collins 2017
M. J. Collins, *Pro HTML5 with CSS, JavaScript, and Multimedia*, DOI 10.1007/978-1-4842-2463-2_28

```
                    img.className = "piece";
                    img.setAttribute("draggable", "true");
                    square.appendChild(img);
                }

                square.setAttribute("draggable", "false");
                row.appendChild(square);
            }
        }
}

function allowDrop() {
    // Wire up the target events on all the black squares
    var squares = document.querySelectorAll('.bblack');
    var i = 0;
    while (i < squares.length) {
        var s = squares[i++];
        // Add the event listeners
        s.addEventListener('dragover', dragOver, false);
        s.addEventListener('drop', drop, false);
        s.addEventListener('dragenter', dragEnter, false);
        s.addEventListener('dragleave', dragLeave, false);
        }

    // Wire up the source events on all of the images
    i = 0;
    var pieces = document.querySelectorAll('img');
    while (i < pieces.length) {
        var p = pieces[i++];
        p.addEventListener('dragstart', dragStart, false);
        p.addEventListener('dragend', dragEnd, false);
    }
}

createBoard();
allowDrop();

// Handle the dragover event
function dragOver(e) {
    e.preventDefault();

    // Get the img element that is being dragged
    var dragID = e.dataTransfer.getData("text");
    var dragPiece = document.getElementById(dragID);

    // Work around - if we can't get the dataTransfer, don't
    // disable the move yet, the drop event will catch this
    if (dragPiece) {
        if (e.target.tagName === "DIV" &&
            isValidMove(dragPiece, e.target, false)) {
            e.dataTransfer.dropEffect = "move";
        }
```

```
        else {
            e.dataTransfer.dropEffect = "none";
        }
    }
}

// Handle the dragstart event
function dragStart(e) {
    if (e.target.draggable) {
        e.dataTransfer.effectAllowed = "move";
        e.dataTransfer.setData("text", e.target.id);
        e.target.classList.add("selected");

        // Use a custom drag image
        var dragIcon = document.createElement("img");
        dragIcon.src = "Images/smiley.jpg";
        e.dataTransfer.setDragImage(dragIcon, 0, 0);
    }
}

// Handle the dragend event
function dragEnd(e) {
    e.target.classList.remove("selected");
}

// Handle the drop event
function drop(e) {
    e.stopPropagation();
    e.preventDefault();

    // Get the img element that is being dragged
    var droppedID = e.dataTransfer.getData("text");
    var droppedPiece = document.getElementById(droppedID);

    if (droppedPiece &&
    e.target.tagName === "DIV" &&
    isValidMove(droppedPiece, e.target, true)) {
        // Create a new img on the target location
        var newPiece = document.createElement("img");
        newPiece.src = droppedPiece.src;
        newPiece.id = droppedPiece.id.substr(0, 1) + e.target.id;
        newPiece.draggable = droppedPiece.draggable;

        if (droppedPiece.draggable){
            newPiece.classList.add("jumpOnly");
        }
        newPiece.classList.add("piece");

        newPiece.addEventListener("dragstart", dragStart, false);
        newPiece.addEventListener("dragend", dragEnd, false);
        e.target.appendChild(newPiece);
```

```
        // Remove the previous image
        droppedPiece.parentNode.removeChild(droppedPiece);

        // Remove the drop effect from the target element
        e.target.classList.remove('drop');

        // See if the piece needs to be promoted
        kingMe(newPiece);
    }
}

// Handle the dragenter event
function dragEnter(e) {
    // Get the img element that is being dragged
    var dragID = e.dataTransfer.getData("text");
    var dragPiece = document.getElementById(dragID);

    if (dragPiece &&
        e.target.tagName === "DIV" &&
        isValidMove(dragPiece, e.target, false)) {
        e.target.classList.add('drop');
    }
}

// Handle the dragleave event
function dragLeave(e) {
    e.target.classList.remove("drop");
}

function isValidMove(source, target, drop) {
    // Get the piece prefix and location
    var startPos = source.id.substr(1, 2);
    var prefix = source.id.substr(0, 1);

    // Get the drop location, strip off the prefix, if any
    var endPos = target.id;
    if (endPos.length > 2) {
        endPos = endPos.substr(1, 2);
    }

    // You can't drop on the existing location
    if (startPos === endPos) {
        return false;
    }

    // You can't drop on occupied square
    if (target.childElementCount != 0) {
        return false;
    }
```

```
var jumpOnly = false;
if (source.classList.contains("jumpOnly")) {
    jumpOnly = true;
}

// Compute the x and y coordinates
var xStart = parseInt(startPos.substr(0, 1));
var yStart = parseInt(startPos.substr(1, 1));
var xEnd = parseInt(endPos.substr(0, 1));
var yEnd = parseInt(endPos.substr(1, 1));

switch (prefix) {
    // For white pieces...
    case "w":
        if (yEnd <= yStart)
            return false; // Can't move backwards
        break;

    // For black pieces...
    case "b":
        if (yEnd >= yStart)
            return false; // Can't move backwards
        break;
}

// These rule apply to all pieces
if (yStart === yEnd || xStart === xEnd)
    return false; // Move must be diagonal

// Can't move more than two spaces
if (Math.abs(yEnd - yStart) > 2 || Math.abs(xEnd - xStart) > 2)
    return false;

// Only jumps are allowed
if (Math.abs(xEnd - xStart) === 1 && jumpOnly)
    return false;

var jumped = false;

// If moving two spaces, find the square that is jumped
if (Math.abs(xEnd - xStart) === 2) {
    var pos = ((xStart + xEnd) / 2).toString() +
            ((yStart + yEnd) / 2).toString();
    var div = document.getElementById(pos);
    if (div.childElementCount === 0)
        return false;  // Can't jump an empty square
    var img = div.children[0];
    if (img.id.substr(0, 1).toLowerCase() === prefix.toLowerCase())
        return false; // Can't jump a piece of the same color
```

```
        // If this function is called from the drop event
        // Remove the jumped piece
        if (drop) {
            div.removeChild(img);
            jumped = true;
        }
    }

    // Set the draggable attribute so the next player can take a turn
    if (drop) {
        enableNextPlayer(source);

        // If we jumped a piece, we're allowed to go again
        if (jumped) {
            source.draggable = true;
            source.classList.add("jumpOnly"); // But only for another jump
        }
    }

    return true;
}

function kingMe(piece) {

    // If we're already a king, just return
    if (piece.id.substr(0, 1) === "W" || piece.id.substr(0, 1) === "B")
        return;

    var newPiece;

    // If this is a white piece on the 7th row
    if (piece.id.substr(0, 1) === "w" && piece.id.substr(2, 1) === "7") {
        newPiece = document.createElement("img");
        newPiece.src = "Images/WhiteKing.png";
        newPiece.id = "W" + piece.id.substr(1, 2);
    }

    // If this is a black piece on the 0th row
    if (piece.id.substr(0, 1) === "b" && piece.id.substr(2, 1) === "0") {
        var newPiece = document.createElement("img");
        newPiece.src = "Images/BlackKing.png";
        newPiece.id = "B" + piece.id.substr(1, 2);
    }

    // If a new piece was created, set its properties and events
    if (newPiece) {
        newPiece.draggable = true;
        newPiece.classList.add("piece");
```

```
        newPiece.addEventListener('dragstart', dragStart, false);
        newPiece.addEventListener('dragend', dragEnd, false);

        var parent = piece.parentNode;
        parent.removeChild(piece);
        parent.appendChild(newPiece);
    }
}


function enableNextPlayer(piece) {

    // Get all of the pieces
    var pieces = document.querySelectorAll('img');

    var i = 0;
    while (i < pieces.length) {
        var p = pieces[i++];

        // If this is the same color that just moved, disable dragging
        if (p.id.substr(0, 1).toUpperCase() ===
            piece.id.substr(0, 1).toUpperCase()) {
            p.draggable = false;
        }
        // Otherwise, enable dragging
        else {
            p.draggable = true;
        }

        p.classList.remove("jumpOnly");
    }
}
```

APPENDIX C

∎ ∎ ∎

References

Part 2

HTML Elements

Name	Meta	Sect	Root	Head	Embed	Inter	Form	Phrase	Flow
a						X			X
abbr								X	X
address									X
area									X
article		X							X
aside		X							X
audio					X	X		X	
b								X	X
base	X								
bdi									X
bdo								X	X
blockquote			X						X
body			X						
br								X	X
button						X	X	X	X
canvas					X			X	X
caption									
cite								X	X
code								X	X
col									
colgroup									
command		X							X

(continued)

© Mark J. Collins 2017

M. J. Collins, *Pro HTML5 with CSS, JavaScript, and Multimedia*, DOI 10.1007/978-1-4842-2463-2_29

Name	Meta	Sect	Root	Head	Embed	Inter	Form	Phrase	Flow
data									X
datalist								X	X
dd									
del			X						X
details						X			X
dfn								X	X
div									X
dl									X
dt									X
em								X	X
embed					X	X		X	X
fieldset			X			X		X	
figcapture									
figure			X						X
footer									X
form									X
h1				X					X
h1				X					X
h3				X					X
h4				X					X
h5				X					X
h6				X					X
head									
header									X
hr									X
html									
i								X	X
iframe					X	X		X	X
img					X	X		X	X
input						X	X	X	X
ins									X
kbd								X	X
keygen						X	X	X	X
label						X	X	X	X
legend								X	

(*continued*)

Name	Meta	Sect	Root	Head	Embed	Inter	Form	Phrase	Flow
li									
link	X								
main									X
map									X
mark								X	X
math					X			X	X
menu						X			X
meta	X								
meter							X	X	X
nav		X							X
noscript								X	
object					X	X	X	X	X
ol									X
optgroup									
option									
output							X	X	X
p									X
param									
pre									X
progress						X	X	X	
q								X	X
rp									
rt									
ruby								X	X
s									X
samp								X	X
script	X							X	X
section		X							X
select						X	X	X	X
small								X	X
source									
span								X	X
strong								X	X
style	X								
sub								X	X

(*continued*)

Name	Meta	Sect	Root	Head	Embed	Inter	Form	Phrase	Flow
summary									
sup								X	X
svg					X			X	X
table									X
tbody									
td			X						
template									X
textarea					X	X	X	X	
tfoot									
th									
thead									
time								X	X
title	X								
tr									
track									
ul									X
var								X	X
video					X	X		X	X
wbr								X	X

Global Attributes

These attributes are supported in all HTML elements

Common

- accesskey - use this to define keyboard shortcut to either activate or set the focus on this element. The actual keyboard command that precedes this will depend on the browser and operating system. For more information, check out this article: https://developer.mozilla.org/en-US/docs/Web/HTML/Global_attributes/accesskey.

- id - a unique identifier, this is a string that cannot contain any space characters and must be unique within the entire HTML document.

- tabindex - an integer specifying the order in which this element is navigated to when using the tab command.

Formatting

- `class` - a list of space-separated classifications, used primarily when applying styles.

- `hidden` - a Boolean attribute, if present ,indicating the element is not currently visible.

- `style` - includes one or more CSS declarations to provide inline styling of an element.

Text Attributes

- `dir` - indicates the text direction, `ltr` or `rtl`. The default is `auto`, which will be set based on the character set of its contents as well as the inherited value. (See Chapter 5 for details).

- `lang` - indicates the language of the contents.

- `spellcheck` - a Boolean attribute, if present, indicates that spelling and grammar validation should be performed on the text.

- `translate` - set to yes if the element's content should be translated when the page is translated by the browser. Set to no if it should not be translated.

Drag and Drop

(see Chapter 24 for details)

- `draggable`

- `dropzone`

Other

- `contenteditable` - set to `true` or an empty string if the contents are editable; set to `false` if not.

- `contextmenu` - indicates the id of a context menu (this has little browser support, currently).

- `data-*` - these are custom attributes not used by the browser but useful in client-side scripting.

- `title` - additional information about an element.

Self-Closing Tags

The following HTML5 elements are self-closing tags, which means that they do not have separate opening and closing tags. This also means that apart from attributes, they have no content either, since the content goes between the opening and closing tags. These are also known as empty or void elements.

- `<area />` - a selectable area of an image

- `<base />` - the root path of any relative path in the document

- `<br />` - a line break that renders like a carriage return
- `<col />` - defines a column within a table
- `<embed />` - embedded content
- `<hr />` - horizontal rule, used to signify a topic change
- `<iframe />` - embeds another web page inside the current document
- `<img />` - an image or picture
- `<input />` - an input field such as a text box or checkbox on a form
- `<link />` - links an external or related resource
- `<meta />` - provides metadata about the current document
- `<param />` - a parameter within an object element
- `<source />` - used to reference the source of a video or audio element
- `<track />` - specifies the track of a video or audio element
- `<wbr />` - a word break opportunity where a line break could be made

The "/" at the end of the self-closing tag is optional in HTML5 as is the space before the slash. However, the slash is required for XHTML such as when the XML MIME type is used, which is generally rare. However, I have seen applications that try to validate HTML by running it through a simple XML validator, which will complain if you do not have the slash character.

There seems to be a fairly passionate debate in the web developer world about whether to include the slash character or not. However, it seems those who argue against it do so primarily for readability sake, which is really a matter of personal preference.

Input Types

A single `input` element is used for all types of data input from checkboxes to date pickers. The `type` attribute defines how the `input` element will function. The supported types are listed here.

Type	Description	Comments
button	A button, with no default action	
checkbox	A checkbox	Use the checked attribute to default to checked
color	Selects a color	The UI for selecting a color can vary between browsers
date*	Selects a date without any time element	
datetime-local*	Selects a date as well as time	No time zone is defined; this is the local time of the browser
email	A text box the accepts a valid email address	Validation only looks at the format. Use the multiple attribute if more than one email can be entered

(continued)

Type	Description	Comments
file	Selects a file from the client device	The accept attribute specifies the file types that are allowed. Use the multiple attribute to select multiple files
hidden	There is no UI but can have a value that is submitted with the form	
image	A button that is displays an image	Use the src attribute to define the image to use
month*	A date picker that selects only month and year (no day)	
number	A text box that accepts a numeric value	
password	The input is obscured such as displaying an asterisk for each character	
radio	Works like a checkbox except only one in a group can be selected	
range	A slider that selects a relative value	The min, max, and step attribute define its functionality
reset	A button that clears the input fields back to their original, default values	
search	A text box that is used to enter search criteria	
submit	A button whose default action is to submit the form	
tel	A text box that accepts a valid telephone number	You must supply the formatting rules through the pattern attribute
text	A single line text box with no additional validation	
time*	Specifies a time (hour, minute, second)	
url	A text box for entering a valid URL	Use the pattern attribute to define formatting constraints
week*	A date picker that selects year and week (1-53)	

indicates that browser support may be limited. For details go to http://html5test.com/index.html

Part 3

Color Units

Keyword	Hex Value	Hex	rgb	rgb(%)
black	#000000	#000	rgb(0,0,0)	rgb(0%,0%,0%)
navy	#000080	No equiv	tgb(0,0.128)	rgb(0%,0%,50%)
blue	#0000FF	#00F	rgb(0,0,255)	rgb(0%,0%,100%)
green	#008000	No equiv	rgb(0,128,0)	rgb(0%,50%,0%)
teal	#008080	No equiv	rgb(0,128,128)	rgb(0%,50%,50%)
lime	#00FF00	#0F0	rgb(0,255,0)	rgb(0%,100%,0%)
aqua	#00FFFF	#0FF	rgb(0,255,255)	rgb(0%,100%,100%)
maroon	#800000	No equiv	rgb(128,0,0)	rgb(50%,0%,0%)
purple	#800080	No equiv	rgb(128,0,128)	rgb(50%,0%,50%)
olive	#808000	No equiv	rgb(128,128,0)	rgb(50%,50%,0%)
gray	#808080	No equiv	rgb(128,128,128)	rgb(50%,50%,50%)
silver	#C0C0C0	No equiv	rgb(192,192,192)	rgb(75%,75%,75%)
red	#FF0000	#F00	rgb(255,0,0)	rgb(100%,0%,0%)
fuchsia	#FF00FF	#F0F	rgb(255,0,255)	rgb(100%,0,100%)
yellow	#FFFF00	#FF0	rgb(255,255,0)	rgb(100%,100%,0%)
white	#FFFFFF	#FFF	rgb(255,255,255)	rgb(100%,100%,100%)

Distance Units – Absolute

Unit	Definition
cm	centimeters - there are 2.54 cm per inch
mm	millimeters - 1/10 of a centimeter
q	quarter of a millimeter - 1/40th of a centimeter
pc	picas - there are 6 picas per inch
pt	points - there are 72 points per inch
px	pixels - there are 96 pixels per inch
in	inches - 96 pixels, 72 points, or 6 picas

Distance Units – Relative

Unit	Definition
em	font size of the current element
ex	height of the font of the current element
ch	width of the "0" character of the current font
rem	font size of the root element
vw	1% of the width of the viewport
vh	1% of the height of the viewport
vmin	1% of the smaller viewport dimension
vmax	1% of the larger viewport dimension

Angle Units

Unit	Definition
deg	degrees - there are 360° degrees in a circle
grad	gradians (sometimes called gon or grade) - there are 400 gradians in a circle
rad	radians - there are 2π radians in a circle
turn	turns - there is one turn in a circle

Time Units

Unit	Definition
s	seconds
ms	milliseconds

Time units can be specified in either seconds or milliseconds. The s or ms suffix is required; otherwise the value will be treated as a numeric value. Spaces between the value and unit are not allowed. Valid time units are 3s, 1.5s, 100ms.

CSS Property List

Attribute	Sub	Chapter
align		14
	-content	
	-items	
	-self	
animation		15
	-delay	
	-direction	
	-duration	
	-fill-mode	
	-iteration-count	
	-name	
	-play-state	
backface-visibility		15
background		12
	-attachment	
	-blend-mode	
	-clip	
	-color	
	-image	
	-origin	
	-position	
	-repeat	
	-size	
border		12
	-top/-bottom/-left/-right	
	-collapse	13
	-color	
	-radius	
	-spacing	13
	-style	
	-width	

(continued)

Attribute	Sub	Chapter
border-image		12
	-outset	
	-repeat	
	-slice	
	-source	
	-width	
box-decoration-break*		
box-shadow		12
break*		11
	-after	
	-before	
	-inside	
caption-side		13
clear		10
color		11
column*		
	-count	
	-fill	
	-gap	
	-rule	
	-rule-color	
	-rule-style	
	-rule-width	
	-span	
	-width	
content		10
counter-increment		
counter-reset		
cue*		
	-after	
	-before	
cursor		11
direction		11
display		10
elevation*		

(*continued*)

Attribute	Sub	Chapter
empty-cells		13
filter*		
flex		14
	-basis	
	-direction	
	-flow	
	-grow	
	-shrink	
	-wrap	
float		10
font		11
	-family	
	-feature-setting	
	-kerning	
	-language-override*	
	-size	
	-size-adjust*	
	-stretch	
	-style	
	-synthesis*	
	-weight	
font-variant		11
	-alternatives*	
	-caps	
	-east-asian*	
	-ligatures*	
	-numeric	
	-position*	
hanging-punctuation*		11
hyphens		11
image*		
	-orientation	
	-rendering	
	-resolution	
justify-content		14

(*continued*)

Attribute	Sub	Chapter
layer-background		
	-color	
	-image	
letter-spacing		11
line-break*		11
line-height		11
list-style		13
	-image	
	-position	
	-type	
margin ·		10
	-top/-bottom/-left/-right	
marks*		11
	-after	
	-before	
marker-offset*		
max-height		10
max-width		10
min-height		10
min-width		10
nav		
	-down	
	-index	
	-left	
	-right	
	-up	
object*		
	-fit	
	-position	
opacity		11
order		14
orphans*		11
outline		12
	-color	
	-offset	

(continued)

Attribute	Sub	Chapter
	-style	
	-width	
overflow		10
overflow-wrap		11
padding		10
	-top/-bottom/-left/-right	
page-break		11
	-after	
	-before	
	-inside	
perspective		15
perspective-origin		15
position		10
quotes		11
resize		
tab-size*		11
table-layout		13
text		11
	-align	
	-align-last*	
	-autospace*	
	-combine-upright*	
	-decoration*	
	-decoration-color*	
	-decoration-line*	
	-decoration-style*	
	-indent	
	-justify*	
	-kashida-space*	
	-orientation*	
	-overflow	
	-shadow	
	-transform	
	-underline-position*	
top/bottom/left/right		10

(continued)

Attribute	Sub	Chapter
transform		15
	-origin	
	-style	
transition		15
	-delay	
	-duration	
	-property	
	-timing-function	
unicode-bidi		11
vertical-align		11
visibility		10
white-space		11
windows		13
width		10
word-break		11
word-spacing		11
word-wrap		11
writing-mode		11
z-index		10
zoom		

these attributes have limited browser support

Part 4

Array Methods

These methods are available for array properties.

Method	Example	Description
concat	var newArray = items. concat(array1, array2, ...);	Returns a new array with the contents of both the original array and the arrays passed as parameters.
copyWithin	items.copyWithin(2, 4, 2);	Copies elements in an array, to other elements in the array. The first parameter specifies the index to copy to, the second parameter specifies the index to copy from, and the third parameter specifies the ending index. So the elements between the 2nd and 3rd parameters are copied to the index in the 1st parameter. The copy overwrites the existing elements.

(*continued*)

Method	Example	Description
every	`var bool = items.` `every(compareFunc);`	Returns true if the specified compare function returns true for every element in the array.
fill	`items.fill("x", 3, 2);`	Replaces the values of the specified elements with the value in the first parameter. The 2nd and 3rd parameters indicate the starting and ending indices.
filter	`var subset = items.` `filter(compareFunc);`	Executes the compare function against every element in the array and returns the set of elements where the compare function returns true.
find	`var item = items.` `find(compareFunc);`	Returns the first element in the array where the specified compare function returns true.
findIndex	`var i = items.` `findIndex(compareFunc);`	Returns the index of the first element in the array where the specified compare function returns true.
forEach	`items.forEach(function);`	Calls the specified function for each element in the array.
indexOf	`var i = items.` `findIndex(compareFunc, 2);`	Returns the index of the first element in the array where the specified compare function returns true. The second parameter indicates which location in the array to start the search (default is 0).
join	`items.join("; ");`	Outputs the elements into a string with each element separated by the specified string.
lastIndex	`var i = items.` `findIndex(compareFunc);`	Returns the index of the first element in the array where the specified compare function returns true.
map	`var newArray = items.` `map(function);`	Creates a new array that is the same size as the existing array. Each element is created by calling the specified function on the corresponding element in the original array.
pop	`var item = items.pop();`	Removes the last element from the array and returns it.
push	`var l = items.push("xyz");`	Adds the specified element to the end of the array and returns the new length.
reduce	`var v = items.` `reduce(aggrFunc, initial);`	Reduces the array to a single value by applying the specified function to each element, starting with the first element.

reduceRight	`var v = items.`
	`reduceRight(aggrFunc,`
	`initial);`
		Reduces the array to a single value by applying the specified function to each element, starting with the last element and going in reverse.

reverse	`items.reverse();`	Sorts the elements alphabetically in reverse order.
shift	`var item = items.shift();`	Removes the first element of the array and returns it. The index of the remaining elements is shifted down one so the second element (which is now the first) has a zero index.

(*continued*)

Method	Example	Description
slice	var subArray = items. slice(2, 3);	Removes elements from an array and returns them as a new array. The first parameter specifies where to start, and the second parameter indicates how many elements should be removed.
some	var bool = items. every(compareFunc);	Returns true if the specified compare function returns true for at least one element in the array.
sort	items.sort();	Sorts the items in the list alphabetically.
splice	items.splice(2, 1, "x", 'y", "z");	First removes elements from the array based on the first 2 parameters (the starting elements and the number to be removed), then inserts the remaining parameters into the array at that location. The index of the subsequent elements is adjusted as needed.
toString	items.toString();	Outputs each of the elements into a comma-separated string.
unshift	var l = items.unshift("abc");	Adds the specified element to the beginning of the array (as index 0) and shifts the remaining indices by one. Returns the new length of the array.
valueOf	var v = items.valueOf();	This is the default function. Returns a string containing a comma-separated list of elements.

Window Members

Property	Description
applicationCache	Provides a list of the resources that have been cached for offline support.
console	A place to write debugging messages and run ad hoc JavaScript commands.
crypto	Returns a Crypto object that is used for hashing, encryption, or random number generation. The specification is still in the early stages. For more details see the specification at https://w3c.github.io/webcrypto/Overview.html.
devicePixelRatio	Indicates the ratio between the device pixels and the device independent pixels.
dialogArguments	For dialog windows, this provides the arguments that were passed in when the window was opened.
document	The HTML document loaded in this window.
frameElement	If the window represents a frame, indicates the element that the frame is embedded in.
frames	Returns a collection of child frames inside the current window.
fullScreen	Indicates if the window is using fullScreen mode.
history	Returns the history object that is used for navigating back to a previous page.
innerHeight	The height of the available area that the windows content can be displayed in. This will include the space used by the horizontal scroll bar, if there is one.

(continued)

541

Property	Description
innerWidth	The width of the available area that the windows content can be displayed in. This will include the space used by the vertical scroll bar, if there is one.
isSecureContext	Returns true if the window is using a secure context.
length	Returns the number of subframes in the window.
localStorage	Provides a place to store data that will be available after the session ends.
location	Returns the location object that provides details about the web address of the current document.
locationbar	Returns the BarProp interface for the web address UI control.
menubar	Returns the BarProp interface for the menu UI control.
messageManager	Returns the MessageManager object that is used to manage interprocess communication. Requires elevated privileges to use.
name	The name of the window.
navigator	Returns the navigator object that provide details of the browser and device.
opener	The window that opened the current window.
outerHeight	The height of the window including browser elements such as toolbars and menus.
outerWidth	The total width of the window including all UI elements.
parent	Returns the current window's parent or the current window if it is the topmost window.
performance	Returns the Performance object that provides utilities for monitor client-side performance monitoring.
personalbar	Returns the BarProp interface for the personalization UI control.
returnValue	Used for dialog windows; contains the value to be returned to the calling function.
screen	Returns the screen object that provides details about the device's display.
screenX	The distance from the left edge of the device display and the left edge of the browser window.
screenY	The distance from the top edge of the device display and the top edge of the browser window.
scrollbars	Returns the BarProp interface for the scrollbar UI controls.
scrollX	The distance that the document is currently scrolled horizontally.
scrollY	The distance that the document is currently scrolled vertically.
self	Returns a reference to the current window.
sessionStorage	Used for storing application data that expired when the session ends.
speechSynthesis	Returns the SpeechSynthesis object that is used to access the Web Speech API.
status	The text that is displayed in the status bar of the browser. This property can be set, causing the updated text to be displayed.
statusbar	Returns the BarProp interface for the status bar UI control.
toolbar	Returns the BarProp interface for the toolbar UI control.
top	Returns the topmost window.
window	Returns the current window.

(*continued*)

Method	Description
alert()	Displays a modal dialog with the specified message.
atob()	Converts a base-64 encoded string into binary data.
blur()	Removes the focus from the window.
btoa()	Converts binary data into a base-64-encode string.
clearInterval()	Cancels a repeated timer that was scheduled using the setInterval() method.
clearTimeout()	Cancels a timer that was created using the setTimeout() method.
close()	Closes the window.
confirm()	Displays a modal confirmation dialog box.
dispatchEvent()	Fires the specified event.
dump()	Writes a message to the console.
find()	Searches for the specified string within the document.
focus()	Change the focus to this window.
getComputedStyle()	Computed all of the CSS declaration that should be applied to the window.
getSelection()	Returns a selection object that indicates the selected items.
matchMedia()	Performs the specified media query and returns a Boolean result.
moveBy()	Moves the window by the specified amount.
moveTo()	Moves the window to the specified location.
open()	Opens a new window/tab.
openDialog()	Opens a new window as a dialog box.
postMessage()	Sends a message to another window.
print()	Opens the Print dialog box to allow the user to print the document.
prompt()	Opens a dialog box and returns the user's input.
resizeBy()	Resizes the window by the specified amount.
resizeTo()	Changes the window size to the specified dimensions.
scroll()	Scrolls the document to the specified location.
scrollBy()	Scrolls the window by the specified amount.
scrollByLines()	Scrolls the document by the specified number of lines.
scrollByPages()	Scrolls the document by the specified number of pages.
scrollTo()	Scrolls the document to a specific set of coordinates.
setCursor()	Sets the cursor icon.
setInterval()	Schedules a function to be executed repeatedly with a specified pause between each execution.
setResizeable()	Toggles whether the window can be resized.
setTimeout()	Schedules a function to be executed after a specified interval.
showModalDialog()	Displays a modal dialog box.
sizeToContent()	Changes the size of the window to fit the current contents.
stop()	Stops the window from loading.
updateCommands()	Updates the state of the commands in the browser UI.

Navigator Members

Property	Description
appCodeName	Indicates the code name for the browser.
appName	Indicates the name of the browser.
appVersion	Indicates the version details of the browser.
battery	provides details about the device's battery; includes the following properties: charging (true if the device is pulled in and charging), chargingTime (the number of seconds remaining until fully charged), dischargingTime (the number of seconds until the battery is completely discharged), and level (a valued from 0 to 1 indicating the current charge level). You can also listen for events that fire when these values change.
cookieEnabled	Indicates if the cookies are currently enabled.
geolocation	Obtains positioning data from the device. This is demonstrated in Chapter 26.
hardwareConcurrency	Returns the number of logical CPUs used by the device.
language	Indicates the preferred language of the user of the current language set in the browser's UI.
mediaDevices	Returns an array of media devices that are available.
mimeTypes	Returns an array of MIME types that are registered.
online	A Boolean value indicating if the device is connected to a network.
oscpu	Specifies the operating system used by the device.
platform	Returns the platform that the browser was compiled with.
plugins	Returns an array of plugins that are currently enabled.
product	Indicates the name of the engine used by the browser.
serviceWorker	Returns the ServiceWorkerContainer object that is used to manager the ServiceWorker objects associated with the current document.
userAgent	A string describing the user agent (browser).

Method	Description
javaEnabled()	returns true if the browser support JavaScript
registerContentHandler()	registers as an available handler for a specific MIME type
registerProtocolHandler()	registers as an available handler for a specific protocol
vibrate()	causes the device to vibrate if the device supports it

Console Methods

Method	Description
assert()	Writes an entry to the console log only if the first parameter is false. Use this to log only under certain conditions such as a function returns an error. The log entry also includes stack information.
clear()	Removes all the entries from the console log.
count()	Logs the number of times this line of code has been executed. If you pass a label to the count() method, the label will be included in the log entry.
dir()	Outputs an object to the console such that its members can be expanded or collapsed in the log.
dirxml()	Outputs the members of an object in either XML or JSON format.
error()	Writes an entry to the console log to represent an error. This method supports string substitution.
group()	Writes an entry to the console log that starts a new group. Subsequent entry to the log will be indented. Use the groupEnd() method to end the current group. Groups can be nested.
groupCollapsed()	Works just like the group() method except that the group is collapsed, requiring the user to expand it to see the subsequent entries.
groupEnd()	Closes the current group.
info()	Write an informational message to the console log. This method supports string substitution.
log()	This method is used for general logging purposes. Other methods such as error(), info(), and warn() imply a severity level, which log() does not. This method supports string substitution.
profile()	Starts the browser's built-in profiling tool. The capabilities here will vary by browser.
profileEnd()	Stops the current profiler.
table()	Displays data in the console as a table. The data must be either an object or an array. If the data is an object, the property names and values are displayed in tabular form. If the data is an array, a row will be displayed for each entry in the array. If the contents of the array are objects, a separate column will be used for each object property. You can also specify the properties that should be included in the table.
time()	Starts a stop watch. Use the timeEnd() method to stop it and log the elapsed time.
timeEnd()	Stops the specified stop watch.
timestamp()	Adds a marker to the bowsers timeline or profiling tool.
trace()	Logs the stack trace to the console.
warn()	Writes a warning entry to the console log. This method supports string substitution.

Element Inheritance

Name	Inherits
a	HTMLAnchorElement
abbr	HTMLElement
address	HTMLSpanElement
area	HTMLAreaElement
article	HTMLElement
aside	HTMLElement
audio	HTMLAudioElement
b	HTMLSpanElement
base	HTMLBaseElement
bdi	HTMLElement
bdo	HTMLSpanElement
blockquote	HTMLQuoteElement
body	HTMLBodyElement
br	HTMLBRElement
button	HTMLButtonElement
canvas	HTMLCanvasElement
caption	HTMLTableCaptionElement
cite	HTMLSpanElement
code	HTMLSpanElement
col	HTMLTableColElement
colgroup	HTMLTableColElement
command	HTMLCommandElement
data	HTMLDataElement
datalist	HTMLDataListElement
dd	HTMLElement
del	HTMLModElement
details	HTMLDetailsElement
dfn	HTMLElement
div	HTMLDivElement
dl	HTMLDListElement
dt	HTMLSpanElement
em	HTMLSpanElement
embed	HTMLEmbedElement

(continued)

Name	Inherits
fieldset	HTMLFieldSetElement
figcapture	HTMLElement
figure	HTMLElement
footer	HTMLElement
form	HTMLFormElement
h1	HTMLHeadingElement
h1	HTMLHeadingElement
h3	HTMLHeadingElement
h4	HTMLHeadingElement
h5	HTMLHeadingElement
h6	HTMLHeadingElement
head	HTMLHeadElement
header	HTMLElement
hr	HTMLHRElement
html	HTMLHtmlElement
i	HTMLSpanElement
iframe	HTMLIFrameElement
img	HTMLImageElement
input	HTMLInputElement
ins	HTMLModElement
kbd	HTMLElement
label	HTMLLabelElement
legend	HTMLLegendElement
li	HTMLLIElement
link	HTMLLinkElement
main	HTMLElement
map	HTMLMapElement
mark	HTMLElement
menu	HTMLMenuElement
meta	HTMLMetaElement
meter	HTMLMeterElement
nav	HTMLElement
noscript	HTMLElement
object	HTMLObjectElement

(continued)

Name	Inherits
ol	HTMLOListElement
optgroup	HTMLOptGroupElement
option	HTMLOptionElement
output	HTMLOutputElement
p	HTMLParagraphElement
param	HTMLParamElement
pre	HTMLPreElement
progress	HTMLProgressElement
q	HTMLQuoteElement
rp	HTMLElement
rt	HTMLElement
ruby	HTMLElement
s	HTMLElement
samp	HTMLElement
script	HTMLScriptElement
section	HTMLElement
select	HTMLSelectElement
small	HTMLElement
source	HTMLSourceElement
span	HTMLSpanElement
strong	HTMLElement
style	HTMLStyleElement
sub	HTMLElement
summary	HTMLElement
sup	HTMLElement
svg	SVGElement
table	HTMLTableElement
tbody	HTMLTableSectionElement
td	HTMLTableDataCellElement
template	HTMLTemplateElement
textarea	HTMLTextAreaElement
tfoot	HTMLTableSectionElement
th	HTMLTableHeaderCellElement
thead	HTMLTableSectionElement

(continued)

Name	Inherits
time	HTMLTimeElement
title	HTMLTitleElement
tr	HTMLTableRowElement
track	HTMLTrackElement
u	HTMLSpanElement
ul	HTMLUListElement
var	HTMLElement
video	HTMLVideoElement
wbr	HTMLElement

Index

A

Anchor (a) element
  download attribute, 116
  href attribute, 115
  linked resource, 116
  target attribute, 116
AdjustWindow() function, 331
Ajax. *See* Asynchronous JavaScript And Xml (Ajax)
alert() function, 493
Animation, 161
  attributes
    delay, 289
    direction, 289
    duration, 289
    fill-mode, 289
    iteration-count, 289
    name, 289
    play-state, 290
    timing-function, 289
  configuration, 288
  Cubic Bézier, 291, 293
  keyframes, 287
  multiple, 290
  shorthand, 290
Application programming interface (API)
  displaying location, 499–501
  using geolocation object, 497–499
  web project creation, 496–497
async attribute, 8
Asynchronous JavaScript And Xml (Ajax), 513
  handling response, 514–515
  request, making, 513
  XMLHTTP, 513
  XMLHttpRequest object, 513, 515
Attribute selectors, 164–165
Audio controls, 375
Audio elements
  autoplay attribute, 123
  Boolean attributes, 122
  change source, 384

controls attribute, 378, 379
endAudio() function, 381
events, 377
file formats, 124
HTML document, 378
load() method, 384
Math.round() function, 379
native controls, 123–124
play and pause button, 379
progress and seek, 381
seekAudio() function, 381
setupSeek() method, 379
setVolume() function, 382
style adjustment, 383
toggleMute() function, 382
togglePlay() function, 380
updateMute() function, 382
updatePlayPause() method, 380
updateSeek() function, 381
volume attribute, 122
volume control, 382
autocomplete attribute, 136

B

Backgrounds, 161, 236
  clipping, 238
  examples, 239–243
  fixed background image, 243
  gradient, 241
  image attributes, 236
    attachment, 237
    origin, 237
    position, 238
    repeat, 237
    size, 238
  shorthand, 239
  table styling, 254
Baseline, 277
Bing Mapping API, 375
Bing Maps account, 501, 503

Get the eBook for only $4.99!

Why limit yourself?

Now you can take the weightless companion with you wherever you go and access your content on your PC, phone, tablet, or reader.

Since you've purchased this print book, we are happy to offer you the eBook for just $4.99.

Convenient and fully searchable, the PDF version enables you to easily find and copy code—or perform examples by quickly toggling between instructions and applications.

To learn more, go to http://www.apress.com/us/shop/companion or contact support@apress.com.

Printed in the United States
By Bookmasters